SERVICE
PARTS
HANDBOOK

OTHER BOOKS
BY JOSEPH D. PATTON, JR.

Instrument Maintenance Manager's Sourcebook (Editor)

Logistics Technology and Management: The New Approach

Maintainability and Maintenance Management

Preventive Maintenance

*Service Management: Principles and Practices
    (With W.H. Bleuel)*

Service Parts Management

SERVICE PARTS HANDBOOK

Joseph D. Patton, Jr.
& Herbert C. Feldmann

New York

THE SOLOMON PRESS   PUBLISHERS

PATTON CONSULTANTS, INC.
4 Covington Place
Hilton Head, SC 29928-7665 (USA)
Phone: (803) 686-6650
Fax: (803) 686-6651
e-mail: jdpatton@aol.com

Library of Congress Cataloging-in-Publication Data

Patton, Joseph D.
    Service Parts Handbook / Joseph D. Patton, Jr. & Herbert C. Feldmann.
        p.   cm.
    Includes bibliographical references and index.
    ISBN 0-934623-73-2
      1. Inventory control—Handbooks, manuals, etc. 2. Spare parts-
-Handbooks, manuals, etc. I. Feldmann, Herbert C. 1942-
II. Title.
TS160.P36 1996
    658.2'7—dc20   96-35417
CIP

The Solomon Press Publishers
98-12 66th Ave
Rego Park, New York 11374
Phone 718-830-9112
FAX 718-830-0351

BOOK DESIGN BY SIDNEY SOLOMON & RAYMOND SOLOMON

Dedication

Service Parts Handbook
is dedicated to our wives,
. MARGE FELDMANN
and SUSAN PATTON,
for their tolerance,
understanding, and support
over the past thirty years
and especially during the
preparation of this book.

CONTENTS

Section II
TOOLS AND TECHNIQUES *99*

Independent parts suppliers
OEM opportunities
Ready for issue
Courier stocks
Parts knowledgebase
Will-fit replacements

23. ASSET RECOVERY *349*

Control excess
Value for excess
Accounting and hazmat obligations
Reverse logistics

24. COMPUTERIZATION *357*

Logistics systems history
Service parts computerization issues
Basic system requirements
Role of bar code and remote data entry
Planning capabilities
Database requirements
Off-the-shelf system selection

Section III
PULLING IT ALL TOGETHER 379

25. PERSONNEL AND ORGANIZATIONS *381*

People are the most important asset
Change, the constant in service
Technology or people?
New appraisal systems
Logistics functional organizations
Part Master qualifications
Planning and forecasting analyst qualifications
Procurement qualifications
Inventory control personnel qualifications
Warehouse personnel qualifications
Training
Parts management pointers

PREFACE

Objectives

T he objectives of this handbook are to:

1. Provide a reference book for service parts that will help both novices and experts become proficient in the effective support of parts for service.
2. Standardize terms, principles, and practices that are important to effective management of service consumables, durable equipment, materials, and parts.
3. Improve knowledge of the considerations and trade-offs between labor and parts, with understanding of how to apply life-cycle cost and profit analysis.
4. Create awareness of the differences between parts necessary for maintenance service and those used for production.

Overview

Performance and financial pressures are increasing on parts for service, maintenance, repairs, and operations (MRO). In the *Fortune 500* largest US industrial corporations alone, an estimated $148 billion is invested in service parts. Inflation means that generally the next parts order will cost more than the last one did. Carrying costs of inventory for space, security, environment, record keeping, computer systems, operations, insurance, obsolescence, personnel, taxes, and the cost of borrowing or alternative uses of money typically exceed 30 percent of a part's value per year. This means that keeping a $1,000 component on the shelf "just in case" will cost at least $300 every year. Financial pressures are great to reduce inventory investment. Fortunately, multivendor, open systems with common components enable considerable cost reduction through sharing of common inventories. The challenge is both human and technological. The hard sciences of mathematics and statistics must enhance the soft art of people skills. We humans must realize that managing resources does not require that we own those resources. We must also have instantaneous, accurate knowledge of the availability and location of a needed part and how it can be acquired and transported to the point of need on time. Those are difficult paradigms to change.

The service parts function in many organizations needs to be afforded higher status. Parts management personnel are becoming much more professional, but they are still often paid low wages to manage millions of dollars' worth of inventory. The parts business should receive attention not only when trouble occurs but also during the routine times that probably indicate good management. That is one reason this book emphasizes measurements and goals. Today, Service Parts is frequently organized as a *profit center*. Many businesses make more profit from service parts than they do from the sale of finished goods. Good parts support should be recognized and praised!

Joe Patton's book *Service Parts Management* was published by the Instrument Society of America in 1984. Experience, management concepts, technology, and scientific modeling have advanced considerably in recent years. Every Service Parts Management training program presented by Patton Consultants, Inc. contains significant new content.

Some of the information in this book has been published in magazine articles and in new chapters to update editions of Joe Patton's other books. His other texts include *Service Management: Principles and Practices* (coauthored with Bill Bleuel), *Logistics Technology and Management, Maintainability and Maintenance Management,* and *Preventive Maintenance.* Even more information is integrated into case studies and hands-on exercises used in training programs. Ideas for better service parts management flow from many sources. Close relationships with consulting clients and friendly executives across the service industry enable the authors to be sounding boards for many concepts. These clients are also the trial locations for many developments that are covered here.

Service logistics, like many professions, contains elements of both art and science. Theory must usually be combined with the art of local knowledge so it can be tuned into a completely positive practice. Many situations exist where we have known for years that rules-of-thumb are effective, without understanding the underlying logic. For example, 85 percent First Pass Fill Rate from a field engineer's vehicle stock has long been the industry standard. When we ask people why they use 85 percent the answer is often, "I read it in a book and it seems to work." Since the book and several related articles are probably by Joe Patton, the blind faith is appreciated. That practice can now be justified by research and logic which are presented in this text. The Logistics Performance Envelope concept developed by Herb Feldmann serves well to enable scientific balancing of the competing measures: Response Time, First Pass Fill Rate, and financial resources.

There are five "rights" of service parts: item, place, price, quality, and time. (In this context the word *right* means *accurate, correct, exact,* and *precise.*) These five utilities intend to achieve the right part at the right place, for the right price, in the right quality, at the right time. The objective of effective service parts support is to satisfy customers by providing the necessary parts, at the needed location, for a reasonable price, in usable condition, at the desired time. It is important to note that the customer of service logistics is often a field technician or an internal support organization who in turn supports the end-user customer.

There is a major trade-off in the service business between parts and labor. As labor costs increase, the trade-off shifts in favor of using more parts and less labor. This is also stimulated by customers' needs for high equipment uptime, which can be obtained better by a quick change of complete modules than by extensive on-site repair with piece parts. The transition to integrated electronics increases the importance of parts, since many capabilities that used to be mechanical, hydraulic, or optical, are now combined into small electronic packages. These factors all put more emphasis on having the right part. Bailing wire, tape, and soldering irons are no longer effective tools for service.

Computer power enables us to process information accurately and rapidly, but parts is still a people business. Innovations in the implementation of our mental processes, many of which are outlined in this book, provide more benefit than do advances in technology. "I don't have the part I need" is probably heard from more field service and plant maintenance personnel than any other complaint. On the other hand, many stockrooms and warehouses contain items that have not been touched for a long time. The key ingredient in balancing people and technology is motivated managers and parts personnel who can apply this knowledge successfully to specific situations.

Billions of dollars are invested in inventories of equipment, materials, and parts. Hundreds of thousands of people hold such jobs as materials forecaster, inventory control specialist, stockkeeper, receiving clerk, distribution manager, expeditor, provisioning analyst, picker, packer, manager of material, service planning specialist, and logistician. The rapid transportation business, including such companies as Airborne, Federal Express, and United Parcel Service (especially their SonicAir subsidiary), has been built around the need to move service parts rapidly, thus verifying that a great need exists for practical information on the principles and practices of service parts management.

Service parts are related to manufacturing production parts. Many people know how to provide parts "Just-In-Time." The problems and opportunities are similar to the challenges of wholesalers and retailers in keeping their shelves stocked. A difference is that service parts are required "Just-In-Case." This book focuses on many additional distinctions. The principles presented in this book are relevant to many different persons who might belong to a number of different professional organizations (The addresses of professional organizations and related publications are listed in Appendix A.) including:

American Institute of Plant Engineers (AIPE)

American Production and Inventory Control Society (APICS)

American Productivity and Quality Center (APQC)

American Society for Quality Control (ASQC)

Association for Advancement of Medical Instrumentation (AAMI)

Association For Service Management International (AFSMI)

Commercial Food Equipment Service Agencies (CFESA)

Computer and Business Equipment Manufacturers Association (CBEMA)

Computer Industry Technology Association (CITA)

Council of Logistics Management (CLM)

Equipment Maintenance Council (EMC)

Farm and Industrial Equipment Institute (FIEI)

Independent Service Network International (ISNI)

Industrial Maintenance Institute (IMI)

Institute of Electrical and Electronics Engineers (IEEE)

Institute of Industrial Engineers (IIE)

Instrument Society of America (ISA)

National Association of Food Equipment Manufacturers (NAFEM)

National Association of Service Managers (NASM)

National Farm Power and Equipment Dealers Association (NFPEDA)

Society for Maintenance and Reliability Professionals (SMRP)

Society of Logistics Engineers (SOLE)

Society of Reliability Engineers (SRE)

A distinction will be made between "equipments," which are considered durable and are individually marked with a unique serial number identifier; "parts," which are stockkeeping units in which many items may be (in fact, should be) identical; and "materials" such as cleaning supplies, lubricants, and paint. All three classes are included in our coverage with note made of important differences as they affect the topic.

The information now in this book has been used to conduct many public workshops for leading universities and professional associations as well as in internal training for many corporations and government agencies. Service Parts Management

workshops are usually well attended, in contrast to people-re-
lated workshops. Improving service parts management will
have a positive impact on commerce, government, and industry with benefit to people around the world. The problems in
the United States are generally the same as they are in Australia,
Israel, or Zambia.

Acknowledgments

Together Joe Patton and Herb Feldmann make a superior
logistics team. Herb excels at the numbers side of this business
while Joe brings strengths on the people side. Since the words
often flow onto paper in a form that is not clear to lay people,
Susan O. Patton provided considerable clarity to the grammar.

Sidney Solomon and Raymond Solomon of Publishers Cre-
ative Services and the Solomon Press have also added tremendously to this sixth book with Joe Patton. Generally, the
authors' motivation declines after the initial words and illustrations are mailed to the publisher. Fortunately, the Solomons
effectively shepherd the manuscript through the production
process to this final publication.

Mary Russell did a marvelous copyediting job, and the staff
at Twin Typesetting, Inc. contributed their usual fine typo-
graphic skills.

SERVICE
PARTS
HANDBOOK

Section I

CHANGES
and
CHALLENGES

1 *TERMS AND DEFINITIONS*

Standard business terms and definitions have been embellished to describe parts-related activities. Most of the words used to describe service parts are derived from their common use in other areas and logical dictionary references. Many readers will wish to skim through the following pages and move rapidly on to the next chapter. Other persons, new to the realm of EOQ, ROP, and SKU, should skim the following terms and definitions as a base of reference. If the meaning of a word used in later chapters is not clear, then a review of this chapter should provide clarification.

ABC inventory policy   Collection of prioritizing practices to give varied levels of attention to different classes of inventories. In manufacturing, ABC is based on (unit cost x quantity). For service, those criteria must be considered separately, along with essentiality, shelf life, and other factors. "A" level parts are most important.

Activity-based costing (ABC)   Cost accounting system that ac-
cumulates costs based on activities performed and then
uses cost drivers to allocate these costs to products and
other bases, such as customers, markets, or projects. ABC
attempts to allocate overhead costs on a more realistic basis
than direct labor hours or units. Activity-based management (ABM) uses the information to improve productivity
and reduce waste.

Adaptive smoothing   Form of exponential smoothing in which
the smoothing constant is automatically adjusted as a
function of forecast error.

Algorithm   Prescribed set of well-defined rules or procedures for
solving a problem in a finite number of steps.

Allocation   Apportionment made for specific purposes to two
or more persons, or things, or locations. If too few parts
are available to fill all orders, then the available parts must
be allocated to best meet the demands.

Amortization   Process of recovering a capital investment over
time via expensing.

Asset   Durable items that appear as a positive category on the
financial balance sheet. The term also refers to humans,
but the investment in people is not considered a financial
asset under current accounting practices.

Assembly   Group of subassemblies or parts that are put together to constitute a major subdivision of a final product.
An assembly may be an end item or a component of a
higher level assembly.

Audit   Objective comparison of actions to policies and plans.

Authorized stock list (ASL)   The part numbers and quantities of
field replaceable units that should be stocked at the specific
location for which the ASL is created.

Average inventory   One-half the average lot size plus safety
stock. The average can be calculated based on observations
taken over several historical time periods. For example, the
quantities at the end of each month may be added and the
result divided by the number of measurements.

Availability   With reference to parts, the fact that the part is on
hand and in usable condition. Product availability is the
probability that the item will work properly under stated
conditions. Inherent availability (Ai) concerns failures

only. Achieved availability (Aa) includes preventive maintenance and planned downtime. Operational availability (Ao) considers total downtime, including administrative time and logistics time, so Ao = Uptime/Total Time.

Backorder An unfilled customer order or commitment. Also, a demand for an item where inventory on hand is insufficient to immediately issue the part.

Bar code Rectangular array of bars and spaces that can be rapidly scanned to send information to a computer that processes the data for identification, pricing, and other information.

Bias Consistent deviation from the mean in one direction (high or low). A normal property of a good forecast is that it is not biased.

Bill of lading Carrier's contract and receipt for goods the carrier agrees to transport from one place to another to be delivered to a designated person. In case of delay, loss, or damage, the bill of lading is the basis for filing freight claims.

Bill of material (BOM) Listing of all components and their quantities (parts, subassemblies, and materials) that go into a parent assembly

Bin Storage device or shelf unit to hold discrete parts.

Blanket purchase order Long-term commitment to a supplier for material against which short-term releases are generated to satisfy requirements. Synonym for standing order.

Book value Accounting worth of items carried on the balance sheet after depreciation has been subtracted. Net book value (NBT) often includes revision for current market value being lower than original cost.

Box-Jenkins model Forecasting approach based on regression and moving average models. The model is based on historical observations at varying time intervals of the item to be forecast and on historical errors in forecast values, not on regression of independent variables.

Break-even point The level of activity at which operations switch from unprofitable to profitable (or vice versa). The break-even point is the graphical intersection of the total cost curve with the total revenue curve.

Buyer   Person who performs supplier selection, negotiation, order placement, expediting, measurement of performance, evaluation, and related purchasing activities.

Calendar time   All days and weeks as contrasted with operating time or work time. For example, a week is seven calendar days, but may be only five operating days. Most service measures are calendar days since most customers need support abound the clock.

Capacity   Capability of a function to perform its mission or output rate. For example, the number of monitors that a repair center can fix per hour.

Capital asset   Durable items with long life or high value that necessitate asset control and depreciation under tax accounting guidelines, rather than being expensed at first use.

Carload lot   Shipment that qualifies for reduced freight charges because it is greater than a specified minimum weight. The higher less-than-carload (LCL) rate may be less expensive for small but heavy shipments since carload rates usually include minimum rates per unit of volume.

Carrying costs   Expense of handling, space, information, insurance, special conditions, obsolescence, personnel, and the cost of capital or alternate use of funds to keep parts in inventory; also called *holding costs*. Carrying costs are often calculated as a percent of gross inventory per year.

Chaining   Procedure whereby on orders for part numbers that have been replaced, the oldest number will be checked and the order filled with it if possible. If those parts no longer exist, the link goes to the stock of parts under the "replaced by" number.

Commodity code   Classification of parts by group and class according to their material content or type for consolidation of procurement, storage, and use.

Component   A constituent part.

Confidence   Degree of certainty that something will happen. The statistical definition defines the range of certainty about mathematical samples. The social definition concerns human perceptions. For example, a low confidence of replenishment means that parts probably will not be rapidly replaced, and is the main reason field service personnel retain excess parts.

Configuration Physical and functional characteristics of systems, items, and related items of hardware or software; the specific parts used to construct a machine; the shape or makeup of a thing at a given time.

Consigned parts Items which are in the possession of customers, dealers, or other business partners but which remain the property of the title holder.

Constraint Any factor that prevents a system from achieving a higher level of performance with respect to its goal.

Consumables Supplies such as fuel, lubricants, paper, printer ribbons, cleaning materials, and forms, that are exhausted during use in operation and maintenance.

Contingency Alternate actions that can be taken if the main actions do not work.

Contract Agreement between two or more competent organizations or persons to perform or to not perform specific acts or services or to deliver merchandise. A purchase order becomes a contract when it is accepted by the supplier.

Cost The total acquisition and usage expenditure to the buying firm.

Cost of sales Cost of transfer from the supplier plus cost for operating the service parts function.

Cost-plus Pricing method where the buyer agrees to pay the seller the costs incurred to produce the goods or services, plus a percentage or a fixed fee.

Critical Category of items that are very important to performance and more vital to operation than are noncritical items; the essential "significant few."

Customer Person or organization who receives a product, service, or information. There may be internal customers as well as external customers. In the service parts business technicians or field engineers may be the main customers who in turn support end-users.

Cycle counting Inventory accuracy audit technique where items are counted on a cyclic schedule rather than once a year. Cycle counting aims to identify and eliminate causes of error.

Dead stocks Items for which no demand has occurred over a specific period of time.

Demand Requests and orders for an item. Demands become issues only when a requested part is given from stock.

Depreciation Financial write-down of the value of an item over its useful life. Parts depreciation ranges from 18 months to seven years. Part depreciation is typically expensed every month.

Direct costs Any expenses associated with a specific product, operation, or service.

Disposal Act of getting rid of surplus property under proper authorization. Typical means of disposal are to sell back to vendor/manufacturer, abandon, destruct, donate, recycle, sell, and scrap.

Distribution requirements planning Replenishment inventory calculations are usually time-phased from the lowest levels needing resupply up to the master repair/production/acquisition schedule. Rather than being limited to only time-phased logic, other planning approaches may be included such as "use one, order one" or period order quantities.

Distribution resource planning (DRP) The planning of key resources contained in a distribution system, including space, money, vehicles, and labor.

Downtime Portion of calendar time during which an item or equipment is not in condition to fully perform its intended function.

Echelon stock Intermediate stock levels in a logistics network between the central supply point and the point of maintenance.

Economic order quantity (EOQ) Amount of an item that should be ordered at one time to get the lowest possible combination of inventory-carrying costs and order/production costs.

Economic repair A repair that will restore a product to sound condition at a cost less than the value of its estimated remaining useful life.

Economy of scale Effect of larger volumes of activity reducing unit costs by distributing overhead across more units.

Engineering change   Any design change that requires revision to specifications, drawings, documents, or configurations.

Environment   Aggregate of all conditions and influences on parts and equipment. Typical considerations are physical location, operating characteristics of nearby equipment, actions of people, and the conditions of temperature, humidity, salt spray, acceleration, shock, vibration, radiation, and contaminants in the surrounding air or liquid.

Error type one/Alpha/Producer   Mistake made when items thought to be defective are, in fact, good.

Error type two/Beta/Consumer   Mistake made when items are thought to be good but are, in fact, defective. The acronym BAB (beta accept bad) should help in remembering the error types.

Error type three/Charlie/Problem   Mistake made when the problem is not correctly identified.

Essentiality   Importance of an item to performance of the mission.

Excess   Items declared to be more than required for current needs.

Expedite   Special efforts to accelerate a process. An expediter coordinates and assures adequate supplies of materials and equipment.

Expense   Those items that are directly charged as a cost of doing business. They generally have a short nondurable life. Technically, nonrepairable service parts should be expensed when installed on equipment; however, many organizations expense these low cost expendable parts when they are shipped to the field technician.

Expensed inventory   Parts written off as a "cost of sales." Material transferred from ledger inventory to expensed inventory is to be used within 12 months. The parts usually remain under the control of field service personnel in order to support maintenance under contract.

Exponential distribution   A continuous probability distribution where the probability of occurrence either steadily increases (positive exponential distribution) or decreases (negative).

Exponential smoothing   Mathematical technique that weights new data differently than old; also called a geometric moving average. Also used to modify future plans based on comparison of forecast plans with actual results.

Failure   Inability to perform the function within specified limits.

Failure modes, effects, and criticality analysis (FMECA)   Reliability analysis of what items are expected to fail, the consequences of failure, and how important they are to system performance.

Family   Group of products or other items similar in design and construction which can be treated as common for service purposes.

Federal Acquisition Regulations (FAR)   Documented conditions governing all U.S. federal agencies in procurement of services and supplies.

Fill rate   Service level of a specific stock point. An 85 percent fill rate means that if 100 parts are requested, then 85 of them are available and issued.

Financial reserves   Money planned for depreciation and the expenses of disposing of excess and obsolete durable items.

Finite replenishment rate   Specific, usually uniform, rate of replenishment; for example, 100 units per month.

Firm planned order   Order fixed in time and quantity, which must not be automatically changed by computer logic.

First in—first out (FIFO)   Use the oldest item in inventory next. FIFO accounting values each item used at the cost of the oldest item in inventory. Contrasts with LIFO (last in—first out).

First in—still here (FISH)   Result of poor forecasting and management. Any FISH parts should be removed from stock unless they are insurance-class parts which are essential and have a long acquisition lead time.

First pass fill rate (FPFR)   The percent of demands that can be met by parts stocked at the specific location.

Fixed costs   Expenses such as facilities and training that do not vary directly with activity rates.

Fixed order quantity   The quantity, or multiple thereof, to be generated due to batch production, repair, packaging, or shipping constraints.

Focus forecasting System that simulates the effectiveness of various possible forecasting techniques on a set of data in order to allow selection of the best technique.

Forecast Prediction of future demand; created by mathematical manipulation of historical data and future projections, possibly tempered by subjective judgments.

Forecast error Difference between forecast demand and the demand that actually occurred.

Fractionation supply Process whereby stocked items are classified as to relative rate of issue, cost, or other significant factors.

Free on board (FOB) Terms of sale that state where title passes from seller to buyer.

Frequency Count of occurrences during each time period or event. A typical frequency chart for inventory plots demand versus days.

Generally accepted accounting principles (GAAP) A group of principles and practices that provides standards for the accounting profession.

General and administrative (G&A) A category of expense, usually added as a percentage of direct labor and material costs, which covers support and management costs.

Gross profit Amount of profit as a percent of sales revenues.

Gross requirement Total of all demands for a component before netting on-hand and due-in quantities.

Hardware A physical object, as distinguished from a capability or function. A generic term dealing with tangible items of equipment—tools, instruments, components, parts—as opposed to funds, personnel, computer programs, and plans, which are termed "software."

Histogram Graphic plot of a frequency distribution by means of rectangles whose widths normally represent class intervals and whose heights represent corresponding frequencies.

Hold for disposition stock Defective material held at a stock location pending removal for repair or for scrap.

Identification Means by which items are named or numbered to indicate that they have a given set of characteristics.

Identification may be in terms of name, part number, type, model, specification number, drawing number, code, stock number, or catalog number. Items may also be identified as part of an assembly, a piece of equipment, or a system.

Incremental analysis   Analysis of the benefits gained versus costs related to change; also called marginal analysis. The cost of a single additional unit is normally compared to its related benefit or cost.

Independent demand   Need for an item that is not related to needs for other items. For example, initial branch startup parts and training parts that are not based on the number of installed products. Synonym is *nonrecurring*.

Indirect costs   Expenses not directly associated with specific products, operations, or services; usually considered as overhead.

Initial demand and supply   Earliest period of field introduction in which pipeline, shelf, training, and failure quantities must be taken into consideration.

Insurance items   Parts and materials that are not used often enough to meet detailed stock accounting criteria but are stocked because of their essentiality or the lead time involved in procuring replacements; similar to safety stocks, except on low-use parts.

Integrated logistics support (ILS)   Composite of the elements necessary to sustain the effective and economical use of a system or equipment, at all levels of maintenance, throughout its programmed life cycle. It is characterized by the harmony and coherence obtained between each of its elements and levels of maintenance.

Interchangeable   Parts with different configurations and numbers that may be substituted for other parts, usually without any modification or difference in performance, since they have the same form, fit, and function.

Interface   The common boundary between two or more items. That portion of anything that impinges upon or directly affects another item.

Intermediate part   Material processed beyond the raw material stage so that it can be rapidly completed into a finished part that may have several varied configurations, depending on the specific need. Cost is an influence. The desired scenario is to incur relatively little cost initially (large time and flexibility savings for little investment) with the major costs coming at completion.

Internal failure cost   The cost of things going wrong before the product reaches the customer. Examples include washout, burnin failures, quality rejects, shipping wrong parts, and work done over.

Inventory   Physical count of all items on hand by number, weight, length, or other measurement; also any items held in anticipation of future use.

Inventory control   That phase or function of logistics that includes cataloging, counting, procurement, inspection, storage, distribution, audits, and disposal, of material. Inventory control assures that we do have the parts we think we have.

Inventory investment   The money value of all levels of stocks.

Investment stock   Materials held for speculation in the hope that their value will increase owing to inflation, supply shortage, or other economic conditions.

ISO 9000 series standards   A set of five related international standards on quality developed by the International Standards Organization (ISO) based on inputs from the national standards organizations of 91 countries.

Isolation   Separation of the good from the bad in order to find and repair or replace the bad items.

Issue   To provide a part that fills a demand.

Item   Generic term used to identify a specific entity. Items may be parts, components assemblies, subassemblies, accessories, groups, parents, components, equipments, or attachments.

Job shop   Facility and organization in which similar equipment is organized by function. Each job, such as an equipment repair, follows distinct processes and routing through the shop.

Just-in-Case (JIC)   Strategy of providing parts to meet the level of support goals, within the contracted response time, for the target cost. JIC is driven by highly variable, stochastic demands compared to the relatively precise, deterministic basis of the Just-in-Time philosophy.

Just-in-Time (JIT)   Philosophy of eliminating waste by providing all activities and parts precisely when they are required, with zero defects, reduced lead times, efficient operations, and minimum costs.

Kanban   A Japanese method of JIT production or repair (developed by Toyota Corporation) that uses standard containers with a card attached. The Japanese word *kanban* means card, billboard, or sign. Kanban is a pull system in which work centers signal with a card that they want to withdraw parts.

Kit   Parts gathered for a common purpose and usually arranged in a special package. For example, a new product installation in remote geography may be supported by a kit of the parts that will most likely be needed.

Labor   Work done by people.

Last in—first out (LIFO)   Use newest inventory next. LIFO accounting values each item used at the cost of the last item added to inventory. Contrasts with FIFO (first in—first out).

Late finish date (LF)   The latest time an activity can be completed without delaying a related project.

Leading indicator   Specific business activity or index that indicates future trends. For example, equipment orders indicate the need to train technicians, order service parts, and plan installations.

Lead time   That amount of time estimated, or actually required, to accomplish a specific task such as acquiring a part. Total lead time normally counts the hours from recognition of the need for a part until the receipt of that part.

Learning curve   The graphic and underlying calculations that show the rate of improvement in productivity as more quantities of an item are accomplished. For example, technicians installing a field change may take four hours to do the first, two hours to do the second, and then do most of the rest in about one hour. Synonymous to *progress curve* and *experience curve*.

Least squares method   A statistical technique to determine the curve shape that best fits given data. This regression analysis minimizes the sum of the squares of the deviations of the given data points from the curve.

Ledger inventory   Items carried on the corporate financial balance sheet as material valued at cost.

Less than carload (LCL) or Less than Truckload (LTL)   Small shipments that do not fill a vehicle or do not weigh enough to qualify for rate discounts. General commodity truckloads are usually set at about 10,000 pounds.

Level of repair (LOR)   Locations and facilities at which items are to be repaired. Typical levels are operator, field technician, depot, and factory.

Level of service (LOS)   Desired measure (usually a percentage) of satisfying customer demands for the "right part, at the right place, at the right time."

Life cycle   Series of phases or events that constitute the total existence of anything. The entire "womb-to-tomb" scenario of a product from the time concept planning is started until it is finally discarded.

Life-cycle costs   All costs associated with the system life cycle, including research and development, production, operation, maintenance, and termination.

Logistics   Art and science of management and engineering, and the technical activities concerned with requirements design, and supplying and maintaining resources to support objectives, plans, and operations. (Society of Logistics Engineers' definition.)

Log normal distribution   Continuous probability distribution where the logarithms of the variable are normally distributed. The log normal form is common in service parts support where many parts are available in few minutes, some parts arrive the next morning, but a few parts take days to obtain.

Lower of cost or market   Value placed on inventory that uses the lower amount of what was paid for an item or what it could be sold for now.

Maintenance concept   Statements and illustrations that define the theoretical means of supporting equipment. It relates tasks, techniques, technology, tools, parts, and people.

Marginal analysis   Synonymous with incremental analysis.

Master part record   Data fields that detail all necessary top level facts about a stock keeping unit.

Material   Metal, wood, lubricants, cloth, and other hard goods generally purchased in bulk and used in smaller variable quantities; also all items used or needed in any business, industry, or operation as distinguished from personnel.

Matériel   Military term that covers all items necessary for the equipment, maintenance, operations, and support of military activities, whether for administrative or combat use, and excluding ships and aircraft.

Material requirements planning (MRP)   Manufacturing techniques that use the master production schedule, bill of materials, and inventory data to calculate requirements for materials. Time-phased MRP explodes the bill of material, adjusts for parts already on hand or on order, and then offsets the net requirements by appropriate lead times.

Maximum inventory quantity   The most parts that should be on hand. Generally this maximum will calculate as the sum of reorder point (ROP) + the reorder quantity (ROQ).

Mean absolute deviation (MAD)   Average of the absolute values of the deviations of observed values from some expected value. MAD is often calculated using absolute deviations of actual data from forecast.

Mean, arithmetic   Average of a series of values; specifically, their sum divided by the number of items in the series. Sometimes simply called "mean" and symbolized by $\overline{X}$ ("X bar").

Mean downtime (MDT)   Average time a system cannot perform its mission, including response, active maintenance, and supply and administrative time.

Mean logistics delay time (MLDT)   Downtime while necessary replacement parts, supplies, tools, or data are being obtained.

Mean time between failures (MTBF)   Average time/distance/events which a part or equipment performs between breakdowns.

Mean time between maintenance (MTBM)   Average time between both corrective and preventive acts.

Mean time between replacement (MTBR) Average time/distance/events between when a part is installed on equipment and when it is removed for any reason. Typically this is MTBF less the interval between scheduled preventive maintenance replacements.

Mean time to repair (MTTR) Average time required to fix a failed item.

Median Midpoint of a series of quantities or values; specifically, the quantity or value of that item which is so positioned in the series when arranged in order of numeric quantity or value that there are an equal number of values of greater magnitude and of lesser magnitude.

Milk run Regular route for delivery of good parts and pickup of defective or excess items.

Min-max system Type of order point replenishment system where the minimum (min) is the order point and the maximum (max) is the "order up to" level. The order quantity is variable. An order is triggered when the sum of on-hand inventory plus on-order inventory is at or below the minimum (reorder point) quantity.

Mode Most frequently occurring value or type in a series.

Model Simulation of an event, or process, or product by physical, mathematical, or verbal means.

Monte Carlo analysis Simulation in which occurrences have a probability of occurring proportionally to expectations in the "real world."

Moving average Mathematical method of considering recent events; for example, averaging the last three months' shipments or averaging the cost of the last ten items added to inventory.

National Stock Number (NSN) Identification number assigned to a stock keeping unit in the U.S. federal supply system.

Network fill rate Percent of orders filled completely at a local stock point plus additional stock points in the distribution network.

Next higher assembly Component level of hierarchy immediately superior to the item in question; "parent" item.

Nomograph Charts that relate mathematical models and provide solutions by connecting scales with straight lines.

Nonrecurring   Demands that are unlikely to happen again since they are for special situations.

Nonrepairable Parts   Items that are discarded upon failure for technical or economic reasons.

Normal distribution   Statistical distribution commonly referred to as a "bell curve." The mean, mode, and median are the same in a normal distribution. Deviations from the mean are equally likely to be plus or minus.

Not-operational-ready-spares (NORS)   Equipment that is not available for use because of a lack of parts.

Obsolescence   Decrease in value of items that have been superseded by superior items or are no longer needed.

Obsolete   Designation of an item for which there is no replacement. The part has probably become unnecessary as a result of a design change.

On-hand stock   Total quantity of good parts available for use.

On-order stock   Total of all replenishment orders. The on-order quantity increases with new orders and decreases when ordered parts are received or orders are cancelled.

Operating days (O days)   Number of days on which production activities take place. There are normally 250 operating days in a year.

Opportunity cost   Value of either gaining or failing to gain projected business. For example, if a customer requests a part that is not available, the customer may well go elsewhere for that part and perhaps also for other future purchases. The opportunity cost of that part would be the potential profit from that customer's business. This is also termed "lost sales" or "lost sales cost." Also defined as the return on capital that would have resulted if the money had been used for some other purpose.

Optimal replenishment model   Mathematical process of determining what quantity to order and when, by using a fixed order point or a fixed order interval.

Order   Demand or request for an item. When the order is filled, it is termed "issued" or "shipped," but is only termed "used" when installation in equipment is reported.

Order costs   All costs related to acquiring an item, including soliciting and qualifying suppliers, selecting the vendor, preparing and communicating the purchase order, expediting, receiving, quality assurance, and paying the invoice. There are normally separate order costs for internal versus external orders, and further variations for blanket orders that should cost less than unique orders and for different commodities.

Order point (P)   Quantity of parts at which an order will be placed when usage reduces stock to that level; also called reorder point (ROP) or trigger level. Yes, the common abreviation is a single letter P. The quantity is normally calculated as the forecast use during the replenishment lead time plus safety stock.

Order entry (OE)   The function of translating a customer's desires into terms used by the supplier. OE includes creating of pick, pack, and ship documents or electronic instructions.

Order quantity (Q)   Number of items demanded. The economic order quantity (EOQ), also called minimum cost quantity, is a specific number; but the actual order quantity may vary as a result of cost, packaging, transportation, discounts, or extraordinary demand.

Original equipment manufacturer (OEM)   A production operation that buys and incorporates another supplier's products into its own products. For example, a personal computer OEM may build its PCs from mother boards, disk drives, and power supplies all manufactured by other companies.

Outsourcing   Process of having external partners provide goods and services that were previously provided by internal employees.

P model   Mathematical logic for determining quantities on the basis of fixed order point (P).

Packaging   Use of protective wrappings, cushioning, containers, and complete identification marking.

Packing   Application or use of exterior shipping containers or other shipping media (such as pallets), and the assembling of items or packages thereof, together with the necessary blocking, bracing, or cushioning; weatherproofing; exterior strapping; and marking of the shipping container.

Pareto principle Critical few (often about 20 percent) of parts or people or users that should receive attention before the insignificant many (which is usually about 80 percent). In service parts, the percentage often goes to 90: 10.

Part A material item (hardware or software) that is used as a component of equipment. A part such as a printed circuit board may be itself made from many components that function effectively when combined into the discrete functional part. Parts generally make up subassemblies, higher assemblies, and complete equipments.

Part numbers Unique identifying numbers that denote each specific part configuration; also called *stock numbers* or *item numbers.*

Parts bank A stock of inventory carefully controlled for rapid issue.

Perpetual record Constantly updated records that will identify the status of parts at any point in time.

Physical distribution Movement, control, protection, and storage of materials. Activities included are freight, transportation, warehousing, material handling, protection, packaging, market forecasting, and customer service.

Physical inventory The actual parts themselves. Also the audit of inventory quantities by actual count, typically done annually.

Picking Process of taking the correct demanded parts from stock for issue or shipment.

Pick list Document on paper or electronic media that describes all parts to be picked.

Pipeline Channel of support by means of which material or personnel flow from sources of supply to their point of use, or from point of failure to the repair point.

Pipeline stock Material moving to or from one point to another, usually from the source to the point of issue, or defective material moving from the point of failure to the repair point.

Pipeline requirements That dynamic part of the total service parts requirements needed to support the flow of parts between static stocking locations.

Planning The process of determining service parts requirements and distribution to meet performance goals. The outputs of planning are multileveled, many and varied including: forecasts, budgets, investment requirements, management action plans, purchase requests, and repair orders.

Poisson Frequency distribution that is a good approximation of the binomial distribution as the number of trials increases and the probability of success in a single trial is small; often used to describe demand queuing.

Predictive maintenance Subset of preventive maintenance that uses nondestructive testing such as spectral oil analysis, vibration evaluation, and ultrasonics with statistics and probabilities to predict when and what maintenance should be done to prevent failures.

Preventive maintenance (PM) Actions performed in an attempt to keep an item in a specified operating condition by means of systematic inspection, detection, and prevention of incipient failure.

Priority order classification Rank of importance and shipping sequence in order processing systems. Typically, P1 = system down and R = routine.

Probability The mathematical number between 0 and 1 that estimates the number of events in which a particular result will occur. For example, a .90 (90%) probability of having a part on hand means that if the part is demanded 100 times then it will be available 90 times. The downside risk is often more painful that the upside, so the goal is often stated "equal to or greater than x%."

Procurement Process of obtaining persons, services, supplies, facilities, materials, or equipment. It may include design, standards determination, specification development, selection of suppliers, financing, contract administration, and other related functions.

Product code Designation used to extract part groups from a master file according to product. For example, "ABN" could be A = product line, B = equipment within product, N = basic equipment, option, or kit.

Provisioning Process of determining and selecting the varieties and quantities of repair parts, spares, special tools, and test and support equipment that should be procured and stocked to sustain and maintain equipment for specified periods of time. It includes identification of items of supply; establishing data for catalogs, technical manuals, and allowance lists; and providing instructions and schedules for delivery of provisioned items.

Purchase order (PO) The purchaser's authorization that formalizes an acquisition transaction with a supplier. The PO should include names, addresses, description and price of the goods or services, and the terms and conditions of the commitment.

Push system Initial supply and replenishment of items from central (wholesale) distribution to field (retail) stocks where decision making is centralized. (Contrasted with *pull system*, where field operations request the parts.)

Q model Type of inventory model that operates on a fixed order quantity (Q).

Queuing Pattern of demand placed on any activity, such as an accumulation of work at a work station.

Quick response program (QRP) System of linking all elements of a supply chain electronically, which may use direct shipments from suppliers to end users.

Range In statistics, the spread from the smallest event to the largest. For example, from 3 to 12. It is important for service parts to state the absolute range of "3 to 12," rather than the relative quantity between the two of "(12 − 3) = 9."

Ready for issue (RFI) Category of good stock available for immediate shipment.

Records Data, facts, and information. The media may range from a small black book in the worker's pocket to an electronic computer file. A computerized part record contains all fields of data about a part.

Receiving Function that takes custody of incoming materials, assures conformance with the purchase order, checks for damage, and notifies both physical handling personnel and Accounts Payable of the status.

Recurring Demand that will probably happen again, so should be planned for in the future.

Reliability Probability that any item will perform its intended function without failure for a specified time under specified conditions.

Reorder point (ROP) Minimum quantity, established by economic calculation and management direction, that triggers the ordering of more items.

Repair Restoration or replacement of parts or components as necessitated by wear, tear, damage, or failure; to return the facility, equipment, or part to efficient operating condition.

Repair code Yes/No designation of whether or not a part can be repaired. May also indicate the facility at which the part is repaired.

Repair component parts Parts below the field maintenance level that are needed to repair failed parts at the repair point. For example, a repair depot may use discrete electronic components that should not be provided to field technicians.

Repair parts Individual parts or assemblies required for the maintenance or repair of equipment, systems, or spares. Such repair parts may also be repairable or nonrepairable assemblies, or one-piece items. (Consumable supplies used in maintenance or repair, such as wiping rags, solvents, and lubricants, are not considered repair parts.) Repair parts are also *service parts*.

Repair point Location at which defective repairables are repaired and returned to a ready-for-issue condition.

Repairables Parts or items that are technically and economically repairable. A repairable part, upon becoming defective, is subject to return to the repair point for repair action.

Replaced by Term applied to a part number that has been superseded by another part.

Replaceable spare parts list (RSPL) The list of parts, usually in the back of an equipment manual, that a manufacturer recommends be stocked to support the product. Those field replaceable parts that should be on the authorized stock list.

Retrofit Part, assembly, or kit that will replace similar components originally installed on equipment. Retrofits are generally performed on a machine to correct a deficiency or to improve performance.

Return on investment (ROI)   Financial measure of the relative return from money (or other resources) put into goods or services. ROI is usually expressed as a percentage of the earnings produced by an asset divided by the amount invested.

Revenue   Money received for supplying parts, labor, equipment, or other products and services.

Run-rate   The rate of demand for a part at a particular stocking location.

Safety stock   Quantity of an item, in addition to the normal level of supply, required to be on hand to permit continuing operation with a specific level of confidence if resupply is late or demand suddenly increases.

Scenario   Description in words and or graphics that describes how an item will be used, or how a situation can develop.

Scheduled maintenance (SM)   Subset of preventive maintenance based on fixed intervals of time or use or events.

Scrap   Items discarded in so far as original use is concerned and which have no reasonable prospect of value except for the recovery of their basic material content.

Seasonal trends   Variations in demand that fluctuate with the seasons of a year. The influencing factors may be weather, vacations, holidays, growing cycles, or similar events that are repeated annually.

Secondary failures   Malfunctions caused by the failure of another item.

Service level   Frequency, usually expressed as a percentage, with which a demand can be filled within the required time. A 95 percent level of service means that 95 out of 100 demands are properly issued. If viewed from the end customer or service technician's perspective, the service level is the percent of parts received on time, out of those requested, from any and all levels of the support system. Synonymous with *support level*.

Serial number   A unique identification number assigned to a single item that will never be repeated on similar items.

Service parts   Parts used for the repair and/or maintenance of an assembled product. Synonyms are *spare parts, spares,* or *repair parts.*

Setup costs   All expenses necessary to prepare for manufacturing or repair of an ordered part. Setup costs are usually assumed to be constant regardless of the quantities produced, so the cost per unit will decrease as order size increases. Setup costs may increase substantially in later stages of the life cycle after routine production is stopped, since additional retooling, material, information, training, and personnel relearning is required.

Shelf life   Period of time during which an item can remain unused in proper storage without significant deterioration.

Shelf requirements   That part of the total service parts requirements needed at specific stocking locations at any given time to meet performance parameters.

Shipment   Item or group of items from one place, released to a carrier for transportation to a single destination.

Shipping   Function that arranges outgoing packaging, weighing, documentation, loading, and transportation of items.

Shrink   Loss of inventory due to loss, theft, and damage.

Simulation   Mathematical process that attempts to model what will happen in the real world. An inventory simulation is usually run on a computer with probabilities of demand and supply injected according to typical patterns.

Single sourcing   Supply of items by only one vendor. (Contrasts with traditional acquisition which used at least two suppliers for every item to foster competition.) Sole sourcing requires high quality, reliable performance, short lead times, and close cooperation. The benefits are less administrative burden, better communications, and sharing of rewards.

Six-sigma quality   Term used to indicate that a process is under tight control. Motorola popularized the term for ∓ 6 sigma from the centerline on a control chart.

Smoothing   Averaging data by a mathematical process such as least squares or regression analysis.

Smoothing constant   The weighting factor in exponential smoothing that is applied to the most recent data. For example, an "alpha factor" of .8 would give most recent data a weight of four times the .2 remainder that $(1.0 - .8 = .2)$ gives to the old data.

Software Efforts, plans, and documentation to support or sustain projects, operations, equipment, and items; including such things as engineering and design, technical data, plans, schedules, and computer programs. Software excludes physical parts, materials, equipment, and tools; and contrasts with hardware.

Spare parts (spares) Components, assemblies, and equipment that are completely interchangeable with like items installed or in use, which are used, or can be used, to replace items removed during maintenance and overhaul. These parts used for maintenance of an assembled product are also called field replaceable units (FRUs). *Service parts* is a more desirable name because "spare" has the connotation of being extra.

Specifications Documents that clearly and accurately describe the essential requirements for materials, items, equipment, systems, or services, including the procedures by which it will be determined that the requirements have been met. Such documents may include performance, support, preservation, packaging, packing, and marking requirements.

Standard deviation Measure of average dispersion (departure from the mean) of numbers, computed as the square root of the average of the squares of the difference between numbers and their arithmetic mean.

Standard item Part, component, material, subassembly, assembly, or equipment that is identified or described accurately by a standard document or drawing.

Standardization Process of establishing the greatest practical uniformity of items and of practices to assure the minimum feasible variety of such items and practices, and effect optimum interchangeability.

Standards Established or accepted rules, models, and criteria by which the degree of user satisfaction of a product or an act is determined, or against which comparisons are made. A document that establishes engineering and technical limitations for items, materials, processes, methods, designs, and practices is therefore a standard.

Statistics Collecting, classifying, summarizing, and interpreting of numeric facts by other than accounting methods.

Stock   Items in inventory ready for issue. There may be good stocks separate from defective stocks.

Stock number   Number assigned by the stocking organization to each group of articles or material, which is then treated as if identical within the using supply system; also called *part number* or *item number* or *part identifier.*

Stock out   Indicates that all quantities of a part normally on hand have been used, so that the items are not presently available. Demand for a nonstock part is usually treated as a separate situation.

Stock-point fill rate   Percent of orders filled completely on the first pass. First pass fill rate (FPFR).

Stockkeeping unit (SKU)   Reference that designates each SKU from others according to shape, size, color, odor, strength, reliability, or other characteristics. An SKU inventory means the stock of an individually described SKU that may contain any quantity of units.

Stockkeeping unit location (SKUL)   Number of units inventoried at one facility. One or more SKUs make up a product line and the sum of all SKUs make up a total inventory for a company.

Supplier   Provider of goods or services. Synonym is *vendor.*

Supply   Procurement, storage, and distribution of items.

Support level   Percent of demanded items that can be issued within the specified time from all applicable sources. (For example, if the requirement is for overnight part delivery, then the local technician can get the part from central stocks.)

System   Assemblage of correlated hardware, software, methods, procedures, and people, or any combination of these, all arranged or ordered toward a common objective.

Terms and conditions (Ts & Cs)   Provisions and agreements listed in a contract.

Third party logistics company   A company that manages part or all of another company's product or part supply, repair, and/or delivery functions.

Throwaway maintenance   Maintenance performed by discarding used parts rather than attempting to repair them.

Time-based competition   Corporate strategy that emphasizes time as a means to achieve competitive advantage.

Trial products   Test items usually built in small quantities for research and development, experimentation, development, testing, and demonstration prior to production.

Turnaround time   Interval between the time a repairable item is removed from use and the time it is again available in serviceable condition.

Turnover   The number of times that inventory cycles, or "turns" during a year. Turnover is measured on either numbers of parts or on monetary value that evaluates how often a part is demanded versus the average number of parts kept in inventory. For example, if two widgets are kept in inventory and eight are used each year, then the turnover is $8/2 = 4$ per year. In monetary terms, however, turnover is the cost of inventory sold/average cost of inventory carried. A common calculation is to divide the average inventory level dollar value into the annual dollar usage. For example, if an average inventory on hand of $1 million supported annual usage of $4 million, that would be 4 turns. Unit turns is a better measure for management since that equates more to the number of customers affected and is not biased by a few high dollar items.

Uncertainty   Lack of definite knowledge that ranges between complete certainty and a total lack of knowledge. Variability of demand and supply creates uncertainty.

Unit cost   The total cost to acquire one part. Make sure that order, transportation, and processing expenses are added to the price paid to the vendor and prorated per part unit.

Universal product code (UPC)   A type of bar code used on groceries and retail goods.

Unscheduled maintenance (UM)   Corrective maintenance (CM), emergency maintenance (EM), or repairs to restore a failed item to usable condition; contrasts with *scheduled maintenance*.

Upgradability   Yes or No code that indicates feasibility of modifying the previous revision of a part to the current revision.

Usage   Quantity of items consumed or necessary for product support. Usage is generally greater than the technical failure rate.

Variable cost   Costs that change as a function of units of time, labor, or material resources.

Warranty   Guarantee that an item will perform as specified for at least a specified time, or will be repaired or replaced at no cost to the user.

Wear out   Deterioration as a result of age, corrosion, temperature, or friction that generally increases the failure rate over time.

2 UNIQUE ATTRIBUTES OF SERVICE PARTS

here are at least fifteen major differences between parts used to manufacture a durable product and the parts used to repair and service it. Production has received considerable attention in recent years. Many Japanese techniques, including kanban and just-in-time, have been effectively adapted, in concert with cellular assembly, team empowerment, and material requirements planning (MRP). Advances in manufacturing and production offer knowledge that can improve service parts. Production of equipment just-in-time is, however, a very different situation from managing just-in-case service parts.

The dynamic environment of the service parts processes is much more complex. In many ways, the process is similar to a double MRP. First, repairable assets are analyzed with the goal of using a part already owned. Then, if a part must be procured from sources external to Service, a second MRP-type process is used to plan that acquisition. A major reason why standard MRP will not work for service parts is that MRP is based on fixed cycles with variable quantities, while service parts planning should be based on fixed quantities with variable cycles. Early versions of the service simile were termed distribution requirements planning (DRP). The advanced techniques of demand and supply planning (DASP) are covered later in this book.

The transition of components from proprietary, legacy items to their being common, open, multivendor parts contributes to further opportunities. The proprietary equipment of yesterday is giving way to equipment assembled from standard components. Production can learn many lessons from Service, and Service can learn much from Production. The major service parts inventory factors are shown in Table 2-1.

TABLE 2-1

Fifteen ways that Service parts are different from production parts

1. Product life phases	9. Risk
2. Future variability	10. Essentiality
3. Replacement causes	11. Flexibility
4. Multiple locations	12. Repairables
5. People influence	13. Diagnostics
6. Confidence effect	14. Gain or loss
7. Demand - supply cycle	15. Systems
8. Pain or pleasure	

Product life phases

The first main difference between the way parts should be analyzed for service and the way they should be analyzed for manufacturing is the life phases which service parts must go through. The approximate length of each phase is shown in figure 2-1.

Manufacturing, by definition, is but one period in a product's life cycle. There are five distinct phases of product life:

Preproduction
Product introduction
Normal life
Postproduction
Termination

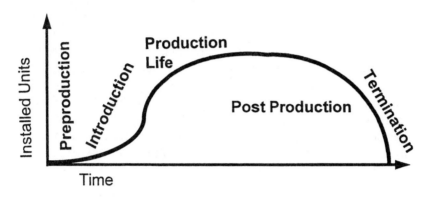

FIGURE 2-1 Service life is much longer than production

The first phase, preproduction, includes tests and training with new equipment, very little historical data, some correlation with prior products, possibly laboratory tests, and reliability handbook predictions; but that is about all the knowledge available at this stage. Initial support is based on people's best engineering experience and educated judgment. Service parts, in spite of all our sophistication and technology, is still very much a people business. Experienced, educated, and dedicated people are vital to help manage service parts.

In the second phase, product introduction, a fundamental concern is having a basic supply of service parts. Provisioning must be carefully done using every possible source of information, and manufacturing must be pushed to deliver the required parts on schedule. Because of frequent configuration changes and resulting obsolescence, buy as few early parts as possible. On the other hand, introduction is the most critical period for Sales, since successful customer reports will increase sales, and negative reports can kill a new product. Parts availability at introduction must be carefully planned, with emphasis on flexibility rather than large quantities.

The third phase a product goes through is the ongoing normal life phase, which should be many, many years. Valid use data is gathered, computer models start to operate well, forecasts can be adjusted on the basis of good field predictions and what engineers say is going to happen to their design changes, and perhaps the numbers are large enough that parts planners can generate accurate forecasts.

Then, one day, an e-mail message comes, "Production of the model 95 stops at the end of next month. How many extra parts do you want us to make for service?" That question strikes fear into the minds of many parts planners. Major decisions are required and involve large financial investment. The source of parts may change in the post-production phase. Often, production can make a final batch of parts before they convert to new products. In some cases, service simply takes over the vendors who were supplying production. In many other cases, as discussed later in this book, service will function with mostly repaired and cannibalized parts.

Eventually end of life comes in the termination phase, when the product has to be withdrawn from the marketplace. Early in a product's life, very few people like to face the fact that their product may die. However, logisticians must think about the idea because they must come up with very specific decisions for the end of life. Not many people say, "We're going to support it for ten years after the last one is built," or "We will support it for seven years after it's delivered to you." There are many products still in the marketplace forty years later, and no one will say, "Sales, it's time you tell the customer that we are not going to support that model 95 any longer." It's an opportunity for Service to do a sales job on Sales and say, "It's your chance to get our latest, greatest product out there and replace that old one that's just limping along." Some service organizations evaluate parts on annual schedules during later years to plan discontinuance. In this way, product support generates life phases that do not generally pertain to manufacturing.

Future variability

Future demand variability does not function like a production schedule. Manufacturing demands for parts tend to be deterministic, given a bill of materials and a build schedule.

Service parts demands are probabilistic, driven by random equipment failure plus human intervention. An overhead projector provides an example of the differences. Production requires every item on the bill of materials to assemble the projector. They need one frame, one lens, one platen, two light bulbs, etc. Service planners now look at the product and think, What will need to be replaced? They know that the light bulb will fail at about 120 hours of use. The designers of most projectors realize that bulb failure will stop the show, so they design in a second bulb that can quickly take over the lighting function. That at least means that a burned-out bulb can be replaced overnight instead of causing an immediate panic. Service planners don't order any frames, because the entire machine will be replaced if the frame is damaged. Planners do realize that they probably need more switches than the reliability failure rate tables predict. The reason is that people like to set their coffee cups on the flat surface from where they often spill sugary liquid into the switch. That failure mode is not considered by many designers, but it does affect service part demand.

Service is a business that must be very flexible. Our judgments are educated, but we are predicting and forecasting the future, so we're planning for tomorrow and the following days with inevitable complications. At the very least we must try at least to forecast what future demand is going to be. Some computer programs will do that, but the logic is only history projected into the future. There is considerable art mixed with the science. The computer cannot accurately predict what's going to happen unless we provide it with information that is modeled to show how the real world is going to operate. This is one area that a well-educated and financially experienced person should control. A good person with effective computer assistance can handle up to 12,000 line items, although 3,000 to 8,000 is typical. As few as 300 line items may be a full load if these are repairables with a high activity rate and if they account for a large percentage of the business.

Service parts managers must have a working relationship with engineering and marketing in order to know in advance what changes are coming. A lot of information is covered informally; you cannot force such communications into an ultraformal relationship. Service management should insist on signing off engineering change orders (ECOs). Any field engineering organization that does not have sign-off of ECOs is never going to be operationally effective. This issue must be forced, but there are many issues and communications that are much better handled over a cup of coffee. "Well, Sam Design Engineer, what changes are you planning? What's going to happen beyond the formal paperwork?" "Marketing, when is that product going to be terminated? Do you really expect to install 3000 units of that superfuser? Are we planning a big promotion that will need a lot of consumables, or are we getting into a peculiar change in the market?" "Is there possibly a new use for the product that is going to alter the usage of those parts?" "Are products suddenly going to be stocked at different locations, or shipped to remote locations, whereas equipment has been geographically centered until now?" These things must be factored into our computations, and only a human can tell the computer what's going to happen. Otherwise you come up with the GIGO problem, which now means "garbage in, gospel out" because it's coming from a computer. Data are not necessarily accurate just because they are in printout form. If you lie to a computer, it will lie to you. People have to help determine causes, risks, and ranges of future demand variability.

Replacement causes

The causes for replacement of service parts are not all attributable to failure. Many parts are replaced because diagnostics are inadequate, manuals give incorrect instructions, or the tech rep can't find out what the problem is and so pulls out the easiest thing to remove. Perhaps the cause is really a loose connection on the board, but when the tech rep replaces the whole board, the problem goes away, so the decision is made that the problem was a defective board. The U.S. Air Force and many civilian industrial organizations find that 30 to 45 percent of all their electronic modules coming back as failed are actually good. Fortunately, a lot is being done to improve design of equipment and the support hardware and software, and to train maintenance personnel in how to troubleshoot problems. Several new, complex products have No Trouble Found (NTF) rates under 5 percent, which is a major improvement.

There are many reasons besides failure for why parts are replaced. Training causes damage when short circuits or overstress conditions occur. Inept operators damage equipment. Even willful damage sometimes takes place. Parts are occasionally replaced twice, owing to incorrect installation on the first repair. Frustrated technicians trying to show customers that they are working hard may replace parts just to show activity.

Multiple locations

Figure 2–2 shows the complexity of a typical service parts network. Most field service representatives have parts in their cars. Parts are also stored at district, area, branch, zone, or regional distribution centers—whatever the facilities are called—even at technicians' homes. Stocking service parts is a much more complex problem than having parts in one or two manufacturing locations. There are advantages to stocking parts in multiple locations if management can learn to utilize those multiple locations. But, more locations usually mean increased parts quantities and costs, and difficulty finding the part you want that might not be where it is supposed to be.

There are economies of scale to consolidation. If all parts are put in a centralized location where they can all be seen in one big area, fine. When parts are distributed to the four winds, management control is very difficult. Only a few service organizations have accurate knowledge of what stock is being kept. However, with the advent of distributed processing and computer systems, perpetual inventories can be kept. It is vital to control inventory by location and quantity. Parts cannot be controlled well by a once-a-year physical inventory that may not be done correctly anyway, at the holiday season, in lackadaisical fashion, over the weekend when people would rather be elsewhere. Once-a-year physical inventory often causes morale, accuracy, and reliability problems. As computer power becomes less expensive and more sophisticated, the link between maintenance reports and the parts used helps to improve effective control of inventory.

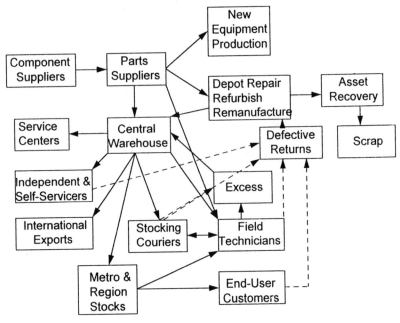

FIGURE 2–2
The service parts network is very complex

Management must keep current on what parts are where. To do that, there are two initial computer reports that will really help. One of these, the New Item Candidate report, documents what parts are used, but have not been stocked. If parts are requested, they should be on hand. If an emergency order was required, why weren't the parts in stock? There we have the information that says, "We should be carrying those parts."

On the flip side of that situation are the parts that a company has in stock but did not use in the last six months. If they weren't used, why are field technicians carrying them around in car trunks? Turnover and use reports provide the information that enables management to go back and take a good look at both supply and demand. The holding of parts and the actual use of those parts has to be tied together. Identification of excess parts means that those valuable assets can be specified for consolidation and reduction.

People influence

People have a major influence on our service system. A production-line approach to service helps to standardize a lot of things in the service area and give people direction. If people don't have direction, they'll do their own thing. Intelligent service managers need to determine the one best way to do things, gain the participation of employees, and work with them so they will do their jobs in the best possible fashion. Service parts is a people business that can be standardized to best practices much better than it has been in the past.

People need to be trained. All parts people should be educated about the service parts business, and about mathematics and how to use the basic economics and statistics that are necessary to understand supply and demand. This knowledge should be taught at a fundamental level so that all service representatives can learn to manage parts for their particular territories. An observer on a recent field improvement program watched a tech rep diagnose a defective microswitch, take the switch apart, and spend 1 1/2 hours rebuilding the switch, including soldering internal components. The technician had four calls waiting and had three good microswitches in the car trunk right outside the door. He spent one and a half hours fixing the defective switch because his manager had recently told him that his parts were costing too much. If there hadn't been a well-qualified observer watching, it would never have been believed! The tech rep said he was doing what his manager wanted him to do. He truly thought he was doing the right thing, and yet that equipment probably failed the next day because he had reduced the reliability of the switch. He wasted one and a half hours that could have been billed at the rate of about $100 an hour. By the time that second call was completed, he had invested over $150 in a $3 switch. And yet might not your reps do the same thing? Do your people have the right kind of guidance to suggest why that was a bad thing to do? That tech rep worked for the service division of a *Fortune 500* company!

The effects of confidence

Confidence is a general human problem, but is listed here because of its influence on service parts. Tech reps must have confidence that they can get a resupply of parts. One of the biggest single factors that causes tech reps to stock excess parts is lack of confidence in being resupplied. It is much better to have a consistent supply system than one that is sometimes very fast and other times very slow. That is like having one foot in the oven and the other in a block of ice: on the average you may be statistically comfortable, but you're burning one foot and freezing the other! A lot of our parts support is done that way. Somebody yells wolf, and all of a sudden the parts are supplied on emergency order overnight, while normal orders take several weeks. Trust will be lost. You can't blame tech reps for wanting to cache away a supply of parts when they don't have confidence in the system. Consistent, good support is a challenge, and a tremendous opportunity for management. Once confidence improves, stock that was once thought essential will be given up as excess.

Both demand and supply can vary

Time requirements for parts availablity vary from immediate need in the case of an air traffic control computer to the next day in the case of most home computers. Rarely do you need to have a part available before the technician is ready to replace it. If a service call is scheduled for tomorrow morning, then the parts can be stocked centrally and delivered overnight. On the other hand, if a critical server goes down, the needed part may be required within an hour or two, and therefore must be available close to the customer site. Parts for installation and preventive maintenance can use the same just-in-time techniques that work for manufacturing.

Any time a tech rep comes into the office in the morning to pick up parts, considerable productive time will be lost. Not only are tech reps not starting their first call of the day at starting time but they're often wasting time talking with other employees, having a cup of coffee, and then starting to drive to their first customer. A lot of time is lost. Get those parts into the tech rep's hands with a "milk run" that travels a regular route, or by direct shipment to the customer or the technician's home, or in whatever way gets the parts efficiently to the point of need.

It is very important that field engineering, field service planning, service program management—people with field experience—participate in the early design stages of any product. It is not possible for the typical design engineer to understand all the environments that products are going to encounter in the field. It is not possible to learn experience from a textbook. You must get out in the field; you must see it. Take engineers by the hand to user locations and show them how the products and parts are being used in the field. Show them what the customers do with parts. Listen to customers. Watch casual operators try to manipulate equipment. It's a challenge because engineers are always working on high priorities, albeit perhaps not effectively. They may be working on the wrong thing. Service should provide guidance and arrange for experienced service engineers to work closely with product engineers during new-product design and development.

Another alternative is to present a "show-and-tell" in-house. Some very effective things can be done with photographs, 35mm slides, and audiovisuals during a lunch hour. Have a lunchtime presentation in the local cafeteria. Show some of the situations in which the equipment is used, how parts are used, and how they're handled. Show all the steps of the demand-and-supply cycle that the parts go through so people can pre-act instead of just react.

A specific blind spot in manufacturing compared to service is the lead times for delivering new parts. Especially with material requirements planning (MRP), a lead time is firmly established, and many operations are scheduled around that number of days (or months). Service lead time is specifically measured to include everything from the time a technician recognizes that he needs the part until that part is in his hand for installation. Often, when a service part is ordered, the scheduler looks up the lead time, adds it to the present date, and keys in that date as the required date. Finished parts often sit on the shelf waiting until delivery on the required date to meet "on time" JIT goals. Service often really needs delivery *as soon as practical*. Watch out so the lead time does not become a self-fulfilling prophecy to deliver parts slowly, because that is what it has always done.

Pain or pleasure

Figure 2-3 depicts several business and psychological factors. Unlike manufacturing, which needs parts for every unit of production, service parts is a one or zero business. The normal need is for one part. If you have that part, I am moderately pleased. After all, your job is to have the part I need. If you do not have a part (zero on hand) then I am very unhappy and probably give you considerable pain. If you have two parts, I may take some satisfaction in knowing there is a backup in case my part does not work, but the pleasure is little. When the quantity of excess gets large and expensive, then the financial burden begins to get painful. It is judged that the pain of too many parts will never get as severe as the pain of not having the one part I need.

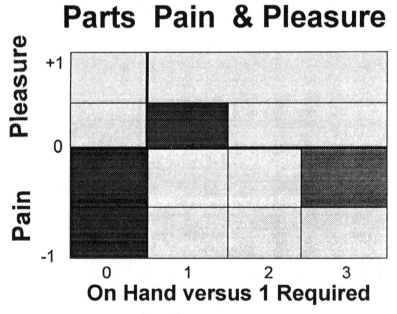

FIGURE 2-3
Parts inflict more pain than pleasure.

Risk

While manufacturing must have every part listed on the assembly bill of materials, no service organization can afford to stock 100 percent of possible needs. Risk is a fact of life with service parts. Service managers have to learn to deal with probabilities and confidence levels. Judgment is rarely going to be right all of the time. An organization that carries all the parts ever needed must have money to burn. The typical service manager can become very emotional over that customer who cannot be supported because of the lack of a part. Ninety-five percent availability of parts means that 5 percent of the parts are not going to be immediately on hand. Risk can be measured as the percent of orders not filled within the specified time limit. For example, if 98 percent of field replaceable units (FRUs) are to be available within 24 hours, then the risk is 100 − 98 = 2 percent. You must learn to live with that kind of quantification and risk in order to manage the service parts business.

Essentiality

Essentiality attempts to concentrate attention on the parts most critically important to equipment operation and customer satisfaction. It often uses a four-point system:

Class 1 Safety or severe damage
Class 2 Not operable
Class 3 Degraded
Class 4 Cosmetic

Basically, class number 1 is assigned to a part if the concern is safety or legality, or if the part is likely to cause severe damage if it fails. A safety valve is obviously a class 1 item. A class 2 rating means the equipment can not operate, and will therefore not produce revenue or fulfill its mission. A class 3 rating means that the part is slightly degraded, substandard, slow speed, or low quality. Class 3 is the default rating. Class 4 applies to a minor cosmetic item. Class 1 and 2 parts will be car stock if they are frequently used and are cost effective. Rarely should a tech rep ever carry a part rated 4. The next service call is usually adequate to replace that glass or panel, or to take the spray paint and touch up the part. Note that essentiality alone does not answer the question, Stock or not? Cost and frequency of need must also be considered.

Manufacturing has no critical parts. Or, depending on how you look at it, all parts are critical. Essentiality considerations are important to service, but they are not so useful to manufacturing. To build a machine requires all parts, with little recourse. Nearly every product serviced has some parts that are highly essential to the safe operation of equipment, while other parts are not. This implies that separate processes may be used to assure the prompt availability of the essential versus the nonessential parts. Joe Patton first described essentiality in a 1971 paper on planning spare parts for preproduction products, which is partially covered in chapter 9. However, few service parts systems today gain the advantage of essentiality. Assign an essentiality rating to every part. A part should be given an essentiality rating when it is entered into the information system by a service engineer who understands how that part is being used in the machine.

The machine itself should also be given an essentiality rating so we know how important it is. If it's a life-support machine, it gets a very essential class 1 rating. If the equipment is an overhead projector, it's less critical. If the projector light goes out, the projector is out of commission but the failure certainly isn't going to be catastrophic. That light bulb would be an essentiality class 2. A particular piece of equipment may be essential to a specific customer. If a medical center has four sterilizers, the situation is not critical if one of them fails. If there is only one sterilizer in a small rural hospital, that one is more essential to the small hospital than any one of the four is to the medical center. Everybody in service should be using the essentiality classification system. Every part and every piece of equipment supported should be rated according to its essentiality. Essentiality is a major factor that should be universally considered in service.

Flexibility

A major service condition is flexibility. Service situations that affect part demand rates are in a continual state of flux. There are many opportunities in service to use management information and make use of multiple part locations to find needed parts: Go to the next higher assembly. Look to other products on which the part is used. Repair a damaged part. Even, as a last resort, cannibalize (dismantle a piece of equipment for its parts). There are many different places where a part can be found, if the information is available on where to find it. Management information systems in the future should disclose perpetual inventory to everyone involved, right down to the field representative/dealer level so that it is known instantly where those parts are—from the central distribution center to the individual technician in the field.

The challenges and opportunities are ripe for flexibility. Outsourcing with supply and repair of parts by independent parts specialists is growing. There is no need to pay money and own parts on the balance sheet if you can instead exchange rapidly, or borrow, or rent, or share needed parts. Too often stocks are limited as a result of artificial measures rather than accurate business-level forecasts based on supported installed units, contracted response times, desired support levels, and benefits of the recommended stock list.

Most leading companies give their service reps and dealers an authorized/recommended stock list and require stocking those parts. The stocking lists are based on the product models in the territory, and the population and use of the equipment being supported. Push-versus-pull inventory is one of the techniques that says, management knows better what inventory you ought to carry. That narrow position can cause problems if a tech rep suddenly has to go on a call out of the territory and may not have the parts for the equipment to be serviced. Logistics business models based on good historical information and accurate projection of the future can accurately forecast the parts and the quantities a technician should carry.

Stocking recommendations for local inventories and car stocks can be greatly aided by the use of worldwide demand data. The distinction between demands and issues and usage is important. Demands are what the technician requests (thinks he needs) to fix the equipment. Not all demanded parts are available to issue. Even if the parts are issued to the technician, he may not need all of them so some are returned to good stocks. Plan based on demands. The more demand data you have, the more accurate your forecast can be. Assure that your computer system logs all part demands, even though they may not be filled. The differences between what parts are demanded, what parts are provided, and what parts are really needed can guide improvements in diagnostics, training, and discipline toward fewer parts and lower costs.

Repairables

The fact that many parts are durable and can themselves be repaired adds greatly to support opportunities. If a part is repairable it may either be repaired or discarded. Since financial investment has been made in the durable item, initial effort should be made to repair the item either for economic benefit or sometimes because a new replacement part is not available. The cost of repair is typically only 20 to 30 percent of the cost of a new part, so recycling defective parts through repair can be very profitable and conserves resources. In many cases, repaired parts will have fewer "dead on arrival" (DOA) or "early life failure" (ELF) occurrences than new manufactured parts, since their weak elements have already been found and eliminated. Do note that any product being sold containing repaired, recycled, refurbished, or remanufactured parts must be labeled as such.

Diagnostics

Manufacturing does not use parts as diagnostic tools. A factory is usually equipped with adequate tools and test equipment to thoroughly test every product. It is cost prohibitive and physically impossible to provide such test equipment to every field engineer. Therefore it is not uncommon in service for a test procedure to start with the directive, Use a good part.

The use of parts as diagnostic tools causes considerable debate between design engineers and service continuing engineers. Testability is one of the technologies that must be improved in the near future in order to accurately test and diagnose hardware and software to tell exactly what is wrong. Eventually simple diagnostics should tell an operator either go or no go. This is necessary to simplify decisions if more maintenance must be done by the operator.

It is logical to state, if a part rarely fails, it should not be carried with a field technician. That same logic presumes that there is little need for a tool part since the one in place will be good. With high volume products, the cost of designing a built-in or remote test is often far less than the cost of many technicians carrying extra parts. Electronic parts do not endure well in a hot, bounce-around, loosely packaged, frequent-in-and-out environment. If a part is to be carried for diagnostic purposes, flag it for special observation, be sure to report every use as a tool or as a failure replacement, and exchange a software or firmware diagnostic for the part as soon as possible.

Gain or Loss

The gain or loss that each service part will bring has a major effect on revenues, costs, and profits. Most organizations supply parts at a profit. A manufacturing ABC inventory level that strictly multiplies the cost of the part by the number of parts used is not adequate for service. Would you rather have one $1,000 part or a thousand $1 parts? Most service reps probably will opt for the thousand $1 parts because the chances of their getting parts that will fix several problems are much higher than if they have only one $1,000 circuit board. Further, both absolute and relative profit should be considered. For example, a $10 part in inventory might be marked up seven times and sold for $70. There's a difference of $60 that is profit. Wouldn't it be better to have that high-markup part available to sell to somebody versus a part that sells for double the price with a gross profit of just $10? Would you rather make $10 or $60? To most persons, $60 is the answer, if the probability of someone needing it is about the same. So there is a positive, optimistic profit-oriented gain for some parts.

On the other side—the loss side, and preventing the loss—look at how much time reps in the field take to get parts. Many persons say, "That's a necessary evil." Not so! If fixed-price contracts or leases require parts, then any money saved is desirable. There is very accurate information from service improvement programs which proves that parts-related activities waste a lot of money. Some accurate parts-related time data from a well-run large service organization are shown in Table 2-2. These data are based on over 700 hours of observation of 65 tech reps.

TABLE 2-2
Tech rep's average parts activity time per event

	Average Minutes
Obtain part number	6
Requisitions	8
Travel to get part	15
Checking on orders	13
Return to stock or defective	18
Cannibalize	15
Pricing	8

Another recent survey of multivendor technicians shows one hour per service call, which is 34 percent of the call time, used to identify, order, acquire, and receive parts. This is a major target for improvement.

If an essential part is needed and not on hand, the service rep has to contact the branch and find out where it is. Perhaps another rep has one. At the very minimum, the first rep is going to have to get the part number, prepare a requisition, travel to get the parts, and go back to the customer. This will probably take at least an hour. What's that hour worth to you? Service labor costs $35 to $100 an hour these days. Multiply that rate by time, plus the cost of transportation, and that quantifies a large loss that can be avoided.

Parts costs can be traded against people costs. If service reps always have the right part, the initial investment may cost more, but having those parts available will make the reps much more productive, customers will be a lot happier; and you're going to do more business and make more profit.

About 3 to 4 percent of a tech rep's time should be devoted to working with parts, getting part numbers, obtaining the items, and so on. That is 15 to 20 minutes each work day. Most organizations probably average 10 to 12 percent of paid time spent to get parts, with many higher. Take that difference and multiply it by an eight-hour day and by the labor rate charge, and the cost is at least $25 a day spent on chasing parts which could better be spent on producing revenue! A lot of parts-related times are hidden today in organizations' data collection and measurement systems. Computerized management systems rarely log the considerable effort and time required for the stockkeeper calling to find available parts, the dispatcher chasing strayed shipments, managers arranging transfers, technicians disrupting customer work to hand off parts in a coffee shop. These are additional opportunities for improvement.

Systems Approach

Finally, a systems approach is vital to effectively fit together all the pieces of the complex service logistics puzzle. Logistics touches almost every function of a corporation. One must look at the total life cycle. From the very beginning, one must plan products and design the support system with the product and

TABLE 2-3
Multiechelon planning enables rapid response
at relatively low cost

STOCK LEVEL	FILL PLAN FOR LEVEL	% OF ORDERS RECEIVED	FPFR FOR LEVEL	RESPONSE TIME FOR LEVEL (HRS)
LOCAL	85%	100	85	0.25
STRATEGIC	10%	15	67	8
CENTRAL	4%	5	90	24
MANUFACTURING	1%	1	100	72

Aggregate response time 2.7 hours

customer in mind rather than afterwards having to react and support the design. Use service-level data to measure performance and adjust the stock levels to meet management's goals. Table 2-3, as an example, shows that with this approach, the service level of a multi-echelon distribution system can be 99 percent, even though the fill rate at each location is 70 percent or less.

3 CHANGES AFFECTING PARTS

$\mathcal{S}$ervice professionals at all levels recognize that both external and internal factors affect what we can and should provide as support. It is critical that we, as service leaders, proactively direct our destiny. Over recent years, service management has progressed from being a cost-centered installation and repair business to becoming a major profit and strategy contributor at a corporate level.

There are about fifty major trends presently influencing the service business. The challenge is limiting the number to the top fifty. Of these, about thirty directly affect parts. These are marked with an asterisk (*) in Table 3.1.

Fifty trends

The following trends (shown in Table 3-1 below) are arranged in subject groups for readers' convenience. Items within each group are in alphabetical order, which is generally not their order of importance. Alpha order both facilitates finding an item and avoids arguments with readers who are persons with varied interests, products, and customers. You will no doubt find that some items have much more influence on your operations than others do.

TABLE 3-1
Parts influence the majority of trends

Customer Changes
  Capability over product
*Comprehensive support
*Customer happiness priority
*Independent and self-service
*Information role
*International considerations
*Quality emphasis
*Response becomes restore
*Single-point contact
  System integrators
*24 x 7

Competitive Changes
  Acquisition and mergers
*Competition growing
*Competitor = Collaborator =
  Customer
  Intangible, value-add
*Legal concerns
*Managing versus doing
  Market growth slowing
*Price cutting
*Profits high, but decreasing
  Vertical market niches
*Warranties and contracts longer

Technology Changes
  Communications integration
*Component reliability
*Diagnostics enhanced
*Equipment costs decreasing
*Micro emphasis
*Multivendor, open systems
*Parts importance increasing
*Predictive maintenance
*Remote support tools
*Software importance
*Systems complexity
*Transport faster

Business Changes
  Assets and cash emphasis
  Emotions lead economics
  Labor rates increase
  Manage versus do
  Information systems guidance
  Organization broad and short
*Outsourcing
*Products develop fast and short
  Profit centers
*Revenue and profits high
  Service selling self
  Support expensive, invisible
  Tax and accounting changes
  Technician travel reduced
*Technician skill shifts
*Trade technology for labor
  Virtual offices

Solder guns can be dangerous weapons

The challenge to you is to take the trends and spin them to your service advantage. Change is not new to product support, but it is complex and now requires more emphasis on logistics. Years ago, Joe Patton wrote regarding future service technicians, "The Lone Ranger with oscilloscope will be replaced by ambassadors of service who deliver the team's solution to the customer." How many 'scopes do you see used in field service today? Technicians with solder guns would ruin more multilayer boards than they would fix. What we do see is the best organizations bringing together solutions to all their customers' needs.

Unfortunately, many other organizations still fail to properly put in place all the resources necessary to please customers. There is a major need in product support for people who can bring both experience and logistics science to bear on customer service challenges. A vision for the future shows service organizations whose small staff are primarily coordinators who bring together the resources supplied by partners and subcontractors. There are career opportunities for people who can visualize the changing strategy and tactics, identify the necessary elements, and bring them together in cost-effective processes.

Service organizations of the future will plan and manage all necessary service resources, but they will own only those assets that are critical to their core business. The most common functional groups will probably be:

Call management and help desk
On-site technical support
Information to the point of need
Hardware
Software

Specialist organizations will provide call management functions with help desks to triage customers' requests. A few large organizations will provide technical "feet on the street" around the world. Other organizations will specialize in providing parts where needed within a few hours. Other experts will provide generic training, on-the-spot information as required, and technical assistance backup. Software will similarly be provided to complete total capabilities. The challenge is to plan and manage all these pieces into a seamless, comprehensive whole that makes the customer happy. The metrics are money, time, and satisfaction.

Financial efficiencies based on economies of scale will drive many of these trends. We all want to have *our* own associates directly helping *our* customers, but that is not economically feasible. Until you can fully utilize at least several hundred technicians on each continent of this world, there will be considerable travel and other waste time. Most organizations have under-utilized territories. So, one company will provide field technicians to many partners. The technicians will wear my company's emblem on their suit coat for my calls, and they will wear your emblem for your calls. Several companies do this already. Genicom, for example, specializes in servicing printers for many other service companies; however, even they try to provide all the logistics pieces within the product niche. There are further efficiencies to be had.

Human performance is restricted by the knowledge required to understand every situation a technician may encounter and to react properly. No one technician can know the intricacies of so many different products. How then can we help a human ambassador appear and feel capable of supporting every product he is asked to service? By providing generic technical training and strong human communications skills, backed up by guidance at the time of need. The abilities to solicit the customer's needs, to listen carefully, to empathize with the customer, and to fix the technical situation while satisfying the customer are paramount. Given the expanding variety of product configurations and high reliability, even a technician trained in the details would probably forget what he is taught before his knowledge is put to use. Portable electronic information devices are necessary. A technician going to call on a new situation can be provided with diagrams, trouble-shooting decision trees, parts lists, and other on-the-spot guidance. The information can be on a magnetic or optical disk, or can even be downloaded along with the service call through phone or wireless communications. This does change the job description for field technicians. The distribution of knowledge will require even less technical ability in the field. Conversely, the field ambassadors must become more skilled in communicating with their customers and in offering to meet other customer needs (often termed *business development* or *selling).*

What about parts?

Fortunately, hardware is very reliable, but when it fails the specific replacement part is vital. In the fast-changing arena of multivendor, open systems you can't be extravagant enough to own all the right parts where you need them to meet contracted response times. Nor can you afford to be caught with excess parts when the product configuration changes and your stock becomes obsolete. The logistics performance envelope, (which is the subject of chapter 26), is bordered by financial investment, response time, and support level. This bears an interesting similarity to the human technician performance envelope, doesn't it?

Repairs of high-tech parts are done best by experts with proper facilities, sophisticated diagnostics, and test equipment. This is another specialist subset of the service parts business. Even system hardware and software integration will become specialized. Consider, for example, bringing together all the pieces of hardware and software necessary for the electronic briefcases carried by insurance agents. Companies like Integron and Unisys find this a profitable service niche.

Software is very similar to hardware, but it has the added ability to move at the speed of communications media. The intertwining of software and hardware will become more sophisticated. Software will eventually simplify human challenges. For example, "plug and play" will relieve users and technicians of the need to detail switch settings, device drivers, and other interface complexities. The intricacy of software requires many coordinated, skilled specialists to detail the requirements effectively.

Virtual facilities is another trend in our business. Many companies are eliminating physical offices. Instead, communications and computers enable road-warrior service personnel to operate effectively from home, van, or the customer's site.

Even technical specialists can be equipped at relatively low cost with everything they need to operate from home, airport, or elsewhere. With databases that can identify who has what skills, experienced technicians on calls can do double duty and help other technicians who need special knowledge. Obviously the management of service personnel must change too. Face-to-face contact may not be frequent with many more reporting persons (or self-managed teams), so contacts must be of high quality. Voice and data communications, such as e-mail, should be frequent and friendly, as well as efficient. Throughout these changes, parts stocks with technicians will become smaller and smaller, with required parts delivered rapidly from other sources.

Logistics reformation

Logistics is the term applied to the sum of all processes that re-form these elements and bring them together to focus on the customer. Logistics has sometimes been regarded as the muscle part of the service business. That mind set is changing. In the future, muscle must be supplemented by mind. Brawn must be replaced with brain. Key to future service success are the people who can visualize the big picture before it occurs, anticipate all the pieces of the puzzle, and put everything in place to thrill the customer. Since providing the correct hardware and software at the desired location, when the technician needs it, in good working condition, for a reasonable cost, is becoming the most important element of service, improved logistics is critical to enhance the service process.

4 *PERFORMANCE GOALS*

$\mathbb{I}$f you ask service parts personnel, "How many words of praise did you receive last week?" The answer is usually, "None." To the query, " How many messages of criticism did you get?" The answer is, "Several." Unfortunately, the service parts business is prone to criticism since it must operate at less than 100 percent instant support. Performance goals are valuable as benchmarks for comparison with other organizations and as measures of process and results against internal standards and customer needs. Without goals an organization has little idea of whether they are good enough, or too good, and perhaps not getting the expected high return for their efforts.

People sometimes use the word "spare" in referring to parts. That is a problem symptom. If the word is defined in the sense of the "spare" tire for a car—that is there for emergency backup insurance use—that usage is fine. Often, however, spare means

57

excess to any reasonable requirements. Stockkeepers are by nature hoarders. Most people in the service business have a cache
of parts that they expect to use eventually. Many parts turn
over less than once a year, and wiping a finger over them often
will show thick layers of residue from lack of use. Also, some
of the parts may be for equipment that has long since been
scrapped. On the other hand, a part that is requested often is
not available. That absence may cause production loss, thus
promoting higher costs, stress, and lack of confidence by users
in the service parts system.

It is necessary for every organization to have objectives and
goals. Service goals should be written, understandable, measurable, challenging, and achievable. The following are goals that
have been adopted by many organizations and discussed with
thousands of service personnel in workshops and presentations. Most organizations can meet a few of the goals; some
meet all of them. The purpose of stating the goals is to set our
sights high and to focus future learning on the practical question of how to meet these goals in your own situation. If your
organization cannot meet a specific goal, then identify how
good (or bad) you are today, and negotiate an improved goal
as the target.

Comprehensive system goals

Three major goals stand above the rest as measures of total
system performance. They are:

$$\text{Operational Availability (Uptime) } A_o = \frac{\text{MTBM}}{\text{MTBM} + \text{MDT}} \geq 98\%$$

$$\text{First Call Fix Rate} = \frac{\text{Quality Satisfied at First Attempt}}{\text{Total Requests}} \geq 90\%$$

Restore Time = Time from Notification of Failure until Operable $\geq$ 99% per Contract

These goals above include failure rate reliability, ease of
maintainability, parts, labor, skill, documentation, remote diagnostics, technical support, and most elements of the total

service process. Note that the symbols stand for *greater than, or equal to*. The symbol < means *less than*. Goals are best expressed with an optimistic bent, so we prefer ≥85 percent correct rather than ≤15 percent wrong. Emphasize the positive. There are goals specific to parts that are subsets of the system goals and add a desired level of control.

Parts primary goals

Parts needed are on hand ≥ 85%, with balance ≥ 99 percent overnight.

This can be interpreted so field personnel have access to parts that fill at least 85 percent of their parts needs within 15 minutes. The 85 percent is a guideline that has scientific foundation and may range 82 - 92 percent for most products and organizations. The remaining parts should be supplied overnight. The reason the final goal is less than 100 percent is that requests for unusual, low use parts may require special acquisition that can take longer than overnight.

As shown in Figure 4-1, First Pass Fill Rate equals the percentage of Demand Accommodation times the percentage of Demand Satisfaction.

$$\text{Demand Accommodation (DA)} = \frac{\text{SKUs on Authorized Stock List}}{\text{SKUs Demanded}} \geq 90\%$$

Identification of the parts which should be stocked at a location is termed an Authorized Stock List (ASL). The list is set to fill a high percentage of demands and to balance that fill rate with desired response time and cost. There should be an ASL for every stock location. (The scientific preparation of ASLs with human critique is discussed in chapter 9.) Demand Accommodation is measured by the number of requested parts that are on the ASL. The Demand Accommodation for the central stock should be managed to nearly 100 percent immediate availability, though the physical parts may be located at and shipped by repair partners, fourth party parts suppliers, shared inventories, and other preplanned arrangements.

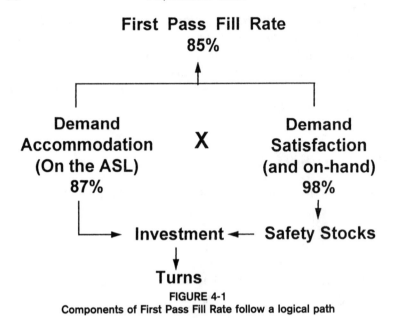

FIGURE 4-1
Components of First Pass Fill Rate follow a logical path

$$\text{Demand Satisfaction (DS)} = \frac{\text{Total Quantity of ASL Parts Issued}}{\text{Total Quantity of ASL Parts Demanded}} \geq 95\%$$

Since Demand Accommodation ∗ Demand Satisfaction = First Pass Fill Rate, for a desired fill rate, the DA may be decreased if the DS is increased. There are natural limits on DA and DS when the FPFR is 85 percent or higher. For example, to meet an 85 percent FPFR, DA 92 percent requires DS 92 percent. The calculation is FPFR/DA = DS = .85/.92 = .92. There is advantage to a high DA, but there is considerable challenge in predicting which parts will fail. Many reliable products today have very few failures scattered over many parts. That is a forecaster's nightmare. Logistics requires less effort and cost to stock more quantities of a few SKUs rather than having to acquire low quantities of many SKUs.

Safety stocks are measured only as a control to alert us if they become excessive. The safety stocks are driven by need for high Demand Satisfaction and are based on statistical tables for confidence and are also related to parts essentiality and cost.

Parts Turns is not considered a valid goal for service parts, because it is a fourth order fallout of the higher goals. The calculations for turns are:

$$\text{Unit Turns} = \frac{\text{Total Demands in Units}}{\text{Average Quantity On-Hand}} = \frac{7}{2} = 3.5$$

$$\text{Financial Turns} = \frac{\text{Total demands At cost}}{\text{Average \$ Value On-Hand}} \quad \text{eg.} \quad \frac{\$70,000}{\$20,000} = 3.5$$

Several problems arise in using Turns as a service measure. To illustrate:

Part L: Demand is 2 with cost $1,000 each, and average quantity on-hand of 1.

Part M: Demand is 12 with cost $1 each, and average quantity on hand of 3.

Unit Turns = 14/4 = 3.5
Financial Turns = $2,012/$1,003 = 2.

Thus we can see that the calculation methods do not agree with each other. At least be consistent if you use turns as an indicator. A second problem is in managing the denominator of the calculation: average quantity on-hand. The easiest way to get high turns is to not stock any parts. That may win accolades for turn rate, but probably loses customers and your job. Outsourcing provides an option to gain high turns since your balance sheet would not hold any parts but the demands can be filled quickly by your supplier partners.

In spite of having been critical of turns as a measure, do realize that low turns can be a warning of excess parts. At the very least, stratify parts so that slow-moving insurance parts for elderly products are kept separate from the active minority. Aim for at least 3.5 turns on repairable parts in normal product life and 12+ turns on consumable and expendable parts.

Figure 4-2 shows the very complex interaction between logistics measures. Part Volume and Support Level are in unique type to show that they are primarily influenced by external factors. The volume is modified by the number of products supported, failures, documentation, diagnostics, technician training, discipline, and other influences. Level of support is determined primarily by contractual agreements and management strategy. Response Time, First Pass Fill Rate, and Investment are highlighted since they are the main components of the Logistics Performance Envelope. That concept is covered in chapter 26.

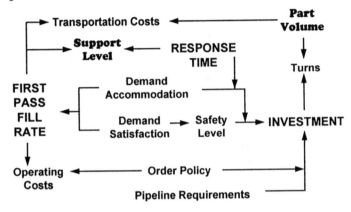

FIGURE 4-2
Logistics metrics have complex relationships

$$\text{Emergency Order Rate} = \frac{\text{Quantity (or Value) Expended}}{\text{Total Quantity (or Value) Demanded}} = 5 \text{ to } 15\%$$

If the rate of emergency orders is too high, the activity and costs will climb to the frustration of everyone involved. When a large portion of effort becomes Priority 1, then routine activities suffer. When the emergency level goes below 5 percent that indicates over-investment in field inventory and probable low turnover of expensive parts. An organization should set a target emergency order rate and then track it for optimization.

$$\text{Dead on Arrival (DOA) Rate} = \frac{\text{Quantity Defective for All Causes}}{\text{Total Quantity Processed}} = 1\%$$

DOA is the main measure of parts quality. Later discussion will focus on curing the underlying causes which often include manufacturing defects, ordering the wrong part, picking the wrong part, mixing up parts in packing, and shipping damage. If a part is not usable for any reason then it is counted as DOA and major actions should be directed at improvement. DOA is serious from a customer perspective. Imagine a field engineer who determines that she needs a part to fix the down critical equipment. She tells the customer that the part should arrive by 8:30 tomorrow morning. When she installs the part, it does not fix the problem! Both the tech (who is really logistics' customer) and the end customer are unhappy. The next part, expedited at considerable cost and effort, had better fix the problem!

New Customer on System =
Hours to Accept an Order from a New Customer ≤ 24 hours

A new customer requesting service or ordering a new part is probably panicked. Many companies have the capability to instantly enter the customer into their online database. Other companies with antique processes, fill out papers that go to credit approval and then the part order is placed. Get a credit card number over the phone for an initial order, or ship COD (cash on delivery), or take the chance and ship with invoice. In most cases, checking credit will cost more that the potential loss if a part is not paid for, and the risk of nonpayment is low. On the other hand, time wasted doing those activities also delays sending the part and satisfying the customer.

Repairable Parts Return = Days from Failure until Receipt at Repair Facility
≤ 7 calendar days

Time-Sensitive Repairs = Days from Arrival at Repair Facility to Good, On-Hand
≤ 3 Work Days

Repair of assets already owned is a "pipeline" that can be shortened in many firms. As discussed later in chapter 21 on Repairs, return of defective parts needs to be given high priority and pushed with field people. All parts do not need to be immediately repaired. Some are excess. Others are in ample supply and should be repaired in a batch for effective use of tools, people, and test equipment. Many companies repair needed parts the day they arrive, burn them in overnight, and ship the next morning. For many repair operations a one week cycle is good. The week is a natural sequence which smooths operations and is a reasonably short time.

Repairable Material Assets (RMA) Information ≥ 99% Accurate and Paperless

Information flow of field failure details to the repair technician provides major assist to diagnostic operations. Many companies require field technicians to fill out a card and attach a copy to the returning part. Tags often contain gems of wisdom like "Failed" or "Quit." The Repair Center should be online with service call records. Field techs should complete all necessary information fields, which should be computer validated. The only marking on a part or package need be the service call number. The receiving technician can then look at the service call report on his monitor and obtain guidance to failure cause and probable repair action.

$$\text{No Trouble Found (NTF)} = \frac{\text{Count of Units with No Defect Found}}{\text{Total Alleged Failures}} \leq 10\%$$

One of a Repair Center's frustrations is not being able to find a problem with an alleged defective part. If a clear defect is found then the part can be repaired. If no defect is found, there is a nagging feeling that field conditions were enough different so the repair tester may not find the specific problem. Advances are being made to built-in test, remote diagnostics, and sophisticated technical support that is reducing historical 45 percent NTF to under 10. The RMA information preceding is one tool to reduce NTF.

$$\text{Complaints to Management} = \frac{\text{Communications to Executives about Parts Problems}}{\text{Total Parts Activities (Service Calls or Sales)}}$$

$$\leq .001\%$$

One complaint per 10,000 actions is a challenge to many organizations. For companies achieving six sigma quality, that is not even close. Do you even measure the level of complaints? How about compliments? They can be measured too and provide motivating pats on the back.

Financial goals

$$\text{Investment to Revenue, at Book \$} = \frac{\text{Balance Sheet Book \$ Value of Parts}}{\text{P \& L Service Annual Revenue \$}} \leq 20\%$$

Even though this measure mixes the balance sheet item for Book Value of Parts with the Profit and Loss (P&L) item of Annual Revenue, this metric is very useful for comparisons. One formerly-large company got into graphic workstations a few years ago. They discovered after several months that they had purchased parts valued at over 120 percent of what they expected in revenues for the next year. There was no way they could make a profit!

Theoretically, this ratio could become zero if all parts are provided by outsourcing partners or you lease parts and your balance sheet contains no assets. In that case, do evaluate the P&L costs of using those parts so they do not exceed 20 percent either. There are indications that this ratio will change higher with concentration on multivendor, open parts. With these standard parts and accurate diagnostics, labor becomes less and parts become a larger part of the expense mix.

$$\text{Investment to Equipment Cost, at Gross \$} = \frac{\text{\$ \quad Invested in Parts}}{\text{\$ Cost of Equipment Supported}} \leq 8\%$$

This measure is useful for new product budgeting and to benchmark one product against another. If the new product is a "child" of known "parents," that can provide comparison data. Use the knowledge that can be gained from actual field analog.

$$\frac{\text{Total cost of parts support}}{\text{Total hardware service revenue}} \leq 35\%$$

For profitable multivendor support, the percentage of parts costs, including all indirect and overhead costs should be driven toward a 25 percent target.

Other parts measures

There are many other measures that may be applicable to your specific business. Suggestions include:

All orders received by 3 pm for stock items shall be shipped the same day.

All back-ordered parts due for shipment shall be shipped the day they are received.

Out of Stock, or nonstock, shall be scheduled within one workday; 90 percent will be shipped within 5 workdays.

The status and expected or actual shipping date of every order received at supplier's Order Entry function shall be available through Order Entry within 3 minutes.

Any customer contacting a parts stock facility or supplier Order Entry function shall receive assistance necessary to accurately order any replacement part with 95 percent success rate on the first request and 100 percent by the second selection.

Repair measures

$$\text{Parts per Unit Repair} = \frac{\text{Sum of Costs of Parts Used}}{\text{Number of Repairs}}$$

$$\text{Repair Rate} = \frac{\text{Number of Repairs Completed}}{\text{Number of Technician Hours}}$$

$$\text{Repair Cost Ratio} = \frac{\text{Cost to Repair Defective Unit}}{\text{Cost of a New Unit}}$$

$$\text{Backlog Days} = \frac{\text{Demand Total Work Hours}}{\text{Supply Work Hours per Day}}$$

$$\text{Operational Productivity} = \frac{\text{Utilized Time}}{\text{Total (Paid) Time}}$$

$$\text{Achieved Productivity} = \frac{\text{Standard Units Output}}{\text{Total (Paid) Time}}$$

$$\text{Effectiveness} = \frac{\text{Standard Units Output}}{\text{Utilized Time}}$$

Please note that many of these measures are shown as simple averages ("means"). Chapter 8 on Statistics emphasizes that understanding the mode, median, and standard deviations is also necessary. It is generally necessary to control the variances before the mean can be improved. For additional measures that cover human labor, installation, and preventive objectives read *Service Management: Principles and Practices*, Third Edition, by Patton and Bleuel.

5 *TOP TEN TECHNIQUES*

$\mathbb{P}$eople often shake their heads and say, "Wow! This service logistics sure is a complex business." Like most operations, service parts has a group of functions that are more important than the rest. This follows Pareto's Principle, which is one of our top techniques. Years of experience lead us to ten techniques that are considered most important for managing service parts:

1. Gain Management Support
2. Emphasize Customer Satisfaction
3. Establish Goals
4. Use Life Cycle Cost and Profit Analysis
5. Minimize Personnel Delays
6. Centralize
7. Concentrate on the Critical Few
8. Control Provisioning, Forecasting, and Excess

67

9. Promote Quality
10. Use Computers to Expand on Human Capabilities.

Gain management support

The best ideas in the world, backed by the soundest of logic and econometrics, will fail unless they are championed by the persons in charge and supported by upper management. A major challenge in managing service parts is that logistics has been regarded as a mundane, but necessary, function that only needs attention when severe problems arise. Now is the time for good men and women to speak out about the virtues and profits of sound inventory management. Manufacturing inventories are getting considerable attention with Materials Requirements Planning (MRP) and Just-in-Time (JIT) inventory strategies. The Japanese have taught Americans much about how to manage manufacturing inventories. There are many reasons why managing service parts requires a different set of techniques, and we are teaching people around the world how to benefit from them.

People always support projects best if they understand that the results have positive advantages to them. "What's in it for me?" is a common, if frequently unspoken, question. Make sure that management understands emotionally, beyond the black ink on a financial report. A bit of showmanship and desk pounding about the 'angry customer who was going to throw the product out and was made friendly by the critical part arriving in time to help him meet the deadline' can go a long way toward arousing management enthusiasm!

Emphasize customer satisfaction

Customer satisfaction is the end measure of success. Too often, service performance is measured by *bitch level*. If there are no complaints, then everything must be running right. Survey your customers. Rank customers according to the amount of business they do with your company. The critical few should receive a personal visit to assure they are satisfied, and handle any problems face-to-face. The next group should receive a telephone call. And, everyone should be surveyed at least once a year and given special attention if any problems occur. The marketing costs of doing repeat business with satisfied existing customers are a small fraction of the costs for gaining new customers. A survey recently showed the rank order in which people are motivated to provide satisfaction to:

1. The boss
2. Self
3. Specifications and goals
4. The customer

Stop and think if you are falling into that same trap. High quality performance should satisfy all of the critics, but over the long run the customer must be at the top of the list.

Establish goals

Every organization should have goals that are written, measurable, understandable, challenging, and achievable. For example, at least 85 percent of all parts that could cause equipment downtime shall be available with the field engineer. By measuring ourselves against such written goals, we can know immediately if we are successful or not. A useful technique in goal setting is to have the persons who must meet the goals participate in the goal setting. With proper leadership, most organizations will set goals for themselves that are much higher than management might dictate. The added advantage of participation is that people will work harder to achieve the target they set for themselves. It also helps to use score boards and frequent reporting on what actual results are compared to those goals.

Use life cycle cost and profit analysis

Business strategy and planning should evaluate the complete "womb to tomb" life cycle of products and parts. Design sets the stage for the following production and service efforts. A product is designed and built once, but must be serviced many times. Since service revenues will exceed the original hardware and software sales revenues for many products, and bring higher profit margins, the influence of service must be carefully evaluated.

Revenues tend to be fixed. Therefore in the basic equation [Revenues − Expenses = Profits], expense reduction is an effective tool to improve profits. There are also techniques such as parts contracts, leasing parts, shared inventories, and confidence kits that can stimulate parts revenues. Make sure that the expected benefit of carrying a part is greater than the expected cost of carrying that same part. The decision is simple: if the benefit is greater, then stock it. If the cost is greater, do not stock it. The decision equation is [Cost of Carrying versus Benefit of Carrying]. On the cost side of this equation, we have the investment to be made in the part and related support systems, which is primarily the cash flow and the carrying cost. There is some difference between the costs of carrying capitalized repairable parts and of carrying parts that are expensed. Single-use parts should not be accounted as expense until they are physically installed in equipment. Holding parts in inventory waiting for a need to occur costs about 30 percent a year. That means if a module costs you $1,000, then it consumes about $300 each year in facilities, labor, information, obsolescence, insurance, taxes, and money tied up that could be better used elsewhere. Capital parts often claim investment tax credit and are typically depreciated each month, so some people assume that the carrying costs are being recovered. That is correct only for the acquisition costs, and even their recovery as a depreciation expense is regained only over an eighteen-month to five-year time period. The carrying cost of fully-depreciated parts is still about 20 percent. The big advantage of repairable parts is their ability to be recycled rapidly at less cost than for acquiring new parts.

On the value side of this equation is the probability of needing the part and the value that will be received (or the cost that will be avoided) by having it on hand. If you sell parts direct to customers, dealers, or distributors, then there is profit to be made if you have the part. But if you don't have the part, and customers can go elsewhere, then they may go to another vendor. In the future they will probably go there first. Contracted service, which is a large percentage of most organizations' revenues and expenses, is a different situation. If you have contracted to support a customer, then parts must be made available regardless of how much effort and expense is required.

Contract revenues are fixed and the expenses vary according to the effort and expediting required. Thus, if parts expenses can be kept low, then profits will be high. If extra effort is required to get people out of bed at overtime rates, make emergency shipments, and have field engineers traveling to get parts, then expenses will be high and profits will be low. Just the direct costs of expediting are usually $20 to $250 and up. Many expediting costs are not quantified as easily in monetary terms as they are in mental anguish.

Minimize personnel delays

If at all possible, avoid having field technical personnel travel to get parts. Parts-chasing time is expensive in both lost revenue and personnel frustration. Part of the solution is an Authorized Stock List (ASL) that accommodates at least 85 percent of all parts needs. The optimum ASL should be calculated and may exceed 95 percent of needs for a specialist field engineer. Supply the remaining parts, which are hopefully of low essentiality, when next convenient. Or, if the parts are required for a down machine, have them delivered to the field engineer by a less expensive person. Roving parts vans, taxis, and even courier services are generally less expensive than diverting an expensive, technically competent person to transporting parts. Recognize and use the distinction between a demand-based and an issue-based parts management system. If a part is requested (a demand) but is not available for issue, often no record is kept and the engineer spends time finding an alternative solution. We need to know if the requested part was on the stock list or not. Often, parts that should be stocked are not, for financial, space, or other dubious reasons. Another situation is requests for parts that are not stocked and possibly not even identified in the service parts system. We need to log the demands for every part so we can periodically evaluate if we are stocking the right parts.

In the future, fault-tolerant hardware with remote diagnostic capability may be largely maintained by a parts courier who will be able to locate the defective equipment, safely open the electrical panel, remove the module with the lit red LED, install a good module, and politely inform the customer that the equipment is again working at full capacity. The technical talent will be at the Headquarters Technical Assistance Center and most of the on-site work will be done by these "Customer Service Technicians" who are qualified to a higher level in customer relations than in technical skills.

Centralize

Information should be centrally known on parts availability at every level of an organization. Part stocks to meet fast response should be located at the point of need, but any additional quantities should be centralized. If you consolidate parts to a central location where they can be found in a hurry, then transportation means must exist to get them quickly to where they are needed. The key is rapidly getting your hands on the parts. One company that produces and services products for the banking industry had three regional distribution centers across the United States as well as the headquarters central stock. By gradually eliminating the regional centers and consolidating inventories, they saved over $1.5 million and are providing a higher level of customer service. Inventory shrinkage that was $300,000 two years ago is now reported to be only $6,000. A major computer company has consolidated inventories into about 14 clusters across the United States and reports significantly better performance than with the previous large numbers of parts at sites and riding with field engineers. Centralization is a matter of balancing part availability and delivery time against costs and benefits measured in both monetary and customer satisfaction terms.

These issues pivot on confidence. If people in the field have confidence that they can get the parts quickly from the central location, then they won't try to keep so many caches of parts in their own possession.

Concentrate on the critical few

Pareto's Principle, which is known to many people as the "80/20 Rule," points out that there are a few critical items in most things we do that make the major difference, and most of the items around us are relatively insignificant. For example, most of our parts demands are for a relatively few items that turn over very fast, but many items sit in our inventory with just one or two uses a year. On the other hand, problems in defective components will come from just a few of the total parts. This Principle of the Critical Few also relates to the authorized stocking list of parts that should be kept in a field engineer's car trunk or on-site. Many service organizations can fill at least 90 percent of demands for parts with only 5 to 10 percent of all the stock keeping units in their inventory.

The critical few will often be high turnover parts. They may also be high dollar, long lead time, most essential, or even those parts that are prone to disappearance. These various factors may be lumped together into a single classification referred to as A, B, or C, or if you prefer, 1, 2, or 3. This is a more sophisticated evaluation than manufacturing uses in their ABC system, which is normally just based on the high extended value parts being the A, with midrange B, and low values being C. Classifications may be much more complex and different actions tied to the individual parameters. However, experience shows that most humans are unable or unwilling to apply the effort necessary to manage detailed criteria. The results are much more effective when all the criteria are combined into a single class rating. Hopefully no more than 10 percent will be Class A items, perhaps the next 20 percent should be termed Class B, and so on. Then you can manage by class for cycle counting, control attention, and stockroom location; with most effort given to the As where we get the most benefit for the effort.

When the very first product goes out the door, it should be accompanied by a kit of parts to meet expected needs. As needs are more accurately identified, excess parts in the kits should be returned and additional parts added to meet those needs. There are several schools of thought on this issue of authorized spares. One extreme says that headquarters knows best and should direct precisely the parts and quantities to be carried. The other extreme insists that only the field engineer knows what parts are required and that he should be allowed to carry anything he wants. The best solution is a balance between the extremes. There should be an authorized stock list determined by headquarters' technical and financial expertise. Quantities should be determined based on the product population to be supported, geography, fill rate requirements, and the cost of carrying the parts versus the expected benefit.

Keep parts as central as possible and manage strongly from that level. A good information system will assure that field needs are accurately reported to headquarters so the information can be refined into a statistically accurate recommended stock list. The field engineer and his manager should have the final say because there are territory changes, unique environmental situations, and other factors that headquarters cannot possibly foresee as accurately as field personnel can. If our friend Charlie Brown, Field Engineer, says "I must have that part;" then let him have it, but track how often it is used. If the part is not used for the next three months, remove it from Charlie's stock and put it at the next higher level. If the part is not used from that level in the next six months, then consolidate it to the central facility. Some parts will only be kept at the World Distribution Center. Today, if we can get our hands on the part, we can transport it rapidly to wherever it might be needed. Yes, customs inspectors may cause some delay, so a few parts may be kept in specific country distribution centers. The important thing is to get your hands quickly on the part. That is much easier to do if parts are centralized than if parts are scattered all over the country.

Control provisioning, forecasting, and excess

The best way of reducing investment in service parts is to avoid ever getting those parts into inventory. Most stock rooms today have excess parts that can and should be eliminated.

But, when we try to sell those parts to recover some of our investment, we typically find that they are obsolete, defective, and worth very little. Stimulate accurate provisioning decisions on what parts should be stocked and how many. The best strategy is to have on hand a small quantity of the parts that will probably be needed, with flexible arrangements in place to rapidly acquire parts to meet additional needs. Initial provisioning based on handbook, laboratory, and "similar to" information can be reasonably accurate. However, there will always be a few parts that were never expected to fail but somehow do; and some parts expected to fail that don't. Watch out for two common problems from manufacturing. The first is, "Don't worry about ordering your spare parts, I've ordered 10 percent extra of everything for you." That approach is naive because everything does not fail, and those few things that do fail will need frequent replacement. The second problem comes at end-of-production when the manufacturing manager says, "We have a million dollars worth of transports left over at the end of our production. I am going to transfer them to Service." That is a gift horse whose mouth should be shut before it bites you.

Forecasting of needs for service parts requires knowledge of demands from the past and especially what supply and demand factors are expected to change in the future. Regression analysis, exponential smoothing, and other techniques can help fit a particular situation. But, there is no substitute, especially with low-volume parts, for timely information gained from friends in engineering and sales and at other organizations who support similar products.

Elimination of excess is one of the most difficult things that any part manager has to do. You know by the laws of probability and statistics and Murphy, that as soon as you let the parts go you are going to need them. That is true for many of the operations we work with. Service is a probability business, unlike manufacturing which is based on deterministic one-to-one direct ratios. Rather, we know that even with a 98 percent delivery rate, it still means that 2 percent of the time that part can not be delivered. We must learn to live with probabilities and manage by them.

Elimination of excess means to get the value out of those parts as quickly as you can. If you can get them back to the vendor while the parts are still useful in manufacturing, then do so. Or, perhaps you can contribute them to a hospital or an educational institution and at least write off the contribution. Put money in your annual budget so that funds are routinely available to write off those parts from your reserve account. The important thing is to get rid of excess parts so they no longer take up space, people's energy, data collection, taxes, and other resources that are better focused on the critical few.

Promote quality

Quality in service parts means more than just conformance to specifications; it means meeting the customer's needs. This then requires starting with an accurate identification of what the customer perceives he wants. For example, if the customer wants an off/on switch, but the description or drawing or identification numbers are vague—or the wrong part is pulled from the shelf—or the wrong part is packed in the right box—or for whatever reason the part is not correct—then the customer is angry.

Then add the result of dead-on-arrival (DOA) parts! A very bad situation is created when the field engineer responds, diagnoses the problem, and tells the customer that the part is special ordered and will arrive tomorrow morning at 8:30 a.m. But, when the part is installed, it does not work! Again, whether the part is new, rebuilt, damaged in shipment, or whatever, makes no difference to the irate customer, the frustrated field engineer, or to the manager whose expenses must reflect the additional service calls and expediting expenses. For those of us who measure (and we all should), 100 percent is often an elusive target. But, anything less than perfect needs to be improved.

Use computers to expand on human capabilities

There are many things that computers can do to help manage the business. A computer can keep the records, do the calculations, and alert us to special needs far better than any human can. Reorder points, economic order quantities, and average pricing can be easily calculated by even a microcomputer.

The reorder point (ROP) should trigger when we order replacement parts to our stocking facilities. Individual Field Engineers should operate on a weekly replenishment for normal use parts stock. A system that reports parts used on each service call can initiate automatic one-for-one resupply of authorized parts. At higher levels however, the ROP should be automated as one tool for optimizing inventory on hand. The reorder point is simply lead time (usually in days)/average parts used per day; so the result is the number of parts expected to be used during the time it takes to get replenishment parts. For example, if I use one part a day and resupply takes 15 days, then I should reorder when my stock is down to 15 parts.

Now come the refinements. First, the reorder point is based on averages. Do I need a safety stock to cover either higher than expected use or slower delivery? Statistically, we can determine what the safety stock should be for specific probabilities and confidence levels. More than that, however, a knowledgeable planner should decide for each part what the penalty of stock-out is, and trade that against the costs of carrying the safety stock. Don't just let the mathematics run rampant. Apply critical thought to classify the parts for essentiality. Evaluate vendor performance. And most importantly, think about how the future may change from the past. Remember that the computer is operating in the past and must have human inputs on pending design changes, supply alterations, and changing demands.

Second, consider not only the parts that are on hand, but also parts in repair, and parts already on order. One organization foolishly designed their new computer system to consider only the on-hand quantities. When that ROP was reached, an order was automatically placed to the vendor. The next day, because the part count was below the reorder point, another order was generated. This happened for several days until the vendor called to ask if they really needed so many parts, since the quantity was more than they had ordered in the past three years. They quickly revised the program and also put the needed human attention onto the situation rather than placing blind faith in the computer.

Repairable parts offer an opportunity for rapid turnaround and reduction of both inventory and costs. The target for turnaround of critical parts from the time they fail in the field until they are cycled through repair into good stocks should be only a few days. You will probably find that return time from the field is a major delay. Target each field engineer with a specific number of days to return, create a Due-in list, and appraise each FE on the speed of returns. As a generality, if the repair cycle is taking you four weeks now and you can reduce that time to two weeks, the inventory quantities can be about cut in half. The points to be made for repairables influencing the reorder point are that their lead time is generally under internal control, can be managed much more directly, and provides a great opportunity for better turnover and more effective use of assets.

EOQ (Economic Order Quantity) is the number of parts that should be purchased at a single buy to gain the least-cost combination of order costs and carrying costs. On the one hand, we have those carrying costs of about 30 percent of the unit cost per year. Of course, the more units we have in our inventory, the higher the carrying costs are. On the other hand, each time we place an order, it costs between $25 and $500 to handle all the paper work, phone calls, expediting, receiving, and quality assurance. You can not do optimum inventory management unless you know what your carrying costs and order costs are. You must have those two facts in order to calculate Economic Order Quantity. Computers can aid in both gathering costs and in performing rapid, accurate calculations of the ROP and the EOQs. Note that a human can often provide additional insights in packaging, convenience, satisfaction and other factors that make the difference between EOQ and Optimum Order Quantity (OOQ). There are still many combinations of judgment and science where computerized artificial intelligence benefits from additional human intelligence.

The payback on a computerized service parts management system is generally under one year. The computer knows when you have issued parts down to the reorder point. It can be programmed to capture demands even though the parts may not be available for issue. It knows which parts are repairable and can provide a follow-up list to assure that all returns are promptly cycled through the repair system. It can rapidly show availability so you can get your hands on needed parts. The computer is a vital link to feed back information and to help service parts become a profitable, sustaining part of our service business, aimed at fulfilling our objective of increased confidence in service parts.

6 QUALITY

It is said that *Quality is the most complex bundle of business concepts ever gathered into one word.* Poor quality angers many of us, with negative results. High quality brings customers back for more and gains us profits, so everybody wins. Customer satisfaction derives from a combination of technological capability and human relations. But, mere satisfaction is not good enough when competitors are striving for customer happiness, delight, and even ecstasy.

Quality of service parts is especially important since they often arrive on the scene after other attempts at correction are exhausted. Service parts probably go directly into the replacement parts inventory. They will rarely be installed in new machines at a factory. Therefore, their first trial in actual functional use may well be as a repair part for a problem that is receiving the full attention of an angry user. It would add insult to injury if the replacement part failed too. People blame parts for human failings. Parts are inanimate, unfeeling, and easily made the target of complaints. It is easier to say, "They sent me the wrong part;" than to admit, "I ordered the wrong part." Quality of service parts includes much more than the correct functioning of the physical part or its fitness for use or conformance to specifications. A part may be software where electronic code has bugs, or the wrong version is picked, or the media gets demagnetized during shipment. The ease of identifying a part number, confirmation of availability, and arrival of the part on time are all elements of logistics quality. Quality encompasses all aspects of service parts.

Service parts quality misconceptions

"Our customers only want low price, they don't care about anything else."

"Who needs service and parts when you have good products?"

"Why should we worry about getting better? We're the only choice they have."

"You can't measure service quality."

"Quality is their responsibility."

"I don't care what they feel, the facts are . . . "

"Any worthwhile investment will pay for itself in less than a year."

"I'm sure if you test enough, it will pass."

"If you want quality, we've got to have a bigger budget."

"Let the phone ring, I've got my job to do."

"If we don't make an occasional mistake, customers won't appreciate what we do for them."

"It's much more cost-effective to let the image get dim before we replace the cartridge."

"It takes too long to see any benefits; we need to save those costs now."

"I don't have time to do it right."

"I don't care if it does have a bug, the shipping schedule is more important."

"Even if I know I don't have the right part, I'll still go to service the call."

Have you heard any of those statements on the job? Did you act to correct the error in those feelings? If you did not, then you allowed problems to perpetrate and fester into major failures. Superior quality requires positive action. Follow the guideline: *Under-commit and over-deliver.*

Increasing effectiveness

Fortunately, equipment produced today is much more reliable than in previous years. An interesting observation in parts support is, if you survey people about their satisfaction with parts, the best support is perceived to be on products that do not fail and therefore rarely need parts. When parts are needed, however, that exact part is more necessary than in earlier products. It is no longer possible to repair on site with solder and tape. As the value of service increases in our economy, the quality of service must become an increasing concern and opportunity. Quality is no longer the purview of only planners, engineers, and production workers. In 1978, when Joe Patton and Bill Bleuel wrote the first *Service Management: Principles and Practices* book, quality was not enough of a priority topic to rate many words. The second and third editions of *Service Management* have major chapters devoted to Service Quality.

Further evidence of attention to service quality is creation of a new senior management position in many corporations called Director of Total Quality, or Vice President of Customer Satisfaction. Further, notice that the word *control* has been removed from most titles and organizations since we now realize that quality should be designed and built into products and services. The total quality management (TQM) concept yields superior productivity; rather than using inspection controls to cull out bad performance after the fact. Control is still part of the process, but we are pushing to plan and produce better quality parts and processes so there is less deficiency to control.

The customer wants a product or service to be fit for use as defined by that customer. Why should we emphasize service quality? The following are main reasons:

1. Profit
2. Customer demand
3. Contract penalties and incentives

4. Legislation
5. Liability
6. Marketability

The main reason is summarized in that one word at the top of the list—*profit*. The desired result of logistics quality is to make a profit. Another reason is the customer's demand for high quality. Quality is a very marketable thing. In the past, service has not received much attention, so the fact that service is now getting high recognition is a very positive thing. Competition stimulates quality. It's a positive thing to say, "We have fewer call-backs, we do the job right the first time, we have the right parts to our field engineers faster, and we satisfy customers to a higher level!" Further, it is necessary to match factual measures with the perceptions so that performance can be benchmarked against both absolute and relative comparisons. Perceptions are far more important than facts.

Those are all positive things. There are some things on the negative side. Because some industries haven't regulated themselves as well as they should, government agencies in many states and nationally have passed laws that regulate us all. Service charges and the effectiveness with which maintenance is done are issues in which society has a very large impact on what is happening in the area of service quality. Liability, no surprise to anyone, is pushed by agencies of the government, EPA, OSHA, and many ambitious lawyers. Parts have major impact on the liability of a product. If you service something in the medical market and a patient gets a lethal shock, it may be the fault of the product, it may be the fault of the surgeon, or it may be the fault of the service organization, but that doesn't make any difference to the person who gets buried! And every one of those people could be involved in law suits and have a very expensive time of it. Your warehouse packer may have had no influence whatsoever on the problem; but the fact that he packed that particular item could be something that puts you into court with expensive litigation.

Penalties and incentives are included in several contracts that guarantee uptime on equipment, for example, 99+ percent uptime on a telephone directory assistance system or a file server. Patton Consultants' surveys show that over 80 percent of service organizations have response time targets. The next step is availability/uptime targets, from the time a capability fails until it is back up again. User customers really don't care how quickly you get a technician there. They expect that upon arrival the qualified technician will have the right parts, the right training, and the right tools, analytic devices, and documentation needed to rapidly restore the capability. Customer expectations set the standards. In most cases, the main customers of logistics are the field technicians/customer engineers. Those expectations may be created by advertising, an order clerk's comments, or actual delivery of the parts. Customers then intuitively compare their perceptions of achievement against those expectations and feel some degree of satisfaction. Logistics organizations must talk to customers frequently to determine the level of satisfaction, what might be done to improve, and what other services might be provided to help the customer.

Quality pays

Does high quality service pay off? YES! Unfortunately, many companies think that their cost of service quality is not significant. At Corning Glass, James R. Houghton, Chairman and CEO and a past chairman of National Quality Month, finds that Corning Glass' cost of quality runs between 20 and 30 percent of sales. That means that the costs of doing things right and fixing things that are done wrong is worth about $500 million each year to Corning. In Gallop Organization polls such as their *Customer Perceptions Concerning the Quality of American Products and Services* conducted for the American Society of Quality Control (ASQC), the conclusions were that American consumers "would be willing to pay a substantial premium to get the quality they desire in consumer products." *The Wall Street Journal* reports that the most important factor in choosing a long-distance telecommunications carrier was "quality of service." Cost was the second most mentioned factor, and most important to only 25 percent of the respondents.

The importance of quality is entering a new phase of maturity. For many years quality was a negative fear to be avoided.

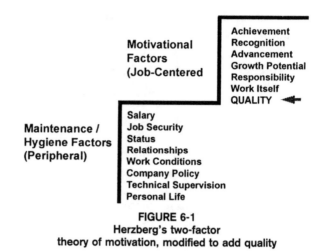

FIGURE 6-1
Herzberg's two-factor
theory of motivation, modified to add quality

Now, management and direct providers alike realize that quality is a critical requirement that comes direct from our customers. If we overlay attitudes toward quality on Herzberg's two-factor behavioral theory of motivation, as shown in Figure 6-1, changes in the behavioral reactions to quality may be modeled. Quality in past years was regarded as a peripheral maintenance hygiene factor. An absence of quality caused problems, but an abundance did not have much added value. The status of quality has grown to that of a motivational factor where special achievements in quality gain profits for the provider.

Ten dimensions of service quality

There are ten considerations necessary for good quality across all support services, including parts:

1. *Reliability*: Honor promises and do it right the first time.

2. *Responsiveness*: Demonstrate willingness and readiness to provide service.

3. *Confidence*: Have skills and knowledge to perform the service.

4. *Access*: Make it easy for customers to do business with you.

5. *Courtesy:* Be polite, respectful, clean and neat.

6. *Communication:* Keep customers informed in language they understand.

7. *Credibility:* Have the customer's best interests in mind.

8. *Security:* Give the customer a feeling of freedom from danger, risk, or doubt.

9. *Understanding:* Strive to understand customers' needs and learn their requirements,

10. *Tangibles:* The physical evidence of service; what facilities, equipment, and even parts packages look like.

How to plan, measure and control parts quality

Quality should be everybody's responsibility. That is a nice platitude, but what is quality? And, if I am to be responsible, what authority do I have? The traditional definition of quality was "performance to specifications." To service technicians, quality is the characteristic that is lacking when part number 50777 is in a box labeled 58777, or if the part is revision B when this specific machine requires revision C. Those events may be gathered under the term "fitness for use." Other people understand quality as "distinguishing features"; or as a "grade, class, category, or brand." A black panel arrives instead of a gray color one. Or, the box looks like it has been reused too many times and the part inside is therefore suspect. What about waiting ten minutes on phone hold while someone tries to find the part you need? Then, what if the promised part does not arrive at 8 am? There are many aspects of parts quality that involve procedures, systems and people, beyond hardware.

Plan

If you provide too much service, you will spend more money than you should and not gain proportionally from that cost. If you do too little service, the customers aren't happy and will complain or may quietly take their business elsewhere. As Figure 6-2 illustrates, you should ask customers first what factors are most important to them. A good way to obtain a forced ranking is to tell the customer that she has $1,000 and

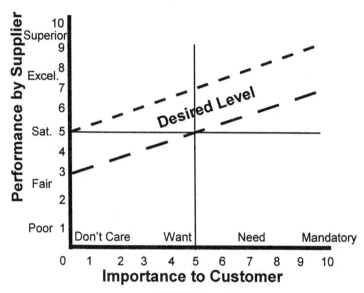

FIGURE 6-2
**Desired level of performance is bound by what the
customer thinks is important**

ask her to buy the amount of each factor she wants. The dollars
spent can then be converted mathematically into rank order
and weight of the factors. The customer is then asked to rank
the supplier's performance on each factor. This data can be
plotted on the control chart. Note that the bounds above and
below the desired level of performance shown in Figure 6-2
allow relatively lower performance on items the customer
doesn't care about, and require superior performance on items
that are mandatory.

Put your money and resources where the parts and processes
are most important to the customer. Establish statistical control
charts. Efforts should be concentrated to keep performance
within the control limits. If a characteristic is not important to
the customer, don't worry about the satisfaction level or the
performance. If you deliver performance that is much above
the upper control limit, you waste resources. Too much of a
good thing doesn't really gain more benefits. It's nice to pat
yourself on the back, but you are probably not gaining much
extra business because of the excess, and it is going to cost a
lot of extra money.

An illustration is managing *restore time*. When signing contracts, customers often ask, "How good are you?" And you say, "We will give eight-hour restore time." You centralize parts, and they can be transported anywhere in North America within six hours. That holds the investment in inventory relatively low. Then, if the fix times turn out to often be a faster four hours, you are probably very proud. But, the customer's expectation changes to four hours every time. When you deliver the promised eight hours the customer says, "Your service has deteriorated; it's lousy now!" Also note that much of a restore time goal may be used by diagnostics and travel, so that parts must respond in shorter time. Often, a four-hour restore requires parts to be on site within two hours of notification.

Comparison to the goal also depends on how you have specified restoration time. If you told customers that you are going to give them a maximum *average* of eight hours, that statistic allows you to go two hours one time and 14 hours another. If you tell the customer that you are going to give a maximum of eight hours on any call, then manage to an eight-hour time. A customer will be happier if you are consistently at a eight-hour time than if you arrive and fix the equipment in one hour today but take 15 hours the next time and vary from fast to slow. The US Postal Service has done a large amount of research in that area, and they find delivering the mail to be sensitive to consistency in the same way. Rather than having fast but erratic mail delivery, most of us would rather know that mail will arrive in three days every time.

Customer-based situational goals are a step beyond universal goals. As customer targets become tighter, logistics managers realize that their organizations cannot do everything at equally high speed without spending excessive money on resources. It is better to provide very fast support when the urgency is great and allow slower, lower-cost support when conditions permit. As a generality, conditions may be divided into either time-sensitive or cost-sensitive. If central equipment such as a file server fails, that affects many people; all possible effort should be put to fixing that problem quickly. The target for down priority equipment might be maximum of one-hour response with two-hour time-to-restore. If low priority equipment (for example, a terminal in an area with many similar terminals) has a minor density problem, then that might be a low-cost, next-day call.

The series brings us back to highly motivated personnel. There is no instant solution to the people challenges. It's not as easy to create motivated personnel as it is to forecast parts (and that's a stretch!). Of all the items that will help achieve high service quality, highly motivated people aimed towards unified goals are the single most effective resource to achieve consistently high service parts quality.

Measure

One challenge is that high reliability products are often serviced by low reliability people. This is evidenced by using the first call fix rate (FCFR), which is the inverse of the number of call-backs out of the total number of service calls. Reliability is defined as "quality in the field." Quality, once equipment comes off the end of the production line, becomes reliability for our purposes. The main source of information is the parts usage reported from service calls. Special emphasis should be put on dead-on-arrival (DOA) and early-life failure (ELF) parts. Parts can use a defect weighting system, because on most products the kinds of defects that can happen are not all essential defects that shut equipment down completely. Many systems code defects as "hard" or "soft," with soft items being things that merely degrade the operation and hard items being things that cause a complete shutdown of the system. Within that coding, put weightings on the failures so that a total weight score can be calculated at the end. Then a product with a weighting of two may be acceptable and anything worse than two is rejected. Defect information should get back to the responsible people so that they can correct deficient areas.

Technical performance includes product-specific things such as, in the copier or printer business, resolution and smears, and how black the lines are, and how white the background is. Or how many times you can dial the telephone and have the connection properly made, or how often a new laptop battery fits without cutting off excess plastic, and what the ratio is of correct part identification versus misses.

The percentage of on-time deliveries of parts addresses how often parts are promised to arrive tomorrow morning and do arrive by the expected time. Naturally, the customer's expectation is that the part is going to be in their hands by then. If it's not there, then bigger problems arise. It is better to promise something on a schedule that is guaranteed to be met and then deliver it a little faster. Under-promise and over-deliver.

The percentage of parts calls that are answered in time and the percentage of calls completed out of the total are a function of the total number and type of telephone calls that come in to a logistics management center. Assure that operators who are supposed to answer those phones do pick them up by the third ring (try for the first or second) and that calls aren't lost as they are being transferred to technical assistance personnel. Slow answers and lost calls are sources of additional aggravation to an already irritated customer.

Costs and revenues are a clear measure in the service parts business. Sources of information include published prices, competitive quotes, and customer complaints concerning how expensive the desired part is. That's based mostly on the number of comments about prices considered out of line with somebody else's, and the percent of return on investment (ROI) or the return on net assets (RONA). It all comes together in business practice, which is where you can tell by repeat business whether the customers are satisfied enough to keep coming back to you. That really is the final decision point. How many contracts are renewed, and how many of the customers on the list for time and materials (T&M) service are still coming back? Are there people in the records who haven't been heard from for six months and yet must have needed parts in that time? Contact those customers and solicit them for future business. The percentage of new customers versus repeat customers is a good measure of satisfaction. It will cost at least eight times more to get a new customer than it will cost to keep an old customer happy: it's a lot better to keep present customers satisfied than to sell new ones.

Benchmarks and surveys

Quality is perceived as both an absolute value and as relative to alternatives. Benchmarking is helpful in comparing your functions to similar functions in other organizations. Those organizations do not necessarily need to be in product service. For example, one of the best pick/pack/ship operations in the USA is considered to be at the sporting goods retailer, L. L. Bean from whom many service parts organizations can learn. Both the numbers and the processes are integral to improvement. Many service organizations actively share information with others. Appendix B is a comprehensive benchmark questionnaire. In many cases, good ideas are only a start. The major challenge lies in the implementation.

Conduct satisfaction surveys by mail, phone, and visits. One recommendation is a survey by mail to every customer at least once a year. Rank your customers in order to designate A-level customers that are big volume. If any of these get lost to competition, business will really suffer. B-level customers are the next most important group, and the remainder are C-level. Use Pareto's 80/20 and 90/45 rule, which is also known as the Principle of the Critical Few, so attention is directed to customers that have the biggest impact on your business. Those A-level customers should get a face-to-face visit. Give them everything and anything they want for a reasonable price so that everybody profits. The B-level customers should receive a telephone call on a regular basis and when there is any problem. C-level customers normally can just be mailed the surveys. This prioritized customer contact system can help keep a measure on how well customers are being satisfied. Little or no concern shown to a customer sends a message that you do not care about his business. Few customers leave due to excessive attention.

Be cautious about bias when asking for parts-specific information. If you come up front and ask about parts, respondents will often say negative things, even though the balance is good. Include questions about parts in a survey covering all aspects of service. Once you have gotten responses on overall service, then bore down to ask ,"Are you happy with parts support?"

Control

Now that we have a plan and can measure performance, the next step is control. The following are some methods used to provide quality controls on service:

1. Goals—written, measurable, understandable, challenging, and achievable
2. Service parts people help plan and design-in support
3. Logistics sign-off of all affecting changes
4. "Stop ship" if all resources are not ready
5. Product service council
6. Installation quality audits
7. Service call report evaluation
8. Failure report and corrective action system (FRACAS)
9. Problem/cause/action analysis
10. Service problem hotline
11. Customer calls and letters
12. Service quality audits
13. Manager of Service Quality
14. Account reviews
15. Quality participation teams
16. Customer surveys
17. Managers phone top customers
18. Service and Sales rate Logistics
19. Logistics rate themselves
20. Motivated personnel

The last item, motivated personnel, is key to most elements of the process. If you set participative goals and write, "Here's where we are now, and three months from now we should be within these control limits," people will work that way. Service parts experts should be involved intimately in planning and designing in support for new products. Logistics should have a sign-off on all affecting changes. Anything that influences a product—every engineering change order—should be approved by service. It may get to the point that you will have to stop shipment of a new product if all the resources aren't ready. Some organizations, particularly those that have put enough emphasis on quality, will have designated someone as Vice President of Customer Satisfaction, Manager of Service Quality, or a similar title, who has the authority to stop any product from shipping until it will perform well in a customer installation. Sometimes the delay is overridden by a top executive who says, "Look, we'll be shot down in the marketplace if we don't get it out there. Yes, we know it's bad, but we must ship in order to get our chunk of the market and to demonstrate at the trade show." Nevertheless, bring the problem to the attention of responsible persons. A Product Support Council that looks at both existing and new products can say, "Here are the things that need to be done to be able to service it. We're having problems out in the field. We should be doing something differently."

An Installation Quality Report System is vital to show that products are being installed smoothly. Installation is the most critical phase of the product's life. That's when the customer's perception of a lemon or an excellent product is determined. It takes a very long time to develop and nurture a good positive quality reputation. You can lose a reputation in service instantly.

Statistical process control (SPC) techniques are applicable to analyze parts information. Evaluation of service calls requires a computer system that ranks calls and identifies problems and causes. The acronym FRACAS identifies a *failure report and corrective action system*, generally including both a reporting system and a task force charged with identifying the top problems on a product. Put short-range solution responsibility on the person or the organization that can alleviate the problem quickly, and then emphasize a separate long-range solution, which may be a design engineering or a manufacturing correction. Quite often there is something in training or publications that can be done very quickly to get "band-aid" improvements, and permanent solutions can come later.

Problem/cause/action analysis is keyed to *What was the problem? What caused that situation?* and *What action made the customer happy again?* What were the top ten causes? Are they material failures? If transformers are failing, is it because of loose connections? Are we spending most of the time board-changing, or what? Again, computer analysis is a big help.

A service telephone "hotline" is another good control. Particularly on new products, the speed and detail of mail isn't adequate. The normal reporting system isn't adequate. It is better to have the ability for tech reps in the field to call or fax or e-mail and say, "We have real trouble, please come out here and help take care of it." As said before, customer calls and letters are a late indicator. Create a separate DOA hotline for technicians to call from the site of any suspected dead-on-arrival parts. In order to get DOAs under 1 percent, every occurrence must be tracked and the cause prevented from ever recurring. Several companies who are successful in almost abolishing DOAs (several are under 0.1 percent) direct those calls to the Chief Engineer or Vice President of Quality. With that kind of management support, the problems are solved in a hurry.

Service quality audits are a good investment of a parts manager's time. Have someone in your organization measure how good customers think you are, how good employees think you are, and what the correlation is between those measures. A manager of service quality could head the process. Where a particular customer has a lot of equipment, get together with sales and service and review everything to support that customer. Quality teams, technicians, and in-house people know what most of your problems are. In many cases, we don't bother to ask for their advice. These audits made by participation circles, self-managed work groups, internally directed project teams, or similar management terms, are very beneficial in identifying problems and helping people develop and implement solutions. Already emphasized is a prioritization system with the most important customers getting visits from your managers, the next group of customers each getting a telephone call, and everybody getting a mail survey. The survey questionnaire should be mailed to specifically named and addressed customer decision makers—not just to the purchasing agent, but to the person who is really making the decision to buy your services.

Consider using double postcard forms sold pre-stamped by the post office. They can be typed by a word processor so that the request instructions and the customer address are on one card, and on the other card are the answer forms and return address. The cards are folded in half when they go out so that only the customer address and answer form sides show. The respondent just tears off the postcard and sends back the preaddressed answer card. Alternatively, you can reproduce the questionnaire as a letter, but it is important that size not be more than one page. If more than one page, fewer people will take the time to fill it out and send it back.

Most customers are quite pleased that you ask them for their opinions. Leave space for any customers who want to complain or detail the problems, and flag those instantly. Don't send all these returning questionnaires directly to the computer people for processing. Make sure a responsible person looks at them quickly and pulls out any that have messages in bright red ink saying, "If it breaks again, your equipment goes out on the street." There is a very positive marketing advantage to this kind of survey. A few really dissatisfied customers will be identified at that point. Most service organizations are very surprised to find how good customers rate their service. In many cases the customers rate service better than internal organizations do.

Since customers are people (with all the perceptual variation which that infers), focus groups and face-to-face individual discussions can be used to find out in detail what the customers really want, how important those wants (or musts or needs or nice-to-haves) are, and then how satisfied customers are with specific levels of performance. We can measure many controllable internal factors in quantitative terms of money or time or rates. Once we have those bench marks established, they can be modeled in comparison to the related customer perceptions and we can tune the quantitative and qualitative factors in parallel with each other. Thus, following the KISS (keep it satisfyingly simple) principle, we establish our plan for quality service.

Also, have sales rate service and parts support. Most of us have very critical things to say about sales persons. On the other hand, how often have we asked sales persons to fill out questionnaires on the parts service of their accounts and general quality level? Our own people can be good critics of our operation.

Special attention to repairs

Repaired parts should be subjected to even more stringent quality controls than a new part going into production equipment. The final test of a part is how well it operates in the final product. For replacement parts, that final product is in front of a concerned customer who wants it operational, Now! As with new parts, quality must be designed and processed in, rather than inspected in. In other words, the diagnostic and repair process must be done logically with quality and reliability in mind at every step. There is little value in finding defects after errors have added expense to repair. Anything less than 100 percent acceptable quality of replacement parts will be much more expensive than the alternative of investing wisely to gain high quality.

Awards and certifications

A wave of quality consciousness is sweeping businesses worldwide. Individual certifications that are applicable to service management include the Computer Industry Technology Association's A + Technician Certification; the American Society for Quality Control (ASQC) Certified Quality Engineering (CRE), Certified Reliability Engineer (CRE), and Certified Quality Auditor (CQA); the American Production and Inventory Control Society (APICS) Certified in Production and Inventory Management (CPIM); the National Association of Service Managers (NASM) Certified Service Executive (CSE); and the Society of Logistics Engineers (SOLE) Certified Professional Logistician (CPL). The national Baldrige Award has been emulated by most states for their own state quality awards. The ISO 9000 series of standards is receiving major emphasis, especially for companies doing business in Europe.

The Baldrige Award is presented annually to the top American manufacturing and service companies at the culmination of a long and expensive application and judging process. The preparation for the competition is valuable whether or not a company wins. Regional service firms may find more value in state quality competitions. The statement that your firm is "Winner of the New York State Excelsior Quality Award" could add powerful endorsement to your advertising. In the future, several states will change their quality awards from the selection of a relatively few top organizations in each category to an absolute Yes/No rating that an organization has achieved the award criteria.

The ISO 9000 series is applicable to service and maintenance organizations in hardware, software, and professional services. The standards require procedures, documentation, training, and consistency, but unfortunately do not set levels of performance. Most organizations working toward ISO certification also set high standards of quality performance. External auditors typically do a pre-audit that will find and correct most problems. After enough time for your organization to make improvements, they follow up with the final audit that counts.

The concept of quality is complex. Of all the items that help to provide superior service parts quality, the most important is highly motivated people aimed at meeting high quality goals.

Section II

TOOLS
and
TECHNIQUES

7 IDENTIFICATION AND RECORD SYSTEMS

Unique identification

$\mathbb{E}$very service stock keeping unit (SKU) must have a unique part number. Characteristics of the part number should be:

—All numeric, with no alpha characters, dashes, or spaces
—Short as possible, five or six digits
—No intelligence

Why not a 14 digit alphanumeric identifier that tells knowledgeable people that the part is a finished motor for a model 201 sorter, the country where the part was manufactured, and that it is repairable? Simplicity enhances accuracy and speed.

Computers can provide the relationships that formerly had to be done by humans looking at tables and lists. The part number is the key to all record keeping. Most data entries are made by people who either write down part numbers or push computer keys. The fewer digits there are to be remembered, the better. Error rate increases as the number of digits increases. To code a connection with a product type is asking for obsolescence and precludes standardization of common parts to multiple products. Combining different systems from acquired companies is simplified if the "All numeric, Short, Non-intelligent " rules are followed.

Most companies can operate with five-digit part numbers, allowing up to 99,999 line items. More items than that, unless supporting a very large organization, indicates a problem with too many field replaceable units (FRUs). Data entry can be done at high speed using the numeric keypad on computer terminals if all the entries are numeric. Injecting a space or alpha character requires hand movement to that key on the main keyboard and disrupts the process. The minus ($-$) key on most numeric pads can substitute for the dash, but should be necessary only in long numbering systems. Alphanumeric data fields require all five digits to be entered, even if they are 00001, so that the part numbers will sort in the proper order. All-numeric fields will right-justify entries and save effort by requiring entry of just 1 instead of 00001. Suppress leading zeros whenever possible, since the human eye takes time to distinguish a zero from other characters (especially "8" on a monitor screen), but does not need the same time to recognize spaces.

Eight ways to identify a Part

Useful ways in which a part may be identified in a complete system include:

1. Organization's part number
2. Suppliers' part identifiers
3. Manufacturers' part identifiers
4. Word description by noun and modifiers
5. List of parts for a commodity code

6. List of parts used on a specific equipment or a product line
7. List of parts made by a specific manufacturer
8. List of parts acquired from a specific supplier

The key information in most systems is the part number, which, as previously described, should indicate a unique stock keeping unit (SKU). All other ways of finding a part should reference to the part number.

Values of an accurate master record

An accurate parts record is a vehicle to:

1. Speed part availability and thereby equipment uptime and productivity
2. Facilitate rapid identification of the part needed for a maintenance action
3. Rapidly determine if the needed part is in stock
4. Eliminate, or at least reduce, duplication of the same SKU under different identifiers
5. Enable different facilities to share parts by common identifiers
6. Reduce equipment life cycle costs
7. Sell parts with equipment, or at least remove parts and reclaim some value in parts when related equipment departs a site
8. Guide purchasing to the best sources for a part
9. Enable alternative parts to be found and used effectively
10. Reduce parts costs, increase productivity, improve revenues and gain profits

A story about implementing parts management software at Eastman Kodak provides good illustration. Several years ago, Kodak headquarters' parts and materials were all on two-part Acme Visi-Record cards. These cards were in tubs that occupied the entire wall of a room about a football field long. Since to start at the first tub and proceed through to the end would require over a year of data entry, it was decided to use Pareto's

Principle of the Critical Few to select the parts with which to start. For three months all record cards used were returned, not to their place in part number sequence, but rather to a small central bin. After two months there were only about three feet worth of cards, with about 1,800 parts used. The first step in conversion to computer database was to assure that those high-moving parts were correctly identified. Those parts were given names according to the new standard.

At a progress meeting, the Kodak manager stated that they had entered the noun descriptions for O-Rings and wondered if it were possible to have as many as 28 duplicates for an item. We answered, "Yes; but please add the *Manufacturer* with *Manufacturer's Part Number*, before you get too upset." They did that, and at the next meeting sheepishly announced that they had discovered 23 different part numbers for the same part. In fact, there were 23 different stock locations and safety stocks and all the other accouterments for each of those part numbers. Those were small O-Rings for injection molding equipment. Apparently every time a new piece of equipment was ordered, some-one said to the junior engineer, "Order us the spare parts we might need." Those words may sound familiar to readers. To continue—they proceeded to enter data, concentrating on the *Equipment Used On.* They were very quiet about results until we asked if there were similar findings like the O-Rings. The manager said, "We hoped you would not ask. The injection machines that those O-Rings were used on were all sold two years ago!" Of course, your company won't find any similar situations! Or will they?

Noun nomenclature

Noun nomenclature is very helpful since it describes parts in the same words that humans normally use, without going through codes such as commodity groups and classes. Persons trying to identify a specific part will usually ask for it in descriptive terms, "I need those little rubber washers and springs that fit inside my single-handle kitchen faucet," or "I need an oil filter for a 1999 Dodge pickup truck." The authors originally discovered the value of accurate descriptions in 1977 while evaluating parts support of a large public utility corporation. Yellow rain suits were noticed in four separate large bins under four different names: CLOTHING, PROTECTIVE; RAINWEAR, YELLOW; OUTERWEAR, PARKAS AND TROUSERS; and GARMENT, SLICKERS. Each had a different SKU identifier, a different order track, and redundant controls. If those large, bright colored garments could be overlooked, there were probably duplicates in smaller, less conspicuous items. Little hunting was required to find many similar redundancies. Consolidation paid for the effort many times over.

Examples of query by noun nomenclature are: "WASHER, KIT W/SPR & TOOL, FOR DELTA SGL-HDL," or "FILTER, OIL, 1/4T TRK, CHRYSLER." The noun nomenclature is related to commodity code as described later. It is even possible to have a computer program that identifies the possible commodity codes for each part description and then allows the operator to decide which is best. Wire nuts, for example, that are used to make electrical connections would be "NUT, ELEC, 10 GA-2 WR." Since the search check for commodity code against the noun would be only against the word "NUT," it would probably show the choice to be mechanical or electrical and the user would select the appropriate code for the group and class. Other ways to find the oil filter would be to do a computer search of all parts stocked for trucks, or all parts manufactured by Chrysler, or all parts purchased from NAPA. A typical catalog page is illustrated in Table 7-1.

Structured part catalog and selection system

The challenge in developing and maintaining a noun nomenclature system is to assure that every part is entered using a valid noun. Converting thousands of existing parts to logical, orderly descriptions is time and talent consuming. Recognize that concentration should be given to frequently used parts. The parts used once a year can be renamed when there is activity. The advantages of standard names and descriptions are great.

A Structured Part Noun Nomenclature System requires software integrated with procedures to catalog and select parts. It

TABLE 7-1

Parts catalog descriptions gain by using familiar words

STOCK NUMBER	NOUN	DESCRIPTION
601	ABRASIVE	,SILICONE,CARBIDE,120:15 DEG
702		,SILICONE,CARBIDE,120:30 DEG
708		,SILICONE,CARBIDE,120:45 DEG
809		,SILICONE,CARBIDE,120:60 DEG
818		,LEAVITT LAPPING MACHINE
49	ABSORBER	,SHOCK,AIR,FOR MOD 6233 COPIER
50		,SHOCK,TEFLON, 2X3X1/2
31249	ACTUATOR	,PAPER FEED,OKI, 3PIN
6243		,PAPER FEED,EPSON,SNUBBER PR
3002	BEARING	,ROLLER,BALL,STNLS,3.6MM
28222		,ROLLER,SEALED,STNLS,4CM
39432		,ROLLER,PHOSBRONZ,1/2"
123465		,ROLLER,PHOSBRONZ,3/4"

is based on common words that allow humans to quickly identify a required part in common terms. These capabilities may be initially stand-alone, but should be incorporated into computerized management systems so that part descriptions are properly disciplined and uniformly validated throughout the corporate information systems. This capability can be blended into multiuser networks with procedures that funnel part requests from authorized persons to a database manager who has final approval authority.

Note that these principles are also applicable to product names and descriptions and similar business records. They can be used to standardize software as well as hardware. Definitions used are:

NOUN   A primary "one-word" description of a part type. Example: BEARING, BOLT, MOTOR, RESISTOR.

DESCRIPTOR   A word that defines and explains how a Noun will be further detailed and categorized to uniquely describe specific parts. Examples: FORM, MATERIAL, COLOR, POWER, SIZE.

CHARACTERISTIC   A value or modifier that a Descriptor may assume. Examples: (for the Descriptor "COLOR") BLUE, GREEN, RED, YELLOW.

At a minimum the database will contain a list of Nouns, Descriptors, and Characteristics to be used to validate part descriptions. Additionally, it should contain a list of part numbers with their descriptions that have been constructed based on the Noun/Descriptor/Characteristic structure.

Parts management software should contain the ability to construct a structured part description using a combination of Nouns, Descriptors, and Characteristics in the database and assigning a part number to that description. Each description must:

- Contain only one Noun
- Contain as many Characteristics as there are Descriptors defined for the Noun selected. Example: If the Noun "BEARING" has been selected, and the Descriptors "TYPE" and "SIZE" have been entered in the database to describe the Noun, then valid Characteristics must be entered (at least one for TYPE and one SIZE) to complete the part description.
- Once a unique combination of a Noun and Characteristics for the required Descriptors has been assigned a part number, no other part number will be permitted for that combination.

Software requirements include:

- An unlimited number of Nouns will be permitted in the database, so long as they are authorized and minimized.
- One or more Descriptors should be associated with a particular Noun to the database. A maximum of 16 Descriptors is normally permitted for each Noun. Two to five are typical. Note that if a Descriptor is being added to the structure of a Noun, and Part Numbers have already been defined for that Noun, the Characteristics for that Descriptor must be input and the part records will not be available to the system until Characteristics for the new Descriptor have been selected for the parts involved in the change.
- An unlimited number of Characteristics are permitted in the database per Noun/Descriptor combination.
- Past Numbers may be located by entering a combination of a Noun and a partial or complete list of Characteristics for Descriptors of that Noun.

- Lists may be either viewed on a monitor or printed to include:
  1. Full structure with all possible Noun, Descriptor, and Characteristic combinations.
  2. Noun Structure List with all Descriptor and Characteristic combinations for a single noun.
  3. Part Number Lists with Part Number and Descriptions.

Deletes and Changes to structure definitions are strong on the side of discipline:

- Nouns can be deleted if no parts have been defined for the Noun in question. If parts have been defined and Part Numbers assigned to the Noun, then the Part Numbers and all other information will be deleted as well. Nouns cannot be changed. Changes require deletion of old Nouns with all Descriptors and Characteristics; and then entry of complete revised information.

- Descriptors can be deleted from the structure. If parts have already been defined for the Noun, then the Characteristics for the Descriptor being deleted will be removed from the part Descriptions. The name of a Descriptor can be changed within the structure provided that the new name takes all of the Characteristics of the old (and in the same order) and the new Descriptor does not already exist for that Noun.

- Characteristics can be deleted if no parts for the Noun and Characteristic in question have been defined. If parts have been defined for a Noun and Characteristic in question, then the Part Number will be deleted as well. Characteristics can not be changed. Like Nouns, they must be completely deleted and replaced with the desired Characteristic.

The computer software disciplines and validates part descriptions. Obviously, considerable human thought is required to load the system with the most effective words. The standard list of Nouns must be established, as illustrated in Table 7-2, with a related word dictionary that lists other common terms that should be gathered under the standard Noun as shown in Table 7-3. Photographs or drawings of unusual items will be a help to assure they get properly cataloged. Conventions for

TABLE 7-2

Part noun descriptions form compartments in which to classify every part

ABRASIVE	BLANKET	CATCH	CRIMPER
ABSORBER	BLOCK	CATHODE	CROSSARM
ACCUMULATOR	BLOWER	CAULK	CRUCIBLE
ACTUATOR	BLUEING	CEMENT	CRYSTAL
ADAPTER	BOARD	CHAIN	CURTAIN
ADHESIVE	BOLT	CHANNEL	CUSHION
ADJUSTER	BOOK	CHART	CUTTER
ALARM	BOOM	CHASSIS	CYLINDER
AMPLIFIER	BOOT	CHEMICAL	
ANALYZER	BOTTLE	CHISEL	DAMPER
ANCHOR	BOWL	CHOCK	DECODER
ANODE	BRACE	CHOKE	DEFLECTOR
ANTENNA	BRACKET	CHUCK	DEGREASER
ANTIFREEZE	BRAID	CIRCUIT	DETERGENT
ANVIL	BRAKE	CLAPPER	DEVELOPER
APERATURE	BREAKER	CLEANER	DIAL
APPLICATOR	BRICK	CLEAT	DIAPHRAGM
APRON	BRIDGE	CLEVIS	DIE
ARBOR	BROOM	CLOTH	DIFFUSER
ARM	BRUSH	CLOTHING	DIODE
ARMATURE	BUCKET	CLUTCH	DISCONNECT
ARMOR	BUFFER	COATING	DISINFECTA
ATTENUATOR	BUM PER	COIL	DISK
AUDIO	BURNER	COLLAR	DISPENSER
AWL	BURNISHER	COLLECTOR	DISPERSANT
AXE	BURR	COMPRESSOR	DISPLAY
AXLE	BUTTON	CONDENSER	DISTRIBUTO
		CONDUCTOR	DIVIDER
BACKING	CABINET	CONDUIT	DOCUMENT
BAFFLE	CABLE	CONE	DOLLY
BAG	CAGE	CONNECTOR	DRAIN
BALANCER	CALIPER	CONTACT	DRESSING
BALL	CAM	CONTAINER	DRILL
BALLAST	CAMERA	CONTROL	DRIP
BAND	CAMSHAFT	CONVERTER	DRIVER
BAR	CAN	CONVEYOR	DRUM
BARREL	CANOPY	COOLANT	DRYER
BATTERY	CAP	COOLER	DUCT
BEARING	CAPACITOR	CORD	
BED	CARD	CORE	E-RING
BELLOWS	CARRIAGE	CORNER	EARPHONE
BELT	CART	CORONA	ECCENTRIC
BINDER	CARTRIDGE	COUNTER	EJECTOR
BIT	CASE	COUPLING	ELBOW
BLADE	CASTER	COVER	ELECTRODE
BLANK	CASTING	CRANK	ELECTROLYT

TABLE 7-2 (continued)

ELEMENT	FUEL	IMAGER	MAGNET
EMITTER	FUNNEL	IMPELLER	MANDREL
ENCODER	FUSE	INDEX	MANIFOLD
END	FUSER	INDICATOR	MANTEL
ENVELOPE		INDUCER	MARKER
EPOXY	GAGE	INDUCTOR	MASK
ESCAPEMENT	GAS	INJECTOR	MAT
EXCHANGER	GASKET	INK	MESH
EXHAUST	GATE	INSERT	METAL
EXPANDER	GEAR	INSERTER	METER
EXTENSION	GEARBOX	INSTRUMENT	MICROPHONE
EXTINGUISH	GENERATOR	INSULATOR	MILL
EXTRACTOR	GLAND	INTERFACE	MIRROR
EYE	GLASS	INTERPOSER	MIXER
	GLASSES	INVERTER	MONITOR
FACE	GLOBE		MOP
FACING	GOVERNOR	JAW	MOTOR
FAN	GRATING	JET	MOLDING
FASTENER	GREASE	JEWEL	MUFFLER
FEED	GRID	JOINT	
FERRULE	GRILL		NAIL
FIBER	GRIPPER	KEY	NAMEPLATE
FIELD	GRIT	KIT	NAPKIN
FILAMENT	GROMMET	KNIFE	NECK
FILE	GUIDE	KNOB	NEEDLE
FILLER	GUN		NIPPLE
FILM		LABEL	NOZZLE
FILTER	HAMMER	LADDER	NUT
FINDER	HANDLE	LAMP	
FINGER	HANDSET	LCD	O-RING
FIRMWARE	HANDWHEEL	LEAD	OIL
FITTING	HANGER	LED	OILCAN
FIXTURE	HASP	LEG	OILER
FLAG	HEADSET	LENS	OINTMENT
FLANGE	HEATER	LEVEL	OSCILLATOR
FLAP	HEATSINK	LIFTER	OUTLET
FLARE	HELICOIL	LIGHT	
FLASHBAR	HINGE	LIMITER	PACKING
FLASHER	HOE	LINE	PAD
FLOAT	HOIST	LINER	PAINT
FLUID	HOLDER	LINK	PANEL
FLUX	HOOK	LOCATOR	PAPER
FOLLOWER	HOSE	LOCK	PAWL
FOOT	HUB	LOCKPLATE	PEDAL
FORCE P		LUBRICANT	PEN
FORK	IC	LUBRICATOR	PENCIL
FORM	IDLER	LUMBER	PENETRANT
FRAME	IGNITOR		PHOTOCELL

TABLE 7-2 (continued)

PILOT	RECORDER	SHOE	TENSIONER
PIN	RECTIFIER	SHUNT	TERMINAL
PINION	REDUCER	SHUTTER	TESTER
PIPE	REEL	SIGHT	THERMISTOR
PISTON	REFLECTOR	SIGN	THERMOCOUP
PIVOT	REGULATOR	SLEEVE	THIMBLE
PLATE	RELAY	SLIDE	THYRISTOR
PLATEN	RELEASE	SLING	TIE
PLATFORM	REMOVER	SNUBBER	TIMER
PLENUM	RESIN	SOCKET	TONER
PLIER	RESISTOR	SOFTWARE	TOOL
PLOW	RHEOSTAT	SOLDER	TOOTH
PLUG	RIBBON	SOLENOID	TORCH
PLUNGER	RIM	SPINDLE	TOWEL
POINTER	RING	SPLASH PLAT	TRACK
POLE	RISER	SPLINT	TRANSDUCER
POLISH	RIVET	SPONGE	TRANSISTOR
POSITIONER	ROD	SPOOL	TRANSMITTE
POST	ROLLER	SPOON	TRAP
POWER SUPP	ROPE	SPRING	TRAY
PRINTBAND	ROTOR	SPRINKLER	TRIP
PRINTER	RUBBER	SPROCKET	TRIPOD
PRINTHEAD		SPUD	TRUNNION
PROBE	SADDLE	STAKE	TUBE
PROCESSOR	SAMPLER	STANCHION	TURNBUCKLE
PROPELLER	SAW	STAPLE	TYPE
PULLER	SCALE	STARTER	
PULLEY	SCALPEL	STATIC ELIM	VALVE
PUMP	SCANNER	STEP	VANE
PUNCH	SCOPE	STOP	VISE
PURIFIER	SCRAPER	STRIKE	
PWB	SCREEN	STUD	WASHER
	SCREW	STYLUS	WAX
RACE	SEAL	SUMP	WEIGHT
RACK	SEAT	SUPPRESSOR	WHEEL
RADIATOR	SEGMENT	SUSPENSION	WINCH
RAIL	SELECTOR	SWITCH	WINDOW
RAKE	SENSOR	SWIVEL	WIPER
RAM	SEPARATOR		WIRE
RAMP	SET	TABLE	WRENCH
RATCHET	SHAFT	TAP	WRINGER
REACTOR	SHEATH	TAPE	YOKE
READER	SHEETING	TAPPET	
RECEIVER	SHELF	TELEPHONE	
RECEPTACLE	SHIM	TELESCOPE	

TABLE 7-3

Noun descriptors with sample characteristics

Note that an objective of this system is to standardize on generic parts. The specific product model "where used," manufacturer, etc. are kept in a separate, related file.

Where several different words may be used for the same noun, those are identified in the list as "is . . ."

Maximum word length is 10 characters. We recommend comma separators and eliminate unnecessary spaces in the database.

Noun	Descriptors with sample Characteristics			
AMPLIFIER	WATTS	#PINS		
ANTI-STATIC	is STATIC ELIM			
ARM	TYPE			
ASSEMBLY	is KIT			
AUDIO	TYPE	DB	RANGE	WATTS
BATTERY	VOLT	AMP HR	SIZE	
BEARING	TYPE	STYLE	MATERIAL	ID	OD
	BALL	SEALED	STAINLESS	
	ROLLER	OPEN	PHOSBRONZE	
	SLEEVE		DELRIN	
BELT	TYPE	SIZE		
	FLAT			
	SLOT			
	V			
BRUSH	TYPE			
	DISCHARGE	is STATIC ELIM		
BULB	is LAMP			
BUSHING	is WASHER			
BUTTON	TYPE			
BUZZER	is AUDIO			
CABLE	TYPE	MATERIAL	SIZE	
CAM	TYPE	MATERIAL	SIZE	
CAPACITOR	UF	VDC		
CARTRIDGE	TYPE	COLOR	SIZE	
CASE	TYPE	MATERIAL	SIZE	
CELL	is BATTERY			
CHUTE	is GUIDE			
CLAMP	is HOLDER			
CLIP	is HOLDER			
CLUTCH	TYPE			
COLLAR	TYPE	MATERIAL	SIZE	
COLLECTOR	TYPE	MATERIAL	SIZE	
CONNECTOR	TYPE	MATERIAL	#PINS	
CONTROL	TYPE			
CORONA	TYPE	MATERIAL	SIZE	
COVER	TYPE	MATERIAL	SIZE	
CUSHION	is PAD			
DAMPER	TYPE	MATERIAL		
DETECTOR	is SENSOR			

TABLE7-3 (continued)

DEVELOPER	TYPE	QTY				
DIODE	TYPE	UF	VOLTS			
DISCHARGE BR	is STATIC ELIM					
DISPLAY	TYPE	ANALOG/DIGI	METRICS	SIZE		
DOCUMENT	PRODUCT	WHO FOR				
DOOR	is COVER					
DRUM	TYPE					
DUCT	TYPE					
ENCLOSURE	is COVER					
FAN	TYPE	VDC	WATTS	SIZE		
FILTER	TYPE	MATERIAL	SIZE			
FIRMWARE	MODEL #					
FOAM	is INSULATION					
FRAME	TYPE	MATERIAL	SIZE			
FUSE	TYPE	AMP				
FUSER	TYPE					
GEAR	TYPE	MATERIAL	#TEETH	SIZE		
GUIDE	TYPE					
HEATER	TYPE	VOLTS	WATTS	SIZE		
HEAT SINK	TYPE	CAPACITY	SIZE			
HINGE	TYPE	MATERIAL	LEFT/RT	SIZE		
HOLDER	TYPE	MATERIAL	SIZE			
IC	MODEL #					
INSULATOR	TYPE	MATERIAL	RATING	SIZE		
JUMPER	is WIRE					
KNOB	TYPE	MATERIAL	SIZE			
LABEL	TYPE	MATERIAL	SIZE			
LAMP	VOLT	WATTS	BASE			
LATCH	is HOLDER					
LCD	MONO/COLOR					
LED	COLOR	VOLT	SIZE			
LENS	TYPE	FOCAL LENGTH	F STOP	MOUNT SIZE		
LEVER	is ARM					
MAGNET	TYPE	FORCE	MATERIAL	SIZE		
MANUAL	is DOCUMENT					
MIRROR	TYPE	MATERIAL	SIZE			
MOTOR	HP	RPM	NEMA FRAME #	VOLT	SHAFTBASE SIZE	SIZE
NAME PLATE	is LABEL					
NUT	TYPE	MATERIAL	SIZE			
PACK	is KIT					
PAD	TYPE	MATERIAL	SIZE			

TABLE 7-3 (continued)

PANEL	TYPE				
PCB	is PWB				
PLATEN	TYPE	MATERIAL	SIZE		
POWER SUPP	TYPE	VOLTS	WATTS		
PRINTER	TYPE	RESOLUTION	WIDTH		
PRINTHEAD	TYPE	#PINS			
	INKJET				
	DOT MATRIX				
PULLEY	TYPE	SIZE			
PWB	PURPOSE	SPEED	PRODUCT		
RECTIFIER	—C TO —C	VOLTS	WATTS		
RELAY	TYPE	VOLTS	AMPS	CONNECTORS	
RESISTOR	OHM	WATT	%		
RETAINER	is HOLDER				
RIBBON	BLK/COLOR	MATERIAL	CARTRIDGE	SIZE	
ROLLER	PURPOSE	MATERIAL	UP/LOW	OD	LENGTH
	FEED				
	FRICTION				
	FUSER				
	REGISTRATION				
	TRANSFER				
RULER	is SCALE				
SCALE	TYPE	IN/MM	SIZE		
SCANNER	TYPE				
SCREW	HEAD	SLOT	MATERIAL	TYPE	SIZE
	FLAT	PHILLIPS	BRASS	MACHINE	4
	OVAL	SLOT	SIBRONZE	SELF-TAP	5
	PAN		STAINLESS	WOOD	1/8
	ROUND				
SENSOR	TYPE				
SHAFT	PURPOSE	MATERIAL	OD	LENGTH	
SHELF	is TRAY				
SOCKET	TYPE	#PINS			
SOFTWARE	TYPE	VERSION	MEDIA		
SOLENOID	TYPE	VOLT			
SPACER	is WASHER				
SPEAKER	is AUDIO				
SPRING	TYPE	SIZE			
	COIL				
	LEAF				
	TENSION				
STANDOFF	is HOLDER				
STATIC ELIM	TYPE	MATERIAL	SIZE		
SUPPORT	is HOLDER				
SWITCH	POLE/THROW	VOLTS	AMPS		
THERMISTOR	TYPE	SET POINT			
TONER	TYPE	SIZE			
TRACTOR	TYPE	LOCATION			
TRANSFORME	VOLT	WATT			
TRAY	TYPE	MATERIAL	SIZE		
TYPE	FONT	PRODUCT	CHARACTER		

TABLE 7-3 (continued)

WASHER	TYPE	MATERIAL	SIZE
	FINISH	BRASS	4
	FLAT	SIBRONZE	5
	LOCK	STAINLESS	1/8
WIRE	TYPE	MATERIAL	SIZE

standard abbreviations must also be set. For example, inches can be " or IN or INCH. (Consulting assistance from an external expert can be helpful, coupled with the personality necessary to negotiate agreements among differing factions.)

Commodity codes

A typical question is, "Should not the part number identify the kind of equipment it is?" The federal stock-number system does that, and a very small system running purely on manual cards could also. In between these very small and very large systems, the costs are generally much greater than the benefits. The typical method of identifying a commodity is by group and class. Table 7-4 shows some examples from the *Federal Supply Classification Cataloging Handbook*.

The advantage of having a group and class embedded in the part number is that the stock-keeping personnel can quickly learn to double-check the parts they are handling. If they are pulling part 61051234, for example, it should be a motor. If it is a relay, they should easily reject it as a mistake. Another plus is the ease of dividing parts into categories for purchasing and pricing attention. The overwhelming disadvantages include:

1. Extra digits are attached to a part number that must be used in every transaction. The few extra seconds necessary to speak or to write down the number and then to check those digits can add up quickly.

2. The commodity group class may change in different uses or the part may fit into several commodities. Items common to multiple products should have a common part number. It would be foolish to have separate stocks of the same SKU with only part numbers different.

3. If different part-numbering systems ever have to be integrated, the commodity designation will probably cause trouble.

TABLE 7-4
Examples of commodity codes

Group		Class	
25	Vehicular equipment components	2510	Cab body and frame structural components
		2520	Power transmission
		2530	Brake, steering, axle wheel and track
		2540	Furniture and accessories
		2590	Vehicle miscellaneous
28	Engine, turbines and components	2805	Gasoline, reciprocating
		2815	Diesel
31	Bearings	3110	Bearings, antifriction unmounted
		3120	Bearings, plain unmounted
		3130	Bearings, mounted
55	Construction materials	5510	Lumber and basic wood
		5520	Millwork
		5530	Plywood and veneer
		5630	Pipe and conduit, nonmetalic
61	Electrical components	6105	Motors, electric
		6110	Electric control equipment
		6115	Generators
		6120	Transformers
		6135	Batteries

Few people have the foresight to know what future products may be developed or what acquired products or merged company identifiers might be.

4. Numbers must be assigned in blocks, rather than in sequence. This takes more time, wastes numbers, and requires more digits.

5. The computer can display or print both the part number and the full description of the part for far better auditing of transactions than a person can do.

A combination that can be advantageous for organizations with high outside customer service components is to define the group and class for each part and use them as a cross check to the part number. Thus if customers are ordering a new wick for a kerosene heater, which will be a frequently ordered item, the added digits can help assure that the customer has ordered and will receive the desired part. The part number should not require the group/class prefix in order to be unique. In other words, the same part number should never be duplicated in another group/class. The commodity group and class should be kept in the part record as separate fields, which will allow a sort on those parameters for purchasing and stocking use. The group and class are related to the noun nomenclature, which is a preferred way of operating.

National stock number

The National Stock Number (NSN) system is one of the most comprehensive in existence. It is well illustrated in *Military Handbook 5* with supplements. The U.S. Government thinks it important to know where a part is manufactured as well as the group and class that defines what kind of material it is, and a unique identifier. The North Atlantic Treaty Organization (NATO) modified the system in order to make it acceptable around the world. Then, especially for commercial purposes, the Australian government developed Auslang, which is a noun and description-based further extension of the system. This is especially necessary for Australia because it relies on many other countries for manufactured goods, especially to support the country's mining and metal-refining operations that are often several days removed from the closest source of resupply. These series of manuals are all cross-referenced so that commodity code groups and classes can be found from the noun and description, and vice versa. For commercial and industrial purposes, many of the groups and classes for weapons systems should be deleted and a few additional ones are required. The Du Pont Corporation found that its effort to develop a commodity code group/class and noun nomenclature system necessitated the labor of five people over a year, and the system underwent further refinement during actual use.

Form, fit, function

These three parameters are used to decide whether a part is different from others. Consider a printed wiring board (PWB) that the engineers want to call "part 456, revision B." (As a side note, this part might more properly be called a "Printed Circuit Board," but the hazardous chemical abbreviated "PCB" has given a bad meaning to those initials. Thus the designation "PWB" is used for electronic boards.) This PWB looks the same as its previous cousins, fits the same card cage and connectors, but has the additional capability of automatically sensing and accommodating varied transmission rates. The question is whether it should be called revision B or should receive a new part number. This is a borderline situation that is best resolved by using a new part number. It will provide better control, unless the organization tracks parts by unique revision levels. If the latter is done, the revision is treated much like extra digits on a part number. Steiger Tractor, for example, uses a T1 or T9 suffix to indicate advancement of a part. Consideration should be given to the fact that as soon as technicians discover that one variation of a part is more reliable or functions better than another, they will push for the improved version. Inventory managers should make sure that stocks of the older part are used whenever possible before the new part numbers are released.

Bill of materials

All manufacturing operations start with a bill of materials (BOM). This list of components in equipment is "exploded," starting with the top system level, into subsystems, then assemblies, then subassemblies, and finally piece parts. Every component then, except the top level, has a "next higher assembly" and also can be categorized "where used." Factory maintenance and field service have little use for the complete manufacturing bill of materials. However, they do need to know the parts that may be repaired during maintenance. These are often referred to as line replaceable units (LRUs) or field replaceable units (FRUs). (The selection and standardization of FRUs is covered later in detail.) Individual electronic components soldered onto a PWB are not normally field replaceable. Complete PWBs, lamps, motors, and power supplies would be listed as field replaceable parts. On computers and office equipment, the steel frames and welded assemblies are not normally field replaceable, but agricultural and industrial operations frequently replace such parts.

The decision to catalog a part number as available for service is different from the decision to hold service stock on that part number. Exterior panels, for instance, are an essentiality class 4 (cosmetic) item and would not be stocked in the field service supply system. Should a need arise for the part in the field, an order is placed and would flow normally through the order system. When the order reaches the analyst, a purchase order is sent to manufacturing. For in-production items, the order can be filled quickly. Out-of-production items may require full manufacturing lead time.

In many service organizations, a *field replaceable unit* (FRU) *list*, sometimes called a *spare parts list* (SPL), is developed in the provisioning process and maintained on a database for access throughout the life of the product. When the last product is removed from field service, the part numbers associated with that product should be purged from the inventory (assuming they are not also used in other current products).

Reference designators are also useful physically and logically to locate parts within equipments, or even equipments within systems. For example, all resistors may be coded with an R and then sequentially numbered as R1, R2 and so forth. Equipments within a large facility might have a system component designator such as "12 MOV 1234," meaning that this is in the System 12 Motor Operated Valve 1234. That is both a functional and a physical location and may be cross-referenced by the "where used" list. A major value of "all parts used on an equipment" is to display any parts stocked. It also identifies which parts should be disposed of along with equipment that is being removed. Too often, equipment is removed and sold but the support parts remain on the stockroom shelves until someone notices the thick coat of dust and lack of activity. Effective asset management will offer the support parts for sale or scrap together with the capital equipment. The "where used" information helps assure that parts are prioritized for essentiality in relation to the equipment they support. Also, standardization is promoted by using the same part on several products. And if one of those products is being terminated, we want to assure that the parts are still available to support other equipment on which they are used.

Special controls

The number of data elements for service parts tends to expand as the effort to control service parts increases. It is not unusual to have 50 or more data elements for each part number on the Parts Master Record. An example of a field list for a Parts Master Record is shown in Table 7-5. Normally these elements are entered through the cataloging organization. Data elements are entered in the part record in several ways:

1. By direct entry through the cataloging organization
2. By data handoff from suppliers
3. By data handoff from the warehouse control system
4. By internal calculation

TABLE 7-5
Parts master data fields

Part Number	Repair Code
Description	Product Code
Unit of Measure	Provisioning Code
Superseded By PN	Equipment Used on (multiple)
Essentiality Value Class	Interchangeable-with ID
Commodity Code	Next Higher Assembly ID
Shelf Life	Capital/Controllable/Expendable/
Environmental Restrictions	Consumable Code
Quality Class	Field Change Order (FCO) or ECO(s)
Cost	applied
Next Cost	FCO Class
Sell Price	Tariff Code
Defective Return Credit	Responsible Inventory Analyst
International Price Code	Primary Repair Facility
Packaging Type	Repair Cycle Time
Packaged Size and Weight	Secondary Repair Facilities
Source Code	Stock Keeping Unit
Vendor Identification(s)	Emergency Reserve Quantity
Vendor Part Number(s)	Repair Center Only Code

In all cases data quality must be a primary concern. Data maintenance is an ongoing task for the cataloging function.

Exception reports that contain data considered abnormal will aid in maintaining data quality. In addition to the fields entered into the database from the cataloging organization, other data enters the Parts Master Record. Some fields are updated by supplier data:

Purchase lead time
Repair lead time
Production status
In/out of current production
Next cost

Some fields are filled by entry or change of related data:

Standard cost date of last change
Base cost date of last change
Retail price date of last change
International price date of last change

Some fields are calculated and displayed:

Control class code (ABC)
Economic order quantity
Reorder point quantity
Safety stock level
Economic repair quantity
Use to date
Returns from users to date
Purchases to date

Change control should be regulated by a central engineering function, with sign-off by maintenance or field service. Changes to part numbers, supersession, revisions, and use of discrepant materials should all be approved by the affected users before implementation. Too often an administrative-type person may judge that these have no influence and yet the stockroom may have large quantities of parts on the shelf or be in the midst of negotiations for purchase or repair. Certainly tools, test equipment, and documentation must also be considered before changes are approved.

Quality assurance of parts requires special attention. At nuclear power stations, for example, every part will be categorized as quality assurance or not, and will have subgroups within the qualification. For example, category lE means a safety-related part that must be qualified to perform in special environments. Concern arises when the same part is used in several locations. A relay, for example, may be a category 2 in many systems and cost $5.50. If it is to be qualified lE category, that same part could cost $250. If the cost difference is relatively small, all quantities of a part should be bought according to the highest qualification and then may be used wherever needed without any special control. If, however, there are large cost differences, the environmentally qualified parts should have a different part number and be treated as completely different parts, which they are because their function is different. It may be useful to retain the "interchangeable with" information on the part record for the lower qualified part since a more costly, more highly qualified part could be used in the lower situation for emergencies. The reverse is not acceptable.

Environmental controls themselves are a concern with parts such as gaskets, O-rings, paint, chemicals, and even bearings that may deteriorate with age or in the presence of certain chemical vapors or temperature extremes. Bearings and rotating equipment such as motors should be revolved every few months to ensure they do not develop flat spots. Lot control presents some unique problems that are presently best handled manually. The relatively few parts that do require shelf-life control, rotation, or inspection controls can be flagged on the computer or manual record and listed so a human can perform the required physical action. Table 7-6 shows another detailed Master Parts Record. Note that in this case quantity and location are on separate records.

Figure 7-1 shows the data displayed on a computer monitor. Figure 7-2 illustrates a simpler format that is suitable for small service organizations, and also includes the functions of location and quantity.

Keep only necessary data. These database fields should cover any event that may occur. If, however, the data are not needed, then eliminate that element from consideration and do not

TABLE 7-6
Data elements for a part object

Item	Abbreviation
Part identification	Part Number (PN)
Description	Noun X (10)
Commodity code	Comm Code
Revision	Rev
Essentiality	Essn
Control class	Ctl
Service only	Svc only
Stock locations	Stk Loc
Stock Level %	Stk Lvl
Use/Year	Use/Yr
Lead days	Lead Dys
Reorder point	ROP
Minimum cost Qty	EOQ
Unit of Measure	Unit
Quality class	Qual
Environmental	Envir
Shelf life days	Shlf
Shutdown use	Shutdn
Sell price $	Price
Cost $	Cost
Margin $	Marg$
Margin %	Marg%
Carry Cost %	Carry%
Order $	Order$
Repair cost $	Rpr$
Return credit	Rtn cred$
Vendor code	Vendor code
Vendor name	Vendor name
Vendor part ID	Vendor PN
Equipment used on E/P	Use
Higher Assembly	Hghr assy
Interchangeable	Intrchbl
Superseded by	Suprsd by
Date Last Invent	Date last
Quantity on hand	Qty-OH
Quantity on order	Qty-OO

waste the time and effort required to gain and keep accurate information. It is even worse to have false information than it is to have none at all. Information can be expensive. The benefits of having information must be weighed against the cost.

Media

The medium used for cataloging parts is rapidly transitioning from paper and microfische to computerized electronic data retrieval. Parts data have historically been written on cards or printed on paper, often in the format shown in Table 7-3. Sequenced in part number order or alphabetically by noun and description, this type of catalog is useful for an industrial parts crib or field service stockroom. As the volume of paper increases, inventory systems specialists usually recommend the use of microimaging. Microfilm that contains a 35-mm photograph of each page in sequential order is handy for high-volume storage, but microfiche that can store 80 pages per 4 x 5 film is more efficiently distributed to many users, and the desired information is more easily retrieved from the flat fiche. Where many field representatives are involved, the cost of mailing alone will pay for the difference in cost between paper copies and the film.

Film image is excellent for typed single-line entries such as parts catalogs, but it is not as good for schematics and detail that need to be closely traced. Revising and updating parts

```
                     P A R T    M A S T E R

Stock Number:   123456    Desc: CONNECTOR ,INSUL,MULT TAP,COPPER,#4
                                SPEC PURPOSE PER DWG 45E

Com Code: 5935        Suprsd by:              Next Higher: 324563
Essn: 2   Envir: Y    Shelf Lf: N   QA Cl: 1M  Outage: N  Value Cl: C
Std Para:   QA21      QA 33      PAS1

Use/Yr:    30     Unit: EA     Lead Days:  60      Last PO#:  XB12H3
Last Cost$:   647.75     Avg Cost$:   657.75    Next Cost$:   685.00

Calc ROP:  11  Adj ROP:       S/P Prod  System   Component   Intrch
Calc EOQ   15  Adj EOQ:  18    S         01198      C122      123467
                               P    Mot

Supl Code: G111
Supl Name: GENEROUS ELECTRIC
Supl Part: GE12345678998M

Supl Code: L355
Supl Name: LINK FOUGHT
Supl Part: LF25443P
```

Figure 7 -1
Master part information is grouped in logical clusters

TABLE 7-3
Parts data for a field stockroom

Part Number	Description	Location	Unit of Issue	Dealer Price	Unit Price
12345	FUSE,15 AMP,SLOW BLOW	A12B1	EA	1.04	1.25
12346	RELAY,20 AMP,DPDT,TI DELAY	E01A3	EA	6.25	7.80
12349	SWITCH ,20 AMP,SPST,FOR COLEMAN X21	B09E8	EA	2.96	3.55

information is a continual challenge. If change sheets and additions are distributed, the receiving people rarely note all the changes on their base documents. Since the objective is to provide accurate information to the end user with minimum effort, complete pages, or even whole documents, or comprehensive CDs should be distributed whenever possible.

Do make sure that information will be readily available in case a computer-based system is interrupted. It is recommended that a complete catalog be printed about every three months, or whenever significant changes occur. Catalog listings should be ordered in the several sequences most useful to parts requesters: Part Number, Noun Description, and possibly Equipment Used On. Computerization is covered in more detail in chapter 24 and as related subjects are mentioned.

```
==================================================================
   P A R T    R E C O R D    A N D    A V A I L A B I L I T Y

Part ID  7001        Desc BEARING    ,ROLLER,STNLS,7MM

On Hand     5  Location    A22B2        Supl     Supl   Equipment
                                         ID     Part ID  Used On
On Order    0  Unit of Issue  EA
                                        4789CW   998INT   EP310
In Repair  NA

  Stock Category  S  Annual Use     45

     Control Code  C  Unit Cost    4.75

       Repairable  N  Lead Days      30

Last Review  06156  Reorder Point    8

                    Order Quantity   7

Enter Part ID, or "Q" to exit

==================================================================
```

FIGURE 7-2
Simplified part record with local availability

Serial numbers

While part serial numbers may be required for identification of specific parts for aerospace, nuclear, security. or quality tracing purposes, the added digits cause extra work and frequent error. Do not use serial numbers on individual parts unless absolutely mandatory. Then, if you must track serial numbers, use bar codes or an electronic means of accurately reading the numbers.

Repair operations often add a unique number to every repaired part so they know if that part has been in their shop before. If an intermittent problem or no trouble found (NTF) is claimed on repeat visits to repair, then the suspect part should be scrapped to avoid further field problems. The identification number added in repair can range from a simple stick-on tag to etching or painting the numbers on the part body. Again, the identifier should be readable by optical or electronic means.

8 WORKING WITH NUMBERS

This chapter establishes a familiarity with the fundamentals of statistics as used for managing service parts. This business revolves around numbers. The customer, field engineer, and mechanic would like immediate access to 100 percent of their parts needs. To achieve this would require immense stocks of parts, people, and money; and is unreasonable in the vast majority of situations. Therefore, the numbers, representing physical parts, must be arranged, analyzed, and communicated so that humans can make necessary management decisions. We should heed the statement of Sir Josiah Stamp of the English Inland Revenue Department in the early 1900s, when he said, "The government are very keen on amassing statistics. They collect them, add them, raise them to the nth power, take the cube root, and prepare wonderful diagrams; but you must never forget that every one of these

127

figures comes in the first instance from the village watchman, who puts down what he damn pleases." The computer era version of the same problem is "garbage in = gospel out." We must begin with good data.

Organizing data

Humans use numbers best when they are organized in a logical sequence of individuals or groups. Assume the data shown in Table 8-1 are quantities used each week of a 13-week quarterly period for part no. 345678, which is a switch.

The first step in preparing the data for effective use is to sort the data into order from the lowest number ascending to the highest number, as shown in Table 8-2.

TABLE 8-1
Original data as received

Week	1	2	3	4	5	6	7	8	9	10	11	12	13
Use	9	3	12	15	9	7	6	18	9	8	5	6	12

TABLE 8-2
Data sequenced in ascending order begins to have rational flow

3	5	6	6	7	8	9	9	9	12	12	15	18

Range

Now look at the range of data, that is, from the smallest number to the largest. Range can be expressed in two ways:

1. As the numerical difference between the largest and the smallest; for example, $18 - 3 =$ range of 15.
2. As 3 to 18. Knowing the absolute numbers, for example, 3 through 18, is a big help in service parts management because it not only tells us what the range spread is, but it also shows the absolute values. A range of 15 between 3 and 18 is much different than the same range between 103 and 118. If the numbers are of major importance, such as for forecasting the needs for expensive parts, it may be advisable to draw a histogram that graphs the numbers.

Cumulative distribution

For managing parts the cumulative distribution will be useful. It is constructed by adding each week's data to the previous sum, so that the data continually increase from the lowest to the highest. In this specific case, it would be termed "quarter to date data," since each week it would tell us the total used to that date. As can be seen in Table 8-3, the first week's data are the actual 9. The second week is 9 plus 3 equals 12. The third week is the previous sum of 12 plus 12 (that week's data), and so on. The slope of the cumulative distribution shows whether demand is increasing, decreasing, or stable. A uniform slope would mean steady demand, and an increasing rate of use would show as an upward ascending line. Zero demand would be shown by a horizontal line. It is not possible on a cumulative distribution to have a decreasing line, unless there were returns credited to stock.

A cumulative distribution plotted as percentages rather than absolute numbers will be shown as very useful for determining levels of support and what parts should be stocked to fill various percentages of demand; as in Table 8-4. The percentages are determined by dividing each number in Table 8-3 by the total of 119. For example, $9/119 = 0.0756$, which rounds to 8 percent.

The cumulative distribution on ordered data is very useful for determining the probability of need for each quantity. Table 8-5 shows the cumulative percentages for the Table 8-2 ordered data. It can be seen from the data that filling 85% of the requests requires 15 units.

TABLE 8-3

Data arranged in cumulative order shows rate of progress

9	12	24	30	48	55	61	79	88	96	101	107	119

TABLE 8-4

Cumulative percentages show progress toward 100 percent

8	9	20	33	40	46	51	66	74	81	85	90	100

TABLE 8-5

Relationships show when cumulative percentages are ordered by units

Units:	3	5	6	6	7	8	9	9	9	12	12	15	18
Unit Percent:	2	4	5	5	6	7	8	8	8	10	10	12	15
Cumulative Percent:	2	6	11	16	22	29	37	45	53	63	73	85	100

Mean, mode, and median

Mean is the statistical term for arithmetic average. It is calculated by:

$$\overline{X} = \frac{\sum_{1}^{n} x}{n}$$

In the above example,

$$\overline{X} = \frac{119}{13} = 9.15 \cong 9$$

In the above example $\overline{X}$ is called "X bar" and is the symbol for *mean*. The $\sum_{1}^{n}$ is the Greek capital letter sigma, and stands for *sum* or *total*. The small "1" on the lower right and the N at the upper right of the Sigma says to add all numbers from the first through the last. In our specific case, that would be 3 through 18, or if you were referring to the week periods, it would be from the first week through the 13th week. The X to the right of the sigma simply refers to all those actual numbers, which are termed X's. The N below the line is the number of events occurring. In our case of 13 weeks, that means 13 events and 13 numbers.

The mean tells us the average of all the usage. That number conveys a lot of information. Be alert, though, to the fact that a person can stand with one foot in a 120° F oven and the other foot in a 20° F freezer and on the average would be at a 70° F temperature, which, in this case, would not be comfortable. Mode is the most frequently occurring number, in this case "9." In the parts business, a frequently occurring mode probably indicates that parts are used in a pattern, such as four bearings at a time. There may be patterns within the mode, as possibly indicated by the multiples of three in our example. The median is the midpoint of the distribution. In our example of 13 numbers, look at the ordered data and count to the seventh number; that is the median, which is also 9.

Graphics

People gain information more easily from graphical displays than from lists of pure numbers. Parts analysts will find frequent use for graphs and plots. Most parts analysts simply enter the data into a computer program and it will display the graphical plot on the monitor screen or printout. It is important that users understand the process that is being developed and be able to do it manually when a computer is not available. For the 13 numbers in our data, a column can be established for every number from either 3 (our lowest) through 18 (our highest) or from 0 through 18. For comparison purposes with other parts, the 0 through 18 is better because it shows the absolute range and where it is on the scale of all numbers. The lowest cell is 0 because it is quite possible that there will be no demand for a part during a specific period. Figure 8-1 shows the histogram of these data. This form could also be called a bar chart, since there are bars constructed for each of the number cells by filling in the blocks on the graph paper.

Figure 8-2 Shows a plot of the same information; it was drawn simply by connecting the midpoints of the tops of each cell.

Figure 8-3 shows a plot of the cumulative distribution of the same data.

Parts usage will often form a normal distribution when plotted. A normal, or bell curve, distribution is evenly dispersed around the center with mean, mode, and median all being the same point, as shown in Figure 8-4.

USE HISTOGRAM

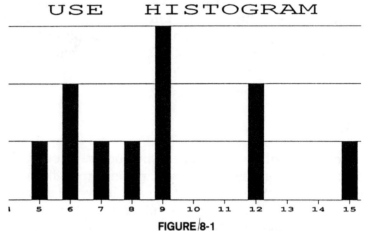

FIGURE 8-1
Bar chart shows the relative number of occurrences for each measure

USE PLOT

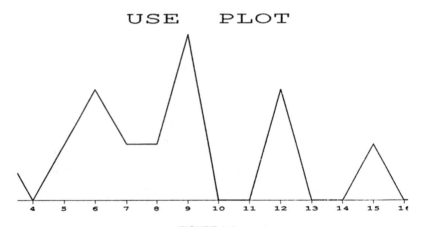

FIGURE 8-2
The number of occurrences may be connected to visualize patterns

Standard deviation

Whether the distribution is wide and short, or narrow and tall, depends on the dispersion of the data from the mean. This parameter is called the "standard deviation" and is represented by "S" or the lower case Greek sigma (σ). It is also referred to as the "root-mean-square (RMS) deviation," because it is the square root of the sum of the squares of the distance that each number deviates from the mean. The formula is:

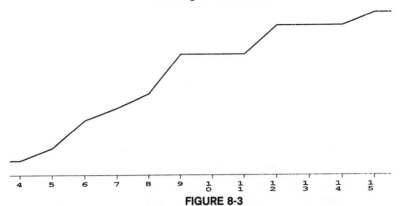

FIGURE 8-3
The cumulative plot always grows up to the right

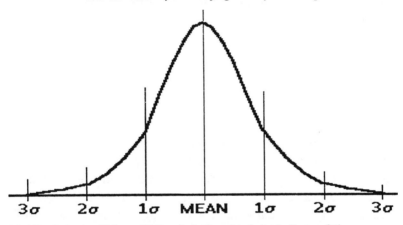

| 3σ | 2σ | 1σ | MEAN | 1σ | 2σ | 3σ |

68.3% of data will be within +/- 1 standard deviation of the mean
95.4% of data will be within +/- 2 standard deviations of the mean
99.7% of data will be within +/- 3 standard deviations of the mean.

FIGURE 8-4
The standard, normal distribution is symmetrical like a bell

$$S = \sqrt{\frac{\sum\limits_{i=1}^{N}(X_i - \overline{X})}{N}}$$

$$S = \sqrt{\frac{(3-9)^2 + (5-9)^2 + (6-9)^2 + \ldots + (18-9)^2}{13}}$$

In our ordered example:

$$S = \sqrt{\frac{210}{13}} = \sqrt{16.1538} = 4.62$$

As it turns out, the equation that defines the standard deviation is very difficult to use to compute this statistic because it requires multiple passes through the data. The following is the computational formula that is mathematically equivalent to the definition formula and only requires one pass through the data.

$$S = \sqrt{\frac{\sum_{i=1}^{N} X^2 - \overline{X}^2}{N}}$$

Fortunately, many calculators and computer programs can do standard deviation calculations very quickly. A large standard deviation indicates a wide dispersion from the mean and a wide, short distribution. This also means it is harder to predict and forecast the actual values. A very small standard deviation represents closely grouped numbers and leads to increased forecasting accuracy. Standard deviations relate to probability so that in a normal distribution the area under the normal curve within one standard deviation of the mean includes 68 percent of all the possible values; 95 percent are included within two standard deviations ("two sigma") and three standard deviations include 99.7 percent. Many industrial processes operate at the two-standard-deviation level, and recognize that 5 percent of all the items may be outside that range. Quality improvements tend toward three sigma to reduce errors under 1 percent. Motorola has made a quality impression with their "six sigma" program. Note that, with regard to parts, we are most often interested in demands that are going to exceed the upper limit. We don't usually care if demand is very low for a short period, if there is reason to believe that it will rise again.

Thus it can be termed that the 50 percent on the low side of the mean will be covered. Our major interest is in the percentage on the high side.

Log-normal distribution

In a normal distribution the data is distributed "normally" or equally around the mean. In a quantitative sense, there is equal volume under the curve on each side of the mean. This property is what makes the normal distribution so powerful from a management point of view. There is another distribution that we see a lot in service, called the log-normal distribution. Log-normal means that the data is not distributed around the average, but if we took the logarithms of all the data points, those logarithms would be normally distributed. Don't be concerned with the math, the data itself looks like Figure 8-5. In

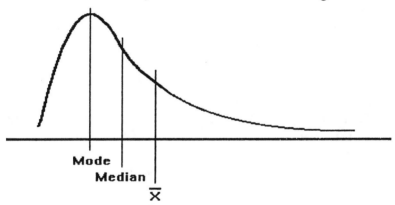

FIGURE 8-5
Many fast repairs and a few long ones skew the log-normal distribution

logistics pipelines this is the most frequently occurring statistical distribution. For proof, ask a repair technician how long it takes to repair an item. The answer will invariably be, "Well, usually ten minutes or so, but it can take one or two hours depending on what is wrong." This is English for "Log-normal" distribution. (Chapter 28 discusses the practical approach to managing this type of distribution.)

Confidence interval

In view of the properties of the standard deviation, we can construct what is called a confidence interval around an estimate. This is true even if the event in question occurs randomly. This is how it works: Suppose we track the time between failures for a sensor and we know that the mean time between failure (MTBF) is 180 days. We also know that failures follow a normal distribution (because we plotted them) and that the standard deviation is 10 days. If a failure just happened, we can say that we are 84% confident that another failure will happen between 170 and 190 days from now. This is because, in a normal distribution, 84% of the data is within + one standard deviation of the mean. Similarly, we can say that we are 95% confident that the next failure will be between 160 and 200 days from now. Confidence intervals can be read from standard normal probability tables such as Table 8-6. (You will see a version of these same numbers in the Chapter 13 discussion of safety stock.) Note also that Figure 8-4 concerns the entire area under both sides of the curve, so it is the sum of both plus and minus probabilities. To illustrate, -2.00 standard deviations gives .0228 cumulative probability, which must be subtracted from the $+2.00$ deviations, which is .9772. The result is .9772 $-$ .0228 = .9544 = 95.44 percent.

Remember that many logistics functions are concerned only with the probability of being on one side of the distribution. For example, management may be worried about having enough quantities of a part (not stocking out) and may have much lower concern about having too many of those parts. That example can be read directly from the table. If you want a 95 percent probability of having enough parts, then you must stock to the mean plus 1.65 standard deviations. A 98 percent probability requires the mean plus 2.06 standard deviations. Please note that if you do not include the variance as computed by standard deviations, then you will be at the mean $\pm$ zero, which gives you a confidence of 50 percent. That is not very accurate when dealing with expensive parts and people, or angry customers. Calculate and use the variance and confidence limits.

TABLE 8-6

Confidence bounds can be read from standard normal probability tables

K density at Zσ from the mean	Cumulative Probability F(k)
−3.00	.0013
−2.50	.0062
−2.00	.0228
−1.50	.0668
−1.00	.1587
−0.50	.3085
0.00	.5000
+0.50	.6915
+1.00	.8413
+1.50	.9332
+1.65	.9505
+1.88	.9699
+2.00	.9772
+2.06	.9803
+2.50	.9938
+3.00	.9987

Moving average

Much part information is kept up to date by the use of moving averages. How many periods should be averaged? Three is a good number. More than that will dampen the effects of most recent data. The moving average is calculated by adding up to three numbers and dividing that sum by the number of events. In our example, if there is no history before the first week, then the actual is the same as the average. In the second week, we can add the totals of the first week and second week and divide by 2, so the average will be 12/2 = 6. In the third week, we add the first three weeks and divide that sum by 3, giving a result of 24/3 = 8. Then in each succeeding week, the newest week's total should be added and the oldest week's total should be subtracted and the result divided by 3. Weeks 2–4, for example, are 30/3 = 10.

TABLE 8-7

Three-period moving averages emphasize the recent three periods

9	6	8	10	12	10	7	10	11	12	7	6	8

Note that moving averages (see Table 8-7) dampen the effects of change so the average never climbs or dives as fast as do the data. The standard moving average gives equal weight to all periods. If more emphasis is desired on more recent data, then weight is recommended, such as 0.6 for most recent, 0.3 for prior one, and 0.1 for prior two. Thus the data for weighted values become

$$9 \quad\quad 6.6 \quad\quad 9 \quad\quad 12.9 \quad\quad 11.1, \ldots$$

For example,

Week 3 $\quad = [(0.6 \times 12) + (0.3 \times 3) + (0.1 \times 9)]$
$\quad\quad\quad\quad = [(7.2) + (0.9) + (0.9)]$
$\quad\quad\quad\quad = 9$

Exponential smoothing

The term "exponential smoothing" sounds very sophisticated, but in reality it is simple to understand and very useful in forecasting parts. The concept is to take some portion of the difference between a result (actual) and what was expected (forecast or plan), and apply that correction to future data. The formula is:

$$\text{Forecast}_n = (\text{Actual}_{n-1} * \alpha) + [\text{Forecast}_{n-1} * (1-\alpha)]$$

In words, this says that the forecast for future period n (usually the next period) equals the actual results for the prior period times the alpha factor, plus the forecast for the same prior period times 1 minus the alpha factor. There is considerable theoretical discussion about what the value of alpha should be. A value of 0.5 means simply that half the difference will be applied to correct the future data. An exponent of 1 means the entire correction difference should be added to the next value. The smaller the alpha factor, the less correction will be applied; this means that more weight is given to historical data over a long term than is given to the most recent period. For example, with an alpha of 0.5, if the actual use last period was 10, and the forecast for the same period was 14, then $(10 * 0.5) + (14$

* 0.5) = 12 forecast for the next period. (Other aspects of exponential smoothing are covered in chapter 12, Forecasting.) Again, it should be remembered that the statistics are only as good as the data provided. If deviations are large, then an analyst should investigate the causes.

Regression analysis

This popular forecasting technique is used to determine the slope of previous data changes so as to determine what was happening and help predict the future, if the same causes are expected to continue. If the points are plotted on graph paper, an eyeball estimate of a line that will connect them may be sufficient. Many pocket calculators have regression analysis programs built-in and standard programs are available as computer software. Figure 8 - 6 shows an example of a regression line fitted between the actual points. The principle is called "least squares" because it minimizes the sum of the square roots of the distances from each actual point to the regression line.

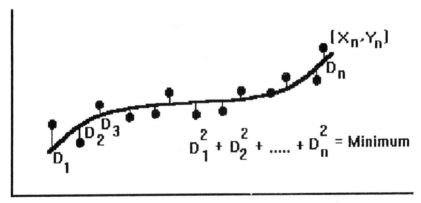

FIGURE 8-6
The regression line shows the pattern of historical data that helps predict the future

Risk, certainty, uncertainty and no knowledge

Risk is a major consideration in data. There is risk that not all data were reported accurately. There is risk that something will change and supply or demand will vary. There is risk that all the good plans on paper will not be completely implemented. Service parts personnel must learn to manage risk. Certainty means that we are absolutely positive about the events. Most of us can say that we are certain the sun will rise in the east tomorrow morning. We know that event has happened every day of recorded history. There is, of course, some probability that it will not happen tomorrow, but that is too small for consideration; and if it does not happen, we will probably not be in any position to worry about it. Looking to the stockroom shelves, we can say that if ten parts a week have been used for the last three years and all related causes are continuing, then the same use rate also will continue.

Anything less than certain is called "uncertain" and has a probability connected with it. A 50 percent probability means there is an equal chance of an event happening versus not happening. This binomial (meaning two events) distribution is often referred to as the "coin toss," since flipping a coin will result in either "heads or tails," either "win or lose." Any percentage smaller than 50 percent means there is less chance of it happening; that is, it probably will not happen. Zero probability would be absolute certainty that an event cannot happen.

Most service parts considerations are uncertain. We usually deal with probabilities in the 60–95 percent range. For example, a service level of 90 percent may be desired. That means that out of 100 requests for parts, 90 of them will be filled. An illustration of probabilities used in pricing parts is shown in the Figure 8 - 7 decision tree.

Some people will say the "highest price" ($575) because they can skim off profits at that price, and then reduce the price. This might be a reasonable choice if it were possible to reduce the price without long-term loss of business. Watch out, because the second time around your customers might decide to wait until the part goes on sale, assuming they have a choice, and you could be left paying the carrying cost. If you have to set just one price and hold it, most people will select the $425 because that has a high probability of clearing out all the inventory at the best possible price. Parts managers don't like to be left holding just a few parts. They prefer to have the job completely over with.

It is important to remember that 100 percent minus percent "yes" equals percent "no." In other words, if 90 percent of parts requests are filled, then 10 percent are not filled. When selecting a percentage target, consider the consequences of failure. It will help to put dollar values on both the success and failure. Too often service people become emotional over a 1 percent event and forget about the value of the other 99 percent, and probably neglect to consider the cost of achieving that final 1 percent.

Marginal analysis

Most service functions operate on a declining rate of return; the same idea as is illustrated in Pareto's principle of the critical few, the 80/20 rule, amplified in chapter 14. The greatest payoff usually comes with initial activity. Improvement per unit usually decreases with an increasing number of units. This is called "declining rate of return." In the parts business, as illustrated with the cumulative distribution, the initial improvement generally comes at relatively low cost but later improvements become increasingly more costly. Rating all parts in order according to their cost and value provides very desirable guidance to management. The ability to sort data in descending order is a standard function on computer spreadsheet and database application programs.

Sampling

Sampling is a technique of utilizing a representative portion of a total population to make judgments about the rest of the items. There are textbooks written on this subject alone. For our purposes it is sufficient to know that a quantity of 30 or more is called a large sample size. Less than 30 is called a small sample size. Small sample size requires special techniques and, of course, much higher risk, since fewer events are available on which to base judgment. Most of the techniques for forecasting and doing numeric analysis are relatively easy with large quantities. Special challenges arise with the small numbers that are

Decision to be made	Possible courses of action	Possible courses of action	Dollar Payoff	Probability of event occurring	Expected Value
		Win	$275,000	20%	$55,000
	Bid $575				
		Lose	0	80%	0
		Win	$200,000	50%	$100,000
Contracts for 1,000 kits	Bid $500				
		Lose	0	50%	0
		Win	$125,000	80%	$100,000
	Bid $ 425				
		Lose	0	20%	0

FIGURE 8-7
Decision trees help humans understand the financial results of each choice

typical of most maintenance service operations. In most cases the service questions is, "What can we do with what we have?" The time and money cost of getting additional data can be investigated. If the potential payoff is greater than the cost, then that may be desirable. Usually, however, service management must work with what is available and recognize the associated risks.

It should be noted that statistical analysis can be used throughout a service parts system, not just for forecasting parts demand. Other examples of useful statistical analysis include:

1. Rate of return of failed parts
2. Time delay between failures of parts and receipt of the failed part at the central repair point
3. Part delivery deviations (delivery date versus part order date) from manufacturing
4. Material in transit (outbound, line items, dollar value, and age of order).

Statistical tools should be applied to as many processes as possible so that statistical control charts are in place for each process. When a process goes out of control (deviates from an established mean plus/minus one or two standard deviations), attention can be focused on the problem. Good management includes knowing what is under control as well as what problems are currently being addressed.

9 CONTROL TECHNIQUES

Average inventory

The average on-hand inventory is calculated: Order quantity/2 + Safety stock. Figure 9-1 illustrates what happens under uniform use.

In the Figure 9-1 example, the service department forecast a need for 40 timing modules during the year. Demand is essentially uniform and averages ten per quarter (40 / 10). If the part is ordered every three months as shown in the left diagram, Option A, then the quantities ordered should be 10 parts at a time. Assuming a safety stock of 0, the inventory will average 10 / 2 = 5, as can be seen from the figure. If the same part is ordered only every six months, as shown in the figure Option B, then the average inventory will be 20 / 2 = 10, or twice as much. The inventory assets carried at any time, or on the average, are of concern to the financial community who want to

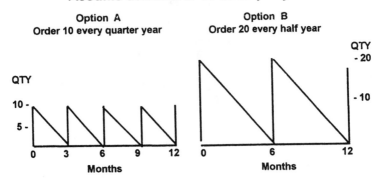

FIGURE 9-1
Average inventory is half the order quantity plus any safety stock

assure that maximum return is gained from those assets. Inventory assets are carried on a corporate Balance Sheet. Direct expenses for warehousing, labor, transport, and other logistics costs are carried on the Profit and Loss (P & L)statement. These financial measures and systems both measure and drive many service parts activities.

Carrying cost

The quantity of parts kept on hand bears expenses that are termed "carrying cost" or "holding cost." Figure 9-2 shows typical components of that cost.

Space considers the square feet (or cubic feet) of space occupied by the parts and support equipment. This can range anywhere from about $2 a square foot for very inexpensive warehouse space to $70–$80 a square foot in downtown New York City. Five dollars per square foot would be a good figure to use if no other figures were known. (As an aside, since space is rented by the floor square foot, it makes economic sense to build up and use as much of the cubic footage as can be safety and effectively occupied.) Furnishings, including shelves, files, drawer units, wall hangings, record systems, and desks, are necessary. The storeroom should be secured. This may be a wire

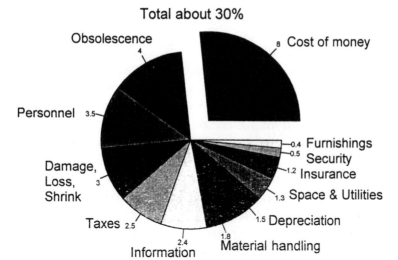

FIGURE 9-2
Components of carrying costs add to at least 30% per year

cage or a locked room with a half-door or window through which all business is transacted. The environment in which parts are stored should be clean, dry, and free of contamination. A stockkeeper should be in charge of this domain. The trade-off between paying for a stockkeeper who will take care of the parts and not having a stockkeeper means that parts may not be available when needed, with undesirable consequences. Labor is expensive but is much less expensive than no control! Collecting and maintaining accurate parts data take time. If a full-time stockkeeper is employed, this person should be in charge of that function and there is little additional cost for each incremental item, up to the point where the stockkeeper is overwhelmed and additional labor must be added. The same is generally true with the information-keeping records on computers and the effort and memory involved. Increases are usually in step functions rather than in smooth increments. Starting and maintaining data and preparing reports involves both fixed and variable costs. In large organizations with many stock locations and catalogs, adding any line item to inventory can cost over $2,000. This means that if the same part is stocked under five different part numbers, it will cost over $8,000 more than it should for a single stock location. One large corporation found the same part under 23 different identifiers!

Insurance will be required by any prudent financial controller or lending institution to make certain that the inventory of parts can be replaced in case of disaster. Insurance on parts generally will not cover obsolescence or damage attributable to neglect or willful mishandling. If a water sprinkler were to break, any damage to parts from water spray would generally be covered. Fire and smoke, explosions of the building's heating system, earthquakes, and floods should be covered, as should burglary where forced entry can be proven. Inventory shrinkage that could be due to internal use or lack of proper security generally will not be covered. Insurance does cost money. It is acquired as compensation in case of unforeseen disasters that could wipe out a company's service business, but prudent management will assure that the risks are minimized in practical ways.

Obsolescence is decreased value due to aging such as shelf life or technical changes that render parts no longer usable. Damage occurs as a result of mishandling, banging around in car trunks, and even use of parts as diagnostic tools.

The major cost, money to buy the original assets, is either the borrowing cost from a lender or the alternate value that can be gained by investing that same money in other uses. The borrowing costs can generally be figured at about 1 percent over the prime rate. That percentage usually sets the lower bound on the cost of money. Profit-oriented institutions should attempt to make as much profit on the money invested in parts inventory as they do on any other investment. Thus if a company plans new projects with a minimum return on investment of 25 percent, then the same objective should be set for parts. Adding all these costs and dividing by the parts value generally results in carrying costs of 30–40 percent. If a round number is needed without accurate data, 30 percent is a good estimate. Note that major opportunity exists for reducing carrying costs by outsourcing parts support. If you don't have to invest cash into parts then the asset never shows on the balance sheet. (That idea of managing resources instead of owning them is covered in chapter 17 on Valuing Service Parts and chapter 22 on Multivendor Opportunities.)

Order costs

Surprising amounts of human energy and information flow are required each time an order is placed. Think through the following scenario: A technician needs a part. Inventory is checked and that part is not in stock. The technician tells this to the parts clerk. Information has to be looked up in an electronic, or paper, catalog to identify the correct part number by description and manufacturer or vendor. The parts clerk fills out a purchase request. Then the purchasing function, which may be the same person or a separate organization, takes over. Several phone calls may have to be made to determine where the part can be best obtained. A purchase order must be prepared, either by hand printing, typing, or computer, and mailed or faxed or e-mailed to the selected supplier. The commitment must be logged for financial and physical control. A confirming copy of the purchase order is probably required from the vendor to assure that it has been received and agreed to.

When the goods or services are received, they must be received into the information system by warehouse personnel. If quality control (QC) inspections are necessary, the parts must be tagged and placed in a controlled area until QC has cleared them. Then the actual parts will be placed on the warehouse shelves or transported to the requestor. These functions are illustrated in Figure 9-3.

Cost of ordering from external sources has been found to range from $18 to over $475. The high end is due primarily to extensive quality assurance requirements. There might be service organizations whose costs are under $150 a line item, but that figure is reasonable to use if no better calculation exists. The related, but slightly less complicated and less expensive functions of orders filled from internal stocks, are shown in Figure 9-4

Order costs should be less for internal orders where a part is on the authorized stock list (ASL). Costs are probably still about $50, as shown in Figure 9-4. Wireless communications are estimated to reduce the $50 to about $30 due primarily to less time required to find a phone, knowledge of up-to-the-minute part availability, and direct contact with the delivery person.

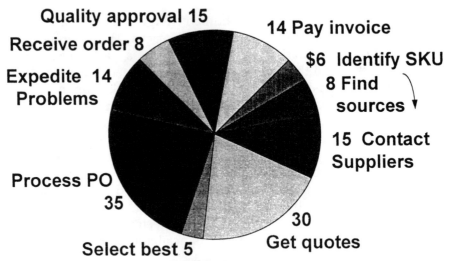

Total about $150

Quality approval 15

Receive order 8

14 Pay invoice

$6 Identify SKU

Expedite 14 Problems

8 Find sources

15 Contact Suppliers

Process PO 35

30 Get quotes

Select best 5

FIGURE 9-3
External order costs often average $150

Before Wireless $50   Vs   With Wireless $30

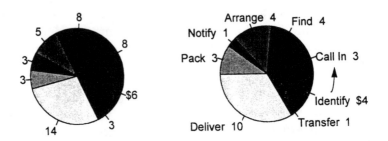

8
5
8
3
3
$6
14
3

Arrange 4   Find 4
Notify 1
Pack 3
Call In 3
Identify $4
Deliver 10
Transfer 1

Conceptual; validate with each organization's own data

FIGURE 9-4
Internal order costs are often $50, but less using wireless communications

How can order costs be reduced? The best answer is through economies of scale. Consolidate orders to a supplier, so that as many similar items as possible appear on a single purchase order. If QC inspections are a major factor, then order larger quantities of those items so that they may all be inspected at once. Each inspection probably involves obtaining the applicable drawings and inspection criteria, special tools and gages, and qualified personnel. Use of blanket purchase orders is another tactic. Commit to buy all your consumable supplies for the year from a specific vendor. You should get a 10–20 percent discount, be able to telephone orders and thus expedite delivery, and receive a confirming delivery list with each individual order and a monthly invoice.

Another approach, which is especially useful on common hardware, is to select the best supplier, probably on the basis of competitive bids, to keep your hardware bins stocked. This can operate in much the same way as a bread salesperson does, who comes by a grocery store once a week to check inventory and resupply stock as necessary. The salesperson will provide a list of what has been resupplied with a monthly invoice.

When doing calculations for economic order quantity and other factors that include order cost, the cost of the most common means of purchasing should be used. For example, if a part is normally ordered as one line item on a long purchase order, and is a standard item with no extra specifications or special receiving inspections, then the cost may be less than $25. If the part is uniquely sophisticated, requires extensive drawings and specifications, and must receive special quality controls, then the cost may even exceed $475. As a starting point for an average cost estimate, add the costs of all the purchasing functions involved with service parts: the technical person who identifies part numbers, the technician who requests them, warehouse receiving, quality assurance, expediting, accounts payable, space, computer power, telephone charges, and all their overhead. Divide that total cost attributed to the acquisition of service parts by the number of line items obtained during the same period. The result will be an average order cost, which then can be tuned for the specific requirements of the groups of parts. Certainly some purchase orders contain many items and, therefore, the cost per item is lower than if only one item were ordered at a time, but the approximation is probably better than what existed previously. It is generally possible to classify parts ordering costs as low, average, or high for use where detailed costs cannot be easily obtained.

Analysis and quantification of carrying and order costs is vital for scientific parts management. A resource to gain these details is your local college. MBA and advanced undergraduate students are often available for practical exercises such as this. Contact the department head of Logistics, Business, or Finance, and outline your needs. This analysis can provide practical benefits for both your organization and the college students.

Since time pressures cause increased expenses, you should compare the costs of planned ASL items that are ordered and transported in routine, low cost fashion, versus the acquisition and transport costs of emergency orders. There is no question but that emergency orders cost many times more than the same part ordered with routine methods.

Economic order quantity (EOQ)

Since the two main costs groups are carrying costs and order costs, we must try to find the least-cost combination that will meet our other goals. Figure 9-5 shows the order costs starting at 0, if no quantities are ordered (disregarding the organization that may be in place to procure parts regardless of whether or not any are ordered) and stepping upward in direct relationship to the number of orders placed during a year. One year is a convenient term to use for most of these calculations, although any period can be used, as long as it is the same for all elements.

Carrying costs will decrease as more orders are made. More orders of fewer parts in each order will lead to smaller quantities in stock bearing the holding costs. More orders will generally cause the order costs to increase—while they may be lower per unit order, the large number of orders will drive the order cost total higher. The total cost curve is the sum (at any order quantity) of the order cost plus the carrying cost:

Total cost = Order cost + Carrying cost

It can be seen that the total cost curve starts high and decreases to a minimum point, where it starts up again. The challenge is to determine where the minimum point occurs. It should also be noted that while there is a mathematically precise minimum cost point, in practical application (due to imprecise information and the relatively small curve slope

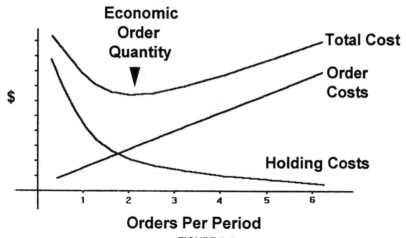

Orders Per Period
FIGURE 9-5
EOQ finds the minimum total cost of carry costs + order costs

immediately on each side of the minimum point) a range around the minimum point that considers practical order quantities can be judged by a human. For example, if the calculation showed 13.5 as the quantity, an analyst would know that you can only order parts to the nearest whole number and that they are packaged in boxes of one dozen, so 12 is the adjusted EOQ that should be used.

In the case of parts that have the potential unit of measure problem, a policy of ordering one order per year per part number may be the best practice. Items such as wire, liquid adhesives and cleaners, adhesive tape, and chemicals may need special packaging and labeling so that once-a-year handling may be much less disruptive to a supply point than the ordering practice suggested by the EOQ formula. Too frequent orders can also cause a problem if testers must be programmed or special checks set up especially for those parts. A rule of thumb is, if the EOQ is less than week's demand, then order one week's supply.

EOQ formula

Fortunately the calculation can be performed with a relatively simple formula that is much easier than the graphical plotting. The minimum cost formula is

$$\sqrt{\frac{2 * \text{Order Cost} * \text{Annual Demand}}{\text{Holding Cost \%} * \text{Unit Cost}}}$$

(If you enjoy mathematical derivations, you can show that this equation results from determining the point at which the slope of the total cost curve becomes zero.)

Suppose we forecast a need for 500 motors during the coming year. They cost us $40 a piece, the carrying cost is 30 percent, and our purchase orders will cost $25 each. What is the best quantity to order at a time?

$$\text{EOQ} = \sqrt{\frac{2 * 500 * \$25}{\$40 * .30}} = \sqrt{\frac{25,000}{12}} = \sqrt{2083} = 46$$

Ask if there are changes coming that might render the part obsolete. Engineering may be planning form, fit, or function changes. Changes may be caused by sales applications in the way the product is used, special events, new technicians, production changes, and so on. Modern computer programs can calculate the EOQ as an integral part of parts management programs. Dynamic EOQ and ROP calculations are one indicator of an acceptable computer program. Some programs still require a human to independently enter the minimum quantity to trigger reorder, and the reorder quantity itself. These calculations should be done automatically every time a part has activity.

Reorder point

Now that we have determined the quantity of parts to order, we need to decide when those parts should be ordered. This is shown in Figure 9-6

The specific trigger quantity is called the reorder point (ROP). To calculate the reorder point, we must forecast both the quantities to be used during future time periods and the lead time. The first thing to look at is the lead time, which is composed of all the time that transpires between when the need for a part

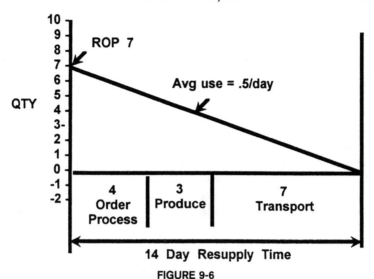

FIGURE 9-6
Reorder point calculates parts quantity that will be used during resupply time

is identified and when it arrives ready for use. These intervening elements may include time to notify purchasing, get quotes, place the purchase order, transmit the purchase order to the vendor; and for the vendor to procure the item, pick and pack it, transport it to the user's location, do receiving inspection, and deliver it to the stockroom or directly to the user. The in-house time from purchase request to orders and receiving parts probably can be accurately measured. It should be less than three days for normal items, but can take weeks in bureaucratic organizations where many approvals and slow paper shuffling take place. Transmitting a purchase order electronically or verbally can be done in a few minutes, while paper and mail require at least several days and much more human effort. Once a vendor knows the purchase order is firm, a reliable estimate of delivery or production time can usually be quoted. An item off the shelf can usually be shipped out the same day the order is received. As an illustration of responsive shipping, you can call a mail-order computer hardware or software retailer after dinner and receive the item the next morning by overnight courier. At the other extreme, quantities of nonstandard PWBs may require 9 months to produce.

The major variable is transportation. Small items may be transported by express mail or one of the several overnight package services. Larger items shipped routinely by truck usually arrive within a week. If parts are required from overseas, however, the transportation and the customs processing time may be several weeks. Air shipment costs, especially of heavy machine parts, can be very high. Lead time should be calculated using the most probable statistical (mode) time. Keep records on how many days there are between purchase request and parts receipt, by vendor. A computerized purchase order system should automatically gather that information by vendor and by part noun and commodity group with class. Remember that records are generally historical data, and purchasing humans must translate that data into a forecast for an order to be placed to support the future. Lead times will normally be consistent by commodity group; thus, as a group, roller bearings will come in short supply, or motors, or electronic components. Let us assume the switches we need have a 14-day lead time (watch out for glibly stated "two weeks" or "30 days" and be sure to add your internal time to what the vendor reports). During the 14 days, we forecast a typical use of 7 switches. That is an average of .5 per day. We realize that it is not possible to use part of a switch. What really happens is that on the first day of our month, three switches are used. On the second day none are requested; on the third day, one; on the fourth, none; and so on. To have parts continuously available, an order should be placed when the number of switches in the bin reaches 7.

If everything holds, 14 days after the order is placed, the technician who receives the last part from the stockroom will turn around and bump into the UPS delivery person with the shipment of replacement parts. For many reasons, that rarely happens in the real world! There is risk that demand may increase and transportation may not deliver as planned. If you can judge these risks based on specific events, then do so and add in those insurance quantities rather than using statistics. (Additional safety stocks are covered in Chapter 13.)

There are organizations that use the concept of a minimum stock level for highly-essential parts. This policy states that a minimum quantity will be held as a safety stock regardless of past demand. If demand increases over a significant period of time, the statistical safety stock will override the minimum stock quantity. The quantity in any minimum stock level will depend on the lead time needed to obtain a replacement part if the stocked part is used. For control, only essentiality 1, 2, or 3 items should be stocked under such a policy.

Remember that those safety stock parts are going to carry the same holding cost penalties as any other part would. If they are not used, then they consume money that could be used better elsewhere. The level of safety stock is a management judgment that should be tempered by the quantitative facts of lead time, forecast, essentiality, and penalty cost if parts are not available. Let us examine some scenarios on the reorder point. Suppose, first of all, that the demand varies. Instead of averaging .5 switches per day, there is an increase in demand to 1.0 switches per day. That means that in the 14-day lead time the total quantity demanded will be 14 instead of 7. The parts analyst should imagine what the worst-case scenario might be and then calculate the numbers to meet that eventuality. In this case, the analyst's thinking was that 14 during the period was the worst-demand case and, in fact, would cover the two standard deviations discussed earlier.

Now look at "What if?" the lead time changes. Suppose a truck strike is looming and could delay shipments by two weeks. Lead time would then be 28 days instead of 14. If demand were to continue at .5 units per day, then the 28 days would require 14 units. So, the reorder point would be set at 14. (You will see in Chapter 13 that the large deviation of either increased demand or slow delivery will adequately cover either or both eventualities.) Do not over-safety stock.

Note that the deviations toward reduced demand and shorter lead time are of little importance to us. We are concerned with not stocking out of parts and are willing to accept some overage on essential items. If those switches cost $9 each, the 7 safety stock switches represent $63 tied up in inventory, with a carrying cost of about $19 per year. Is that a reasonable price to pay for the safety stock insurance against stock-out? That is cheap compared to the costs of $1,000 electronic modules. As described in the trade-off equation, the algorithms are available to do the calculation, but management must provide the judgmental input on risk, value, and cost.

When a part quantity is reduced to the reorder point or below, the system should trigger an automatic order if the parameters are within normal bounds. If parameters deviate, the computer should generate a notice to review the situation and allow a human to decide whether an order is necessary, and if it is, whether the quantity should be the EOQ or some other number. Note that the order notice algorithm must consider quantity on hand plus quantity on order plus quantity in repair. This helps to avoid the problem of the organization that foolishly orders more particular parts every day without realizing that a stream of excess parts will overflow the bins. Highly embarrassing! Also, the ability to set ROP = -1 enables some nonstock parts never to show on the reorder notice.

Variable quantity or time models

Not every situation is conducive to using a reorder point with fixed quantities at variable times. Reorder points based on time may be used instead of those based on quantity. Weekly routine shipments are a means of reducing transportation costs and providing consistency of delivery. If a distributor ships parts every Wednesday, then all parts obtained from that source should be reviewed close to the cutoff time, probably by 3:00 p.m. of the preceding day, so that the most up-to-date needs can be communicated to the supplier. If there is confidence that the parts will be available and will be shipped on Wednesday afternoon, then safety stocks may be kept low. Emergency support is usually available for extreme cases sooner than the next delivery. Note that the lead time should consider the time from order placement until the delivery arrives. Thus, for a part ordered soon after the cutoff, lead time could be 10 days (seven days to shipment plus transport time). The quantity ordered will be the difference between the quantity on hand and the maximum quantity that includes safety stocks. The concept of maximum/minimum stock works well for timed orders, but is not as generally effective as are ROP and EOQ. The types of order models are shown in Table 9-1.

Speculative stocks

Little is to be gained, and potentially a lot lost, by buying and holding service parts on the speculation that their value

TABLE 9-1
Orders can be based on quantity, date, or how many parts

Type of Element	Quantity	Interval
Order Point (P)	Fixed	Variable
Order Quantity (Q)	Fixed	Variable
Order Interval (R)	Variable	Fixed

will increase. Several parts organizations are alleged to have purchased large quantities of electronic components containing gold and silver in the belief that the increasing value of the precious metals would increase the parts' value. In fact, carrying costs of the excess parts (more than 30 percent per year) was greater than any increase in value. Then, when the design changed and the parts became obsolete, the effort involved to redeem the precious metals was barely worth the recovered value. High-volume resource recovery facilities regain value from the integrated circuits and gold and silver components of scrap circuit boards, but the economies of scale must be great. Service parts managers should stick to managing parts and not attempt to gain financial rewards by speculative purchasing.

Authorized stock list (ASL)

Authorized stock lists are a control method that provides every inventory location a precise catalog of which parts they should keep and in what quantity. Scientifically the ASL is determined by modeling the products to be supported for the logistics performance envelope parameters of response time, support level, and financial investment. Those factors are detailed in chapter 26. Since the first pass fill rate is directly related to the percent of demand accommodation times demand satisfaction (see chapter 4), it can be seen that identification of the vital parts and then stocking them in adequate quantity is a combination of science and art. Humans need to identify how the future is likely to be similar to the past, what part number changes are anticipated, how part usage may change, and what technicians will be supporting the equipment. A scientifically determined ASL can significantly reduce financial investment while support level improves. That is a win-win situation in everyone's book.

Once the ASL is detailed for each planned inventory location, the list should be given to the responsible person and his manager. Every stock location should be under the authority and accountability of one responsible person. You will pay for that stock control whether you have it or not, as discussed in chapter 15. The technician may have reasons to request additional parts. If he often crosses into another tech's territory to support a unique product, then critical parts may added if they can not effectively be stocked at the unique site. After the emotions of wanting to control all their own parts settle, technicians are usually pleased to have a scientific basis on which to manage their inventories. The ASL facilitates control since an authorized part will be automatically resupplied, without human intervention. In many situations the reorder point is zero, so that when the tech uses a part and closes the call, that part is automatically resupplied to the authorized location. If the part is used more frequently, the tech may be authorized two or more to assure that he always has one on hand. As described earlier in this chapter, a reorder quantity of several parts may be shipped at one time to minimize total costs. Note that the central stock will have an ASL that must support all the field ASLs, either by parts on hand or by arrangements for rapid acquisition and shipment direct from suppliers.

10 _NEW PRODUCT PART PROVISIONING_

$\mathbb{T}$ he need for initial provisioning of parts for new products is driven by requirements to have replacements available in case of damage or early failure. The natural questions that arise are:

1. Which parts should be stocked?
2. Where should these parts be stocked?
3. How many should be stocked?

These questions are particularly difficult to answer during initial product provisioning since there is no usage history and no field service experience of any type with the product. Nonetheless, these questions need to be answered one at a time and in the order that they have just been asked. The process is diagramed in Figure 10-1.

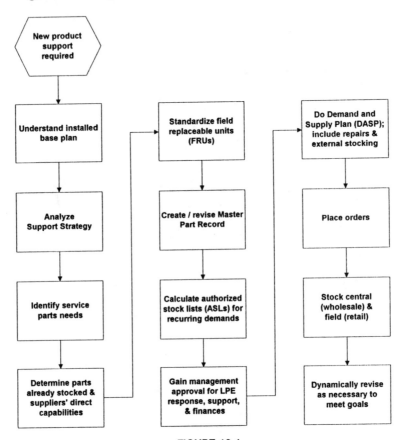

FIGURE 10-1
New parts should be selected based on logic

Service Parts Selection

A very human response to this question is "Well, let's stock everything!" This approach would even be practical if there were only one stocking location for which to plan. But let's look at the response more closely. For starters, what does "everything" mean? To some people this might mean the manufacturing Bill of Material (BOM) that lists every component in the product as well as all the assemblies and modules. If there has been adequate support planning, however, this question has already been answered. It is the Field Replaceable Unit (FRU) List.

FRU Approach

FRU is common enough in the field service industry. Many companies use the term. In the military the similar term is *line replaceable unit* (LRU). In practice it loosely means a part that the field service organization uses at customer locations to service equipment. The problem is that this leaves room for a lot of omissions, so a more structured definition is necessary considering several elements:

1. All parts, assemblies or complete products that are designated for replacement in the field.
2. A FRU list should be developed for each product considering physical construction, required repair time, skill levels of field personnel, field conditions, economics, available field diagnostics, transportation, customer environment, time required to get parts, and so forth.
3. The FRU list covers all potential field failures.
4. There are no overlapping part numbers (except for routinely replaced component parts—such as batteries, and PROMs, that may be replaced without replacing the board that they are installed on).
5. The product FRU list for field technicians will be at a higher level of components than the list for repair depots.

The advantages of developing this list during initial provisioning of field parts are many:

- It reduces number of SKUs that must be planned and managed. In actual experience, the number of parts that must be planned and managed in field distribution is usually cut by at least a third.
- This FRU approach supports 100 percent part availability. At least it guarantees that there will be a part identified that will fix any problem expected to occur in the field.

• The approach fosters fix consistency. All personnel will use the same parts list and there will be only one part (or combination of parts) to fix any problem. This means that all field personnel will be using common solutions to problems. This consistency is obviously controllable (with the list) and is the cornerstone of service quality assessment and improvement.

• Significant value-added is realized from this approach in that the common FRU list reduces time and costs associated with hiring, training, documentation, technical support, and diagnostics development.

This is not to say that other parts cannot be used, but FRU discipline means that the use of a non-FRU item in the field is a deviation from company policy and should require the same management approvals that any other exception to policy would. A distinction should be made between the FRU list and an authorized stock list (ASL). (The latter is the list of parts that are authorized to be stocked at a particular field inventory location and is discussed in chapters 9 and 30.) It is sufficient at this point to note that by definition, the ASL is a collection of FRUs for products that are supported from that stocking location, but not all of the FRUs for any one product. The field technician and local ASLs contain high use, generally low cost parts. The lower demand FRUs will be stocked, but only at the central logistics level. Low use, expensive but essential parts that must be delivered within six hours will often be stocked at a courier's strategic city location.

If FRU lists are not developed for new products, logistics organizations are forced to potentially stock the entire BOM. They are strained to stock and plan the quantity of part numbers that are involved in this ill-defined support strategy. Further, Logistics and Finance are then continuously at odds regarding the investment required. Similar problems exist in other support functions that are charged with technical support, training and developing field level diagnostics.

The FRU lists should not be unchangeable. There will be some nuances that are not immediately evident. For example, if a item which is part of the factory Bill of Materials (BOM) is selected as a FRU, theoretically all items beneath it on the BOM are precluded from being FRUs. But if that item is a circuit board and one of the components on the board is a fuse that is routinely replaced in the field, is the fuse a FRU? It could be. *Or* it could be part of a standard service kit which is a FRU in its own right and has a part number that is not on the original BOM.

Kits

Kitting parts is a common shorthand for planners. Indeed, consolidating all the parts needed for standard specific types of work makes good sense. These prepackaged materials should be prepared for installation, preventive maintenance, modifications, and standard multipart repairs. Everything necessary to do the job should be in the kit, including a list of kit contents, installation instructions, clean-up materials, any reporting forms, and even special tools. Standard service kits may also be developed for a product. These are collections of small incidental parts that are needed to service the product. Such a kit might include nuts, bolts, screws, grommets, seals, gaskets, and so forth. When more of this material is needed, the entire service kit, which should have a unique part number, is ordered. The major objectives of kits is to help parts personnel and users make effective use of their time, minimize customer disruption, and reduce logistics transportation and packaging costs. Kits should be avoided for any reasons other than those discussed above.

Computing requirements

Data requirements

MARKETING FORECAST. This data should come from the Product or Marketing group and indicate the initial product distribution for the first year. It should include sales plans in terms of how many, where, when and in what configuration at the product level. Many people take this information with a grain of salt since it is usually optimistic and the bottom line is that sales persons will sell whenever and wherever they can. It is really more valuable than that since it is the sales plan of what they will try to do. In any case it is much, much better than nothing. To gain best accuracy, tune the forecast at least monthly and place firm orders as late as possible.

FRU LIST. This is the list of Field Replaceable Units for the product as discussed above. It is the list of candidate parts to be spared. The data table should indicate how many of each FRU are contained in the product and the Mean Time Between Replacement (MTBR) for each FRU. Note that the MTBR may include more parts use than just failures. Also on the FRU list is the field level diagnostic equipment needed to support the product under field conditions and preventive maintenance kit requirements, if any. If FRUs are needed for field level diagnostic routines, this should also be indicated. This information should be provided to logistics by the team that develops the service support plan.

LOGISTICS DATA. The following information is also useful depending on the final provisioning heuristic that is developed to compute the initial buy quantities.

- Order versus Use Ratios.
- Logistics Pipeline Parameters.
- FRU repair capability.

It may or may not be possible to support FRUs with repair during the period that is covered by the initial buy. This should be known since a repair program during this period will reduce the initial buy requirements. Shop level tools and test equipment should be defined to the repair facility by the team that develops the service support plan. One of the major challenges is determining what failure/replacement rate to expect.

Forecasted use computations

Forecasting demand during initial fielding of a product requires a *Poisson* distribution rather than a *Normal* distribution because of the low product installed density. Mathematically the question is asked this way: "How many parts should be on hand so that we are confident to a specified degree that no more will be needed during the planning period?"

TABLE 10-1
Major sources of information for improved analysis.
1. Benchmark/Bestmark™
2. Friendly service organization
3. Your own data "similar to . . ."
5. Fourth party parts supplier
6. OEM
7. Industry handbook
8. Component part manufacturer or supplier

Definitions:

P The confidence level. How confident do we want to be? (Expressed as a percentage).

FRATE The failures per 1,000,000 hrs of operation. This is the mean time between failure (MTBF) at the part level. The hour rate is converted to the probability of failure per hour (1 / MTBF) and called λ (lambda) in the calculations.

DAYS The number of days of service. How long do we want to provision for? This will be converted to hours of service and called T (for **time**) in the computation.

K The number of parts supported. This is equal to or greater than the number of products. If you have two of the same part per product, then you have twice the number of items supported.

The following are the equations to compute the probability of failure based on the factors above. For example, the probability of zero failures is:

$$P_0 = e^{-K\lambda T}$$

and the probability of exactly N failures is:

$$P_N = (K\lambda T)^2 e^{-K\lambda} / N!$$

The easiest way to approach the computational problem is to decide on the confidence level you wish to have of forecasting enough parts. Then starting with 0 parts, keep adding units until the desired confidence level is achieved. A short computer program to do this would look like this:

```
STORE 0 TO Q,PROB,N
NFAC = 1
KLT = K * FRATE/1000000 * DAYS*24
MCONF=MCONF/100
FIRST = .T.
DO WHILE PROB >CONF
  IF FIRST
    PROB = 1 / EXP(KLT)
    FIRST = .F.
  ELSE
    N = N + 1
    QQ = KLT ** N
    NFAC = NFAC * N
    Q = QQ / (NFAC * EXP(KLT))
    PROB = PROB + Q
  ENDIF
ENDDO
```

When the "DO LOOP" stops, N will equal the number of parts that will provide the desired confidence level.

It should be noted that the above computation must be done for each stocking location and each part that would potentially support the product. Given computer power, time and effort are not an issue. Due to deviations from the sales plan, a problem exists with computing requirements for stocking locations that may or may not support the item. Further, assuming a very low density at each of the field locations, there will be so much forecasting error "rolled-up" to the aggregate level that generation of excess quantities becomes a certainty.

Essentiality

Another consideration in planning stocks is the essentiality of the part to the product. This concept greatly aids determination of what parts should be stocked. A part that has safety implications on major facilities or equipment should be rated essentiality class 1. Parts that are critical to the operation of major facilities and equipment should be class 2. Without them, that equipment would be down and revenue loss would be great. Class 3 parts contribute to degraded operation, as in cams or snubbers that wear and begin to cause jams and lower production rates. Class 4 parts are cosmetic, such as knobs and labels. To relate the parts need to the maintenance priority, a class 1 or 2 part need will generally be a special "drop everything and run" emergency service call. Class 3 parts will be used on work scheduled in the normal work scheme. Class 4 parts can be installed the next time a person is at the equipment and can do the job conveniently. These four classes are summarized in Table 10-2.

TABLE 10-2
Part criticality helps prioritize resources

CRITICALITY	CONDITION OF EQUIPMENT OR PROCESS
1	Creates a hazard to humans in and around the equipment or process.
2	Equipment or process has stopped. All revenue is lost until part is replaced.
3	Equipment or process is operating at a reduced capacity.
4	All others.

Where to stock

The initial field distribution plan of parts generated by Logistics is obviously central to success of new product support. The mathematics discussed below will predict the demand, but not the distribution. Two approaches are offered for consideration:

Traditional approach

This approach uses the marketing plan to develop a stocking plan of product support "kits" to be placed in the field prior to product introduction. Typically, kits for a national product launch are initially stocked in about 20 field locations to cover major concentrations of equipment. This approach has the advantage of providing a relatively high "comfort level" for customers and field personnel. It should be noted that it is contrary to the policy of optimizing field inventories at the stocking location rather than the location or product level. This means that after the initial provisioning period is past and level setting based on experienced demand takes over, some or all of the parts stocked in the field as part of the initial product fielding will have to be pulled back as excess. This approach used to be the best way to go in the face of uncertainty. Today, however, developments in the transportation and remote storage industries have given us additional options.

Minimum investment approach

This approach makes no assumptions about where in the field that demand will materialize. It forecasts the entire service part requirement as if it were being experienced in one stocking location: central logistics. As products are installed in the field the available stock is distributed to the appropriate field stocking locations. When demand in these locations stabilizes, levels are set and permanent stock provided from "follow on" buys. This approach has the advantage of minimizing investment at a time when demand for specific parts under field conditions is not known, the product design may not be stable, and the density of supported product is very low.

Pipeline Requirements

The final consideration for determining how many parts to provision for a new product are the logistics pipelines. For each part these pipelines are:

1. Procurement. This may be significantly different for new products even it they use parts that have been used in previous products. This is due to the fact that manufacturing and vendors must adjust to the changes in demand patterns generated by the new product. Often service may have to share parts with manufacturing, which creates a conflict in priorities.

2. Field Replenishment. Disruptions in supply of parts from vendors and manufacturing will increase the variability of this pipeline if not its length. Priority transportation should be used even for routine replenishment, to overcome pipeline variability problems.

3. Defective Return. The management and control of this pipeline is critical to the initial support of new products. Procedures should be established to track and control parts in this pipeline. Field technicians should return excess and defective parts for new products on a daily basis.

4. Repair Pipeline. Repair support may or may not be possible during the initial provisioning period. If this support is possible, then the initial buy quantities are computed by adjusting *down* the forecast demand by the number that will be obtainable from repair during the period and *up* by the quantity necessary to fill up the return and repair pipelines.

All of these pipelines should be monitored, managed and controlled using the procedures discussed in chapters 12, 21, and 30. When a new product is introduced, either to field customers or within a factory, the concern is for a basic supply of replacement parts. Looking at it first from a factory perspective, reliance must be placed on the manufacturer of the equipment to provide a recommended spares list. (Be cautious about simply accepting the list as published in the back of a catalog. Often such lists are prepared by a novice engineer during the rush of getting a manual ready for the marketplace, and have not had the benefit of experience.) The best information will come from the field service personnel who maintain the equipment and from other users who have gained experience. Be sure that the most essential parts that require a long lead time are stocked. If possible get a signed statement that the supplier will take back any parts that are in good condition if they have not been used after one year.

There should be a recommended stock list provided to all field locations and individuals. That list should be used as a guide, and also should be tempered by what the users perceive as necessary. In other words, the basic stock should be negotiated rather than dictated. It should be controlled by central logistics and changed rapidly if necessary. Do not let new product provisioning just happen! Establish new product parts provisioning as a legitimate, straightforward process that is planned and controlled.

11 *END-OF-LIFE PARTS*

"Engineering designs it for six months—Manufacturing builds it for nine months—Service maintains it forever." That adage may not be true in all cases, but it fits many situations. At a client location we observed an IBM PC-AT still in full service 12 years after production, being used as a printer driver on a network. When asked why the machine had not been donated to the Smithsonian, our client replied good naturedly that it would be when it broke. Our client had the right idea, of course, to use this "elderly" product to failure and then replace it. Unfortunately, other people want to retain equipment indefinitely, and expect service providers to offer full service contracts for them at "reasonable" prices.

Next to the problems associated with providing logistics to brand new products is the challenge of providing it for products that are nearing the end of their service life. Parts for elderly products always encounter great difficulties. The problems are so great that companies like Compaq, Dell, and Gateway 2000

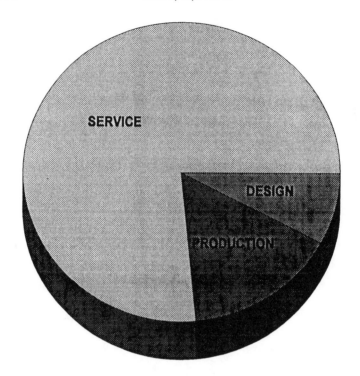

FIGURE 11-1
Service is the longest phase of a product's life cycle

with strong design, production, and sales cultures are usually glad to out-source the support of these products after they leave production. This change of phase invariably puts these companies in a quandary, since "getting out of the business" involves the transfer of tooling, technology and technical data to a third party vendor. Most companies are reluctant to transfer the knowledge and give up the responsibility, since they must retain accountability for good after-sales support.

Regardless of who provides the support, the service organization is faced with a situation where the installed base of the product will decline and the major source of parts is no longer producing them. These situations tend to offset each other, but there is another factor—increasing failure rates. The failure rates of even highly reliable electronic parts follow the traditional "Bathtub" curve.

As shown in Figure 11-2, many parts experience relatively high initial failure rates. This is why we "burn in" new and

Composite Failure Patterns

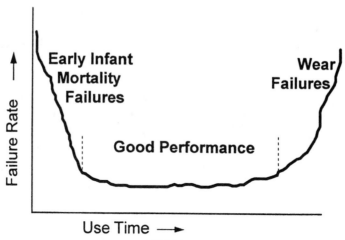

FIGURE 11-2
After "infant mortality," failures are few until wearout increases

recently repaired electronic parts. Parts that survive "infant mortality" perform to specification for a relatively long period of time, but then they start to wear and the failure rate increases. The implication for profitable service contracts is that we could watch the failure rates of the parts in a product increase over time to the point when we should either increase prices or stop offering service contracts. Where is that point?

How long should you support a product

BUSINESS REQUIREMENTS The best legitimate reason to continue to support older products is because the business is profitable. On the surface this might be the only reason, but the decision is not as easy as that. The first question to ask ourselves is—Do we know what is profitable? As the installed density of a product declines, the profitability of supporting it is slowly eroded. Often we have no way to determine when the "critical mass" is lost. This may be because the installed product database is not accurate. Other times it is because we do not have a clear picture of the real costs. Part cost may have been depreciated to zero and other costs are sunk or are included with corporate G&A expenses. In this case, what looks like a profitable business on paper, may be bankrupt in reality. Sometimes continuation is merely a matter of habit. We have been supporting the product for a long time. It is familiar to us and no one questions whether or not continuing support is still good business.

Even when we know absolutely that it is no longer directly profitable to support a product, we may elect to do so for customer satisfaction reasons. It may be that the product is bundled with other products so that the overall contract is profitable. It may simply be to retain customer "good will." These actions are not wrong. In fact they may be good business, but they set a precedent that can be difficult to overcome. These actions set customer expectations and encourage similar acts that will sooner or later become bad business. The real challenge is to know where the line is and be committed *not* to cross it.

LEGAL REQUIREMENTS Does a manufacturer have a public obligation to provide maintenance support (or at least parts) for the products that they make?—*Surprisingly, in most cases, no!* Moral obligations notwithstanding, there is no uniformly applicable law that says how long parts must be provided by the manufacturer. There is a legal precedent. The Uniform Product Liability Law states that a manufacturer must provide parts for their products for seven years after production. This law originally applied only to the automotive industry. Since it did set a precedent, it was for many years the de facto standard for all industries. The rapid advance of technology with the associated compression of product development cycles has changed this practice. Many companies in the computer industry have reduced the length of time that they will support products to three years. This trend started with "low end" products such as PCs and is rapidly expanding. There is little objection to this on the part of business customers since these products are depreciated over 18 to 36 months and turn over in the company's asset base. The small-office/home-office (SOHO) market retains products longer and is expected to complain increasingly about diminished parts support. There is a good niche business opportunity for organizations to specialize in parts for older products.

How to terminate

The hardest part of terminating support for a product is making the decision to do so. The best time to make the end-of-life decision is in the initial product plan. A product should be designed and support planned for a finite period of time, after which it is replaced by your latest, greatest new product. The biggest obstacle to termination is the lead time necessary to terminate the process in an orderly manner without creating customer dissatisfaction. Marketing and sales people should obviously be involved in announcing that support will cease. If properly done, the process should also contain built-in sale leads to assist with the sales of new products. Another consideration is to avoid leaving the company with large quantities of parts and support equipment that will have to be written off over a short period of time. Termination often takes as much as a year because existing contracts should be allowed to expire before support stops. Even after full service contracts are stopped, labor with "best effort" parts may continue.

The termination process goes public with a written notification to customers, (at the time of sale or renewal of a service contract), that the agreement can only be extended for the next year or two. The letter should make clear that support may continue beyond that time on a time-and-material (T&M) basis, but that full service contracts will be discontinued. Notification should be provided early, often at budget preparation time, to give the customer time to plan. Entering the Time & Material (T&M) phase may be difficult since the customer may apply pressure to extend service contracts. If T&M support is continued afterwards it should be done on a "best effort basis" with no guarantees of part availability.

Internal reluctance to terminate

Most managers are reluctant to make such a decision to terminate years in advance of the event. Termination creates problems in the market place. "If you are going to terminate the support on Product A in two years, what are you going to replace it with?" The company may not be ready to answer that question, particularly since customers may delay buying decisions or cancel orders for Product A and wait for Product B. This disrupts the cash flow that is probably needed to develop Product B. However, realistic customer expectations and planned replacement of equipment with a new product of your own usually lead to continued service relationships that generate profits.

In the short term, middle managers responsible for sales and revenue generation are understandably reluctant to turn away the established business represented by service contracts. Often this service business is looked at as a cash cow that is part of an established revenue base. "Why turn it off? Even if it is getting smaller, whatever we get is gravy." This statement is probably not true. At end-of-service-life trained technicians are harder to find, the products are regarded as inferior, technology has probably advanced beyond that used in producing parts years ago, providing the service is increasingly more costly, and profit margins are declining rapidly. The managers who want to retain these contracts are usually not positioned organizationally to see the big picture, or they wouldn't think of these contracts as gravy.

Implications for service parts management

Indefinite support

In view of the conditions described above, it is prudent for logisticians to plan as though support for a product would continue indefinitely. This is true even if an end to the support life of the product has been announced. How is this done? A good rule of thumb is that if the product is out of production, plan to support it for three more years. What will happen is that as the supported density of the product goes down, the quantity of parts needed to support it for "three more years" goes down faster than the stock is used. If the next generation of product is in the field and you do not have an accurate installed base plan, then plan for two more years of support.

Increasing costs

Even with such planning approach the cost will rise. This too has to be planned. The corporate budget plan process is a good vehicle to educate finance and management on the realities of supporting older products. Even if there is a stock of written off parts, the repair expense budget can be expected to rise or remain the same as repair requirements decrease.

End-of-life (EOL) parts planning

Lifetime buys

At the time that production is preparing to terminate assembling a product, the service organization is usually asked to forecast the part requirements for that product over its remaining service life. Further, Service is asked to conduct a "Life Time Buy" for those parts. This is always a dicey situation. If too many parts are bought, excess assets will be generated and logistics planning may be criticized. If not enough parts are bought, shortages will occur and the parts may need to be acquired in a costly manner. Logistics planning will also be criticized if this happens. (Chapter 12 on forecasting reminds us that, for any given part number, the probability of exactly hitting the forecast is virtually zero. Some parts will be over and some parts will be under.) Logistics planning has to therefore strike a balance so that the effect of one type of forecasting error is offset by the effect of the other. If this seems like a no-win situation, it should because it is.

The mathematics

The mathematical situation of parts planning for EOL products is similar to planning for new products. There is a relatively low density of product involved. This produces a low part demand volume. The one planning advantage is that the field failure rates at the part number level are known. These rates may be shifting as a result of the parts wearing out, but the data is usually sufficient for statistical forecasting. The major issue is *how to forecast* this demand. Averaging and smoothing techniques produce forecasts that lag demand since they tend to interpret trends as "spikes" and discount them. This may not be as detrimental for EOL products from a customer service point of view, but it does retain excess longer than necessary. Regression forecasting methods produce qualitatively more accurate results, since they do not discount trends as much.

The object of the logistics planner is to run out of parts just as the last product is taken out of service. This can't be done exactly, but it will help to switch mathematical tools for the final end play. When the installed density of the product is reduced to under 40, it may be useful to use to convert to "Poisson forecasting." Table 11-1 shows an example:

Note that this forecasts the failures for the next two years. It shouldn't be the final forecast however. We should also consider the phenomenon of the "Product Half-Life." The example above assumes that all 40 items will remain in service for all of the two-year forecasting period. We know that this will not happen. If we assume that the average installed product base for the next two years will be half of its current level, the same forecast generates a reduction to 12 items. Alternately, if we use the installed product assumption of 40 but reduce the confidence level from 95% to 50%, the forecasted failures becomes 14. *This is the preferred approach* because we really don't know how fast the product will be removed from service. The forecast should be regenerated at least every quarter. Assuming that the product reduction is uniform over a two-year period, the comparison of the installed product to the part failure forecast at the 50% confidence level is shown in Table 11-2:

Notice at the end, when there are only 5 units still in service, that 2 parts would be enough to cover expected failures for the

TABLE 11-1
Information necessary for EOL planning

For PN 1234:

Products Remaining in Service:	40
Number of PN 1234 per Product:	1
Number of PN 1234 remaining in Service:	40
Failure rate per Million Hours:	20
Desired confidence level:	95%
Forecast period:	730 days

Output:
Failures predicted for PN 1234 will not exceed 20 with 95% confidence.

TABLE 11-2
Accurate installed base information is key to valid forecasts

FY Qtr	Installed Parts	Forecasted Failures for the Next Two Years at 50% Confidence
1	40	14
2	35	12
3	30	10
4	25	9
5	20	7
6	15	5
7	10	3
8	5	2

next two years. We plan for another two years at the current level and let the reduction of the installed product drive the "end play" of our part levels.

"Product remaining-on-contract" data essential

This planning approach is the best available for end of life products in the environment we have described. But, it is entirely dependent on the availability of installed data for the product. The best source for this data is the contract data base. It may not cover products on which you receive time and materials calls, but the mathematics will compute an exaggerated failure rate and cover them that way. Moreover, when the contract base is reduced to zero, you are out of the business anyway.

Sourcing EOL parts

After the normal sources for parts have dried up; (manufacturing has stopped making them, and vendors have stopped selling them), there are still three sources for parts—cannibalization, repair and special build.

CANNIBALIZATION AND DE-MANUFACTURE The difference between cannibalization and de-manufacture is that cannibalization is the selected removal of parts from a product at the time that the parts are needed to repair other products of the same model. De-manufacture is the programmatic stripping of parts from products for stocking against future need. Determining the remaining service life for parts removed is a problem. Parts that are sourced this way often experience higher-than-usual failure rates. Electronic parts are more reliable and have a better track record when stripped from used product. Electromechanical parts wear out faster because of moving parts, but they can be inspected and rejected at the point of tear-down if the wear is excessive.

This process is valuable under two conditions. First, the parts may be so critical to operations or so expensive to purchase that it makes business sense to recover old product from the field and strip it for parts. (Costing these parts is discussed in Chapter 17.) Secondly, it is a fall-back option based on the philosophy that you should always have more than one source for a part. Thirdly, there may be environmental reasons for controlling disposal of hazardous components such as batteries. Finally, you may want to keep used parts out of the hands of competitors or repair shops that might do an inferior job which could harm your products and reputation. Even if you don't use this approach it might be useful to develop the capability in case it is needed. (Asset Recovery is the topic of chapter 23.)

One of the complications of cannibalization is that often there is a period of time in a product's life cycle when additional profits may be gained by recovering the product from the field and refurbishing it for resale. Since the product is likely to be out of production at that point, the repair center operated by logistics is often tasked to do this refurbishment. The parts needed to refurbish the product are the same parts that are needed to support the product in the field. This can lead to subordination of the primary repair mission and the unhappy situation in which the field organization is competing with the repair center for the parts that the repair center is supposed to provide *to* the field.

REPAIR The repair of old parts will be the primary source of parts during the terminal support of products. Even this function is not without challenges. The calibration and maintenance of test equipment may become difficult as this equipment also nears the end of its service life. As the installed product base declines, the number of repair technicians with the necessary technical skills will deplete through personnel turn over. Those who remain will find it increasingly difficult to keep their skills sharp because the demand volume for the parts is also low. New failure modes develop as the parts age. Vender sources for components will disappear and these components will have to be cannibalized from assemblies that are no longer repairable. Components that can not be found will have to be replaced by new ones that will have to be "reverse engineered" at far greater cost than the original components.

SPECIAL BUILD The worst case scenario for the acquisition of a service part is a "special build" of that part by an external job shop. This involves finding and updating the specification for the manufacture of the part, finding a vendor willing to make it, communicating these requirements, and quality testing the parts received. All this is done at very high cost and for a small quantity of parts. Custom building parts is obviously not a good business practice, but does become necessary at times.

Keep costs visible to management

The best way to assure the availability of resources that are needed to supply the parts *and* to assure that business decisions are being made with a full knowledge of the costs involved is to keep the costs visible to management. This often involves special reports initiated by the logistics organization and distributed to product, sales and management groups. Particular importance should be paid to product refurbishment programs which should be terminated when they become unprofitable. This point is usually reached when the existence of the refurbishment programs begins to drive up the cost of supporting the existing product.

Added EOL costs

Areas that should be tracked include those where additional costs are being incurred strictly because the parts involved are for end-of-life products. Here are some areas to look at and questions to ask:

OPERATING COSTS Are the parts being handled any differently (e.g., priority transportation because of short supply)? Are we operating a de-manufacturing program? What does it cost?

PROCUREMENT Are special vendor management procedures required? Is vendor qualification taking longer than usual?

REPAIR Is product test equipment costing more to maintain? Is shop productivity for end-of-life products below that for normal parts?

TRAINING What is our personnel training cost per unit under contract? What is the trend? What training costs are sustained only to support the EOL product?

INVENTORY HOLDING COSTS Part holding cost is discussed in chapter 9. These costs are equally valid for EOL parts and likely to be even higher than early parts. This is sometimes overlooked since the parts are probably depreciated, fully reserved or expensed. Just because parts have no book value from a financial accounting perspective does not mean that it doesn't cost anything to retain them. The original standard cost is the best benchmark against which to judge whether holding costs are increasing or not. Review the breakout of holding costs in chapter 9 and use them as guides to search for unusually high costs.

The End-of-Life phase of a product life seems long, but the end comes all too quickly. Since the products must be supported right up to the end, some excess is unavoidable. Proper planning techniques can lessen the amount of excess parts as the product concludes. How the shift in planning techniques is timed is a major factor in keeping cost under control. That shift is now happening earlier and earlier in product life cycles. Currently there are products that are planned for a one time production run of six months duration and a product life of 18 months. Under this scenario, parts management enjoys no "mid life." Logistics managers are forced to plan the phase-out of parts before they have any field failure experience with them. If this trend continues, planning skills in the logistics organization may become the most important factor for the profitability of service contracts.

12 *FORECASTING*

Landing an airplane has been described as a "Controlled Crash." By the same token forecasting service parts requirements can be described as a "Controlled Guess." When flying an airplane, the weather conditions, fuel supply, cargo, and other factors, are always changing. The only constants are the forces of weight (gravity and mass) and drag. The best you can do is to get on the ground, in more or less the right spot, without breaking the airplane. When forecasting parts, the business conditions, money supply, user demands, and other factors, are always changing. The only constant is the law of probability, and the best you can do is to have a percentage of the right parts without breaking the company.

Overview and terms

In service parts management, demands for parts fall into one of two general categories. Those that can be scheduled accurately and those that cannot. Requirements for particular parts at specific times do not require the mathematical forecasting described in this chapter. Requirements of that *just-in-time* type include the support of installations, preventive maintenance, scheduled upgrades, and training courses. The type of demand that does require mathematical forecasting is termed *random*. These demands may follow a pattern, but there is no guaranteed way to determine when the next demand will occur, or for what, or where. The parts planning process should address both types of demands. Each should be done separately and added together before they are communicated to manufacturing, vendors, suppliers, or other interested parties. It should be understood that this chapter will deal with the forecasting techniques needed to deal with random demands. Many techniques used in service are about as wild as the darts shown in Figure 12-1.

FIGURE 12-1
Many forecasts hit the bullseye as often as do darts.

From time eternal people have wanted to predict the future. Mathematical forecasting provides the illusion of doing just that. The problem is that forecasting is *just an illusion*. The assumption (done in mathematical terms) is that by proper analysis of the past we can understand why things happened. Then, by inference, we can predict what will happen it the future. While it is true that we can often explain the past with the benefit of twenty-twenty hindsight, there is no guarantee that past conditions will exactly repeat themselves. For that matter, what appear to be the same conditions may produce entirely different results. In the service parts world, here are a few things that can change without your awareness:

• Customer use patterns may shift as a result of changes in the customer's business. This induces alteration in failure and replacement rates for parts.

• Failure rate changes may change as a function of age, independent of use patterns.

• Field personnel can change. The new people have a different level of training, new attitudes and approaches to repairing equipment. This changes the demand rates for the parts.

• As well as many other things that you can't—or don't have the time to—predict.

The reality is that you can't sit around and ponder what might happen. If you did that nothing would happen. Sooner or later we must act. So in spite of the fact that forecasting is an inexact science, *it is an indispensable tool* because human effort must be organized and directed in order to be effective. Forecasting helps establish these directions in ways that are rational and can be explained. Without this structured method to predict future requirements, these projections would be based entirely on human judgment (gut feel). These guesses can be amazing and spectacular when they are correct. The reality is that, more often than not, they are wrong. (What gambler tells you about his losses?)

The following definitions are included in chapter 1, but are repeated here to provide a quick reference for this chapter:

Forecast Prediction of future demand; created by mathematical manipulation of historical data and future projections, possibly tempered by subjective judgments.

Planning The process of determining service parts requirements and distribution to meet performance goals. The outputs of planning are multileveled, many, and varied including: forecasts, budgets, investment requirements, management action plans, purchase requests, and repair orders. *(For the purpose of this chapter please note that forecasting is an important planning tool, although not the only one.)*

Run-Rate   The rate of demand for a part at a particular stocking location.

Shelf Requirements   That part of the total service parts requirements needed at specific stocking locations at any given time to meet performance parameters. These requirements are expressed in stocking location, part number, and quantity. Part ordering policy minimum/maximum is frequently used instead of a fixed quantity. Alternatively this requirement can be expressed as *days-of-supply* or *dollar investment.*

Pipeline Requirements   That dynamic part of the total service parts requirements needed to support the flow of parts between static stocking locations. These requirements are based on the length of the pipelines, the volume through the pipelines, and the amount of variance in the pipelines. It is expressed as part number and quantity per unit time for each pipeline. Alternatively this requirement can be expressed as *days-of-supply* or *investment dollars.*

Forecasting methods

There are many different forecasting methods. Whole books are written to discuss just one method. The reader should be aware at the outset that there are different types of mathematical approaches to forecasting and for most specific techniques applicable to service parts these approaches are mechanical, barometric, survey, and causal.

Mechanical

Mechanical methods are the simplest in numerical complexity and usually involve only simple algebra to compute. Some common examples of mechanical forecasting methods are:

TIME SERIES. A Time Series forecast usually involves simply the inspection of the known data and deriving a simple formula to use in future forecasts. For example, the series

1, 2, 1, 2, 1,

implies that the forecast for the next time period would be 2 since the pattern is always +1, -1. Another might be 5, 6, 8, 12, 20,

This is a bit harder on the brain, but with a little inspection one comes to the conclusion that each successive value is the preceding quantity times 2 and minus 4. Therefore the next value of the forecast is 36.

MOVING AVERAGES. This uses the sum of a certain number of preceding periods as the forecast for the next. For example, a three period moving average for an April forecast for an item is:

JAN = 38
FEB = 43
MAR = 48

Then the forecast for APR is: $\dfrac{38 + 43 + 48}{3} = 43$

WEIGHTED MOVING AVERAGE. This method is similar to moving average but each month is weighted to give it more influence over the resulting forecast. This might be used to give more credence to the most recent experience. Weighting the preceding example would result in the following:

JAN = 38 (weighted 10%)
FEB = 43 (weighted 30%)
MAR = 48 (weighted 60%)

Then the forecast for APR is: $(38*.1) + (43*.3) + (48*.6) = 45.5$

Note that the weighting must add up to 100%.

EXPONENTIAL SMOOTHING. This is an exotic sounding, but simple, estimating technique. It involves weighting like the weighted moving average. There are variations of the technique but the most straightforward is:

Last Month's Forecast (LMF) = 43
Last Month's Actual (LMA) = 51
$\alpha = .2$ (20%)
Forecast for this month is $(LMF*\alpha) + (LMA*(1-\alpha)) = 49.4$

Note that α is the weighing factor. The value of the estimate is greatly influenced by the value of α, which must range 0 - 1. The larger the alpha factor, the more weight is on the forecast in our example, and less weight goes to the actual. The equation may be written in reverse, so watch out for where you want the emphasis to go. Alpha = .5 means 50:50, which is good if you don't have better rationale.

Barometric

Barometric methods takes advantage of an aggregate index as a key factor to generate a forecast. For example, the cost of living index is used to generate many forecasts in the retail world. The index may be developed by others (as with the cost of living index) or you may have to develop it yourself. It is important that the index has strong relation to the item being forecast. Sometimes you do as best you can. Herb Feldmann tells the story of developing the first production cost estimate for the Patriot Missile System when he was in the Army during the mid 1970s. Since it was new technology at the time and no one had any production data, estimators came up with an index of "Production Cost per Missile Foot" based on the production data for the Hawk Missile and multiplied by the design length of the Patriot Missile. As it turned out, the biggest problem with the estimate was the double digit inflation rate in the actual production period. The planning guidance provided by the Office of Management and Budget (OMB) at the time the estimate was put together was 3 percent per year. Inflation sky-rocketed and greatly exceeded plans.

Survey

Survey forecast methods involve gathering data from all or a representative sample of sources. The data is then averaged, weighted, or manipulated in some other way to produce the actual forecast. This usually is a polling of some sort, whether it is a complete survey (like income tax), a voluntary survey (like an election), or a selected survey where the forecasters select the sources to be surveyed. The classic example of this is the Delphi Technique where the experts are polled to forecast what will happen in the stock market, national politics or foreign affairs. (You see this approach, live on CNN, every day.) The underlaying issue is of course, who decided who the experts are! For those who think this a bit far fetched for the service parts world, consider asking field engineers what part demands they will experience next year. We have seen that done on occasion.

Causal

This approach assumes that there is a relationship between past and future, that the appropriate cause and effect relationship can be found mathematically, and can be used to project the future. Two fundamental causal methods are applicable to forecasting—Regression analysis and Input/Output analysis.

REGRESSION ANALYSIS This method uses mathematical analysis to find an equation for a curve that "most closely matches" the historical data points in history. It then uses this equation to extrapolate the forecast into the future. There are significant benefits of this type of forecasting. The mathematics can get very complicated but it produces a straightforward and defensible forecast. (It is discussed at length below in the sections on Forecasting Systems and Linear Regression.)

INPUT/OUTPUT (I/O) ANALYSIS This type of analysis also assumes there is a cause and effect relationship at work, *but makes no attempt to determine what it is!* Instead it concentrates on an examination of the input and the output to discern the relationship between the two. Once found, the math is used to predict the future.

Forecasting systems

In the mid 1980s, two years after the merger of Sperry and Burroughs to form the Unisys Corporation, we were working with the combined logistics planning and distribution center in Elk Grove Village, IL. That group had just completed a project that had started in Sperry ten years prior to build a "world class" automated forecasting system to take advantage of the power of a large mainframe. The project was a great success, but the planning group was disappointed with the usefulness of the resulting system.

The design of the system called for automated analysis of the historical data for each part, going back three years. Approximately twenty mathematical forecasting methods (time series and causal) were tested, one at a time, for "Goodness of Fit" to the base data. The method that fit best was selected and used to generate the forecast for that part. *This process is similar in design to several forecasting systems that are being marketed today.* The conclusions of the Unisys experience was a follows:

1. The amount of time it took to run the programs was an original concern but turned out not to be an issue. Although operations went to "batch run" methods, they did have the power of a mainframe and the processing time was acceptable.

2. If a part was used in high volume with multiple demands per week, the system worked well.

a. The basic forecasting equations produced a 50 percent estimate. That means you are equally likely to need more or less the quantity forecast. For this reason the system was modified to "over" forecast initially, and then generate a "rolling net" quantity moving forward in time. Today this approach is part of what is referred to as DRP.

b. If the system made a mistake on a volume part any excess was used up quickly.

c. Linear regression was usually the selected method, but if not, it was usually the second or third selection. Frequently, when linear regression was not selected it was because the part followed a seasonal demand pattern.

3. If the part was not a volume part, no mathematical equation would fit the base date closely enough to produce a forecast with an acceptable degree of accuracy. Another way to look at this is that all mathematical forecasting methods produce equally bad results when the number of events is small.

As a result of this project, Unisys took apart the system that they had built and replaced it with one that was much more

more straightforward, though not technically correct from a mathematical point of view. The system was modified to:

1. Stop the Goodness-of-Fit testing (with the exception of seasonality).
2. Use linear regression for volume parts and adjust forecasts for seasonality if necessary.
3. Use directly transposed history as the forecast for very low demand items, with human adjustment for known change factors.

There are other problems with this approach. Unisys was forecasting total service parts requirements for demand at the central logistics facility and they had a reasonable number of parts that fell into that high volume category. Recently, we have worked with companies that were attempting to implement "auto-method-selection" systems at the field level, where the volumes at that level are typically much lower than the volume at central logistics. The accuracy of forecasting at that level is exponentially reduced and leaves the company with a real conundrum about how to generate the summary forecast—either roll up forecasting error or start over with the base data and have the summary forecast bear little resemblance to the detailed ones.

But, wait, there's more! What is a forecast anyway? It is a quantity of a part that you expect to use during a given time. Or it may be varying quantities that you expect to use in different time periods. Besides the part identification, the common element is a measure of time. The forecast is a predicted "run rate", "use per month," "orders per day." This is all well and good, but it does not answer the question "How much stock do I need to have in place to fill up my shelf and pipelines?" Further, "What stock do I need to have just-in-case demand should become extreme?"

As valuable and necessary as it is, forecasting is only a piece of the planning solution. As technically correct and as glamorous as they are, automatic forecasting systems have limited usefulness. They are good if you are operating in a large scale environment with a large number of high volume parts. Otherwise, simpler approaches are just as good and not nearly as expensive. Sadly, you are more likely to find the high volume environment in retail distribution than in service parts.

Methods that work

Before we discuss specific methods, it should be noted first that they all can be over-implemented and that they are all data-driven. Over-implemented means that the specific technique is so imbedded in the planning process/ystem that it is very hard to change; that the people involved have lost awareness of what it is and how it works. The best advice here is "KISS—Keep It Simple, Standard."

Data-driven means much more than "Garbage-In/Garbage-Out". It means that the input *shapes* the output. For example, what data should be used to plan field stocking—field usage history, field order history, or field shipping history? Theoretically they are all the same, but in reality they are quite different. The first, usage, is what the field reports as consumed. The second, orders, is what the field requests which is typically more than they use. The last, shipments or issues, is what central logistics gives to them regardless of order or use. Orders will often be greater than issues or use. Issues will often be greater than actual use (especially reported use).

Imbedded in the selection of which data set to use for forecasting is a philosophy of field support. Now the methods:

Direct translation of history

This might sound like a trite forecasting method, but it is often the best you have. Suppose you are doing a rolling forecast for the next year and you have less than 6 demands for a part. Six per year is about the limit for regression (in fact way below it for strict statisticians). Why not just duplicate last year's pattern? Unless you know something about the product that the part is used in (new product, end of life product, etc.), just repeating history is usually the best answer for low demand parts.

Moving Average/Weighted Average/Exponential Smoothing.

These are good methods to use if you are only trying to forecast the next period (week, month, etc.). They are simple and direct—see examples above. The biggest shortcoming with all of them is they dampen trends. For example, what is the forecast?

1, 2, 3, 4, 5, 6, . . .

Most people would say 7 just from inspecting the data and automatically discerning the trend. The three period average would say 5, the weighted average would say 5.5, and the exponentially smoothed forecast would produce similar results depending on the value of α. This doesn't seem so bad, but think about it. The forecast will always lag demand since these techniques interprets trends as "spikes" in demands and tends to ignore them.

We were recently contracted by a company to examine their forecasting methods. It seems that the field organization was constantly at odds with logistics about not planning enough parts for new product. Our recommendation was to simply switch from exponential smoothing to linear regression as the basic forecasting method for products that were in initial fielding (the first year after introduction).

Linear regression

Regression analysis was described earlier in this chapter. Linear regression is the type of regression analysis in which the regressed curve is a straight line. This has some major advantages:

• It significantly reduces the regression problem, since all we are looking for is the straight-line that most nearly matches the data.

• It is easily computed and programmed.

• It is more responsive to trends than averaging or smoothing.

• It can be used for a single period or multiple periods and is easily adjusted for confidence. (See discussion about interfacing with MRP in the applications section below.)

• It is easily adjusted for seasonality.

COMPUTATIONS The equation for all straight-lines is

$$Y = M \cdot X + B$$

where X and Y are the coordinates of the line on a grid, M is the slope of the line and B is the point where the line crosses the vertical Y axis. See Figure 12-2 below.

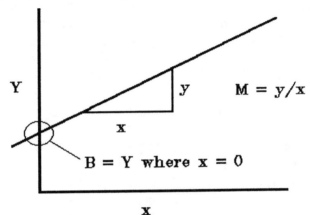

FIGURE 12-2
All lines can be described by a mathematical equation

Since each of the data points have X and Y coordinates, these coordinates can be manipulated to find the values of M and B for the line that most closely matches the base data. The equations are:

$$M = \frac{N \cdot \sum (X \cdot Y) - \sum X \cdot \sum Y}{N \cdot \sum X^2 - (\sum X)^2}$$

$$B = \frac{\sum Y = (M \cdot \sum X)}{N}$$

The standard error of the estimate is a statistic that works with a regression line the same way that the standard deviation statistic works with an average. This gives us the capability to over-stock in a controlled way. (A reason to do this is explained in the coming section, Unique Applications.) The equation for the standard error is a bit cumbersome but, once programmed, the computer gets it right every time.

$$\text{STDERR} = \sqrt{\left[\sum Y^2 - \frac{(\sum y)^2}{N} - \frac{M \cdot \sum XY - \overline{X} \cdot \sum Y)}{N\text{-}2} \right]}$$

ADJUSTING FOR SEASONALITY The chart in Figure 12-3 below is a seasonal item. Demand peaks in the spring. There is a slight downward trend in the data.

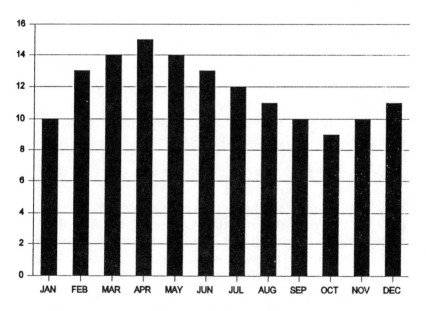

FIGURE 12-3
Typical pattern of use per month

The equation for this regression line is:

$$Y = -.3 \cdot X + 13.79$$

This equation translates the past data of:

10.0, 13.0, 14.0, 15.0, 14.0, 13.0, 12.0, 11.0, 10.0, 9.0, 10.0, 11.0

into regressed forecast data of:

9.9, 9.6, 9.3, 9.0, 8.7, 8.4, 8.1, 7.8, 7.5, 7.2, 6.9, 6.6

There is no impact for seasonality, however, the total demand in the base period is:

$$\sum_{1}^{12} x_i = 142$$

where i is the base period month number.

The total forecast for the coming year is:

$$\sum_{13}^{24} x_i = 98$$

where i is the forecast period month number.

If this quantity is prorated the same way that the data in the base period is, the forecast line becomes:

7.0, 9.0, 9.7, 10.4, 9.7, 9.0, 8.3, 7.7, 6.9, 6.3, 6.9, 7.7

A bit more manipulation is necessary to assure that base period data and the forecast period data flow together smoothly. Initially the issue of "partial parts" should be resolved to the next higher whole unit. Following partial units are accumulated until they add to a whole unit, which is then added.

INSTALLED DENSITY (BOX COUNT) FORECASTING This method relies on knowledge of the product and the part failure rate to forecast part requirements. An example is shown in Table 12-1.

Note that the table forecasts next year's usage for a single part that is used in three products. Since use rate per product

TABLE 12-1
Box count forecast data

PART NUMBER 1234

PRODUCT	PRODUCTS LAST YEAR	PARTS USED	USE PER BOX	PRODUCTS NEXT YEAR	FORECAST PER PRODUCT
PROD A	400	200	0.50	375	187.50
PROD B	375	100	0.27	450	121.50
PROD C	32	25	0.78	250	195.00
	USED LAST YEAR	325		FORECAST FOR NEXT YEAR	504

is known, the future installed density of the product is what drives the part forecast.

Theoretically this process produces the same quality results as part level forecasting. The reality again is quite different. The biggest drawback of this approach is that it depends on knowledge of current and future installed product. Based on our work in the service industry, companies rarely have this data at an accuracy level necessary for good forecasting. Proprietary mainframe equipment typically has good data. Multivendor product lists by location are rarely accurate for long. There are other problems as well. Many companies do not update their engineered Mean Time Between Failure (MTBF) for parts at the product level with actual field experience. Replacements are often greater than failures. Occasionally, users do not care about what we call a *failure*, so the *failure* is not replaced. Additionally, at lower level stocking locations, it is assumed that part usage is uniform across products, customers, field engineers, and geographically locations, which is definitely not the case.

Still there are situations where shortcomings can be minimized and this method applied with good results. For example:

• This approach can be used whenever there is a "step function" in demand based on product moves—(usually new product, planned modifications, and so forth).

• A split in the geographical responsibilities of field stocking locations without a way to separate part level demand history would necessitate this approach.

● Contract cost estimate could use this approach to forecast additional logistics costs to add contracts in an existing service area.

POISSON DISTRIBUTION This technique is explained in chapter 10 in conjunction with new product planning. It can be used to even greater effectiveness with demand rate derived from actual field experience. The criterion for its use are:

Low number of parts subject to failure.
Demands not randomized.
Failure rate known.
Fixed length of time to forecast.
Desired confidence level known.

Unique applications

Forecasts have many purposes: budget planning, gross requirements planning, material buy forecasts, repair loading, capacity planning, transportation cost, and capital investment planning just to name a few. All of these present few problems after the forecast itself has been generated. By far the most problematical area in service parts forecasting is the interface with manufacturing. There is a reason for this.

Service parts materials management uses a Fixed Quantity/ Variable Period model. We simply do not know for sure how many of anything we will need to meet unplanned equipment failures next month or next week. This means that Just-in-Time methods are out of the question for rapid repair service. JIT presupposes that the "Time" is known. The least cost approach for a service environment is to wait until you have reached a certain level of stock (regardless of how long that takes) and then order some more.

This is contrary to the manufacturing material planning model. MRP is based on a production period and the production plan (master schedule) for each production period. It is a Fixed Period/Variable Quantity model. Interfacing these two diametrically opposed models is one of the biggest technical problems of system integration. The following is a proposed solution, but it requires some compromise on both sides to achieve a "best balance" process for both organizations.

Planning cycles

Manufacturing typically uses a monthly planning cycle. It fits well with the master schedule and with financial plans. A month is much too long a cycle for service parts. Too much can go wrong in a month. This statement implies that neither manufacturing nor service can work on the other's cycle. So the first step is to establish or confirm the validity of separate planning cycles and processes for manufacturing and service.

Forecast segmentation

In order to assure smooth translation and communication of requirements the service parts forecast is segmented into three distinct sections. See Figure 12-4. The sections are the Production Lock-In Period, the Logistics Planning Cycles and the Forecast Roll-Out. Each of these sections have different Rules.

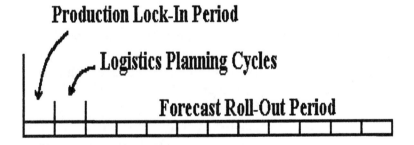

12 Month Rolling Forecast

FIGURE 12-4
Forecast are just plans until locked-in with commitments

MANUFACTURING LOCK-IN This period is essentially the manufacturing lead time. During this period Service "guarantees" minimum perturbation of the manufacturing process. Safety levels are set in central logistics to target no more than 2% out of stock. This means that only emergency (customer down) orders will be allowed to penetrate to manufacturing. Service also guarantees no stretch outs. Once an order makes it into this lock-in phase, Service is obligated to take the stock rather than request schedule extensions.

FORECAST ROLL-OUT These are the out months of the forecast. Service and Manufacturing agree on a certain amount of over-forecasting to facilitate manufacturing. (In Manufacturing it is easier to reduce order quantities than to add to them.) Manufacturing may work ahead on the schedule, but at its own risk. There is no guarantee that Service will convert the part numbers and/or quantities to "hard orders" for the following production period (or at all, for that matter).

LOGISTICS PLANNING CYCLES During the production period immediately prior to the lock-in period service logistics run one or more planning cycles. The focus of these cycles is to assure that sufficient shelf stock is available in central logistics. Forecast part numbers and quantities are converted to hard orders based on the level requirements of Service's Fixed Quantity/ Variable Cycle Model. These orders are then "locked in" with Manufacturing.

One of the issues that often arrives with this approach is that of minimum-make (or minimum buy for purchase parts) calculations. This calculation is used in manufacturing to compute the quantity of parts that optimize set-up costs. When problems arise, it is typically something like this. Service wants 2 of an item and manufacturing wants to make 10 and then insists that Service takes 5 times more stock than it ordered. It usually turns out that this is a very low demand item. In fact it is likely that 2 is a year's worth of demand. From Service's perspective Manufacturing wants to make fours years of excess. This is a no win situation unless you take the company level view. If the cost of carrying excess is in the minimum-make computation, then it really is a good deal if the company assumes the product will be supported for the required length of time. If either case is not so, then Manufacturing needs to do more homework. In these cases it is recommended that the Corporate Comptroller resolve differences.

Confidence builder or crap shoot?

In the final analysis, what can be said about mathematical forecasting is that it is a necessary tool. The real challenge of service parts forecasting is not the volume parts. It is the low volume parts! As noted above, many companies have spent fortunes to improve the accuracy of their volume parts. The improvements are often lost in round off error and moreover only apply to a relative small number of the active part numbers. Forecasting systems are often a Linus' blanket that generates a false confidence.

We have seen companies where more that 10 percent of their part demand is new—unplanned and unexpected each year. These low volume parts cannot be forecast mathematically with great accuracy. There are planning techniques that address this problem well, but the solutions are separate from forecasting.

13 *LEVEL SETTING*

The use of levels for service parts management is often misunderstood, even by those in the service community. We tend to think of stock sitting on the shelf and not being used. While this happens, the purpose of levels is not to tell us how much stock to have, but when to trigger action to get parts moving. In the manufacturing environment it is easy to visualize the timing of part movements. That is what the "Just-in-Time" concept is all about—to manage stock so that it arrives just in time to meet a need. In service we do not know when the next need will arise. So we must have another method to determine when to initiate part actions and in what quantity. The use of stock levels is that mechanism.

Three types of levels

SAFETY LEVEL This level is the most difficult to understand and explain. Simply stated, it is a quantity of parts necessary to absorb the variances in logistics pipelines.

PIPELINE LEVELS These levels provide for the pipeline cycle times.

ORDER QUANTITY LEVELS These levels result from the need to minimize processing cost and inventory holding costs.

Why safety levels are needed

We will now look at these types of levels starting with the most complex, *Safety Level.* Many companies have tried to use their Manufacturing Resource Planning (MRP) System to plan and manage service parts. They usually failed! With the exception of the inventory control process, the management of service parts is vastly different from the management of the same parts destined for manufacturing. There is even a different mathematical management model. Service parts management is a demand driven environment and the "engine" for this demand is random equipment failure. To put this in layman terms—If you can provide the master schedule of equipment failures then you can use a MRP system to plan the part. You do know your average demand for the part and could schedule part requirements based on that. The problem is that an average is just an average! It is like flipping a coin. Half the time it will be too much and half the time it will not be enough. Often, when the decision is too much, we can simply retain the excess for future use. When it is not enough, there may be a big problem! Our management, let alone our customers, don't think much of having the right part in the right place only 50% of the time. So, in order to be "right" more of the time, we have to stock more parts than we think we will need. This is a safety level. To take the emotion out of determining how much safety level is enough we must understand distributions. Not the physical distribution of parts, but the statistical distributions that were discussed in chapter 8.

σ *(Sigma)*

When we order a part it has a replenishment or a procurement cycle. The cycle times have an average (mean) that is usually called the lead time. But lead times are seldom completely consistent. They are different almost every time, if only by a day. This variation in replenishment time introduces uncertainty into our planning efforts. See Figure 13-1

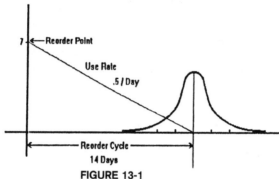

FIGURE 13-1
If we use 7 parts in 14 days, the use rate is .5 parts per day

But, the replenishment cycle is not the only thing that is variable. There is also the variance in demand during the replenishment cycle. This variance is represented in Figure 13-2.

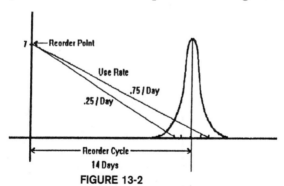

FIGURE 13-2
Delivery can vary with breakdowns, strikes, and weather

It should be noted that the distribution used is not the distribution of demands per day. It is the "inverse" distribution—the distribution of days between demand. This is done to facilitate the combination of this distribution with the cycle time distributions which are in days.

Three things should be noted from looking at these two diagrams. First, we don't care if the stock arrives early or if the demand is lower than average. We are only concerned with late deliveries and higher than average demand. A lack of parts is what we have to hedge against. Second, if these distributions were consistent we wouldn't need safety level at all. Finally, we wonder if these distributions are really normally distributed (i.e., do the percentages cited above really apply). As it turns out, most of our distributions are not normal if left to themselves. Without attention they will form log-normal distributions. This situation can be dealt with mathematically, but it is better to make the distributions normal by managing them. (The technique to do this is explained in chapter 27.) At this point the reader should be assured that if we compute levels as if the distributions were normal no harm will be done. The levels will be somewhat larger than they need to be, but justifiably so. As our pipeline management efforts succeed we are rewarded with lower and more accurate levels.

Combined distributions

As a further complication we see that we are dealing with two distributions. Both are variable. Both operate simultaneously. These are presented in Figure 13-3 graphically.

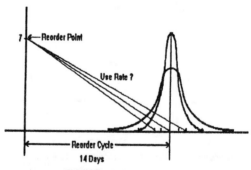

FIGURE 13-3
The larger of the distributions will also include the smaller

Fortunately mathematicians have discovered a procedure for combining the distributions of two independent variables. That rule is that "the variance of the sum is equal to the sum of the variances." This is not as simple as it sounds. The variance being talked about is the square of the standard deviation. So to compute the standard deviation of the combined distribution you have to compute the standard deviation for each of the distributions, square each, add them together and then take the square root of the total. Finally we can develop a workable formula to compute Safety Level.

$$SL_{qty} = Demand/Day * RISK * \sqrt{\sigma^0_{Replenishment} + \sigma^0_{Days/Demand}}$$

In words—The Safety Level Quantity is equal to the Average Use per Day times the Risk Factor times the Standard Deviation of the combined distribution of Replenishment times the Days between use. That leaves us only to explain the Risk factor. We saw in chapter 8 that when data is normally distributed, the standard deviation assumes properties. Specifically:

- 68.3% of the data is ± 1 Standard Deviation from the mean
- 95.4% of the data is ± 2 Standard Deviation from the mean
- 99.7% of the data is ± 3 Standard Deviation from the mean

This is *always* true regardless of the actual value of the standard deviation and this we can literally plan on. The challenge is to decide the number of standard deviations that must be used based on the amount of risk you are willing to take of running out of stock for the part in question at the stocking location in question. Table 13-1 translates the percent of risk to the number of standard deviations that must be used.

One more complication

The safety level equation shown above works for all parts in field stocking locations and for nonrepairable parts in central stocking locations. It does not work for repairable parts in central stocking locations that are supported by repair operations.

TABLE 13-1
Select the deviations from the mean based on the percent risk you can accept

% *Out of* *Stock Risk*	*Number of* *Standard* *Deviations*	% *Out of* *Stock Risk*	*Number of* *Standard* *Deviations*
0	3.00	26	0.65
1	2.33	27	0.62
2	2.06	28	0.59
3	1.89	29	0.56
4	1.76	30	0.53
5	1.65	31	0.50
6	1.56	32	0.47
7	1.48	33	0.44
8	1.41	34	0.42
9	1.35	35	0.39
10	1.29	36	0.36
11	1.23	37	0.34
12	1.18	38	0.31
13	1.13	39	0.28
14	1.09	40	0.26
15	1.04	41	0.23
16	1.00	42	0.21
17	0.96	43	0.18
18	0.92	44	0.16
19	0.88	45	0.13
20	0.85	46	0.11
21	0.81	47	0.08
22	0.78	48	0.06
23	0.74	49	0.03
24	0.71	50	0.00
25	0.68		

To modify the formula for this situation we have to add two more statistical distributions. These are the defective return time distribution and the repair cycle distribution. When this is done the formula looks like this:

$$SL_{qty} = \text{Demand/Day} * \text{RISK} * \sqrt{\sigma^2_{\text{Replenishment}} + \sigma^2_{\text{Days/Demand}} + \sigma^2_{\text{Return}} + \sigma^2_{\text{Repair}}}$$

The calculation does tend to get complicated, but once set up, it is a process that a computer of any size can repeat indefinitely. By computing safety level this way we can assure ourselves of two things. First, we will have safety levels that are as accurate as possible without generating unnecessary excess.

Second, we will be out of the "gut feel" business. Our calculations will be defensible to management and to our financial organization.

Do remember that variances are based on worldly occurrences. Like any forecast, history is only valid as a sign post so long as the future is expected to follow the same path. The numbers merely record the deviations in weather, environment, personnel, use, equipment demand, motivation, seasonality, and other factors. If you know that an event was caused by an Act of God which is not likely to affect the part lead time or demand again, then discount that factor. If you know that another factor will definitely affect the outcome, then include a variance for it in the calculations. You may also want to consider the essentiality of a part in safety stock calculations. Emphasis should be placed on investing in assets which gain big benefit for the cost. If the part is highly essential to equipment operation, then cover a higher level of risk than you would on less critical components.

Pipeline levels

These levels are all easily computed by multiplying the average demand rate times the average pipeline cycle time. As stated previously these pipelines are repair, defective return, field replenishment and procurement. For the purpose of computing levels the pipeline is "owned" by the receiving stocking locations. In other words the quantities necessary to fill these pipelines is built into the levels at the location to which the stock is directed.

We emphasize that the average times can be very misleading if the variance is not considered. Return of defective parts from field locations should be a few days, but there are often negligent and undisciplined technicians who hord parts. Consider a mean return time of seven calendar days with a deviation of seven days. This does not sound bad until you realize that getting back all the parts for repair will take one month (7 days mean + (3 * 7 days deviation) = 28 days). If you use a part every other day (.5 parts per day) then, unless repairs are very fast, you will need to buy up to 14 additional parts to cover the pipeline delay time. Reducing the pipeline delay times is a major opportunity for improvement in most companies.

Order quantity levels

The use of a consistent ordering policy is essential to the containment of both the logistics investment and logistics operating costs. (This is explained at depth in chapter 26.) The standard EOQ calculation is used in this chapter and is shown below. As we will see, when used for the procurement we will alter it to allow for assets that are recovered from repair programs.

$$EQQ = \sqrt{\frac{2 * \text{Order Cost} * \text{Period Demand}}{\text{Carrying Cost} * \text{Unit Cost}}}$$

Unit cost is the standard cost of the item without including depreciation of reserves. (Carrying Cost and Ordering Cost are discussed in chapter 9.)

How levels are used

Looking at Figures 13-4 and 13-5, these are stock level diagrams and show how levels are computed and built up. Figure 13-4 is the level calculation for nonrepairable parts in a central stocking location and for all parts in field locations. Figure 13-5 shows the development of levels for repairable parts in central stocking locations.

As stated in the introduction to this chapter, the purpose of levels is to trigger movement. Here is how it works:

For the diagram in Figure 13-4—When the On Hand Quantity of an Item plus the quantity already on order (less quantities back ordered to customers, if any) is less than or equal to the reorder point then order a quantity equal to the Maximum Quantity plus Customer Back Orders minus the On Hand Quantity and the On Order Quantity.

Central Stocking Location - Non-Repairable Items
Field Stocking Location - All Items

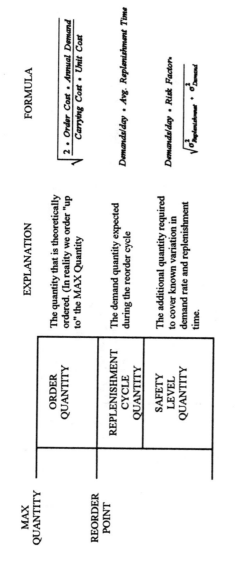

	EXPLANATION	FORMULA
ORDER QUANTITY	The quantity that is theoretically ordered. (In reality we order "up to" the MAX Quanity	$\sqrt{\dfrac{2 \cdot Order\ Cost \cdot Annual\ Demand}{Carrying\ Cost \cdot Unit\ Cost}}$
REPLENISHMENT CYCLE QUANTITY	The demand quantity expected during the reorder cycle	$Demands/day \cdot Avg.\ Replenishment\ Time$
SAFETY LEVEL QUANTITY	The additional quantity required to cover known variation in demand rate and replenishment time.	$Demands/day \cdot Risk\ Factor \cdot \sqrt{\sigma^2_{Replenishment} \cdot \sigma^2_{Demand}}$

MAX QUANTITY

REORDER POINT

FIGURE 13-4
Stock level diagram

	EXPLANATION	FORMULA
MAX QUANTITY → PROCUREMENT ORDER QUANTITY	The quantity that is theoretically ordered. (In reality we order "up to" the MAX Quantity	$\sqrt{\dfrac{2 \cdot Order\ Cost \cdot Annual\ Demand \cdot Washout\ Rate}{Carrying\ Cost \cdot Unit\ Cost}}$
PROCUREMENT ORDER POINT → PROCUREMENT CYCLE QUANTITY	The replacement quantity expected during the procurement cycle.	$Demands/day \cdot Washout\ Rate \cdot Avg.\ Procurement\ Time$
RETURN QUANTITY	The demand quantity expected during the return cycle.	$Demands/day \cdot Avg.\ Return\ Time$
RFI MAX QUANTITY → REPAIR ORDER QUANTITY	The quantity that is theoretically ordered to repair. (In reality we order "up to" the RFI MAX Quantity or the number of detectives available.)	$\sqrt{\dfrac{2 \cdot Order\ Cost \cdot Annual\ Demand}{Carrying\ Cost \cdot Unit\ Cost}}$
REPAIR REORDER POINT → REPAIR CYCLE QUANTITY	The demand quantity expected during the repair cycle.	$Demands/day \cdot Avg.\ Repair\ Time$
SAFETY LEVEL QUANTITY	The additional quantity required to cover known variation in demand rate, return time, repair time and procurement time.	$Demands/day \cdot Risk\ Factor \cdot \sqrt{\sigma^2_{Procurement} + \sigma^2_{Demand} + \sigma^2_{Return} + \sigma^2_{Repair}}$

FIGURE 13-5
Stock level diagram
The equation for central stocking includes new repairable parts.

For the diagram in Figure 13-5 there is a two step process. First, when the On Hand—Ready for Issue (RFI) Quantity of an item plus the quantity already in repair (less quantities back ordered to customers if any) is less than or equal to the repair reorder point, then order a quantity equal to the RFI Maximum Quantity plus Customer Back Orders minus the On Hand—Ready for Issue Quantity and the In Repair Quantity. Second, when the On Hand Quantity of an item in central locations (and regardless of its serviceability), plus the quantity already on order or in repair, plus the quantity of defective due in from the field, (less quantities back ordered to customers if any) is less than or equal to the procurement reorder point, then order a quantity equal to the Maximum Quantity plus Customer Back Orders minus the On Hand Quantity (regardless of condition), Defective Due In, In Repair and the On Order Quantity. Fortunitely a computer can be programmed to follow this logic more consistently than a human can.

14 CENTRAL WAREHOUSE OPERATIONS

Challenges

Deciding the best locations for service parts is a challenge. The extremes can range from every individual tech rep and mechanic carrying an extensive supply, to a centralized supply with rapid delivery to the user. Another question arises as to who should control the parts stocks: maintenance service, production, or a separate materials management organization. Then what physical facilities are required effectively to receive, store, control, pick, pack, and issue parts?

This chapter addresses the special needs of a central warehouse. As this book is being written there is controversy over whether a service organization should run their own facility or should outsource the warehouse and physical distribution functions to specialists. Either way an effective warehouse is required. Since the service business needs parts for rapid delivery *just-in-case,* and those parts often have long production lead times, a stock of parts is needed somewhere. If a SKU is generally required more than eight hours after request, then a central warehouse should be the only parts inventory in the country. It is much better to have one good center for parts stock than to allow each function to have its own cache of parts. Transportation today can get a part from a warehouse in Chicago, Dallas, Atlanta, Memphis, or many other locations near major airports, in less than six hours. Overnight flights via Airborne, DHL, FedEx, UPS, or even the U.S. Postal Service can have parts ready for pickup about 6:30 am, special deliveries in major cities by 8:00 am, and to the rest of us by 10:30 am. Now that much of the transportation challenge is solved, the remaining issue is to have at least one part on the shelf so we can get our hands (or automation) on it quickly to pick, pack, and ship. *To stock* parts and the term *stocking* imply action. The location may be virtual, meaning that a stock may be in a large warehouse, in a van, in a customer locker, or any location that is controlled so we know where the part is.

Control

In theory, one stockroom should have parts both for production and to support service on those same products. Economies of scale would be better than with separate stocks. One safety stock, one group of people, consolidated receiving and inspection, all help keep costs low. Unfortunately consolidation rarely works. Why not? The answer is, because of distrust, lack of confidence, politics, favoritism, poor management, and different focus of effort. A split of service to an independent stock will usually occur as the number of parts, amount of activity, and differences in parts configuration between production and service increase.

In an industrial plant, facility, or separate service organization, the parts should be controlled strictly by the maintenance organization. A durable-product manufacturer who supports its own products with after-sales service probably will establish an independent logistics-parts-support function as service revenues approach $25 million. The authors have seen only two successful joint warehouses in all their years of experience. Those exceptions worked because top management paid special attention to assuring cooperation between the production and service people. Many logistics warehouses support both field service and repair depots. That combination is in many ways more difficult to combine than service and production, but the similar mentality and objectives of repair and field service usually manage to cooperate. If the warehouse function is outsourced with a good set of goals, then the conflicts seem to go away.

Facility layout

"Bin" is a common word denoting the location where a part is stored. It may be a shelf, a section of warehouse rack, a floor pallet, or a small container drawer. Every part should be linked to a physical location so that it can be found rapidly. There should never be more than one part in a physical location. If a shelf needs to carry several line items, then sub-bin designations should be applied. The physical layout usually can be designated by the row, vertical section within the row, and then shelf within that section. For example, AlA would be found in the first row (A), first section (1), bottom (A) shelf. The number of digits assigned to the sections depends on how many rows there are. Generally two digits, which allow up to 99 rows, are adequate. The use of alpha characters in the designation has the potential, in a single digit, to include 26 locations since there are 26 letters, A–Z, in the alphabet. Both people and computers are capable of determining the sequence whether it is 1, 2, 3, or A, B, C; although stockroom people are slightly faster on numbers than on alpha characters.

There is little practical difference between a system with bin designations as alpha-numeric-alpha or numeric-numeric-numeric or numeric-alphanumeric. All-alpha designations are more difficult to work with because the phonetic pronunciation of the letters by different people injects errors. An all-numeric sequence is preferred for rapid data entry because all the numbers can be keyed from the numeric pad on a computer terminal. This is faster than seeking alpha characters or a combination of alpha and numerics. If an all-numeric system is used, it should be stated as three different groups, for example, 3-21-13.

Start with the first designated row nearest the main entrance. The shelf units should start nearest the main aisle. Figure 14-1 shows a typical layout. The pickers can work most effectively if the parts to be selected are arranged on the pick list in bin order. The picker on his or her physical route through the facility can pick both sides of an aisle. For example, section 1 of row D would be directly across from section 1 of row C and all the parts in section 1 of either row C or D should be picked before section 2 in any of those rows. If the rack sections are numeric, then another option is to give the aisle a designation and put even numbered sections on one side and odd numbers on the other. When the picker completes picking all parts from rows C and D and turns the corner to come down between rows E and F, he or she starts at the high end and works down. To make the picking easier, the parts in rows E and F could be listed in descending order. For example, if the sections are numbered, then in rows E and F, section 9 could be listed before 8, and so on. A computer is obviously helpful in doing these sorted listings. The end objective of any stockroom location and picking system should be to make the job as accurate, easy, and fast as possible.

Separate traffic patterns are advisable receiving and issuing. Most items will be received in large quantities contained in big bulky containers, often on pallets, and will be shipped as individual items. The receiving area should have easy access, if possible, to a loading dock so that delivery trucks can unload directly into a receiving area. Any materials that require quality control receiving inspection should be put in a separate, preferably secured, cage until they are inspected.

Since the receiving papers usually indicate only the number of packages and not the contents, a responsible person should inventory the contents against the shipping invoice to assure that what was ordered is what was received. Any discrepancies should be noted for acceptance or follow-up. It is standard procedure on large-quantity items to allow some overage (depending on the purchase order terms) up to 10 percent above

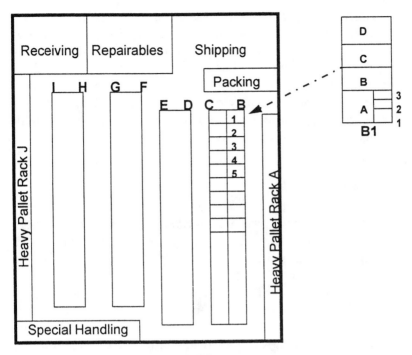

FIGURE 14-1
An effective warehouse provides for minimum movement of parts

the quantity ordered. If 100 PWBs were ordered, the manufacturer probably started the production run with enough to assure that after any problems the 100 would still be achieved. If the process were working well, then perhaps an additional five boards would be produced and shipped. Quantities received over and under, damaged materials, and back orders all need to be identified at receiving and followed up. It is especially important to identify parts that are backordered for rush jobs so that they can be expedited directly to the point of need, and not put in a warehouse bin.

Once parts have been checked and passed by quality assurance, they should be put on the shelves. Wherever possible they should be put in the back of the same bins that hold earlier parts. Why in the back? Because first in-first out (FIFO) is a good physical rule for any parts. That means that the older parts will be in the front of the bin where they will be easily picked and used first.

There are other methods to achieve FIFO, such as lot control, where each incoming shipment is assigned a separate bin, and outgoing orders are picked from the oldest lot. Date stamping puts labels on parts when they are received and pickers are instructed to pick the stock with the oldest date. Shelf-life-sensitive components may also be separated physically and those items put under the management of a few specially trained people who control access to them.

Breaking bulk

Since parts often arrive at a central warehouse in palletainers and bulk cartons, the warehouse may need to "break bulk" and package the parts as an item to issue. PWBs, for example, often come from production in antistatic bags, but slotted in vertical handling racks. Those PWBs must be carefully packaged in protective boxes with accurate identification labels so they can travel individually without damage. Small objects are often put in transparent bags. All items needed for a field job should be packaged together just like a kit of parts at a hardware store to repair a water faucet. A computer program at receiving should print a label for every part. If 20 parts are to be individually packaged, then the printer should spew out 20 labels.

Location assignment

Location of parts within a stock area should be based on four functions: safety, frequency of picking, size, and weight. Hazardous substances should be put in a safe area immediately. Parts picked most frequently should be kept near the issuing counter so the stock clerk can get them quickly. An analysis by part numbers of the numbers of parts processed in the past 12 months will assist bin location selection. High movers can be stocked in the most accessible areas, with slow movers assigned to more remote locations. Large, bulky items usually will be kept near the entrance through which they enter and leave. If they are light weight, they may be put high on racks where they do not use space that is better utilized by small items;

otherwise they are probably kept on the floor or in a special pallet area. Heavy items should be kept near the floor so they can be handled easily and safely. Fast moving, frequently issued parts should be stored close to the place of need.

The central service parts organization should obtain, from the supplier or by counting, the normal quantity per container (such as 12 power supplies per carton). This can help the planner place orders in multiples of the standard container quantity, if the economics and bulk of that strategy makes sense. Nonstandard container quantities must frequently be ordered, but standard quantities require less labor and handling, and sustain less damage.

The development of a forecast for each part can be very valuable in bin location assignment. Once the EOQ and safety stock quantities have been determined, the minimum and maximum stock levels can be calculated for location sizing:

Minimum stock = Safety stock

Maximum stock = Safety stock + Reorder quantity + Reorder point

As forecasting techniques and methods improve, a week-by-week stock projection is possible. Both the minimum and maximum stock levels can be forecast for the planning period. If length-width-height measurements plus weight are entered in the database, then several plans can be developed:

1. Cube (volume), to show total storage volume required.
2. Bin size mix, to show bin sizes needed.
3. Bin change, to show when present bin size will become too small.

Packaged part volume (cubic feet) x Maximum forecast on-hand quantity
= Part space requirements (maximum cubic feet)

Placing similar parts together can make sense in a small stockroom that has no computer system and is often accessed by the personnel who need to identify and select the specific part. For example, all bearings might be placed in orderly sequence so that they can be compared and the correct one selected easily. In a computerized stockroom that handles a large volume of picking and issues, relational shelving can cause problems because a picker working from a computerized number list probably moves the cart rapidly down the row and literally picks the parts on the run. For example, if the order calls for part 5555 in bin 8-22-13, it is relatively easy to miss bin 13 and pick a part out of bin 14 instead. If the nearby parts are all bearings, then the mistake might not be caught until the technician discovers the error and has to explain to the angry customer why the air conditioner will be down for another hot day. If the number and description are significantly different, the error should be identified by the picker who selected a relay instead of a bearing, or certainly should be caught by the quality checks at packing.

A computer program may be developed that can assign parts to the available locations. To do this, the database on each part must include the length, width, height, and weight of each part in its shelf package. The computer program then calculates the space required and searches its list of available bins to find the next large enough location, to which it assigns the parts. The program should look first at any existing locations for that part to see if the shipment can be placed there, or if all the quantities of that part should be moved to another location where they can be stored together. Such a program can also locate heavy parts near the floor on pallet racks and fast moving parts near the pack area.

As picking of such orders probably will be computerized, the pick list is organized in the most efficient sequence. The warehouse may also be automated with computer-directed narrow-aisle fork trucks that can move rapidly in both horizontal and vertical directions. Those systems are vital for high volume, well-packaged products such as for a mail-order house where large volumes of orders must be rapidly shelved or picked. They are less justified in the typical factory or field service stockroom where parts come in many shapes and sizes. There are systems operating that automatically retrieve the container of parts and bring it to the counter where the stock keeper may take out the necessary quantity and then push a button to send the container back to its computer-determined location. While these storage systems make efficient use of vertical space, they, unfortunately, are often slower than a human picker and are even less reliable.

Automation

Portable radio frequency (RF) scanner terminals provide an effective way to gather data in real time. In a large warehouse, the continuous pick and pack activity can be significantly speeded and made more accurate with handheld information devices. A scanner is basically a computer, display, keyboard, laser barcode scanner, and a radio transmitter, all in one battery powered package. Data transmissions between terminals and the system file server log every activity by operator, time, and date. Every user logs into the system by scanning the barcode on his employee badge and enters a personal identification number (PIN) for extra security.

This paperless system shows on the scanner display the next part to be picked . As each pick activity is entered, the system checks the order. If the computer detects an error it will not allow picking to proceed until the error is corrected. Thus, quality assurance is performed at the bin level and errors are nearly eliminated, greatly reducing efforts that used to be required for corrective action. Real time data processing capability provides accurate status for work in process and eliminates the need to freeze part locations for cycle counts. Essential productivity data is also collected for management guidance. To quantify the gains, in one large warehouse the prior error rate was three percent. Three percent of 48,000 orders per month was 1,440 errors per month! Reducing those errors to under one percent saved $111,000 per year plus all the aggravation and field costs.

Large warehouses often find problems in picking orders that combine large items from pallet racks with smaller bin items. That problem was alleviated at Pitney Bowes by a directed pallet pick workstation. This workstation is used to scan a group of orders and produce a logical pick label list in sequential location by row. Pick operators can then pick with the most efficient process and least amount of travel.

As parts are picked, labels (with barcodes) are attached. These labels, which are printed at this station, are scanned to tell which stock order the picked parts belong to. A pick leader then combines picked parts with stock orders. The parts are placed in tubs to go to packing, or go on a conveyor for more picking of additional smaller parts. It is helpful for both training and public relations to post signs at major stations which describe the functions performed there.

Typical reports that can be generated with such a system include for every person, team, shift, and entire group:

—Picks per hour (by part SKU) actual versus standard; for present day, prior day, week, month, and year to date

—Orders per hour actual versus standard, with above same variations

—Packs by individual technician, by end user, geographical territory; also by day, week, and month

Lines per hour

Cases per hour

Orders per carton (for consolidated geography and reduced transport cost)

—Cycle time from order receipt until shipped per day for the last five, week average for the last five, and month averages for the last twelve.

—Where an open order is in the cycle. (Note that this should be on special request only, since prompt order filling will reduce the need for queries.)

—How well we did yesterday

Start backlog order quantity

New orders received; Emergency / Routine / Total

Total to be filled: Emergency / Routine / Total

Completed: Emergency / Routine / Total

End backlog; Emergency / Routine / Total

Interruptions

Defects and errors

—Today's plan

Orders to fill

Requests to pick

SKUs to pick

Estimated work load in standard hours and people.
Progress at specific periods like break times
—Costs for prior five work days, five weeks, and 12 months
Labor, per order: by function
—Transportation:
By mode: Emergency / Rush / Routine / Total
By destination: Service Organization / Technician / Customer
—Accuracy (of problems caught at Packing, before shipped)
—By person / team / function
Percent perfect orders
Discrepancies: wrong item, under, over
—Picks per part number of orders and quantity, for the top 1,000 parts. (This is to enable better location of high-moving parts near balanced pick stations.)

Physical inventory

The works *complete physical inventory* creates dread in most people involved with service parts. For centuries accountants have insisted on full counts of every physical item on the books so they can assure bankers, investors, owners, and other interested people that what ledgers show to be on hand is really there. Unfortunately, a once-a-year physical inventory is usually several percentage points away from accurate, and even that rough estimate begins to deteriorate quickly unless procedures are in place to maintain accuracy. Cycle counting, as described in the following section, is a much better answer to maintaining parts accuracy. A typical inventory taking list is shown in Figure 14-2 especially to illustrate that the count must be "blind." This means that the quantity of parts expected to be present is not shown. (Note that the sort order is by location to facilitate physical movement.)

After the inventory is recorded, usually on paper or hand-held terminal, the results of the physical count must be entered against the perpetual count to determine variances, if any. Figure 14-3 shows helpful information to reconcile variances.

```
             I N V E N T O R Y    T A K I N G    L I S T
             Part
Location     Number                    Description              Quantity

B9C2         599324      SWITCH     ,DPDT,5AMP,110V                _____
B12A2        489320      FILTER     ,HEPA,CLASS100,LAM HOOD        _____
B12C1        920331      FILTER     ,50 MICRON,VENT #5             _____
B13B2        817274      PHOTOCELL  ,PAPER SENSE,OCE 1800          _____
B13C         243589      TERMINAL   ,12GA,COPPER,W/FIT TO MOD12    _____
B13D         423443      SUPPRESSOR,VOLTAGE FOR MOD 61C            _____
B14A         872345      CABLE      ,CONTROL,STNLS,14CM,W/FIT      _____
```

FIGURE 14-2
Inventory taking list ordered to minimize movement

```
             I N V E N T O R Y     V A R I A N C E S

PART     NOUN       PHYS PERP VAR  VAR  PHYSICAL  PERPETUAL  VARIANCE
NUMBER   DESC       QTY  QTY  QTY  Q%   $         $          $

599324   SWITCH     11   9    2    122   22.00     18.00      4.00
489320   FILTER      6   5    1    120  204.00    170.00     34.00
423443   SUPPRESSOR  1   2   -1     50   59.50    119.00     59.50
```

FIGURE 14-3
Variance report shows only unmatched counts

Cycle counting

The objective of cycle counting is to confirm on a statistical basis that parts are being properly managed and that the physical stocks on the shelves equal the perpetual stocks carried electronically in the computer. Accurate cycle counting should eliminate the need for warehouse or stockroom shutdown and complete physical count. Cycle counting is done to reduce or eliminate the errors that creep in as a result of people taking or returning parts without updating the data. Cycle counting is a far more reliable method of inventory verification than annual physical inventories.

The cycle length is the time or units needed to reach the target accuracy. The cycle length is calculated by:

(1−Accuracy level desired)/(Accuracy level desired × P of a variance)

The target accuracy level is usually determined by management auditors, and is often 98 or 99 percent. Probability of a variance is the chance of a mistake occurring during the period, for example, 50/week. The cycles should be based on the most important parts (which contribute to the success of the facility or can cause the most harm if they are not correctly available).

The recommended approach is to assign every SKU to one of three classes: A, B, or C. No more than 10 percent of the items will be class A, no more than 20 percent class B, and the remainder class C. The cycle count will be planned and controlled to a plan such as: class A parts will be physically counted at least every 90 days, class B parts at least every 180 days, and all parts at least once every year. Exceptions are items not picked and not put away, and possibly inexpensive items that could be counted every two or three years since more frequent counting is not justified.

Cycle counts should be done as an integral part of operating the stockroom and should present little impediment to ongoing operations. In fact, cycle counting should provide continual benefit in confidence that the inventory is accurate. Factors that determine the class of a stockkeeping unit, and thereby the amount of attention paid to the part and frequency of cycle count, include:

1. Essentiality
2. Forecast use for year
3. Unit cost
4. Control requirements
5. Frequency of picks and putaways

Other factors that have bearing on this challenge include:

6. Lead time to get additional parts in case of downside error
7. Extended cost on hand, since big dollars get big attention

Lead time effect can be properly managed through reorder point and safety stock. Extended cost is related to the forecast use and unit cost that are the real drivers for our need in accuracy and control. It is better to be able to control a few things well than to do a poor job trying to control many, so these last two factors are not considered in the rank.

Essentiality is the importance of each stockkeeping unit to the equipment it is used on and to the plant. The values of essentiality were discussed in chapter 2.

Forecast use for the next year picks one year as the convenient forecast horizon. The future is obviously what we need to manage for, so historical use data should be updated by any special needs that may cause it to change. *Unit cost* of the parts is generally the cost at last purchase, but may be a weighted average, or it could be the *next cost*.

Control provides impetus to avoid theft, obsolescence, and shelf life. Items such as batteries, popular PWBs, copper pipe fittings, and hazardous chemicals would be rated as control class 1 to provide a high level of control. Most other parts with detailed stock accounting would be the medium control level 2, and any summary stock items, (such as common hardware) would be class 3, low control.

The challenge now is to consolidate the five factors into a single A or B or C class. This is a human function that must be done by intelligent people who understand where the parts are used. The matrix in Table 14-1 should help guide the decision.

TABLE 14-1
Class criteria guide

Value Class	A	B	C
Essentiality	1 or 2	3	4
Forecast Use	100+	10–99	1–9
Unit Cost	$1,000+	$100–999	$0–99
Control Need	High	Medium	Low
Demand Pattern		Separate algorithm	

There are obviously some combinations of these factors that cause the value class to differ from the matrix slots shown. Any one of the factors falling in the A group should put the part into the A value class. Also, a B class part should move into the higher A class if at least four of the five factors are rated B. Likewise, a part should be rated B if two or more of the five factors fall in the B category. Otherwise the parts should be ranked C. If in doubt, push the parts to the lower level because there will be too many clamoring for priority attention. It is better to give A-level attention to the critical few. The number of A class items should be fewer than 10 percent of the items carried.

There should be an override on activity since the last physical count, so that if a part has been requested (i.e., a person has gone to the bin or, in the case of zero stock the part was demanded) five times for A class, ten times for B class, or 20 times for C class, then a physical count should be taken. This is necessary because the more activity there is, the more opportunity there is for an error to occur.

Note, however, that the bigger problems will probably come from an activity such as theft or negligence that is not entered into the computer. Those shortages are at least discovered, if not precluded, by routine cycle counting. Another variation that should be investigated is to stimulate the cycle count at reorder point (ROP). This helps because ROP is a very sensitive time in the part's cycle. It is the lowest quantity in inventory that normally would be checked and thus makes the physical effort easy. It is also the time at which any expediting action could be stimulated if the physical count happened to be lower than the perpetual expectation.

The best procedure for cycle counting is to have a printed list available first thing in the morning when people arrive at the warehouse. They can then take inventory in pairs with one person reading the stock numbers and a second confirming the description of those parts, counting the parts quantity, and reporting the count back to the first person, who writes it on the sheet. The data would then be entered to the computer system. Persons taking inventory should not be easily able to find out what the actual quantities should be. The actual quantities should never be printed on the printout. The parts for count should be displayed in bin sequence. This means there will be gaps, of course, but the physical movement of the people counting should be in a continuous pattern from one end of the stockroom to the other. To reduce error, data for quantities being keyboarded back into the system should be entered following the exact same order of the printout sheet. If there are large quantities of parts to be counted, the several pages of printout can be separated and given to different people so that each group counts perhaps only one or two pages of the total.

Obviously, automation such as handheld RF or infrared terminals will speed both the count and reconciliation of variances. The handheld display can give the same information as a sheet of paper can, and brings several advantages. First, because a wireless system operates in real time, there is no need to stop putaway and pick from bins being counted. The computer time stamps every entry, knowing exactly how many parts should be in the bin every second. Second, any suspected miscounts can be caught on the spot so the counter can validate the quantity without having to return to a bin.

The software program determines how many parts are in each class and divides that quantity by the number of workdays that will be available in that class period. For example, in an inventory of 15,000 parts, there might be 1000 class-A parts that have to be counted within a 90-calendar-day (three-month) period. That would normally be 63 workdays. Thus $1000/63 = 16$ class A parts to be counted each day. If there are no more than 3000 class B parts to be counted during 126 workdays (six months), that adds 24 parts a day. The remaining 11,000 or so C class parts to be counted every year add another 44 (11,000/252) parts. The sum of those is 84 parts a day. There will be, of course, additional counts because of activity or special questions, but 100, or even 200, parts a morning, before activity really gets started, is easily accomplished. The computer database should record the *Date Last Counted* for every part. The software then simply selects the 16 class A parts with the oldest Date Last Counted, the 24 oldest Bs, and the 44 Cs with the oldest last count date. A variation is to have the program first indicate the parts that are to be counted because they are at the reorder point, then the frequent-access count list, and then the balance selected from A, B, and C classes. This should all be presented as one integrated list arranged in location sequence, indicating which parts are selected for count because they are at reorder point and which are selected because of the frequent-access criteria.

Auditors often look at the variance analyses over a period of time to determine the need for a physical inventory. If the variances were consistently (or on the aggregate) under about

3 percent in units and 5 percent in dollars, the cycle count results would be officially accepted. If the variances were more than that, then a complete physical inventory might be ordered. This would mean running a counter for date periods for the total number of line items counted, the number that were in variance, the unit quantity of those variances, and the dollar amount of the variances. The variances are symptoms that should lead to the problems and, to avoid recurrence, the problems must be solved. Problems may be as diverse as people motivation, discipline, and training; or procedures, documentation, security, or management priorities. The variance data generally could be grouped by the month, or four-week periods (which are commonly used with about a 13-period total retention) with under- and over-variances listed separately so the auditors can review the data for any trends. Typical accuracy goals are shown in Table 14-2.

TABLE 14-2
Unit accuracy brings financial accuracy

Category	Goal%
Items valued $1,000 or more	99
Items valued less than $1,000	97
Pilferable, sensitive items	99

$$\text{Gross Shrink} = \frac{(\$ \text{ Written Up}) - (\$ \text{ Written Down})}{\text{Starting } \$ \text{ Valuation}} \leq .5\%$$

$$\text{Unit Shrink} = \frac{(\text{Qty Units Up}) + (\text{Qty Units Down})}{\text{Total Quantity of Units}} \leq 1\%$$

Moving to a new facility

Moving parts to a new facility has challenges that can be met well with planning. This may involve movement to a new building, or perhaps reestablishing the service parts operations in a better location in the existing facility. The major need is to avoid shutting down customer support while the move takes place. The physical layout should be determined in advance to give a smooth traffic flow to shelve and pick parts, with enough space between shelves for the pickers and any vehicles to move. Acquire storage racks, shelves, bins, and drawers to handle anticipated parts volume. Every location is uniquely identified by aisle/section/shelf/drawer box. Decisions made whether parts will be placed according to stock number sequence, by commodity group, or randomly with consideration for the frequency of use, size, weight and other factors were covered previously. Naturally the high-use parts are separated from low-use parts and placed near the access point. A large stock location should use random storage. If the locations are randomly arranged, parts may be moved in physically with little attention to where which part goes as long as it is identified. That way a part can be retrieved for service use at anytime, even before all parts are in and located. If specific parts are to be grouped together or placed in a particular sequence, tags should be prepared from the parts catalog and placed on every bin. Duplicate tags are helpful so that one can be placed on the existing parts and another on the destination location. A typical tag is shown in Figure 14-4.

If a computer system is used, the first set of labels could be sorted in order of the "From" location and then easily applied in sequence to those parts. The "To" location labels can be separately sorted and applied to the new bins. That assistance will allow inexperienced persons (with strong backs) to go to the old location, place the parts in a move container with the tag on top, and move them to the new location. There is great value in planning such a physical move well in advance and using simple systems such as move tags to assure that parts get to the right location with a minimum of disruption. It is also worth the effort to have the initial quantity of the parts indicated indelibly on the tag and to have the moving person put his/her unique number, initials, or name on the tag. Again, this sign of responsibility helps assure a thorough, accurate job. If parts are subject to theft, the personalization also helps reduce that potential for disappearance.

Self-sticking, reusable, adhesive labels are available for rapid processing through a computer printer. Those same labels can be prepared by hand. If most of the work will be done by hand, labels using the 3M "Scotch Post-it" yellow label pads can be

Stock Number: 567345
Description: RELAY, SOLID, 5W

From: A-21-3

To: 9- 12-10

Quantity: 7

Moved by: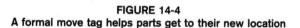

FIGURE 14-4
A formal move tag helps parts get to their new location

worth the small added expense. Any materials cost will be insignificant compared with the amount of labor and need for accuracy. When the parts are placed in their new location, the old tag that accompanied them during movement can be removed and given to data entry personnel (or read with a scanner) as audit confirmation.

If the new location is not to be controlled and parts are to be placed randomly, or possibly within zones or commodity groups and classes, then only the parts that are going to a special area need to be tagged. Once all parts are moved into the new location, inventory teams must go to each bin and record the stock number, validate the part description against that stock number, count the quantity, and enter it into the record.

Bar code and other identification technologies

Bar code for part identification is a technology whose time has finally come. The methodology has been available for decades, but service organizations are only recently utilizing the

Figure 14-5
Bar code used by 3M and UPS

improved capabilities it brings to part identification. Typical bar code labels are shown on a package in Figure 14-5. One label on the box of parts was applied by 3M when they processed the order. The other label is the "UPS Deliverytrac II" identification number which allows real time status of the delivery to be followed. The labels may be prepared by relatively inexpensive printers on adhesive label stock, and then stuck to the part bin and onto packaging. This type of label is similar to the Universal Product Code (UPC) label that is familiar to anyone who buys groceries in a modern supermarket where the checkout person passes the bar code across the reader and sees the computer-translated name and price appear on the screen. The U.S. Department of Defense, Ford, General Motors, Sears, and Wal-Mart now require all suppliers to label their packages with bar code descriptions.

The bar code is typically read in a service parts situation by use of a portable wand reader/recorder. The bar code is recorded in digital format that can be later transmitted via telephone modem or tape or radio to the central computer. Obviously, the error rate is reduced and speed is increased over what is possible by writing and/or key entry of data. So called 2-D PDF symbology is becoming available which can contain about 100 times more data than the linear labels illustrated.

Optical character reading (OCR), optical memory, magnetic strip, holograms, and both passive and active radio frequency (RF) devices are also used for part identification. The military had problems in Desert Storm when large cargo containers were off-loaded from planes and ships and they could not find out, without opening each one, which held clothes, or food, or missile parts. Maintenance people needed to know which container held the critical parts that had fighter aircraft grounded. Now those containers wear an integrated circuit package that will transmit the detailed list of contents when it is queried by a proper scanner. Automatic identification now tags cars, convicts, livestock, medicines, and service parts for rapid, accurate identity.

15 *FIELD STOCK OPERATIONS*

$\mathbb{F}$ield inventories are referred to as *retail* stocks, as contrasted to the *wholesale* stocks held in the central warehouse. Parts should be held in the field only if justified by rapid restoration requirement, frequent need, relatively low cost, high essentiality, and positive tradeoff of parts costs versus labor. This differs with years past when most parts were carried by technicians in their vehicles. Today, resistors, capacitors, oscilloscopes, and soldering irons have been generally replaced by very expensive, fragile integrated circuit cards. The cost of individual parts is much higher and failure rates are lower, so fewer replacements are required. These and other factors lead to the consolidation of parts to a central location where they can be found in a hurry, and then transportation means exist that can get them quickly to where they are needed. The key is to rapidly get your hands on the parts.

Information should be centrally known on parts availability at every level of an organization. One company that produces and services products for the banking industry had three regional distribution centers across the United States and local inventories, as well as the headquarters central stock. By gradually eliminating the regional centers and consolidating inventories, it saved over $1.5 million and is actually providing a higher level of customer service. Inventory shrinkage that was $300,000 is now reported to be only $6,000. A major computer company has consolidated inventories into about 75 clusters across the United States and reports significantly better performance than with the previous large numbers of parts at sites and riding with field engineers. Of course, these decisions require balancing investment, handling, transportation, labor, and other logistics costs against field effort and customer satisfaction.

These issues pivot on confidence. If people in the field have confidence that they can get the parts quickly from the central location, then they won't try to keep so many caches of parts in their own possession.

Responsibility and accountability

A single person should be responsible for every stock of parts. Team responsibility rarely works. Too often, people rush into a stock room, grab a part, and depart in a hurry without any evidence that they took the part. Later, another person sees that the information system shows the part is available so he drives across town only to find the expected part is not in stock. (You pay for control over parts whether you have it or not.) Team parts stocks are fine, if justified by modeling, but one person must be in charge and should assure that everyone follows the rules. As ex-Army officers, the authors remember signing for every important item of equipment their unit had, with the expectation that if any vehicle or weapon or radio were lost, then the officer in charge would be expected to pay for it. In turn, that responsibility was passed on to the subordinates who controlled each property asset. Even in our rapidly changing world of service parts, that is still a workable concept.

Field technicians' job descriptions should include accountability for parts, rapid return of excess and defectives, and immediate reporting of part use or movement. Field managers must inspect what they expect. Frequent checks of vehicles and stock locations are necessary to validate the contents and assure proper care of parts. Since field managers these days have span of control that is often 25 to 30 technicians, traveling together to accounts happens only a few times a year. Make the most of those events. One vital inspection is to inventory the technician's parts against his authorized stock list (ASL). He should possess no more and no fewer parts, except for special orders to unique equipment and replacement parts already on order As discussed in chapter 9, the ASL is agreed to by the technician and his manager, and then forms the firm specification for what parts and how many are carried. Ordering replacement parts is simplified with an ASL because when an ASL part is reported as used the system automatically orders the replacement. The technician does not have to perform any additional steps to obtain the replacement.

Stock locations

Rapid restoration is a major reason for stocking parts close to the point of need. Figure 15-1 shows the typical number of locations required to provide specified delivery times. Note that these times are the hours required to get a part on site after the order is placed. If help desk diagnostics are accurate and part needs can be identified over the phone, and response or restoration entitlement is for the next day, then the part can be scheduled to meet the technician where the technician desires. When restoration is required today, the scenario often finds that additional service call time is used to get the technician on site, diagnose the problem, determine need for a part, identify the part number required, and place the order. Those elements often eat two hours of a four-hour restore requirement, leaving only two hours to get the part on site and into the equipment.

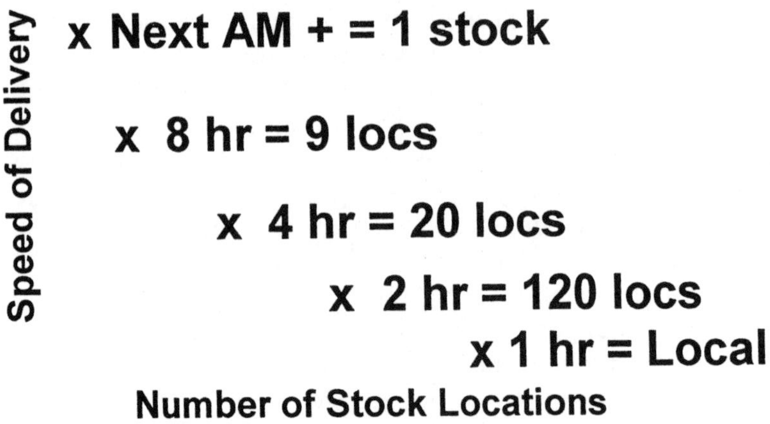

Speed of Delivery

x Next AM + = 1 stock

x 8 hr = 9 locs

x 4 hr = 20 locs

x 2 hr = 120 locs

x 1 hr = Local

Number of Stock Locations

FIGURE 15-1

Faster delivery needs more, closer stock locations

Ship direct

Whenever possible, parts should be supplied direct from vendors to the point of need. The only justification for owning parts and stocking them in your own facility is if that can be done at lower cost and is necessary to provide the required level of service. Certainly security issues and related concerns may require internal control, but even those can often be handled as well, or better, by specialist suppliers. Proprietary parts will normally be kept inhouse, though even those legacy parts may well be handled through external physical distribution channels. A key point is to eliminate unnecessary movement and especially collecting points. Any time a package has to be transferred to another vehicle or held until a complete pallet is packed or a full truck load gathered, time is lost and revenue money is often lost with it.

Most parts suppliers are equipped to ship parts directly to a technician within a few minutes of order receipt. They will ship by whatever means you specify. Their overnight transport service is probably the same as yours.

Advance exchange of repairable parts is standard procedure. This means that the supplier will ship the good part you need instantly, and your people return the defective part within about a week. Actually the allowable time from many suppliers is up to 30 days, which is judged too long. If the defective core is returned, then you are billed at a credit rate, often about 50 percent of new. If the core is not returned within the specified time, then you will be billed the full new part price. (Return of repairables is discussed further in chapter 21.)

Vehicle stocks

Personal stocks of parts are often referred to as van stocks, car stocks, or locker stocks; depending on the mode of transport. Locker stocks are common in metropolitan areas where technicians must travel by foot, bus, subway, or taxi and can not easily carry many parts. Customers in those territories often donate locker space for parts, knowing that they benefit by having parts close in case of need. All of these refer to the basic parts that a tech should have available for every service call. One group of parts are the frequently used, low cost common hardware and expendable items. Fuses, nuts, terminal connectors, air filters, and cleaning materials are typical expendables. Most companies set a dollar limit such as under $25 and expense those parts when they are shipped to a technician. Generally, no further inventory accountability is required because the cost of control would be greater than the cost of accounting for the item.

Do note that return of excess good expendable parts should be encouraged. For example, several companies who were observed with big stocks of expendable parts in field locations, responded to query, that the field people wanted to return the expendable parts but the accountants allegedly would not allow it! When the error of their way was made clear to the accountants, a few thousand dollars from each of over 100 locations added up to real profit.

The other group of parts is the expensive, durable, generally repairable, SKUs. These are the parts that should be centralized whenever possible. Analysis should be done for every potential ASL part to evaluate the cost of carrying the part versus the cost of not carrying it. (That logistics business model logic is covered in chapter 28.)

A rule of thumb for organizations without computer modeling capability is to allow a technician to carry parts that he uses at least once every three months. This will result in turns of four times a year, which is good for most service organizations. The three month rule is easy to check. You can use the computer to list all parts used in the last three months, and then identify any stocked part that was not on that list. There may be reasons to keep highly essential, low cost parts that have high probability of use in the near future; but examine those desires closely. If a part has not been used in the last three months then it should be returned to the central warehouse. As mentioned earlier, if the central warehouse has a part on the shelf and will ship it immediately, then confidence of field people will lead them to return excess parts. Low confidence in central support drives high field stocks. Figure 15-2 shows the sequence of steps and stock locations necessary for various times to acquire parts. The abbreviation *Suplr* stands for a third or forth party parts supplier who specializes in providing service parts to many organizations. *Source* can mean the original equipment manufacturer (OEM), importer, distributor, producer, or whomever is the authorized available root source for the item.

City, metro, and region stocks

When parts are justified in a geographical territory, but can be shared among a group of technicians, rather than being carried by everyone, a convenient location may be selected for the parts. This facility should be run by a captive organization only if it supports a very high traffic volume. It is better to use stocking courier companies such as ADL, Choice Logistics, and SonicAir both to stock the parts in their facilities and to transport them rapidly to points of need. Effort should be made to concentrate technician's attention to the customer and equipment, rather than on chasing parts. Let the courier or taxi or messenger service deliver the part to the technician. Do model and direct the locations where a courier should hold the parts, consistent with required delivery times and costs. Most stocking couriers are willing to open locations beyond their standard list, where justified by profitable business. Geomapping software using installed equipment locations can determine the

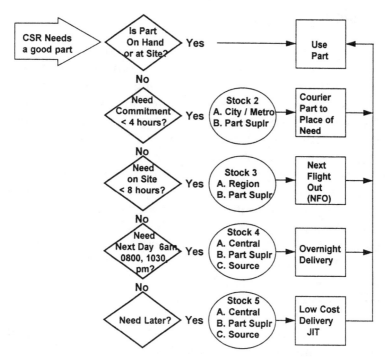

FIGURE 15-2
If parts are needed fast they must be stocked close

optimum locations for stocking facilities. Most important is the ability to get parts to the requiring location rapidly in order to avoid labor delays and nonproductive downtime while waiting for parts.

Getting the ordered part directly into the hands of the requesting technician is a challenge. If a part is delivered to a hospital loading dock or a business reception area, that may be the equivalent of sending it into a black hole in space. Parts have been known to enter such facilities and never be seen again. Two way radio and cellular communications between delivery persons and technicians have been tried with little success although the concept has excellent merit. It remains under-used after several years of availability. Most courier services and even UPS will deliver parts to a technician's home or parked vehicle, leaving the new parts as well as picking up any returning parts. That fail-safe delivery service relieves technicians of travel and inconvenience of returning defectives and excess.

Physical layout

We have all probably seen vans that look inside like a trash dumpster. Technicians with slovenly loading, little organization, and dirty vehicles will not last long as service providers. Careless habits do not support service success. Vans should have racks installed on which the packaged parts can be neatly organized. Tool cases should be kept near the door so they can be removed to carry at any call. Heavy parts should be kept low and secured so they do not move during sharp turns or sudden stops. Lighter boxes should be braced or bungee corded so they do not fly around in traffic. All parts should stay in protective packaging until on site. Typically the packaging for the new part should be used to protect the defective replaced part during return. Technicians should be trained to treat defective parts physically as carefully as new good parts, so that further damage is not caused during transport.

In parts lockers and closets that may be located on a customer's premises, parts should be ordered by part number or commodity. If direct viewing of parts or part numbers on boxes is not possible, then a list should be posted for easy determination of available parts. Defective parts should never be retained. Too often, technicians say that they would rather have a questionable part than none at all. That is dubious logic. Push your people to return any defective, excess, or questionable part so that it can be repaired and quality certified for service use. If parts are used as diagnostic tools, the using technician should be empowered to mark the part package as either good for future use or to be tested. Responsible technicians will assure to the best of their ability that a part is a good part. Requiring the technician to seal the package and sign his name on the seal helps personalize responsibility.

In most small stockrooms it is easy for a human who has a part to store to assign its location to the first vacant rack. There may be a general area for standard normally stocked parts and a separate section for those special ordered direct to projects. Usually the stockkeeper looking for a place to put a new part merely starts at bin 1A and walks down the shelf area until a vacant spot is found, places the part in that bin location, and notes the identifier for stockkeeping records. If the part is already stocked, the receipt stock slip or scanner screen should show the bin where the new quantities are to be put. Visual layouts of parts such as V-belts and gaskets can be hung on peg boards. A physical reminder of when to reorder common parts can be maintained by a card punched and placed in the line of parts at the reorder point. Thus if the computer does not pick up the need to reorder because someone forgot to record the taking of a part, then the physical card will remind the computer to get current and place the order.

Parts for unique equipment

Special parts which are used only on specific equipment should be stored near that equipment. Remember that we said central information should be maintained for all parts, but all parts do not have to be physically at a single central location. The Part Availability information may show that a part is sourced directly from a supplier like Service Electronics, or perhaps the part is located at the Choice Logistics facility in downtown Manhattan.

Physical security

It should be no surprise that parts for open computer systems are often lost, strayed, stolen or otherwise disappear from inventory. The problem was bad enough with proprietary systems when parts were stolen. Now both the supply and the demand are greater with the proliferation of PCs. Of course, none of your technicians would ever do a Saturday afternoon repair job for a friend and use your parts without paying you for them. It's only other peoples' technicians who record parts use against a service contract when the part went into a T&M machine. A complete microcomputer can be created part-by-part "off the books."

One client, desiring to provide a high level of customer support, provided 25 loaner high resolution display terminals to their field districts. At physical inventory time, 11 of them could not be found! Most have been recovered from personal systems, and other locations, but the example remains. One major third party service organization presently has an $11 million shortage variance in their physical inventory. Much of the problem is in missing or erroneous transactions, but some parts are undoubtedly missing. Heads have already rolled over that problem.

Parts security is a problem! You are going to pay for security whether you have it or not. In most cases, you can pay a little now or a lot later. Like many things in our society, even if you are not immediately affected, you should be aware of preventive measures and solutions so you do not become part of the problem. There is a mix of concerns here. One is ethics and honesty. Another is responsibility. Add in overt stealing, ease of access, lack of controls, low accountability, labor-intensive, paper-based, time-delayed systems, low priority attention, uncontrolled stocks, "every body does it" attitudes, annual audits instead of routine cycle counts, and it is easy to see how shortages occur.

How, then do we eliminate covert and overt shrink? The focus should be to let everyone know that they are responsible for inventory in their domain, and then hold them accountable. Conduct regular physical audits to assure that the computerized inventory is correct. Provide timely, accurate information so that every person can keep his parts information up to date. Analyze special orders to make sure those parts are going to legitimate business uses. Compare parts usage across technicians and analyze the causes of high use rates (technicians may need remedial training in diagnostics and repair). Physically destroy any parts headed to scrap. Have a security expert conduct an audit of warehouse and stock facility procedures. Validate a sample of outbound shipments to assure that all FedEx and UPS boxes are going to legitimate technicians and customers for authorized purposes. Confront and strongly discipline any person who steals parts for their personal gain. If people know that managers are watching and are serious about enforcing accurate, legitimate uses of parts, then everyone involved will likely provide high security for parts in their possession.

Serial number control and expensive parts

Management must balance the benefit of controls against the aggravation and financial costs. Like most service items, management attention and discipline must be number one on the list of controls. Serial number control at the field level is even more time consuming and error prone than it is in a central facility. Do not track serial numbers for field parts unless you absolutely must! If you must, then assure that field technicians have automatic identification devices such as bar code scanners. Management attention, discipline, and responsible people will achieve more that serial numbers to encourage positive inventory control.

16 *INTEGRATING PARTS IN THE TOTAL SERVICE PROCESS*

S ervice parts have influence across the entire spectrum of service, and are in turn influenced by many other functions. Studies have been done by the Boeing Commercial Aircraft Company, FMC, Xerox, and other high technology equipment producers which show that 90+ percent of life cycle maintenance costs are determined by the time a product goes into production. This is because the alternatives have been locked-in, configurations are frozen, parts are imbedded in the maintenance concepts (if such detailed planning were done), component reliability is set, and the service path is established. Thus, it makes considerable sense for management to involve logistics in the earliest stages of product development to do the job right the first time. By now many readers are saying, "But I have no chance to influence the products I must support." That is true in more and more products as systems become less proprietary and more open. Do note that the 5 to 10 percent of remaining maintenance life cycle costs are still very big dollars, plus those cost analyses are targeted at only the preventive maintenance and repair business. The other 85 percent of costs over a typical product's life for moves, upgrades, new applications, training, backups, disaster recovery, etc., offer major opportunities for support, and involve parts. Disks, manuals, training programs and similar items; (whether physical, optical, or electronic) require the same management techniques that are effective for physical service parts. Our studies, backed up by others, show that the lifetime costs of a business computer will average at least seven times more than its purchase price.

Affect on uptime

The measurable numeric affect of parts on product uptime, as well as on response, restoration, profitability, and other parameters, is illustrated in Figure 16-1. This copy of a screen from a Patton Consultant's personal computer model displays the choices an analyst can make and what the results will be. This logistics tool enables What if? evaluations of higher percentages of phone call clearance, shorter travel time, reduced diagnostics, faster fixes, centralizing parts instead of stocking locally, and many other tradeoffs. Managers' eyes open wide when they see calculations for contract profitability. Obviously, this is a top level model that requires a buildup of details. In the total picture, it is quickly shown how important various factors are, including parts frequency of need, availability, delivery time, and cost.

How logistics is often victimized

A high First Call Fix Rate depends on five steps:

- Knowing what equipment is defective

```
=====================================================================
              U P T I M E     A N A L Y S I S

Annual Contract Fee      $   4500.00   Phone Clear Time:      0.50
Phone Clear Percentage   %     20.00   Dispatch Time    :     0.25
Mean Time Between Service:   2200.00   Travel Time      :     1.00
                 (hours)               Diagnostic Time  :     1.00
Equipment Down Percentage%     80.00   Fix Time         :     0.50

Logistics Percentage     %     80.00   Loaded Labor Cost$    87.50
Logistics Cost per Event $    700.00
Logistics Level / Fill Rate / Time     Call Back Percentages:
       Level 1       85.00%    0.25 Hrs First Call Clears  %  85.00
             2       10.00    24.00   Second Call Clear  %  10.00
             3        5.00    48.00   Third Call Clear   %   5.00
_____

Response Time     :    1.00 Hrs    Uptime          %      99.56
Repair Time       :    1.20
Logistics Time    :    4.01        Contract Profit $    2280.22
Call Back Time    :    5.73
Average Down Time :   12.04        Profitability  %      50.67
=====================================================================
```

FIGURE 16-1
Logistics has major influence on uptime

- Diagnosing to the problem component
- Recognizing probable defective parts
- Identifying the correct replacement parts
- Supplying those good parts to the point of need

These steps are imbedded in Figures 16-2 and 16-3. (See pp 254–255) The first of these illustrates the interactions from the time a customer calls for help until satisfied. The second figure shows the steps necessary for closing the call, returning parts, and entering information to improve future service.

If a failure occurs in any of those steps, then service parts is usually blamed since they are last on the list. (After all, parts are unfeeling, inanimate objects and we humans never make mistakes, so it must be the fault of parts.) The foundation to effective support is knowing what equipment is to be supported. This requires an accurate database of installed assets.

Good business practice requires that a service organization and the client know what assets are being supported. The client needs to know for legal accountability that the money being paid for service is correct. The client also needs assurance that all software is licensed and has security controls. The service supplier needs to know in order to have the correct parts when and where needed, and to charge the correct amount for service. Too many contracts are assumed knowing only that there

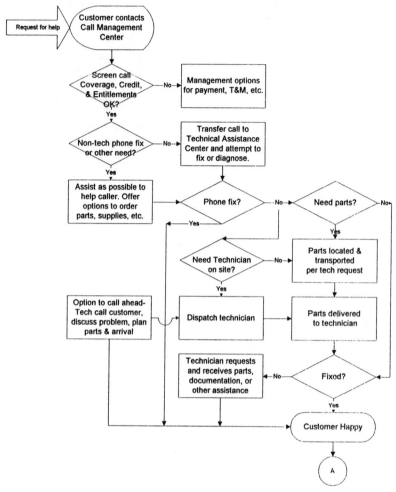

FIGURE 16-2
Parts are integral to customer satisfaction

are "about 300 486's, 500 pentiums, 150 laptops, 200 laser printers, and a few pieces of odd stuff." That is a prescription for win-lose. The customers usually win because they get free service on many products that the servicer is not billing for. The servicers lose revenue (actually direct profits) even though they did the work.

Service planning for both parts and labor requires knowing the brand, technology, and size of components; for example, Compaq ProLinea, P5, 1 Gb hard drive, 28.8 modem, 15 inch

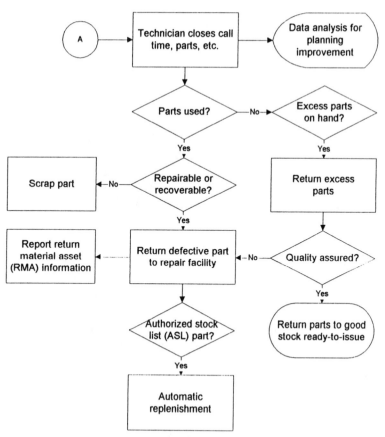

FIGURE 16-3
The call is not complete until returns and reporting are done

.28 SVGA monitor, and HP LaserJet 3P. We will not worry about the motherboard clock speed, but we need to know that it is a Pentium versus 386, 486, P6, or something else. The disk will probably be classified as "mid size" and we could substitute a 1.2, 1.4 or similar size for the 1.0 Gb. We would need to stock either the exact modem or a interchangeable model. The monitor can probably be replaced by one of many similar products, if the contract specifies generic replacement with comparable form, fit, and function. That means that a component need not be the identical logo item, so long as it works just as well. That is a sticking point with some customers who want the keyboard or monitor to look identical, down to the logo. These configuration identities are necessary to quote a fair price, to determine if we have parts already on hand to fix the equipment when it breaks, and to determine what additional arrangements must be made to acquire parts or to arrange to get them as needed.

Sales should be charged with providing an accurate installed base before a contract can become effective. Service may agree to start support based on a rate, with the proviso that the accurate asset list will be available within 30 days. Many companies require that the servicer's control tag be put on every contracted machine, preferably across a cover joint or screw that if opened would destroy the tag. This prevents defective parts from non-contract equipment being exchanged for good components in contracted gear. A better answer is to require all equipment at a site to be on contract. (Even then, defective parts from home computers mysteriously find their way into covered machines.)

Keeping the information up to date is a major challenge. Every service call should validate the equipment record and update it as necessary. New installations and moves performed by company technicians should update the information system. Require that the customer's purchasing people send electronic copies of equipment receipts for entry and addition to billing. At least annually, require an updated list of equipment in electronic form that can update your records. Such asset inventory activity costs money, but it is worth far more money than it costs.

Promote similarity

Where you have influence, push for your customers to purchase similar equipment. The advantages are great in set up, software, training, backup, diagnostics, technician skills, speed of repairs, and parts investment. (Certainly the seven times lifetime cost reduces to four or five times, which equates to many thousands of dollars.) Work with Purchasing to get good deals on preferred products, and publicize the advantages to everyone who might need to procure new equipment. From the service sales perspective, develop a list of:

a. Preferred products that we want to service

b. Products that we will service, but at increased remuneration

c. Products that we will not service, except under extreme need and high reward

Candidate equipment should be placed on each list based on the factors mentioned previously plus consideration for the product density necessary for economies of scale and potential profit. Assure that all elements are considered. (One-of-a-kind expediting can take a lot of time and effort.) Stimulate sales people to promote the "A" list products and avoid the rest, except at additional charge. Standardization goes a long way toward enhancing satisfaction and profit in equipment service.

Sell next-day service

Sales people should be educated and disciplined to understand that same-day response time will cost much more for parts and labor than if the call could be handled tomorrow morning. As detailed in chapter 15, the faster parts must be available, and the more parts must be purchased (instead of exchanged) and the closer they must be stored to the account. Those elements add significantly to cost. If the requirement is for same-day service, then the additional money charged should be allocated about equally to parts and to labor operations.

Expectations must be matched with entitlement. If customers are paying for 24 hour restore, then they should be held to that, except under special circumstances. They can always agree to T&M help at higher cost if they need immediate support. If we can identify required parts and order them from our central warehouse, from an independent parts supplier, or as advance exchange for a warranty repair, then the parts will cost far less than if we had to stock them with every technician. A call management center phone helper can set the expectation level by saying, "I see that you are contracted for 24 hour response, could John Tech have access to the equipment tomorrow about 11 am?"

If parts are not on hand then assure that they are available and know the expected delivery time before committing to technician arrival and restore times. There is little use in sending a technician on site without a must-have part, except to stop the clock on physical response time. Customers quickly tire of technicians arriving only to say, "Now I have to go get a switch." That is also very expensive and wasteful for the service organization, and frustrates technicians. (Was service parts at fault? No, they are being blamed for process failures.)

Parts used as diagnostic tools

As many as two of every three service parts ordered or installed, are unnecessary! Experience shows that service organizations must invest significant dollars in replacement parts to make up for deficiencies in diagnostics, training, discipline, quality and confidence. There are situations where customer engineers order parts before they even talk to the customer about a problem which could involve several different modules. These same people often "shotgun" repairs by installing several parts, and then claim that this haphazard replacement is necessary to quickly restore equipment to operational status. Unfortunately, then the replaced parts are returned for repair with often inadequate documentation about the condition under which they may, (or may not) have failed. This results in no trouble found (NTF) rates often 30 to 50 percent.

If the return and repair cycle is slow, then as many as 30 percent more parts must be purchased to cover the slow, often erroneous, returns. Cycling good parts through the logistics pipeline wastes investment dollars and hinders field support. Design for serviceability is basic. Many cases are noted where a few dollars spent on diagnostics could save many times that expense in parts investment and in customer satisfaction.

Technicians often claim that they need to carry a part for use as a diagnostic tool. Logic, however, says that if a part rarely fails then it is not needed as a diagnostic tool. Logic and reality are frequently different when it comes to technicians. One way to convince technicians that a part is not needed for diagnostic purposes is to track the failure rate of those parts and also determine if those parts returned for repair were really defective. When confronted with facts, most technicians turn in their tool parts.

If a part is required as a diagnostic tool, add a flag to the master part record related to the product it is required to test. Then, that part should be added to the ASL if the technician services even one of those products. That added part will cost money. When you calculate the total costs of putting parts with every product technician, you might find it less expensive to commission the design of a diagnostic tool or software to examine the defect.

Right part

Many times a technician will locate the defective part in a machine and have the part in his hand, but not see any identifying numbers or know more than a general description of the part. This function of part identification is best done by a small technical group who has computer, microfiche, and paper documentation of every product known to be supported. Remember that if the product is not in our installed base, we probably do not have adequate documentation. Good relationships with original manufacturers and distributors is a big help. Changes occur so quickly that the best information usually comes direct from the source. Independent parts suppliers may also help since they gather information about part demands from across the service industry. The Part Master record is another aid. It should contain noun nomenclature descriptions that can be searched on key words to find substitute components. Note that the database will have information about parts we do not stock but can obtain from independent parts suppliers, if we plan for them or have ever used them before. When the part number is known, the part can usually be quickly ordered.

Right place

The next challenge is getting the part into the technician's hands. Logistics should deliver the parts to the technician rather than requiring the technician to chase parts. It is recommended that every technician have a standard method of delivery. This might be Airborne leaving the part in the front left corner of his garage, FedEx dropping parts in the branch office, or UPS/SonicAir arranging by wireless communications to meet and hand over the part in the customer's lobby. Whatever the transportation, it should be direct from the supplier to the technician. Do not arrange for parts shipments to go to a company warehouse if you can avoid it. Staging packages anywhere takes time and costs money. Ship direct. The return of defective or excess parts carries the same message. Return direct.

One client's control process mandated a consolidation point to assure that parts due in were, in fact, received. The collecting point looked like the scene from *Raiders of the Lost Ark* where the box containing the ark was wheeled into a cavernous warehouse containing many similar boxes. Just getting a part out of that facility and into repair averaged 15 days!

Control is not improved by collecting things under your auspices before sending them to repair or back to good stocks. If 30 percent of all the parts collecting are really good, they are just wasting time and money sitting there when they could be put to good use. Control is probably better for parts sent direct to independent repair vendors, since they have to report accurately to realize their revenue.

Low-tech swap out

If a part or equipment is needed and the customer can safely exchange or install it himself, let him be part of the solution. Customers like to participate in fixing products, especially if they can do it faster than your technician can arrive. Gateway 2000 and other mail order computer sellers handle most of their parts by sending them direct to customers. Whole unit replacements are typical for monitors, but assemblies and integrated circuit cards will be FRUs in a CPU if the customer can safely replace them. Instructions are complete and oriented to the abilities of the lowest skilled user. The packaging can be reused to return the replaced part or equipment. The UPS label is enclosed. The customer is clearly notified that the exchanged part must be returned within two weeks, or else the full charge for a new part will be levied against the customer's credit card.

If the customer is not willing or able to replace parts himself, perhaps a courier can be trained to do simple tasks. Most courier operations are busy early in the morning and late in the afternoon, but have time available in midday when they could handle plug-and-play items. Fax machines, speaker systems, telephone answering machines, and laser cartridges are just a few of the parts or equipment they can deliver and install. The cost for such effort can be much lower if done by courier personnel than if by highly qualified technicians. Likewise, it may be possible at even lower cost to hire trade school students part-time to do minor equipment modifications and standard part changes, where parts stocking and transport is a minor factor.

Pipeline demonstration

The four pipelines—procurement, field replenishment, field return, and repair—are the inventory in motion. Many inventory control systems count static parts as well and forget that most service parts activity is parts in motion. For example, if field return of defective parts averages 7 days, but has a standard deviation of 12 days and a 98 percentile of 42 days, that information tells us that most technicians are returning parts promptly, within a week, but a few are taking six weeks! Those few laggards should be identified and helped to realize the time-value of expensive assets.

Figure 16-4 demonstrates the financial influence of various combinations of pipeline measures. This is a micro computer-based model that can be very effective to show the relationships between variables and to stimulate improvement based on real numbers.

```
=====================================================================
          P I P E L I N E     D E M O N S T R A T I O N
```

Demands / Year	:	20	Washout Rate %	:	10
Unit Cost $	:	650.00	Procurement Cycle Time	:	21
Deviation in Days			Deviation in		
Between Demands:		9	Procurement Cycle	:	4
Ordering Costs $	:	150.00	Field Sites	:	50
Carrying Cost %	:	30	Repair Cost %	:	20
Repair Cycle Time	:	14	Return Cycle Time	:	14
Deviation in Repair			Deviation in Return		
Cycle Time	:	3	Cycle Time	:	5

		Quantity	Investment	Annual Cost
Administration	:			2685.
Average On Hand	:	5	3250.	
Procurement Pipeline	:	1	650.	1300.
Repair Pipeline	:	4	2600.	2340.
Field Supply Pipeline	:	0	0.	
Defective Return Pipeline:		1	650.	
Totals		11	$ 7150.	6325.

```
=====================================================================
```

FIGURE 16-4

Computer models enable rapid analysis of pipeline changes

17 *VALUING SERVICE PARTS*

$\mathbb{T}$his chapter addresses how to improve several major deficiencies in common practice for service parts valuation. One deficiency is failure to keep current costs up (or more accurately, *down*) with "lower of cost or market." Several service companies have been involved in mergers or acquisitions where the service parts assets were greatly overvalued. A second need is to use *Next Cost* for logistics evaluations. A third challenge is to include acquisition and carrying costs in the true cost. Methods are described for depreciation and matching write-downs with the related parts usage, as are valuation methods for parts obtained in special deals or from de-manufacture.

Challenges of true value

Many companies with inventories of service parts are significantly out of touch with reality regarding the true value of those inventories. Life cycles of durable products have become much shorter than in past years. Products are designed in less than a year, produced for a few months, and are rapidly made obsolete by following generations of products. Proprietary products are replaced by open, multivendor systems. While modern products generally provide more capability in smaller packages, they are typically very reliable. However, everything will fail sometime. When these high-tech products fail, the exact repair part must be rapidly provided.

A financial challenge with service parts is to maintain book value at the generally accepted accounting practice (GAAP) "lower of cost or market." These parts typically decrease in value over time and product phases. *Open systems* means parts that are in common use, are not OEM proprietary and are, (after initial product introduction), available from many new and repair sources. Personal computer parts from Apple, AST, Compaq, Hewlett Packard, and IBM are typical items. The products assembled into integrated systems will normally come from different vendors, hence the term *multivendor*. Obsolescence is the major cause of declining value, driven by rapid development of new products, multiple variations of configurations, rapidly dropping hardware prices, and capabilities to repair parts at lower cost than new procurement.

The objectives for accurate evaluation are:

1. Enable calculation of accurate profit
2. Satisfy balance sheet requirements to auditors and bankers
3. Know asset value as a major, tangible portion of company worth
4. Minimize taxes
5. Stimulate Service to repair or purchase parts cost-effectively.

Standard, FIFO, LIFO, specific and average

The manufacturing heritage of many companies leads to service parts being initially valued at standard cost. Companies usually carry a variance account for a year and then revalue parts once a year. While this is reasonably accurate for new product parts in their early life, it quickly falls behind reality. As parts are recycled through repair and become available from de-manufacture, trade-ins, and other external sources, the standard cost is often blindly used for pricing and evaluations without consideration for the large related variance account. Standard cost in a part database often lags falling real costs.

First-in First-Out (FIFO) is used to keep physical stocks moving, but is not often used for accounting. Last-In First-Out (LIFO) gives more accurate valuation in these times of inflation. At least LIFO means that the cost of the last part purchased is listed in the master record. Even that last purchase may not accurately represent either all the parts in stock or the cost of procuring the next needed part. Watch out for FISH. That stands for First-in Still-Here.

Specific cost is tied to individual parts, which must have a serial number or other means of unique identification. For parts of a nuclear reactor or an airliner, where serial number tracking is a normal requirement, specific costing can go along with little penalty. Serial number tracking is an expensive control, that should not be done except to meet specific quality or legal requirements. Resist specific costing for financial reasons alone. Where there are quantities of the same SKU, the parts should be grouped into age strata for financial purposes.

Average cost is the recommended costing method for service parts. The calculation is simply the total cost of all the parts divided by the quantity of parts. During the early stages of a product's life, all the costing methods will be about the same. However, average costing more accurately represents the real world costs over the long haul. For example, let's start with three parts that cost $1,000 each, for a total cost of $3,000. A salesperson negotiates a trade-in that nets us two more good parts that carry a cost of $500 each. We now have five good parts that cost a total of $4,000. $4,000/5 = $800 cost per part, which is what our database should now show.

Do note that, while these costs fairly represent the book values of the actual parts in inventory, they may not keep up with either repair technology or the external market place. Both those factors often cause future parts costs to be lower. Thus, we should consider writing down the values of these assets to keep pace with their true market value. Similarly, we should be aware of the true next cost of those parts so that we can do accurate evaluations. For example, you might consider buying a new piece of test equipment for the repair center. Based on the standard cost of a part, the proposed purchase might have high payback. However, if you can now buy as many as you need of that same part for less than half of what it cost new three months ago, your decision may better be to buy all new parts and not repair any.

Reserves

Realizing that money must be planned to cover scrap, obsolescence, and other write-downs, each year's budget should have a line for Parts Reserves. Depreciation and other write-downs are classed as expense. Since Revenue − Expense = Profit, the expense dollars are carefully minimized. That often leads to controllers saying, "Sorry, I know that you need to get rid of those parts, but we just can not afford the expense right now." Unfortunately, a really good time may never come. Planning with reserves provides the necessary foundation.

Routine write-offs is good in theory. In practice, some products do not sell as well as forecast, so manufacturing has extra parts and service has extra parts. Other products are more reliable than predicted, so service parts are not used. Short response time requirements or anticipated high failure rates may necessitate parts located in many stocks within a short delivery time of the potential users. Many other service situations also result in extra parts. The service parts business can rarely use just-in-time techniques, since service parts must be available just-in-case.

You may ask, "Why not just keep all the parts in case they are ever needed?" You are probably aware of the Murphy's Law which says that as soon as we scrap the part it will be needed. Risk is an everyday companion of service parts managers. So are the economic costs of holding parts. These carrying costs should be accurately determined by every service company since they are a major factor in scientific parts management.

Costs for space, utilities, security, personnel, insurance, taxes, MIS, and the cost of money are typically about 30%. That means that the expense associated with having a $1,000 part on the shelf is about $300 per year, whether you use it or not. That is expensive availability insurance. Of course, if you don't have the part when it is needed to fix a down customer machine, then the pain is even greater!

Depreciation

Many service companies depreciate parts over time related to the expected service life of the products on which those parts are used. This can be as short as 18 months for very short-lived products, and is now typically 36 months. On the other hard, hospital sterilizers and similar long-lived equipment with little anticipated change may use seven year depreciation. Five years is typical. This translates in practical terms to expensing 1/60 of the part's cost each month over the five year (60 month) life. Internal Revenue Service (IRS) regulations state that depreciation of parts must be tied to the life of the equipment which those parts are produced to support. Thus, service companies can tie parts depreciation to the life of a service contract, rather than to generic products. Obviously, depreciating parts over a one year contract will result in high expenses. In some cases that can be a sales tool which encourages a customer to a longer contract, since depreciating the same parts over three years will result in about 1/3 lower parts expenses each year. (Note that you must have an accurate record of the installed base of products in order to identify the related parts.)

Accounting would be a major task if this needed to be done for each individual part. Instead, quantities of parts that are acquired during the same month are gathered into a strata, often named for the SKU (stockkeeping unit) and month. For example, the group might be identified as "Part 1234, 7/99." If that strata has an original cost of $6,000, then 1/60 ($100) is expensed each following month. The value of those parts is then $5,900 in August 1999; $5,800 in September, etc. The book value should translate to each individual part. Thus, if the $6,000 were composed of six parts each initially costing $1,000, the second month each part is valued at $983.33.

Another approach, that can be used also on proprietary parts, is to base write-down on usage. Rules used by several open systems service companies are:

1. If a service part SKU is not used in the previous year, all parts of that SKU will be written off 100%.

2. If there is less use in the past year than on-hand inventory, 50% of the cost will be written off. This should be compared to the value determined in 3 below to assure this is equal or lower.

3. Of the remaining parts with usage, the book value will be maintained at the average cost for which those parts are available in the marketplace.

Another company that Patton Consultants advises uses rules:

1. The next twelve month's projected support revenues are multiplied by 25% to determine the maximum parts investment. Products are grouped by category for effective forecasting, calculating, and management. Investments above this limit are 100% reserved.

2. This analysis is updated monthly to determine the installed base, project annual revenue, and determine inventory investment.

3. Reserves may be established with rates directly matched to the age of the part numbers in the catalog. For example, there would be no reserve for the first twelve months, 33% for the second twelve, 67% for the third twelve months, and 100% thereafter. (Make sure that you keep at least one of any part that you might need in the future.)

Gross, book, and next cost

The initial gross cost of a part starts the parade. Often the initial cost will be significantly higher than the following new or repaired costs for the same SKU. Book value is important since that is the current cost of the part. The selling price of parts is usually based on a multiple of the gross cost. True cost of a part should be based on the book value. Obviously, the higher the selling price and the lower the cost, the greater will be the profit, and the taxes. Taxes are going to cause concern sooner or later. Experience shows that a service business should be managed with emphasis on customer satisfaction and profits, and then figure out the taxes. (If taxes start guiding much of a business, then associates will aim for the wrong targets.)

Note, however, that the Next Price for some parts can be higher. Expect an increase if you have to special order small production quantities of high-end parts, often with retired technology, produced from assembly and test fixtures that are long-since scrapped. Add a field for *Next Cost* to your part master record. That way the accountants can have their data fields and the logisticians will also have their special purpose data fields. *Next Cost* is important for logistics evaluations. For example, life cycle costs and profits should use replacement (next) costs of parts, not necessarily what previous parts cost. This is a critical distinction that many financial evaluations neglect. This concern is closely related to current valuations of existing investments.

Maintaining accurate present values

Several schemes are offered to keep the values of parts close to current market. Note that, due to the effort required, only active A and B class (top usage, unit cost, and essentiality) parts will be kept current. It can be effective to concentrate on the top 10% parts that are the fast-moving SKUs with most affect on the inventory value. A structured FRU (field replaceable unit) process is a major help to minimize SKUs with related reductions in financial investment, procurement, documentation, training, skill requirements, and people costs.

For open systems, several vendors will supply the current prices of common parts on computer disks. Several major repair companies send their disks and software to vendors and get automated quotes for the specific parts and repairs they need.

Other vendors supply paper catalogs. Still others are on-line with bulletin boards and Internet Web pages that show pricing almost up-to-the-minute. Simple programming can retrieve current cost information for your active parts.

Do assure that total procurement costs are considered and prorated across the part units. Time and money are both currencies of the service business. The main reason you invest in parts is to make them available in short response times to needy customers. If response requirements are at least eight hours, then parts can be sent from strategic depots or even a central location. This effectively trades transportation costs for carrying costs. For low use parts, this trade is usually to a company's advantage, especially if the parts are high cost.

The process of entering current prices to the computer system will involve:

1. Part price should calculate as weighted average. The calculation is: Unit Cost = Total Cost/Number of Units. For example, if the part inventory starts with two units that cost $25 each, the calculation is $50/2 = $25 unit cost. If one more unit is acquired at a cost of $16, then the unit cost becomes $66/3 = $22. This weighted averaging helps keep parts costs current, and motivates service procurement of the lowest cost quality part that in turn holds down expenses.

2. The part database software must be modified to accept the *OEM cost* and at least three vendor records that display costs for a part *new, exchange,* and *repair.* The records should include the *name* of each vendor, *vendor part number, date of quotation,* and flag for the *preferred source.* This data should interface with the Vendor Database that has *contact names, phones, fax, address, terms,* etc.

3. When a part is first available, enter the *standard, exchange,* and *repair costs* from the single available source.

4. When a part is available from common sources, those prices should be entered into the computer system. The equations should calculate averages from the one, two, three, or more costs in each category.

5. An automatic report should be generated each time a part cost changes.

In every case, a report should be generated to show accounting exactly which parts will be decreased in value, and by how much. The capability should be automated, with an electronic approval before the master parts records are updated.

Valuing parts from deals and de-manufacture

Whole units can be an effective source of parts. There are initial advantages to cannibalizing parts from whole units:

1. A whole product will cost much less than the sum of its individual parts bought separately.
2. At product introduction, whole units will be more available than specific parts.
3. Parts in whole units are more thoroughly tested since they are proven to operate in a system.
4. Failure rates of specific parts are often not well identified until the product is in field use.
5. If parts are not required, the unit may be sold as an untouched new product.
6. If many different parts are removed as needed, the equipment may be made whole with replacement parts and sold as a refurbished product.

Practical use of de-manufacture means that one or two units of whole equipment should be set aside for initial service use. If a customer's new unit fails, the customer may be offered the choice of exchanging the defective unit for a new one, or the customer's own unit can be repaired with a part from the whole service unit. This allows rapid repairs and high customer satisfaction. After a few weeks, the parts with high failure rates can be identified and ordered as piece parts. The whole unit product can then be used as an internal machine, or sold as a whole unit. A part removed from new equipment should be valued at the OEM piece part cost.

There will be opportunity to reduce service costs by acquiring reduced-cost whole product for its parts value. Costing of cannibalized parts obtained from equipment of reduced value may be done either based on their ratio to list (weighted average) cost, or to percentage of real cost. For example, Sales gives a customer $1,000 trade-in for their 486 PC. $500 (or some agreed-to amount) of that is sales discount. $500 is the value of the PC to Service. Present list cost of the PC is $1,750. What value should be put on the parts? Tables 17-1 and 17-2 show two legitimate approaches.

TABLE 17-1
If you want only a few of the parts, use ratio to list valuation

$500 actual cost / $1750 list cost = .286
Identify the needed parts and their list cost. All else will be disposed. Let's assume that we need the disk drive, controller, and power supply.

Disk drive	$300 × .286 =	$85.71
Controller	$135 × .286 =	38.61
Power supply	45 × .286 =	12.87

$500 cost − $137.19 value = $362.81 expense write-off

TABLE 17-2
Ratio to cost covers the entire value without any writeoff

Disk drive	$300/$480 =	.625 × $500 =	$312.50
Controller	135/ 480 =	.281 × 500 =	140.62
Power Supply	45/ 480 =	.094 × 500 =	46.88
	$480		$500.00

Make sure that you do a "sanity check" to assure that the cost of the parts you need will be less that those parts will cost on the open market.

Support software

The part master database should be developed to show interchangeable and substitutable parts. This will allow use of fewer SKUs that can concentrate on the lowest cost part to meet quality and availability criteria. Weighted average costing should be used as the cost value of parts. This requires the software to have sets of fields for alternate vendors that can supply each part.

The equivalent form, fit, function part, which may in fact be from the same manufacturer, will often be available from several suppliers under their own different part numbers. Add your master, super-part number that the computer assigns randomly. This master part number should be five or six digits (smaller is better, and five digits are 99,999 SKUs), all numeric, no dashes or spaces, no intelligence. The computer's part record will relate this master number to the specific part by:

Noun nomenclature
Product(s) used on
Manufacturer(s)
Manufacturer part number
Vendor(s)
Vendor part number
Commodity code (may help procurement, but not always needed)

Parts should be entered to the master database when a product is shipped.

Special issues

Be aware that not everyone wants to maintain accurate part values. If a company borrows funds based on inventory value, they have a bias toward keeping the perceived inventory value high. A few companies even keep defective parts rather than spending the money to have them repaired, since the parts probably appear to an untrained auditor or banker to be good, and therefore worth full loan value This flaw usually surfaces when a business is acquired and the parts are determined to be of much less value than represented.

Repair only required parts. As part usage declines, keep defective, repairable parts in a separate area. Return them to the OEM for credit as that opportunity presents itself. Keep repairable, defective parts on the books at the same value as good parts, but inventory them separately for physical and financial accountability. Expense the cost of repairs.

Continue to return excess new parts when they are identified as possible excess.

Parts such as modems and memory that are available for Retail sale and also in Service should be stocked only in Retail.

When Service needs those parts they can be purchased from Retail. There should be a cost-plus transfer cost at lower than full retail. Even if Service pays full retail this benefits a company by avoiding the carrying charges on two inventories.

Pay attention to pricing of service repairs so that the value of repair is perceived by a prospect as better than a new product buy. Repair done for out-of-warranty revenue is definitely more profitable than selling new retail product.

18 MARKETING AND PRICING

$\mathbb{Y}$ ou should profit from parts in every way possible. Service strategy must consider that future products will be reliable and therefore will require service less often and will need fewer replacement parts. On the other hand, labor costs are increasing at a faster rate than are parts costs, so both cost containment and speed of repair dictate a movement to parts instead of labor; and when a part is needed, it must often be specifically the exact, expensive part. Also consider that legally you could be forced into expensive litigation if you do not agreeably sell parts to almost anyone who wants to buy them. Charge a fair price for the parts and sell documentation, information, technical assistance, manuals, training, certification, and other related items that are needed for support. These factors should stimulate management attention to the marketing of service parts, and special focus on parts pricing.

275

This section of the handbook is oriented toward persons who must price for selling. This information will also help service managers to understand how pricing structures operate so that better purchases can be negotiated. Cost generally refers to acquisition value. Price generally relates to selling value.

Considerations

Any organization that provides service parts must at least cover the cost of buying those parts and having them ready for their customers, whether these customers are internal or external. The base cost of goods is the build or buy cost of acquiring the parts plus the internal carrying costs plus the costs of direct order entry, picking, packing, transportation, billing, returns, handling, and information. Make sure that your "cost" reflects all these elements. Oftentimes a part will require special handling or expediting charges which should be considered. It is better to address as direct costs those elements that can be pinned to the specific part actions, rather than lumping all logistics costs into one big overhead bin and then sharing the costs equally among parts. Lumped overhead costs are a step better than not knowing at all, but direct costs provide much better management tools.

Most manufacturing functions that produce parts and transfer them internally to service organizations raise the transfer price of those parts above their direct cost to cover overhead and support functions. The amount of that internal transfer markup can be the subject of considerable debate. Many managers feel that interdivisional transfers should not include burden. It is, however, a good way to transfer revenues and profits from one organization to another. Some service organizations that are very profitable shift some of those profits to manufacturing by paying higher transfer prices for parts "bought" from manufacturing.

Try to look at the pricing question from the outside, as through the customers' eyes. Other considerations include alternate sources for the parts, competitors' prices, speed of delivery, expediting cooperation, payment terms, warranty, return policy, packaging compatibility, clarity of information, rapid communications, and responsiveness to special requests. The ultimate pricing criterion is the value of those parts to the user who needs them. Service parts prices are considered elastic, which means that increasing prices will decrease sales, and vice versa.

When you consider the "five rights" of parts, however, if you can provide the right part, at the right place, in the right quality, at the right time, then the definition of right price can be reasonably high and is probably the last deterrent to the sale.

Markup categories

Every service business operated for profit should add a profit contribution margin to the costs. The margins will be greater on some groups and classes of parts than on others. The main markup categories are shown in Table 18-1.

TABLE 18-1
Prices are higher if sources are limited

Category	Markup Multiplier
Proprietary unique	4-7
Modified	2-5
Common/universal/will fit	1-2

The markup multipliers are applied to the standard cost of the part. For example, a unique PWB purchased from manufacturing for $250 (manufacturing cost plus transfer cost) may be priced in the range of $1000–$1750, which is four to seven times the cost.

Proprietary unique parts are those for which an organization owns sole rights to manufacture. The designs may be unique or there may be a special manufacturing process involved. The outside appearance should indicate that these are parts that cannot be easily found in common sources. Electronic modules, specialized castings, and rare materials are often found in this class of parts. It should be noted that software also fits into this category and has many pricing characteristics similar to those of hardware.

Modified parts may look like universal, off-the-shelf items. Because of this, efforts should be made to distinguish them by color, special mountings, and packaging. Differential packaging may include a warning that substituted parts can be less reliable, or even unsafe. A valve with stainless-steel inserts instead of phosphor bronze, or an electronic circuit board with different timing are examples.

Common/universal/will-fit parts include common hardware, batteries, bearings, fuses, inks, toner, switches, and V-belts. Many of these items can be purchased at a hardware store or an electronics hobby shop. These items are usually not durable or repairable, and may be considered consumables and expendables, but service organizations should provide any and all parts that a customer may require. Certainly any of those items that fail while under warranty should be replaced without charge. Equipment serviced under contract should normally provide the parts also. Most customers prefer to buy everything from a single source. Even though the parts costs more, that cost includes ordering, expediting, time delays, and other items that cost the customers added time and money, and detract from their business.

Top management must set policy as to whether an organization will attempt to get all possible parts business, or alternatively will provide all necessary assistance to customers so that they can get their own parts. If it is possible to provide complete contract service and/or rapid availability of parts, then it is recommended that service try to sell all possible parts. If, however, the products are remote geographically, require few sophisticated parts, and the customer maintenance personnel are competent to acquire and install the parts, then drawings and specifications for the parts can be provided directly to the customer. This tradeoff has long-term implications that must be thought out carefully before a final decision is made. If service known that customers are going to buy their own common items anyway, service should assure that the proper specifications for these light bulbs, V-belts, and bearings are in the product's replaceable-parts list.

Pricing sensitivities

Customers may be knowledgeable about the price that they would pay for parts from other sources. The news media have featured stories of parts for military applications that cost the government many times what an identical part costs at a hardware store. Many common parts are advertised in mail-order catalogs and supplier salespersons drop by to disclose how much lower their prices are than anyone else. Therefore, the margin should be kept low enough that the perception to the customer is no more than a small premium for your one-source superior service. Universal parts are equivalent to the bread, diapers, milk, and eggs in the grocery business, purchased frequently and, therefore, obvious pricing sensitizers to prospective customers. Items purchased infrequently, such as table salt, which also sell at a very low price, are not significant pricing items because they are purchased infrequently. Consumables such as paper are particularly sensitive and may be priced low, often barely above break even, to create the impression that other prices will be equally reasonable. Realize that volume is a big multiplier! If you can sell loads of paper, like Xerox does, you need to profit only a few pennies on each ream and the result is millions of dollars.

It appears that a price differential of 10 to 20 percent is the threshold that sends customers searching for other sources of parts. Obviously the absolute price has influence, so that a 20 percent premium may be acceptable on a $5 part since a $1 difference is not worth a separate order. However, on a $500 part that 20 percent becomes $100, and a less expensive source would certainly be considered. Special consideration should be given to pricing parts for obsolete equipment. Prices should be increased over time to cover carrying costs on slow turning parts that are held as insurance parts because they are critical and without them, essential equipment would be out of commission.

A minimum price, or at least a minimum order value, should be put on parts. A minimum price of $1 is frequently used, so that even a 12 cent cotter pin will be priced at $1. That is reasonable if a typical order is for just one or two of those items. If, however, many inexpensive parts are needed, such as a fountain dispenser service person who requires mainly O-rings and gaskets that should sell for 35 to 60 cents each, then a minimum order charge is more practical. Terms such as a $2 handling charge on orders under $20 should cover the fixed costs of packaging, with shipping additional. To stimulate consolidated larger orders, incentives such as free shipping for orders over $100 and additional volume discounts are effective. Emergency "equipment down" orders disrupt a parts system. Most organizations charge a handling premium of $5 to $50, or a percentage such as 5 or 10 percent additional for rush orders, and probably also then charge for courier or overnight shipping.

It is desirable to construct a computer program to recommend prices based on desired margins with minimum and maximum guidelines. Retail prices should be monitored for their relationship to the transfer cost. Transfer costs tend to vary over time. Left unattended, fixed prices could fall behind cost increases and actually become less than cost. Alternatively, in the multivendor market, street prices tend to fall, and you could be left pricing parts high and wondering why you are not selling any.

Expect to pay more for a part when you need it in a hurry; or conversely, charge more if you are the seller. Table 18-2 shows examples of purchasing in planned quantities of 1 to 25 parts versus buying one of those parts when needed. You can see that the savings are impressive. Given the need of more than a few of these parts each year with carrying costs about 30 percent, you will save money by buying planned quantities.

Selling through distributors

A multitiered distribution system may go from producer to wholesale distributor to retail dealer to end user. If suggested list prices are published, dealers usually use these prices. Some dealers sell for less, but in some industries dealers sell at a 5 to 10 percent above the manufacturer's list price as a premium for fast supply. The standard procedure is for manufacturers to sell to distributors at a discount off list price, and for distributors to discount to dealers so that each echelon can cover its costs and make a profit. Twenty-five percent is a typical discount, and the actual amount is probably based on volume, with high-volume purchases or purchasers getting larger discounts.

TABLE 18-2
Purchasing planned quantities is usually less expensive than emergency buys

Part #	Bulk (1-25) price $	Emergency expedite price $	Dollars saved by planning	Percent saved
CIE-C701	350.	525.	175.	33
101474-001	105.	192.	87.	45
105370-001	70.	157.	87.	55
Y16450900	52.	160.	108.	67
580027-001	18.	78.	60.	77
103188-001	5.	64.	59.	92
810574-002	2.	55.	53.	96

Profit margin and return on assets

Pricing structure is intended to generate a specific gross profit on parts sales. Specific markup multipliers may be chosen for particular categories of parts to achieve a specified gross margin on parts sales for the period. The calculation is

$$Percent\ gross\ profit = \frac{Sales\ revenues - Cost\ of\ sales}{Sales\ revenue} \times 100$$

$$Cost\ of\ sales = Transfer\ costs \times 1 + \frac{Cost\ of\ operating\ the\ supply\ system}{Cost\ of\ material\ handled\ during\ the\ same\ time\ period}$$

The overhead cost of operating a supply system is usually about 20 percent. In the calculation this is best applied as a multiplier of 1.20. For example, if parts revenues for a year are $500,000 and the direct cost of those parts was $375,000 plus 20 percent operating overhead, then the calculation is

$$Percent\ profit\ margin = \frac{\$500,000 - (\$375,000 \times 1.2)}{\$500,000} \times 100 = 10\%$$

Return on assets is based not just on the profit margin but also on the number of times a profitable sale is made. The formula is

Return on assets (ROA) = Profit margin × Inventory turnover rate

Thus, if the turn rate is 3.5 per year and the margin is 10 percent, then the ROA is a very nice 35 percent. Note that the actual average inventory value was probably under $110,000. If a $200 part was sold for $20 profit margin, then another was ordered to take its place. This happened an average of 3.5 times during the year. High-turn items such as consumables can be sold at low margins. For example, a package of colored ink cartridges might cost (total of direct plus overhead) $14.55 and sell at a 3 percent markup for $14.99 ($0.44 margin). If turnover can be 12 per year, then the ROA is 36 percent or $5.28 on the $14.55 invested in assets to sell. Many industries operate on margins lower than this, however, in computer/electronic parts a few clients average 60 percent gross margins across their parts business, and many are above 40 percent. Service parts can be an attractive business when the parent equipment is selling for margins under 10 percent.

Price control

Parts records should include costs, and may also include list price and our price, if different. This practice is relatively simple and realizes that if customers are going to buy their own common items anyway, the Service should assure that the proper specifications for these light bulbs, V-belts, and bearings are in the product's replaceable-parts list.

Note that the price is referred to as "recommended list price" since to fix prices is illegal. Street prices for computer equipment are nearly always lower than the manufacturer's list. Commodity parts such as disk drives usualy have lower street prices but, following the laws of supply and demand, the less available parts such as laptop screens sell for premium prices.

Publicizing your offerings

If you want to sell parts then you must make buyers aware of what you have to sell and for how much. There are thick paper catalogs published every week. These are useful to keep your company's name in the minds of potential buyers, along with a general indication of what manufacturers and types of parts you specialize in. On-line electronic media is the only way to get current availability and pricing of parts. Bulletin boards and Internet web pages are effective, especially where direct orders can be placed and confirmed on-line. The best parts suppliers will have electronic data interface (EDI) with their customers. This is a definite selling advantage that gives real meaning to the term *wired to a customer*.

Quoting and invoicing

Every organization that sells parts is concerned with quoting and invoicing the correct selling price. Three methods are typical. The first provides a parts list with prices in paper, fische, or electronic form to all field personnel who are then expected to put the proper price on the invoice. Another procedure is to have field personnel list only the part number and quantity on the service call report and the headquarters function, (probably computer automated), applies the correct price, prints the invoice, and sends it to the customer. A third method is to provide the technician with a computer printer, ala Avis, Hertz, and National car rental returns, so the entire invoice can be calculated, printed, and handed to the customer on-the-spot.

Each of these methods can work, but each has advantages and disadvantages in specific situations. Don't use the printed price books, if you can possibly avoid it. Field personnel will rarely keep printed price lists up to date; somehow the latest revision is rarely in the book when it should be. The price books are easily copied and quickly fall into the hands of competitors. Above all, do not send cost information to field people as there is too much risk of it getting into unfriendly hands.

Knowing the prices of parts should help field personnel manage their territories better. For example, the facts should be available to decide whether it is better to replace a part at a cost of $35 or spend an hour trying to repair the problem. On the other hand, looking up prices on a list consumes time that might better be spent doing technical service. If prices are entered by a field person, then headquarters staff can audit them and the accuracy of two people is better than one. Electronic communications should eliminate the need for printed or filmed price lists. Instead, accessing the headquarters computer or a database on a technician's laptop provides accurate prices, availability, ability to instantly order, and even invoicing at the customer's location.

19 *PROCUREMENT (IN-BOUND)*

Procurement, or purchasing as many people call it, is the acquisition of materials and services necessary to operate an enterprise. We advocate the term Procurement because it does not infer ownership. Modern logistics strives to obtain use of a service part without having to invest in the title for that asset.

Part of the process was discussed in chapter 9 under the subject of Reorder Point lead time. Material purchased for service parts is obtained from manufacturers or other suppliers. In many cases firm orders are loaded in a manufacturing requirements planning (MRP) system and are produced along with products in the normal production cycle. Materials managers in a service parts organization should work closely with major suppliers to share information on requirements. Automatic transfer of data for forecasts and purchase orders greatly improves performance of a MRP-driven process as shown in

Figure 19-1. Figures 19-2 and 19-3 illustrate the full procurement process.

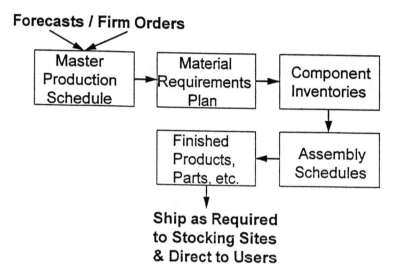

FIGURE 19-1
MRP begins with forecasts but requires firm orders to build

Borrow, exchange, lease, repair, or share

Our first principle of modern procurement is: Don't buy a part if you can employ an asset you already own or use an equivalent part without investing permanent funds. A related principle of parts forecasting is: The only way to maintain full value for money invested in service parts is not to spend it in the first place. Just as leasing has caught on as an alternative to buying a car for cash, so renting or leasing parts has begun to be accepted by conservative service managers. There is a big balance sheet difference between owning title to a part or equipment and gaining use of that same item. Why buy a part if you can get it to use whenever you need it? Therein lies a rub.

There are many innovative ways to gain use of a part that is not already in your possession. Unfortunately, most of them involve parts stocked at a central warehouse where they can be available to anyone authorized "by the drink." This means one at a time, whenever you need it. If you need parts for same-day restore times, you probably need to buy those parts. We predict that partnerships will develop soon between independent parts suppliers and courier firms, so that parts will be stocked at the courier's parts depots. When an order is received at the central order terminal, it will be routed immediately to the depot that can transport the part to the point of need fastest and at lowest cost. Even then, service organizations will have to buy some fast-response parts until an independent parts supplier (IPS) agrees to take over all of the parts support, including parts on consignment. It will happen.

Independent parts suppliers such as Aurora/Century, Cerplex, PC Service Source, Service Electronics, and TOPS Computer Company are sources of many multivendor parts for computers and related equipment. Maintenance, repair and operations (MRO) supplies are being procured with the help of A.R.M.M.'s Maintenet and similar services that electronically link factories with part information and potential vendors. Original equipment manufacturers and assemblers of high technology equipment usually provide advance exchange of parts and send a good part overnight so you can quickly restore their product to operation and return the defective part afterward.

In addition to supplying individual parts when needed, independent part suppliers are interested in providing all the parts a service organization might need in return for a share of the revenue. The ratio of parts cost to revenue on multivendor products is now about 35 percent (and needs to be 20 to 25 percent). Thus, if complete service for a $3,000 Pentium workstation costs about $180 (6 percent) a year, then the revenue share for parts now would be .35 x $180 = $63 per year. These parts are provided on a rapid exchange basis. Obviously it is expected that most products will not fail during the year. One CPU motherboard or power supply or hard drive would consume an individual machine's annual parts budget (and then some), but on the average the actuarial odds should be profitable. The remaining challenge is to reduce the annual cost of those parts to under $45 per year.

Make or buy

A classic decision for both manufacturing and service is the choice of whether to make a part internally or to buy it from an

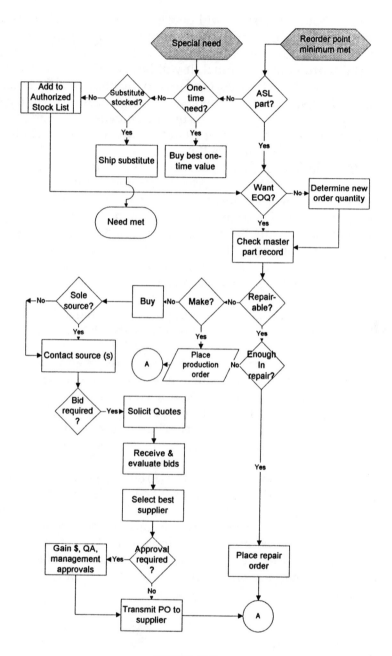

FIGURE 19-2
Procurement should follow logical process steps

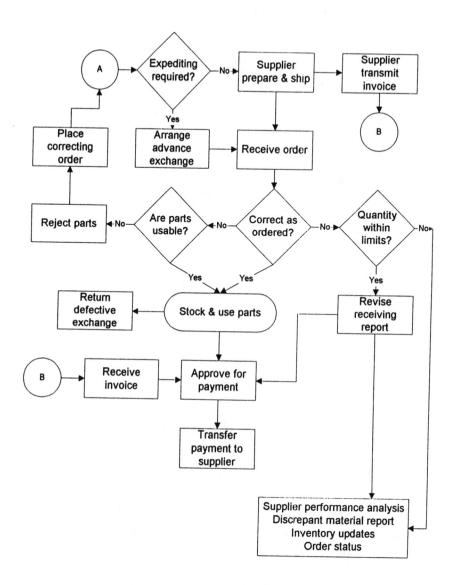

FIGURE 19-3
Followup is necessary after the purchase order to assure satisfaction

external vendor. Economics is the most important determinant although considerations will also be given to continued employment of personnel, use of production capacity, quality, and assurance of supply. If a choice between make or buy exists, the equation should be:

$$Minimum\ total\ cost = C_i D + \sqrt{2C_o C_h D(1 - D/R)}$$

where:		Make	Buy
C = item cost \$		6.00	6.10
D = demand per period		3	3
C_o = order or setup cost \$		50.00	8.00
C_h = holding cost per period \$		0.004	0.004
R = replenish items per day		18	infinite
T = lead time in days		12	16

Substituting:

$$Make = \$6.00\ (3) + \sqrt{2\ (50)\ (\$0.004)\ (3)\ [1 - 3/18]}$$

$$= \$18.00 + \$1.00 = \$19.00.$$

$$Buy = \$6.10\ (3) + \sqrt{2\ (8)\ (0.004)\ (3)\ (1)}$$

$$= \$18.30 + 0.44 = \$18.74.$$

So in this case the least financial cost is to buy.

Note that the rate of supply probably will vary from a fixed rate of production internally to as much as is required instantly from an outside source. Every part should be available from at least two sources if procured externally, even if vendor partnerships are very good. Two or more sources lead to healthy competition that keeps prices as low as possible and assures availability in case of strikes, transportation difficulties, material shortages, disasters, and other detrimental conditions. If the parts are produced internally, then the production organization should assure backup through multiple material vendors, production lines, and so forth. The point is to make sure that you can get parts when you need them at a fair price.

Recent practices concerning vendor-user relationships include using fewer vendors in an effort to improve quality and delivery. Many organizations strive to work more closely with supplier partners and share knowledge of forecasts and special events. Vendor selection should be a weighted evaluation of quality, speed, delivery to schedule, technical assistance and information, ease of ordering all needed parts, and price.

Economic incentives

Another challenge (or opportunity, depending on your perspective) for the parts manager arises with high-volume parts when the salesperson offers to sell $9.00 switches at a discounted price of $8.10 each in quantities of 144. If we need 30 switches a month, our first thought is that 30 switches per month divided into 144 means 4.5 months' supply and the average inventory will be 72 (144/2). If the calculated EOQ is 22 (with average inventory 11), then the difference of 61 (72 − 11) units will have a carrying cost that must be at least offset by the discount and reduced ordering cost for the larger quantity. It is a good deal if the total cost equation is solved using the price of $8.10 for 144 at a time, all other factors remain the same, and the result is significantly under the total cost of 22 at a time for $9 each. In this case the calculations for a one-year supply are:

Total cost = Acquisition cost + Carrying cost + Order cost
   = (Unit cost × Quantity) + (Average inventory × Carry cost/Unit) + Order cost
   = Extended cost) + [(Quantity ordered/2) × Carry % × Unit cost] + [(Annual use × Order cost)/Quantity per order]

Total cost of 22 = ($9 × 360) + (22 / 2 × 0.30 × $9) + [(360 × $ 18) / 22]
   = $3,240 + $29.70 + $294.55 = $3,564.
Total cost of 144 = (8.10 × 360) + (144/2 × 0.30 × $8.10) + [(360 × $18) / 144]
   = $2,916 + $174.96 + $45 = $3,136.

So, buy in quantities of 144 at $8.10 and save $428 ($3,564 − $3,136) over the order period. Of course, you may wonder what the break-even price is. The way to answer that is to solve the algebraic equation, representing the unknown price by "P," and set the result equal to the proposed purchase quantity. For example,

($P × 360) + (22 / 2 × 0.30 × $P) + [(360 × $18) / 144] = Total Cost of 144
(360P) + (3.3P) + (45) = $3,136
363.3P= 3,091
P = $8.51

Any price less than the break-even $8.51 is a saving for you.

Vendor records

The screen image shown in Figure 19-4 illustrates a typical vendor record. This information is linked to applicable part records to provide information on all parts purchased from a vendor, and also to list all vendors for a part. When requests for quotes and purchase orders are processed, the vendor information can be electronically retrieved. Also, some service parts operations do not become involved in the procurement process and merely pass the purchase requests on to a separate purchasing function. Even in those situations, a recommended vendor is good information to have. If service parts management has a vendor preference, that certainly should be noted.

Purchase order types

Types of purchase orders vary from a single order for a single part to blanket orders that cover all purchases from that vendor for a year. Since the administrative cost of processing a purchase order is significant, covering as much activity as possible under a single order minimizes costs. The challenge is to do that and still retain control over exactly what is purchased and paid for. Low cost expense parts such as common hardware and stationery supplies should be procured on an annual arrangement negotiated with a supplier who will both respond to phone orders and have a representative routinely check the

```
================================================================
                  S U P P L I E R    M A S T E R

Mfgr (M) / Splr (S): S      Acct #   : S234
                            Name: RELIABLE ELECTRONICS
Last Act  :  10/12/99
     PO#  :  99173          Addr: 3699 WEST HENRIETTA ROAD

Vol/Yr $  :  31,350         City: ROCHESTER          St: NY
   Max  $  :  25,000         ZIP: 14623-3560
                            Attn: JOE D. PATTON
Rank:  2                    Tel : (716) 334-2554   Ext: 4223

Blanket  Expire            Pay : ACCOUNTS RECEIVABLE
  Order    Date   Orgn            RELIABLE ELECTRONICS
                            Addr: 14 COMMERCE DRIVE
C3955   12/31/99   512
                            City: HILTON HEAD ISLAND St: SC
                            ZIP: 29928-7665


                            Disc %/Days: 2/15      Net Days: 30
                            Buyback (Y/N)?: Y       Charge%: 15
                            Minimum $: 50         Ship Via: FedEx
                            Comment: SPECIALIZE IN ASIAN PARTS
================================================================
```

FIGURE 19-4
All vendor information should display on one screen.

amount on hand and replenish stocks as necessary. An invoice should be submitted based either on regular time periods, such as weekly or monthly, or when the resupply occurs.

Another method of purchasing especially applicable to multivendor parts is to negotiate open orders with volume discounts. For example, initial purchases gain 20 percent discount, when purchases pass $100,000 the discount becomes 25 percent, and above $250,000 the discount is 30 percent.

There is a special challenge in accounting for advance exchange parts and processing a specific purchase order for each part is inefficient, expensive, and time consuming. The easiest way to procure those parts (which are often covered under warranty) is to send a confirming PO after the transaction and do assure that the defective part is returned for credit. If your computer system will not handle blanket purchase orders, a procedure around that deficiency is to create a standard supply contract with an account number which supplier invoices will reference. Process a confirming PO after each transaction, thus creating separate PO numbers which satisfy administrative needs.

Standard order words

The use of standard paragraphs greatly facilitates preparation of requests for quotes, purchase requisitions, and purchase orders. A typical paragraph could be:

QA 214
All materials supplied must conform to the requirements of NRC QA regulation 214, including Amendment 1 dated 1/27/99.

Standard wording can be kept in a word-processing system or a computer-based purchasing network for accurate recall whenever required. This reduces typing time significantly, helps assure that necessary requirements are included, and keeps records accurate. The standard paragraphs pertaining to specific parts should be listed on the "part record" of a computer system for automatic recall at any time they are required.

Order terms and conditions

For buying from vendors as well as selling from your own stock, terms and conditions (called *Ts and Cs*) will generally be net 30 days. Some independent parts suppliers want their money faster and other companies insist on paying net 45 days. Some vendors allow a discount such as 1/10, which means deduct 1 percent if payment is made within 10 days. The last date of the 10-day discount period, or the 30-day net period, should be noted on the invoice. Most interpret the date to be 30 days from the date of invoice and some companies automatically mail the check 30 days after they process the invoice. (That money can be a long time in coming.) Technically the date should be 30 days from the date of parts delivery. Differences of opinion arise over back-dated invoices or invoices that are not sent immediately but arrive days later and require payment by the end of 30 days (10 days from now) with penalties. It should be clear whether the date means payment must be in the vendor's accounts receivable department by that day or "the check is in the mail." The natural inclination of vendors is to collect payment as soon as possible, while purchasers try to pay as late as possible. Effective organizations try to sell the parts and receive revenues before the invoice must be paid. Cash flow is very important in service parts management.

Most vendors have penalty clauses for accounts that are not paid after a defined time period, usually 30 days. That interest charge is related to the cost of borrowing money. It will rise when interest rates rise and fall when the interest rates fall. A typical rate would be 1.5 percent per month, which translates to over 18 percent a year. It means a parts organization must assure that received goods are quickly verified and if the receiving documents and the invoice come to them that they are passed quickly to the people who pay the vendors. Most vendors give better service to customers who pay within the prescribed terms.

Returns for credit are sometimes allowed by suppliers. Electrical components, however, are rarely accepted back again because the risk of hidden damage and of restocking a defective component is great. Mechanical items, motors and devices that can be tested, and items in the original sealed package are often accepted for a 10 percent restocking charge. The payment terms, penalties for late payment, and credit return must be clearly stated

Checks and balances

Inaccuracies and theft are problems in the inventory business. To prevent such problems, a procurement system should be planned with checks and balances built into the process. Another good rule is to have different persons involved: one person should order the part, another should receive it, and a third should pay the bill.

Dollar approval limits for purchasing should be instituted. For example, the stockroom supervisor can approve purchases up to $500. Anything above that goes to the service parts manager, who has a limit up to $5,000. Orders above that dollar limit would be approved by the plant superintendent, director of logistics, or whomever is the superior manager with financial responsibility. Limits, of course, should differ depending on the typical kinds of parts and materials that must be purchased. If the business involves $1,000 PWBs that have little resale value, then the control limits may be higher. If many items are involved that have high use outside the business, such as quarts of oil and batteries, then careful checks should be put on lower limits. It is possible to have separate guidelines that provide tighter controls for consumables than for the dedicated-use parts.

A personal signature, initials, or identifying number should be placed on every order, receipt, and issue. This personalizes the process and assures that accurate transaction records exist. Managers should occasionally check every step of the process. The temptation to steal will be greatly hindered by the knowledge that someone will be checking. If a manager does not want to imply that the checking is to avoid theft, it can be done under the guise that a good manager should know how the system operates. Most personnel are pleased when management takes enough interest in their jobs to find out, in detail, what they are doing and to ask for their opinions. To observe the relationship between incoming delivery personnel and receiving clerks receiving dock, (with attention to how carefully the receiving orders are verified) will pay dividends. Watching the detailed check of received parts may suggest how vendors can improve the packaging of the shipments and better ways to handle internal processes. Following parts through the entire process of locating what bin each part should go to, seeing how it gets there, and verifying the count in the bin will help a manager understand the workings of a service parts system.

As previously emphasized the secured stockroom is necessary for assuring control once parts are in the facility. The secured area should include items such as tools that are subject to pilferage, while other items such as common hardware can be less controlled.

Vendor performance analysis

The main measures of vendor performance are delivery time, quality, and price. Data gathered on each supplier's performance should be frequently evaluated and shared with the suppliers. Additional considerations include suppliers sharing of technical information, breadth of parts stock, buying back excess, notification of good deals, and electronic interface capabilities. The priority order of those considerations will vary among organizations. In the service parts business, quality and delivery to a reasonable schedule are generally more important than price. The purchasing function personnel should keep track of performance by vendor as measured by (1) percent of deliveries on schedule, (2) percent of shipment complete, (3) percent of received items acceptable, (4) average lead time, and (5) relative price.

Sophisticated purchasing functions have developed weighted measurement systems that can quantitatively recommend the best vendor for a specific commodity or part. For service management purposes, our intent is to point out the major considerations. The typical person ordering service parts is either restricted as to possible sources, or must rely upon quick experienced judgment and a relationship that has been established with suppliers. If Business is concentrated to one vendor at least one other supplier should be ready in the wings as backup and to assure healthy competition.

It should be remembered that while procurement must be an honest arms-length transaction process, it is always better to work with the vendors instead of against them. What is good for the service parts function should also be good for the vendor, and vice versa, so that everybody wins.

Pareto's principle of the critical few applies to vendors just as to other service concerns. Determine who the most important vendors are, work with them, and develop a mutually successful relationship that will result in quality parts delivered on time at a reasonable cost.

Status progress

Requests for parts often go through many stages. These may include:

Initial request
Immediate superior approval

Stock control approval
Budget control approval
Quality assurance requirements
Purchasing
Transmittal to vendor
Acknowledgment by vendor
In transport
In receiving
In QC
Available for use

Time from start to finish of this process can be a few minutes, but is often several weeks. In many organizations, especially subsidiaries of overseas parent companies, the lead time consists mostly of the time necessary to get a purchase order through the process checkpoints to the supplier. One way to track the progress of requests is to use status codes. A simple way is to use a countdown series. If 12 events are to take place, then start with 12 when the part is first requested. Change the code to 11 when the superior has signed it, to 10 when stock control has approved it, and so on. In an order-tracking system, every part request can have a status code that then progressively counts down to code 0 (available for use), at which time tracking can be dropped. With computer interfaces to procurement, each function responsible for part of the process can enter its status code and see an instant listing of all parts in the queue waiting for its action. When it clears the action, the status code proceeds to the next required function. A date can be associated with each action so productivity and responsiveness of these specific functions can be evaluated. Some organizations use only a date for each step in the process.

Having detailed the steps of a typical process, let it be said that 90+ percent of all orders should flow automatically to the supplier without other human intervention. Boundary parameters should be soft-coded and, so long as the situation fits within those bounds, the order should be automatic. This use of Pareto's principle frees considerable time from clerical matters and allows people to concentrate their intelligence on important changes in parts.

Parts for specific jobs

Special order (SO) or direct to order (DTO) parts should be added to stock only if they are highly essential, are frequently used, have a long lead time, and/or are low cost. Of course, part data may be kept on the Master Parts Record so that details are readily available when needed, but the part is carried at a stock quantity of zero, meaning that it is not normally on the shelf. Occasions will arise when parts and materials have to be obtained on special order.

Purchase requests and orders for special parts normally should be tied to a specific work order, facility, or piece of equipment so that service calls might be on hold, "waiting for parts." This link to an individual service call helps to identify all parts ordered for a project, and their status. It also facilitates expediting the parts to the user as quickly as possible after they arrive. Accounting also is aided since costs can be directly obligated against the work to show future commitments and then accounted for when the parts and invoice arrive.

The question will arise as to "What stock number should I give these special parts?" The best option is to assign a part number in the regular part number sequence structure. This option supports the shipment of the items to an automated field parts management system, control to the field, and billing to the customer. Some people identify unique parts with the purchase order and line item number, or just the suppliers identification. This PO and line has some advantages if the requestor will be tracking the part by the way it was ordered, (which would be on the confirming copy of the purchase order). However, it is awkward if a decision is made to make those parts regular stock in the future because the identifying number then should be assigned in the regular sequence. The computer can easily reference a supplier's identifier to our master part number and that helps universal cross-referencing. Either way it is helpful to have a flag on the part record that indicates this was a special order part. Forecasting needs to know that the demand is nonrecurring. (Some computer systems delete non-stock part information from the record when the quantities on hand and on order reach zero.)

It is helpful to treat special parts as much like regular stock parts as possible, so that the record keeping system will not have too many variations. It is also beneficial to have a method of reviewing all special orders every six or 12 months to determine whether some parts are being ordered frequently enough to put them in regular stock. Patterns may also be observed that indicate the opportunity for better stock procedures. For example, a facility's construction and maintenance organization frequently ordered paint in special colors. This naturally led to leftovers, difficulties in matching, and other expensive problems. The opportunity was obvious to standardize on a tint base that was purchased in bulk for stock and then the specific colors could be mixed as required, in the amounts required. Over the long term, additional effort is being applied to standardize the colors so that only one tint of each major color would be used in the future. Similar standardization can often be applied to hardware, V-belts, gaskets, and other will-fit common items.

Receiving procedures

Standard operating procedures should be written, taught, and enforced to assure that the right items are received in good condition, accounted for, and accurately recorded as efficiently as possible. Most parts are delivered by truck and the driver has little or no relationship to the vendor. The driver's only mission is to hand over a carton that has the name of the receiving organization on it, and receive a signature as verification that the carton was delivered. A receiving person should at least look at the container to see that it is not obviously damaged. If it is, that fact and a description of obvious damage should be written on the waybill. As the next step, the container should be opened and the contents verified against the shipping list. For example, if the contents are listed as three each, part number 1256, SWITCH, DPDT, and two each, part number 211, SWITCH, SPDT, then at least someone who knows that DPDT means double pole double throw and SPDT means single pole double throw, and how to tell the difference, should check the received parts. This will often be a quality control function staffed by inspectors with the necessary drawings, specifications, and measurement devices who can check for obvious damage and look carefully at any parts that may be damaged even though the outside container is not. (Large air filters, for example, are sometimes received damaged in undamaged cartons.) Any discrepant parts should be immediately tagged. Responsible persons should be notified so that a decision may be made as to use or rejection of the part. The person who made purchasing arrangements should be involved, since the vendor must be notified if the part was discrepant and, if possible, advised as to the deficiency and how to avoid it in the future. If the receiving service organization incurred additional costs for rework of the part before use or other situations arise from the discrepancy, adjustment in the price should be negotiated.

The quantity received, as discussed earlier, may be over generally by 10 percent. If more than that or it is under the ordered quantity, procurement management should be notified to take whatever action is necessary. In many organizations, the inbound quantity must be exactly the quantity on the purchase order. If an overship occurs, the excess material is set aside for a disposition initiated by the buyer, such as return, hold, or receive.

Early shipments (over one day prior to requested delivery date) should be held for disposition by the buyer. An early shipment, unless specifically authorized, will tend to disrupt the normal flow of in-bound material. It can have a negative impact on prepackaging activity, bin assignment, bin sizing, and other warehousing. In addition, early shipments cause unnecessary carrying of inventory. Dispositions for excessively early deliveries can include return, hold until requested delivery date, and receive if needed. The leverage normally used to obtain just-in-time delivery is to hold the supplier's invoice and delay payment until the specified delivery date and terms.

International dealings

Many products and parts today are procured in the world marketplace outside the country of use. A central purchasing organization in England may procure parts from a vendor in

Japan to be shipped to the United States. Prices for goods purchased overseas will usually be quoted on the basis of a specific stable currency exchange rate at the time of delivery. For example, parts from an Israeli company probably would be priced in U.S. dollars. Transportation and customs tariffs are additional and should be included in analyzing the purchasing decision. Delays in customs are one of the more important considerations, and generally depend upon which country the goods are coming from and into which country they are going. Shipping parts into Spain, Argentina, and Brazil is a present problem that can result in many weeks, and even months, of delay. Setting the reorder point higher to provide for safety stocks may be necessary in case of customs delays.

Packaging is also a concern in shipments. Several service companies have success shipping large parts that obviously have little universal value on pallets covered with clear shrink packaging. Their visibility seems to make fork truck drivers and other handlers more careful, and reduces damage. On the other hand, goods that would appear to have some universal value should be shipped in containers that have only the part number displayed. Obviously a package emblazoned with the words "microprocessors," "television components," or even "flashlight batteries," would be a target for thieves. This problem is not unique to the international marketplace. If you buy a high-fidelity stereo from most manufacturers, it probably will be in a plain brown box marked only with the stock number.

If an organization is starting to operate in the international marketplace, it should solicit advice from friendly service managers who have already encountered the problems and solved them. Knowledge can be very helpful about what transportation method to use, which brokers and freight forwarders can be fastest at expediting, the paperwork that is required, and the words to be used. Free trade zones should also be considered. Make sure that all publications are written so that they can be translated accurately into other languages. We live in a global economy now that must arrange to procure service parts from (and supply parts to) every corner of our world.

20 ORDER ENTRY AND SHIPPING (OUT BOUND)

Parts orders

Service parts exist primarily to fill the needs of employees and outside customers. This chapter on receiving and filling orders covers situations that range from the mechanic who comes to the stockroom window, to the field engineer who telephones that parts are needed in a remote location, to the customer or third-party service organization who wants to buy a part. The general flow of order entry and supply is diagramed in Figure 20-1.

Recognition of the need for parts comes in many ways. Many customers and field service representatives have their own reorder point established to trigger orders before panic sets

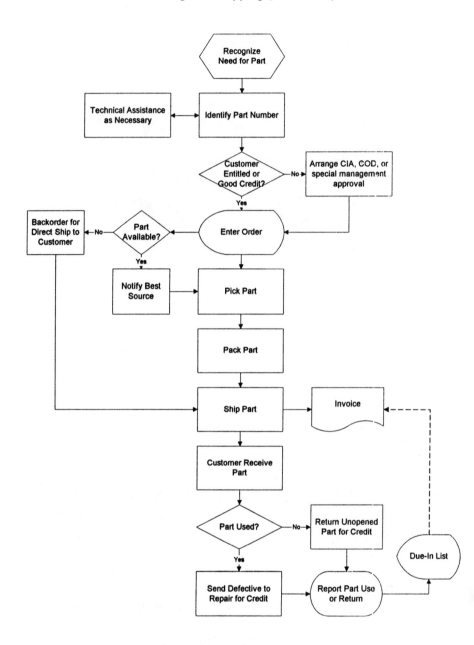

FIGURE 20-1
Order entry requires many steps

in. Others, because of lack of knowledge, negligence, lack of money to invest in parts, or unexpected use, will place emergency orders that need special handling. If an organization supports external customers and personnel, a regular mail/ telephone/e-mail/facsimile order system should be developed. Mail can be appropriate for routine orders that are not time sensitive and it is generally less expensive than the other media. E-mail and facsimile have the advantage of written numbers and identifiers which reduce errors that may creep into a telephone conversation. A telephone customer service order entry function is always necessary as a backup where time, availability of another medium, or the need for two-way conversation is important. Many organizations provide a toll-free 800 area code telephone number allowing outside personnel to call in their orders without incurring long-distance telephone charges. It should be mentioned, however, that the 800 number charges are very expensive and generally result in longer conversations than if the customer is paying for the call. Nuisance calls will also be placed over a free telephone number but may be eliminated if the caller has to pay directly. Wide-area telephone service (WATS) lines can be a competitive marketing advantage, but they should be carefully evaluated to assure that benefits exceed the costs.

A scheduled routine for order placing can be effective. For example, all orders for the week should be placed by Wednesday noon to be picked, packed, and shipped on Thursday morning. The field tech rep's service call should close with a detailed list of parts used, their quantities, and source. If those parts used are on the technician's authorized stock list, opportunity should be provided for the tech to cancel the automatic resupply. Otherwise the ASL part will be automatically replenished without further human decision.

Order priorities

Most service parts systems have two priorities for orders—*Routine* and *Emergency*. Some add a stock classification for filling *Reserve* supplies. Other companies have several variations of emergency, most of which seem to clutter and confuse the true emergencies. The emergency classification (sometimes also called *Priority, Urgent, Ship Same Day, Expedite* or *Rush*) should be used only in cases of extreme need, when equipment would be shut down as a result of need for that part, or you are contracted for a fast restore time with penalty charges if terms are not met. Emergency classification should be used on only 5 to 15 percent of the orders. If the percentage becomes greater, then the priority system is being abused and the special-effort cases will overwhelm normal operations. An increasing use of emergency orders indicates reduced confidence in the authorized stocks lists and normal resupply, all of which begs for management attention.

Several rules regarding emergency orders will be helpful. First, any emergency order received at the ordering location should be installed within four hours. If it takes longer to install the part, then the need was obviously not of emergency classification. Second, the cost for special emergency handling should be recognized. Will-fit parts should be procured locally if the quantity, cost, and speed of acquisition are better than through the emergency channels. For example, fuses that can be obtained at a local electrical store should not be emergency ordered. Fastener hardware should be routinely replenished by the service representative well ahead of need. Numerous emergency orders for this type of item indicate a need to monitor routine replenishment better. Third, not more than twice the normal emergency quantity should be ordered at the same time as the emergency part; for example, if the reorder point on lasers is one and sudden demand causes stock-out, then no more than two should be ordered on emergency. If a special need for more can be detailed as a result of reliability failures, then more can be ordered; but allowing this as a normal situation will abuse the classification and special handling of emergencies. On the other hand, it does make sense to pick, pack, and ship two parts as emergency instead of sending one as emergency and the other one through routine channels. When large quantities of parts are ordered emergency it should raise management suspicion that the system is not being properly supervised.

Availability

While the ordering customer is still on the telephone, two checks need to be made. The most important concerns the availability of the requested part. The other is of the customer's credit standing. Availability should automatically be indicated by any computer program used for order entry or internal parts transfer. If an interactive on-line computer system is not available, then a printout should be at hand that at least shows availability status as of the night before, or a stock record card that is updated with every order. If we are talking about a one-person order entry and issue function, then a card can be adequate. Even with three or four people, a rotating tub of cards can be satisfactory.

For internal availability additional information should be on hand for *On Reserve, On Order,* and *Back Order.* The additional information gained from knowing what parts are on reserve will allow them to be diverted to an emergency situation, with management approval. Parts held on reserve are normally not under separate lock and key, but have been designated for a work order or service call. Often the stockkeeper will have picked those parts and have them assembled in a special location ready for pickup. If those are the only parts available to meet a high priority need, then they can properly be used for the more important job and replaced when available for the lower priority one. The *On order* status lets people know that the parts order cycle has been started. Sophisticated programs can even show how many parts are on which purchase order and the expected date of delivery. Note that a reorder point calculation should include both parts on hand and on order to avoid triggering additional reorder points signals every day until the new parts arrive. At the same time that calculation should indicate whether demands exceed both what is on hand and the number expected in, and what the timing will be.

Parts lent to another organization are easily accounted for as *On Hand* with that other organization. *Back Orders* may be used as a category, although it is not vital. That status of *Back Order* does convey the knowledge that the part order proceeded to the supplier and was acknowledged, but that the supplier is out of stock. From the central service warehouse perspective, a back order usually denotes an unfilled customer order that will be filled as soon as materials arrive. A replenishment is for materials to add to central stock against which there is no customer claim. Items on loan should be placed in the open order replenishment system with the appropriate return or due date. Of course, accounting for the loan item is separate. Again, knowing the expected date of delivery is important.

Figure 20-2 is an order entry screen that shows addresses, credit standing, and other information necessary to serve both inside and outside customers. Note that part availability is displayed here as a simple "Y" (for yes), "N" (for no parts on hand or on order). If parts are on order, the software should display the date parts are expected. This logic answers several questions before they are asked. Note that this one screen can also handle transfers between technicians and returns to stock. Figure 20-3 shows a typical screen layout for parts availability details.

Credit

If outside customers are involved, then concern must be given to the ability and willingness of such customers to pay

```
================================================================
        P A R T    O R D E R    A N D    T R A N S F E R

Rqstr: PAUL CARLOR  Ph: (540) 949-1754      Date: 5/18/99 Ti:1635
Cust#: 234876  Account: GENNYCAME   PO#: 9AB235    Order#: 92435

        Ship To:              Bill To:              Relieve:
C/S/E: E #: 721                C    234876              S   1
Name:  KIT KABOUDLE            GENNYCAME               MAIN
       SERVICE REPAIR DEPT     A/P
Addr:  ONE GENNY WALK          148 CONFERENCE CTR DR
       DOCK R2                 STE 4
City:  WAYNESBORO  St: VA      CHANTILLY    VA
Zip:   22080-1999             22021-9400
                                          On
     PN         Description        Qty  Hand  Unit$    Extd$
345123    SWITCH,ELEC,PAPER FD,12V   1    Y    4.85     4.85
782431    CABLE,ELEC,MAIN PANEL, M213  1    Y   48.55    48.55


Total PNs   2  Total Units   2          Total Part$  52.40
Weight   3                                    Tax$    2.88
Priority: 2  Ship via: FedEx           Ship/Hndl$    7.50
Shipped Date: 5/18/99 Ti: 1735 Doc# 816996951  Total Cost$  62.78
================================================================
```

Figure 20-2
Order entry should have key information on one screen

```
=========================================================================
              P A R T      A V A I L A B I L I T Y
Part #:   463247 Desc: CONNECTOR ,ELEC,6 WIRE,MALE,FOR THERMOSPLIT

Orgn(O)/Stkr(S)/Empl(E): O #:98     Name: BOSTON BRANCH

                                        On      On      On     Back
      ID          Name           Bin   Hand    Rsrv   Order   Order
   ALL         BOSTON BRANCH            5       1      2

   STK91       BRANCH STOCKROOM  A23    2       1      2
   922         NOAH ARK                 1
   924         LONG JOHN                1
   927         HERB BASIL               1



=========================================================================
```

Figure 20-3
Part availability details should be easily accessed

for the parts being ordered. While a service parts organization normally reacts to credit situations that are determined by a financial accounts receivable organization, service management should understand what is going on so it can play its role in intelligence gathering and enforcement. Naturally, if service sends out invoices and is responsible for payment collection, then their paychecks may depend on getting the bills paid promptly. If parts support is furnished as a follow-on to a capital goods lease or sale, then credit information should already be available. (The "how to" of establishing credit arrangements for a customer are beyond the scope of this book.)

Initial parts orders may be received from someone who has not been heard of before. This is very common in the case of durable goods such as home appliances, small sterilizers, and machinery that may be sold and easily installed at a new owner's location. The first knowledge a service organization may have of this is a telephone call (or letter) saying that the potential customer has the equipment and needs some parts. Obviously, being able to supply those parts quickly with a minimum of fuss can establish a profitable future relationship. The best answer is a valid credit card number. Most corporations and the government today authorize credit cards for business expenditures. In multivendor parts, for example, it may make more sense for a technician to buy a keyboard or mouse at the local Computer Warehouse instead of ordering it *Emergency* from headquarters. When you consider again that the cost of handling such an item adds $35–$50 to the cost it is easy to see why local buy with credit card and audit checks is the lower cost way to go.

Several organizations have been encountered where credit departments take three to ten days to approve credit, and meanwhile a new customer anxiously waits for a part that is said to be readily available. Considering the cost of credit checking, a limit guideline could be established at about $100. If the order is for any amount under $100 and the customer appears legitimate, the order could be shipped immediately without a credit check. It naturally would be followed closely to assure that the customer does pay, and then that payment is recorded as an indication for future credit. Higher order costs and orders to questionable or poor paying customers without credit cards should be sent cash on delivery (COD) or cash in advance (CIA). Letters of credit (LC) and similar "cash against" documents are useful for foreign orders. COD can be arranged through most courier services and the U.S. Postal Service. Those collection costs should be added to the price the customer must pay. The amount to be collected will consist of the cost of merchandise, plus shipping, plus COD charges.

Some agents require either cash or a certified check for the order. The usual procedure is to tell the customer the exact amount and have the customer mail the check. When the check arrives, the part will be sent. Customers may pick up such parts in person with check in hand. If a tech rep is required to install the part, the customer can be notified what the service call will cost for both parts and labor and agree to have a check waiting when the tech rep arrives. This should be done only in exceptional circumstances, as it is definitely preferred that field personnel not have to handle money in any form. This is a precaution against both temptation of the personnel themselves and the possibility that thieves might try to rob someone they thought was carrying money. An invoice/receipt already filled out should be sent with the parts and then a signed copy returned. These financial precautions may seem stringent, but they are intended to prevent illicit financial omissions or commissions. Service parts management is a business.

It is hard to imagine a business today without a computer, but just like in the computer, in case you have to operate in manual, each customer (even each piece of equipment at a customer's location) should have a place on the record for the credit to be indicated. A flashing cursor can be useful to indicate CIA and COD status. Those warnings can be applied when the credit people say it is necessary, and can be removed when the problem is cleared up. The customer order personnel should be able to say, "Yes, we have that part in stock. However, your credit standing is cash on delivery. Will you be prepared to pay the delivery person when it arrives?" Credit problems are not reserved for small companies. Many large hospitals, government organizations, and even divisions of *Fortune 500* companies have been put on restricted credit until all obligations are promptly paid.

Pick, pack, and ship

These three functions can be combined under one person in small facilities or, in large facilities, may require many people. They can be done manually or be in large part automated. Self-contained parts rooms are available that can be operated by a single person who keys the part number into the computer that guides the robot to the correct location, retrieves the part, and brings it to the counter. Those automated installations are most justifiable in locations that support high turnover of small parts, such as in a machine tool crib that supports a large factory. The same principle is in use in large warehouses built around retrieval and movement devices such as narrow-aisle fork trucks that can reach hundreds of feet into the air and lift several pallets at one time. In most service picking situations, however, people can gather the few parts on each order faster than a machine can.

When an order is received at a parts location, it is best displayed in visual form either on paper or on a display screen. (Watch the effectiveness of an order display at your local Burger King or McDonalds.) Handheld wireless devices are even more effective since they can be carried to the spot and will provide quality control on the spot. Planned orders can be transmitted in advance so the parts can be staged in a location ready for quick pick up. The pick list should be printed in location sequence so the picker's route through the racks is as short as possible. In a manual system with under a dozen parts on a typical list, the picker can look at the locations and write on the list the sequence 1, 2, 3. In a computer system, the program logic can sort the pick list into the most efficient order. Having pick lists sorted this way is a mark of a good service inventory system. (Inexperienced persons often develop lists in part-number sequence.) Very sophisticated systems, particularly in mail-order retail centers such as L. L. Bean can even consider the volume and weight of each order and direct the picker as to the size of cart to take and how the containers should be arranged.

When the picked parts are delivered to the packing area, a quality control inspection should be performed to assure that all ordered parts are present and in good condition. This check need not be very time consuming, but it is vital to the field personnel on the receiving end to have the right parts to satisfy customers. Accuracy of parts picking is usually a function of the personnel involved. Inaccuracies in parts picking normally point to specific pickers who are in need of improved motivation and training. A visual display, possibly as simple as a chalkboard, can be a very effective announcement of each person's progress in number of orders picked, number of line items, and accuracy. Posting that information publicly provides a goal for everyone to strive toward excellence. (Examples are covered in chapter 25.) Persons who are below the norm generally try hard to equal their peers. There will be some people who continually try to improve on their previous performance and strive for 100 percent accuracy.

Packing and shipping normally will operate close together so that parts are prepared for the most suitable means of transportation. Protection of the parts while keeping weight at a minimum is the main constraint. If there is a large volume of packaging, advice on the best means can be obtained from professional packaging consultants or manufacturers' representatives. Sheets of air-bubble packing, plastic and paper pellets, expanding foam and standard forms are available for packing parts. Special attention must be given to electronic components such as PWBs, instructing all personnel who may handle these components about the damage that can be caused by static electricity and how to prevent it. Microelectronic devices should be kept in individual nonconductive packaging.

Shipping

The economics of shipping depend on how much the package weighs, how far it has to go, and how soon it has to be there. Traditionally, heavy equipment to be shipped long distances at the lowest possible cost would move by a combination of truck and ship. Increasing pressures from financial inflation and need for increased productivity now often put that same shipment on an aircraft for delivery in days instead of weeks or months. Many shippers provide combinations of truck pickup at your door and airplanes to fly the parts to the airport closest to the customer, where they are picked up by another courier truck and delivered directly to the customer.

A service parts manager must be continually on the alert to changing services and to prices offered by competitive shippers. Locations within 400 miles may be served best by truck, whereas a combination of truck and airplane may be necessary for longer distances. For low price and delivery to rural location, a package sent UPS ground offers a good combination of low effort, assured delivery, and tracking. For local deliveries, a taxi or even the service organization's own van may be effective.

Routing depends on the shipment priority, weight, and distance; with additional consideration for size and special handling requirements. Overnight delivery services abound with offers to pick up packages by 8 pm or allow drop off as late as 11 pm in major airport cities for delivery to other major airport cities by 8 am and to almost anywhere in North America by 10:30 am. A package under two pounds can be shipped anywhere in the United States for under $15 by the U.S. Postal Service for next day delivery including Saturday and Sunday. Normal shipping includes weights up to 70 pounds. The USPS charge increases with weight and distance. FedEx, UPS, and other overnight services typically negotiate volume rates for one pound packages, presently about $5.50 for overnight delivery and $4.25 for second day (often delivered late the next day). For comparison, routine UPS ground for 5 pounds is about

$2.75. Packages weighing more than 150 pounds usually require special arrangements. Next flight out (NFO) costs about $115 for pickup and delivery, including the $59 air ticket. Table 20-1 shows typical shipping arrangements within North America.

TABLE 20-1
Shipping options ordered by speed and cost

1. Courier—Fastest method to get a small package delivered directly to the work site. This combination of truck and plane is also highest cost. Some couriers stock parts.

2. Counter to Counter—Parts delivered to special airline counters move as baggage and can be picked up at the destination airport. High cost, but can go on the next flight that an airline flies to the destination.

3. Next Flight Out—Shipments of any size, but generally air cargo, with as few transfers as possible and not consolidated with other shippers' freight.

4. Overnight Delivery, Hold for Pickup—This enables technicians to get parts at the shipper's office after about 6:30 am, and always by 9 am.

5. Overnight Delivery with Special or Weekend Delivery—Packages are delivered as soon as they arrive (e.g., FedEx "First Overnight"), rather than waiting until the next business day delivery.

6. Priority Overnight Delivery—Delivery by 10:30 am the next morning.

7. Standard Overnight—Delivery the next business afternoon.

8. Two Day Delivery—Delivery to destination no later than second business day.

9. Routine Ground—Delivery from one to seven days depending on distance from point of shipment to destination.

Consolidating routine shipments to once a week is cost effective. It means packages can be consolidated by geography and shipped in the most economical fashion. That is, of course, a trade-off against carrying larger inventory quantities for safety stock. One expensive part on the shelf that can be quickly resupplied when used may be more cost effective than an average inventory of five of those same parts with normal resupply only once a month. A smart manager will keep a separate list of emergency shipments and review them frequently to assure that the expediting system is not being abused. A range of 5 to 15 percent is recommended. Too few emergency orders may mean that field inventory is excessive and money is being tied up in truly "spare" parts that are not turning over very fast.

Financial responsibility

An issued part usually also involves a financial transaction to invoice a customer, or at least relieve the part cost from the inventory records. In the simplest form, (that of a central stockroom that issues parts for internal work) the accounting may be no more than a slip of paper dropped in an "Issued" box or a line entry in a log book. There is no need for extensive bookkeeping if proper reordering and controls can be handled simply. As more money is invested in parts and more people become involved, planning and controls must become more sophisticated.

When an individual comes to the stockroom to get parts, a transaction record should be made. This can be a line in a log book or an entry on a computer screen. The important elements are to know:

1. The person who issued the part.
2. The person who received it.
3. Work the part is intended for.

The same information should be used for returning a part to stock. In principle, a part could be transferred directly from one person to another; however, in practice it is best to have the stockroom involved in the process and receive the part from one person and issue it to another. If direct person-to-person exchanges are permitted, valuable parts may disappear and the alleged receiver can say, "I didn't get that part!"

If all inventories are carried on-line, then the inventory quantity can be transferred from the central stockroom to an individual's own stock inventory, and then further transferred to the specific customer or equipment when the call report is completed. If the customer is to be charged for the part, an invoice should be generated. The best source for that invoice is the stockkeeping financial function, although it may be given to the customer directly by the field service person who delivers or installs the part. Under any condition the invoice should be prepared promptly upon delivery or shipment. Cash flow is important. The psychology too is desirable, of getting a bill very soon after the satisfactory service has been provided. And especially if the invoice is for a large amount of money, the sooner it is received after the restoration of uptime, the more willing the customer will be to pay the charge.

Some organizations have their field service representatives present the customer with the invoice when the service is completed. Copies of the invoice then go back to headquarters for accounting, but the customer is expected to pay the presented copy. The problems with this are that the field service rep must (1) carry up-to-date costs for every item, (2) be accurate and businesslike in presentation of full charges, and (3) have the time and skill that are necessary to prepare and present an accurate invoice. It is generally preferable for the service rep to fill out the service call report and allow a central billing function to prepare and mail the invoice and worry about collection. Naturally, a one-person service organization is going to do everything and can prepare the bill most efficiently on the spot and present it to the customer for prompt payment.

To avoid any confusion over payment timing, a specific statement of when the invoice should be paid is helpful. A useful format is terms: "Net 20. Please send payment to arrive at Patton Consultants, Inc. by December 31, 1999. Interest rate of 1.5% per month is due on any amount unpaid after that date." That simple statement makes it easy and direct for a customer's accounts payable function to pay the invoice on time.

Regardless of whether or not a part is being charged, a receiving person's signature should be obtained on the issue form. That proof of receipt should be entered on the transaction log. The signed receipt should be retained as long as proof may be necessary. For a central facility, that may be only a day or two. For a field service time and materials job, it may be 30 or 45 days until the bill is invoiced and paid. It should not be necessary to send a copy of the signed receipt with the billing invoice. Reduce paperwork as much as possible and use electronic communications.

Returns

Returns of unused parts to stock by internal personnel should be encouraged. The accounting mechanism should relieve the person or work order of those parts and credit them back to the stock inventory. Quality assurance can be built into the returns by assuring that personnel know the same part may coming back to them in the future.

Quality of returns from external customers is a concern. Parts should be accepted for return only if good. An unopened package should be acceptable, as should a mechanical component that has obviously not been used or damaged in any way

Electrical components, on the other hand, rarely should be accepted for returns. Most service organizations refuse to allow returns of any electrical or electronic parts, because such items can be damaged by an electrical deviation and the fault may not show up until later.

A restocking charge of 10 to 20 percent is typical for those parts that are accepted for return. It does cost the supplier to put parts back on the shelf and adjust inventory and billing records. Special orders rarely are returnable since they may be difficult to resell. Business practices for returns vary depending on the amount of business done with the requesting customer. Like most situations in the service business, special attention should be given to the significant few, most important customers.

Redistribution

In large supply systems, the concept of an excess parts redistribution pool may be employed. Excess parts from a field service organization are returned to one or more excess control points. Those stock points are managed as redistribution pools. Orders from lower level field locations are passed electronically through the excess pool(s) before going to the central stock point. A good place for an excess redistribution point is a small distribution center. This concept has the advantage of allowing the excess to "burn off" in the field organization without impacting the central stock point. It avoids the quality problems that exist when a field organization returns parts of questionable quality to a central stock point that makes retail sales.

Movement of parts among members of industrial or field organizations requires close control if knowledge of the location of parts is to be accurate. Top-level accounting may remain correct, but lower levels will deviate unless some tracking procedure is used. An "internal parts transfer" procedure is recommended. This is usually a formal system that requires all parts to be returned physically, (or at least in data form) to the stock-keeping location, which then reissues them to the requesting person or organizations.

Procedures often allow the giving person to input data which transfers the part without an acknowledgment from the receiver. This does open the possibility that people will cheat the system by saying they have transferred parts off their inventory, but those parts never show up on the alleged receiver's physical inventory. This problem will usually be corrected when the latter complains that the parts were never received. Investigation shows specific persons to be habitual senders of "ghost" parts. Acknowledgment takes time and effort, but may be necessary to avoid illegitimate transfers. Redistribution of parts at financial checkpoints should also be watched. Mid-December transfers from field locations to higher stock points help the field location to close out the fiscal year looking good financially, but it can make the higher locations appear to be poor managers. This game playing is often overlooked because it does at least put parts at the higher level where they can benefit a larger group of potential users.

21 *REPAIRABLES*

To begin the discussion of the management of repairable service parts it should be emphasized that the primary mission of repair operations is to repair and return items to good on-hand stock. Repair operations are cost-justified by procurement cost avoidance. We want to use assets we already own and avoid the need to spend cash for new parts. After all, if a part could not be fixed, then a new part would have to be bought. Any other activities that repair centers engage in are secondary. In many companies, secondary jobs such as "repair and return to customer" or "repair for down equipment" are more visible and urgent than keeping parts on the shelf ready to ship. If secondary jobs are allowed to continuously take priority over routine repair, the result is more secondary work and a growing inability to meet routine and replenishment orders in the warehouse. The confidence of FEs then deteriorates and they order two parts with priority expedite, just so they will have one when they need it. That descending spiral of unnecessary demands causes more disruptions of the repair system. Shop capacity must be structured to accomplish the primary mission so that secondary work diminishes.

Repair versus discard

Many service parts have the virtue that they can be repaired, refurbished, or rebuilt. That means their value can be restored by replacing damaged components, joining broken pieces, or reforming materials. This capability makes it possible to retain the materials and labor value that would be lost if the part had to be discarded. It also provides the capability for restoration to use in difficult situations where new parts may not be available but the means of repair can be.

Historically, maintainability and manufacturing strategy have tended toward discard rather than repair. It was generally less expensive to manufacture parts that are to be discarded. The production process can use epoxy, welding, encapsulation, and other techniques that save money in production. Unfortunately they render the components unrepairable. Trade-off analysis often showed that was the correct way to go since there can be advantages to service by not having to train personnel in repair techniques or spend money on repair tools and facilities. However, there are three factors that work against success with a discard policy:

First, there must be an adequate supply of replacement parts since every failure requires a new replacement. This impacts heavily on older products that are out of production. In this case repair may be the only source of serviceable parts.

Second, international customs barriers between countries still require extensive paper work to ship parts back and forth. There are countries that do not distinguish a failed part from a new one, and thus the same duty will be charged on a defective part unless it can be proved that it is a specific replacement. If these parts can be repaired in-country the necessity of having to pay customs can be avoided.

Third, motivated technicians would repair parts classified as a throwaway, using locally purchased components. The only real problem is that the component used in replacement is often of inferior quality and the workmanship involved may cause unreliability and future failures. Pennies saved on part costs may result in dollars lost through additional service calls and customer dissatisfaction.

The second and third problem above are rapidly diminishing as technology proliferates, but the economic and availability reasons to operate repair parts still prevail.

Defective return

Probably the most frequently overlooked segment of the logistics pipeline is defective return. This lack of interest is partly because these assets are not immediately usable. The returning defective parts are, however, a significant portion of the logistics investment. The recommended pipeline performance parameters are seven days, with a two day standard deviation. This is easily achieved if field personnel return parts once a week and use routine ground transportation as a shipping mode. The following are aspects of this task to be considered.

Pack and ship services

In recent years local shipping offices such as Mail Boxes, Etc. have developed to provide packing and shipping services to the general public. Their operations are ideal for the return of repair parts. It is relatively easy for a FE to simply drop off his returning parts at these centers, and the service will pack and ship the parts.

Repair tags

Paper forms are a target of opportunity for elimination by electronics. Repair tags are not necessary if the service organization has a fully functional call management system. In that case the service call number can be used as a Return Material Authorization (RMA) number and the electronically recorded data on the service call will contain all the data that would otherwise be recorded on a repair tag. Regardless of the recording medium, "Repair Tag" information should include:

- The equipment the part came from and the reason for removal.
- What financial account gets credit for the returned part.

• Symptoms of failure causes that could be a major help to repair personnel.

A typical repair tag is illustrated in Figure 21-1.

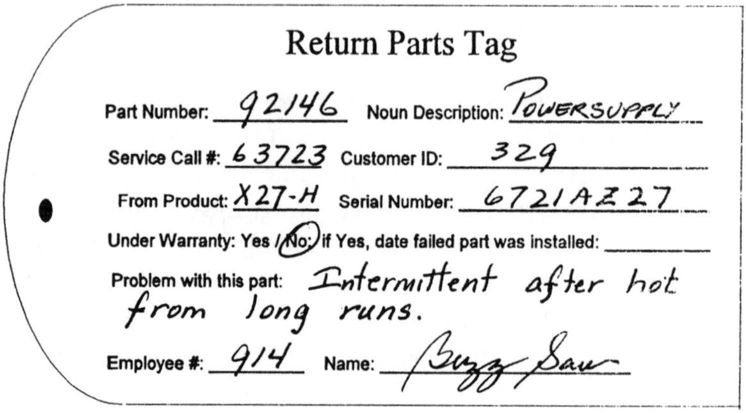
Return Parts Tag

Part Number: 92146 Noun Description: POWERSUPPLY

Service Call #: 63723 Customer ID: 329

From Product: X27-H Serial Number: 6721AZ27

Under Warranty: Yes / No: If Yes, date failed part was installed: ______

Problem with this part: Intermittent after hot from long runs.

Employee #: 914 Name: Buzz Saw

FIGURE 21-1 A paper repair tag

Any part that is designated as repairable should be packaged in returnable containers if there is any transportation involved. This is true even when packing and shipping services are used in the return pipeline. Packaging for new parts should be plainly marked to indicate that it is a reusable container so that the opener does not destroy it. Inside the container should be the defective parts information tag (if applicable); complete instructions on how to exchange the new part in the box for the failed one; the return address label (possibly several, if the part might go to different repair locations depending on geography), prepaid postage or other transport arrangements; and sealing tape. The part recipient should only have to remove the new part from the box, complete any applicable return tag, put the old part in the box, seal the container, apply the address and postage label, and put it in the mail. FedEx, UPS, and other courier organizations will arrange "Round Trip" shipping to deliver the new part in the morning and pick up the repackaged defective part in the afternoon.

If a large, fragile unit such as a complete CPU or a monitor is to be returned, the repair center will usually arrange to send packaging when they get the RMA information. Even though returning parts may be defective, they should be treated with care so that no more harm occurs inroad to repair. Note that this same treatment should be applied to good parts that are being returned as excess.

Return credit

One question frequently asked is, "How much credit do I get for return of this repairable item?" Most organizations provide an exchange price that credits the reusable value of the returnable, defective parts. That figure is usually the average value calculated over many repairs and considers scrap rate, shipping damage, and the range of repairs required The value is usually 30 to 50 percent of the new part's price. Of course, the higher the credit, the more motivation there is to return parts.

Credit should be given promptly on receipt of the failed part. One way to credit for returns effectively is simply to invoice for the new part assuming trade-in. If the failed part is not received in 10 days, then a second invoice is sent for the credit value plus handling charges. Some organizations invoice the full amount and then give credit on a voucher when the returned part is received. That requires two invoices, whereas only one is usually necessary with the first option. One invoice is better than two. Another alternative is not to send a new part until the defective one is returned, but that is slow and causes longer downtime.

Location

The benefit of having regional repair centers used to be that you could shrink response time and reduce pipeline investment by repairing items close to the customer. With the transportation infrastructure that has grown up in the United States in the last 10 years, this is no longer true. So long as the FE gets the part rapidly into the hands of the courier service, transport time is a small consideration. It is better now to concentrate repair expertise and capital investment in a single location.

For most service organizations, a single repair center can effectively handle all parts and equipment repairs for North

America. The location should most effectively be within an hour of a major airport so that emergency shipments may be easily expedited and the cutoff for evening shipments will be at least 9 pm eastern time to include the 6 pm end of normal business on the west coast, which is three hours time zone difference. The southern USA is a preferred geography because weather rarely hinders flights, taxes on inventory are low, and skilled labor is available. Having said southern, the exception is Chicago. From Chicago, a part can be anywhere in North America in six hours. Weather is a negative, but O'Hare airport is prepared to handle bad weather. The 1,200 flights out every day are rarely delayed over half an hour. Industry average for all deliveries of small packages on time is about 93 percent for major airlines and 95 percent for commuter airlines.

Dallas, Texas, is the next best location with 1,100 flights out every day. If factors beyond fast, frequent flights are considered, Dallas may be on top. Considerations include cost of facilities near the airport, labor rates and productivity, and taxes. Atlanta has 950 flights out each day. Boston, New York, Philadelphia, Pittsburgh, and other northern airports are close to customers, but suffer from frequent weather delays and labor problems that make them less desirable locations. The western airports at Los Angeles, San Francisco, Seattle, and Phoenix are not good choices since the last flight connections with the east coast leave in early afternoon. Note that it is often possible to put parts on a night flight from Los Angeles, San Francisco, Phoenix, or Dallas headed east and have those parts at an east coast airport even earlier than the FedEx office has its parts.

As volume grows, consideration should be given to a second center, located across the country. One reason is disaster insurance, so that a fire or labor strike in one location would not destroy a company's entire capability. If a service organization has related manufacturing or repair operations, then one warehouse should be co-located with those facilities. Consider also that the manufacturing or repair facility might serve as the disaster backup, if they can stock the required parts. If there are enough units to be repaired that can fully load several technicians at each center, then shipping should be considered and bulky, heavy units such as monitors and complete printers should be repaired at the facility closest in total transport cost.

If a courier is to be the main transportation, then a location near the courier's sorting hub can obtain late shipment times and also regional expediting. FedEx has their main hub at Memphis with regional hubs at Chicago, Indianapolis, and Newark. For example, FedEx shipments can be dropped off at the Memphis Airport hub up to 1 am for shipment that day. UPS shipments can also be dropped off at their Louisville, Kentucky, main hub up to 1 am. Drop off at 9 pm is typical of regional hubs including Columbia, South Carolina; Dallas, Texas; Chicago, Illinois; Newark, New Jersey; Ontario, California; and Philadephia, Pennsylvania.

Repair center management

A repair shop which supports service logistics operations is a first cousin to manufacturing job shops. Service repair centers usually concentrate on repairing modules which are used by service technicians to repair customers' equipment. The following principles have been adapted for repair operations from more traditional manufacturing operations. In either environment, the correct application of these concepts consistently produces productivity and/or throughput improvements in the 15 percent to 25 percent range. Modern "Team" approaches do not contradict these guidelines. Self-directed work groups primarily place more emphasis on sharing responsibilities and motivation.

The supervisory imperative

Everyone needs a supervisor. The more chaotic or disorganized an environment is, the closer the supervisor needs to be to the work. An interesting outcome of time management studies of repair shop supervisors is how little time they are able to devote to their primary job. This main job, of course, is *facilitating the work that is ongoing today.* It is not going to meetings, talking to vendors, chasing components or filling out personnel paperwork. Administrative tasks must be accomplished, but when they require the majority of the supervisor's time, something is wrong. One of the truisms of productivity improvement is that unsupervised effort is inherently unproductive. Just giving the supervisor back to the technicians will alone produce a dramatic improvement in shop throughput. If supervisors are not supervising, it is usually management's fault for requiring nonsupervisory activities to be performed in such volume that it detracts from supervisor's primary duties. There are also times when it is the supervisor who prefers other tasks (particularly technical ones) to supervision. If this is the case, the responsibility can again be laid at management's feet for not providing supervisory tools and the expectation that they will be used daily. You must inspect what you expect.

Work management

Manage the work, not the people. The vast majority of technicians are willing to work. If there is a problem it is usually with the work, not the people. One of the pitfalls of productivity assessment is that it can be used to "beat people up." This is a misuse of the measurement tool. Systems and measurements are not needed to identify poor employees. Those people stick out like sore thumbs! Practical experience suggests that people do resist measurement but, when they find that the measurements are fair and for the right reasons, they do not resist. More often than not they respond competitively. The successful application of the approach is in the hands of the supervisor. If John Smith's numbers are not right, the answer is usually found in the work that John was doing, not in John himself. If he is approached this way he will view the exchange as giving help and assistance, not personal criticism.

Time awareness

Time, more than money, is the common denominator. It needs to be spent wisely. In the "job shop" environment of a repair center, the speed of production is largely a matter of managing the time of the technicians. It is everyone's responsibility to be aware of the time (person-hours) going into the product. The philosophical issue is—Who controls the speed of the "line"? Most people will agree that, while workers should not be pushed beyond a reasonable limit, the responsibility for setting the pace of efforts belongs to supervision. In the case of a repair center, work should be assigned by the supervisor to the technicians with the communication of job time expectation. "Here is the task - You should be done by 3:00 p.m.—If you see any problems in finishing by then let me know." This approach does several things. First, it helps communicate the scope of work before the work begins. If the technician is thinking two days and the supervisor communicates two hours, there may be a misunderstanding as to what is to be done and a chance to gain agreement before the work starts. Second, it gives the technician a benchmark to judge whether or not this particular job is an exception to the norm. Finally, it tells the technician what to do if a nonstandard situation arises. Talk to the supervisor! The supervisor may authorize additional diagnostic time or more extensive work. On the other hand, he/she may reassign work or scrap the part. In any case management has been given the opportunity to do its job before the time is wasted.

Group effectiveness

What one technician does on any given job is not a major concern. What counts is the entire shop. In a repair center there is a statistical reason for this. Unlike manufacturing job times which are invariably normally distributed, repair times are exponentially distributed. You can prove this to yourself by simply asking a technician how long it takes to repair a particular item. The answer is most likely to be something like "Usually about 2 hours, but every once and a while it's an all day job."

Fortunately there is also a statistical answer to this situation! It is called the Central Limit Theorem and it states that work sample averages are normally distributed regardless of the shape of the distribution from which the samples were drawn. Mathematics notwithstanding, this means that we can consider all the jobs in the shop during the week as a work sample. We can then track and trend this effort with assurance that our measurements are meaningful. So what do we track? Certainly, the number of units produced to the schedule is useful and should be tracked. There is also a more meaningful metric, that is harder to track but immensely more descriptive. It is the ratio between the "should take" labor hours for the items that were completed and the total man-hours that were available for work in the repair center during the measurement period (a week is recommended). This ratio is commonly referred to as *labor productivity*. While the term is passé and probably should be called something else, it is just as valid a measurement as it was when Frederick Taylor and Lilian Gilbreth first started to measure human effort for time and motion study in the early part of this century.

Work visibility

As Frederick Hertzberg states, *"Work itself is a motivator."* There are several maxims that allude to this human phenomenon. Two might be "If you want something done—find a busy person" and "Work expands to fill the time available." The fact is that when people visually see the work remaining, they do not slow their efforts. A preferred method for doing this is called the "backlog wall." All of the pending work is kept in one place rather that being distributed to technician work benches. It is important that this is not just unserviceable units which may or may not be repaired someday but actual work which must be done in the near term. As technicians see the items being removed from the area they gain a sense of accomplishment. As they see other defective parts added to the demand they know that they are not running out of work.

Work readiness

What is there to do today? What are we going to do tomorrow? Shop throughput is directly related to our ability to keep the flow of work going steadily. One of the easiest ways to destroy smooth and productive flow of work is not having the work available when the human resources are. Prescreening work for certain conditions may be beneficial if repair technicians cannot complete items once they have started them because of these conditions. Another technique is the multiwork-station approach. Here diagnostics are performed by one group of technicians, component replacement by a second, and final testing by yet another. These groups are "balanced" so that the flow of work through the shop remains uniform and there are no major buildups of work in process between steps. Most importantly, work should be planned and prepared before it goes to the "floor." Common experience is that the addition of one administrative work planner and expediter usually provides an increased throughput equivalent to three technicians.

Measurement consistency

Rough standards are better than no standards. The use of job standards was implied above and there is a common misconception that job standards cannot be applied to repair work. *This is not true!* What is true is that job standards cannot be applied to repair operations *in the same way* that they are applied to manufacturing operations. First, remember that repair times are exponentially distributed. This means that perhaps 75 percent of the jobs routinely are finished in less that the average time. Therefore, the median (50th percentile) of the work time distribution should be used as the job standard for any given unit. Second, remember the "Central Limit Theorem" and don't try to measure productivity based on individual jobs. Measure a number of jobs for the same unit and/or group effort over a period of time. Most importantly, remember that productivity is a ratio. It doesn't much matter if we are 34 percent productive or 134 percent productive! What is important is the knowledge that we are getting better or worse? Do we even know? These questions can only be answered if we consistently apply the same standards (good or bad) as the measurement baseline.

Erroneous perceptions

If you want to use "gut feel," please do so in the privacy of your own home. The squeaky wheel is not always the biggest problem. While we are busily fighting today's fires are there other, bigger ones, smoldering that we don't see? Sure there are! As human beings we automatically service the current interrupt first. Did you ever wait in a line only to have the telephone ring just as you got to the service counter? Who got serviced first? I bet it was the person on the phone. That is not good customer service. Another human tendency is to assume that the past repeats itself and that yesterday's most important problems are also today's. In fact, if we did our job yesterday, today's problems should be something else altogether. Since our perceptions of the world around us is not always the best way to decide where our efforts should be placed, it is important that we approach the decisions about the expenditure of human efforts using all the quantitative data we can acquire.

Pareto's principle

Eighty percent of the solution can be achieved by solving twenty percent of the problems. Concentrate first on the critical few. One of the simplest and easiest techniques to master for turning data into information is the Pareto Analysis. Everyone experiences the 80/20 rule. For example, 80 percent of our grocery dollars go to 20 percent of the items that we buy in the grocery store. It isn't always 80 percent and 20 percent either. It might be 75/25 or 90/10. Pareto analysis is a way of organizing data to see if a few important items will stand out from the rest. The principle is named after Vilfreado Pareto, an Italian economist, mathematician, and sociologist, who in the late 19th and early 20th century, used the technique to describe the distribution of wealth in the population. It can be used to determine if a problem is broad in scope or limited. If a critical few cannot be found in a set of data then, assuming that there is a problem, the solution is usually a general one to be addressed with policies and procedures. If a critical few are found, then the solution deals only with those items or with the situation in which those items occur. For example if 80 percent of our manpower is consumed by 20 percent of the items that we repair, then we might do well to examine the work methods used for those items.

The ineffective productive indirect

If we don't constantly examine how we do what we do, how do we ever get to do it better? Our processes should be constantly subject to review. Often a big time eater is indirect time. Not the work itself, but the necessary actions required to facilitate the work. Things like moving items within the shop, acquiring components, and technical research. These actions are required if the work is to be done. What is not recognized is that these are functions of the environment in which the work is being done. For example, if commonly used components are distributed to technicians, then they don't spend a lot of time obtaining these parts. To be sure, environmental improvements cost dollars. However, it may be found in the example above that there is the equivalent of one man-year of technician time being spent in the acquisition of components. If this is so, it is usually cost effective to hire a shop parts expeditor at significantly lower pay. What is important to remember is that we shouldn't accept the environment as it is and should constantly seek improvements. Continuous improvement—the Japanese call it *Kaizen*—is the relentless quest for a better way and higher quality craftsmanship.

Reliability

The only thing better than doing a good repair job is not having to fix it at all. Repair centers are seldom looked to for reliability improvements. Sadly so. The necessary technical expertise to advise the field of work practices and field conditions that cause parts failures is inherent in all repair centers. Often what is missing is the process of communicating the conditions under which the parts failed in the field and the feed back loop for information to the field. Another case is the replacement of "standard" components with more reliable ones. This should be within the purview and charter of the repair center. These decisions should be based on the economics of the old and new components as well as the usage rates that influence the number of man-hours that the part consumes annually both in the shop and in the field.

Managing the repair cycle

Just as with the defective return cycle, the repair cycle must be managed to specific pipeline parameters if excessive investment is to be avoided. This is best done with the use of a fixed planning cycle. As noted above, a repair shop is very similar to a manufacturing job shop. Manufacturing organizations usually use a monthly planning cycle. In the volatile service world, however, a month is too long. Too much can go wrong! Certainly, repairs for single items can be effected in a matter of minutes in an emergency, but this does not allow for an orderly flow of work. A good compromise is a weekly planning cycle. This gains some efficiency from shop processes and reduces chaos to a minimum.

The pipeline performance parameters best suited for a weekly planning cycle are an average of seven days with a three day standard deviation. That means that the average repair time will be completed in seven calendar days and 98 percent of the items will be processed in two weeks. Remember from statistics that 2.06 standard deviations will include 98 percent of all elements. All items for a given week's work should be processed in three weeks even if this has to be forced with scrapping.

The shop work plan is straightforward. A "work order" is generated for each week. When the material is received in the shop, a 100 percent screen is conducted. This will cause "no-problem-found" items to fall out immediately and thereby guarantee the first pipeline parameter (one week average). At the same time, needed components are identified early so that they can be obtained in the following week; thereby guaranteeing the second parameter (98 percent in two weeks). The last 2 percent will always be problematical, but the disposition of these items should not be postponed beyond the end of the second week. This guarantees the last parameter of the repair cycle distribution (100 percent resolution within three weeks).

Electronic guidelines

Electronic modules such as printed circuit boards are prime candidates for repair. When circuit boards are job-ordered for repair, outstanding engineering change orders (ECOs) should be installed before testing. Why? The answer is that the changes must be done anyway, their installation may eliminate the problem, and if the unit tests good then repeat testing is eliminated. After the boards are repaired, time and materials should be logged against them so costs and repair performance can be measured.

Bar-coded part numbers and serial numbers help in data collection and analysis. Tracking components replaced, labor, problem/cause/action, and turnarounds, will provide information to improve many situations. On completion of repair, the boards should be marked to show that they have been through a repair cycle. If a computerized data base is not used for this purpose, a good way is a dot of colored paint or ink or a stick-on colored tab. If a defect was found and corrected, a yellow mark is suggested. If a defect could not be found, then use a red mark. If a board with a red mark comes in for repair a second time and a defect cannot be found, then the board should be scrapped. The reason for this drastic discard action is that there is probably a defect such as an intermittent electrical fault that may not be found in testing but does appear in the user's equipment. Further time should not be wasted trying to find the problem. The level of quality and the cost of service are enhanced by eliminating the board from further use.

Quality control and assurance

One organization states that their parts will be "new or better than new." In fact, repaired parts may be better than new because any manufacturing bugs have been found and eliminated. Repaired parts should be subjected to the same quality controls as any new part. As with new parts, quality must be designed and processed in rather than inspected in. In other words, the diagnostic and repair process must be done logically with quality and reliability in mind at every step. There is little value in finding defects after they have added expense to repair. Above all, it should be remembered that repaired parts are probably going directly into the replacement parts inventory. They rarely will be installed in new machines at a factory. Therefore, their first trial in actual functional use may well be as a repair part for a problem that is receiving the full attention of an angry user. It would be adding insult to injury if the replacement part failed too. Anything less than 100 percent acceptable quality of replacement parts will be much more expensive than the alternative of investing wisely to gain high quality.

Requirements calculation

Calculating the number of parts required within the whole-sale logistics process is different for repairable parts than for throwaways because central logistics must maintain the quantities necessary to support the defective return and repair pipelines. Once the initial pipeline quantity is calculated, demand is filled by turning over the repairs quickly and getting those parts back into good use. The time from user to repair location is a major element. With a captive service force, this is motivated by making it an item on the job description and performance appraisal. Economic trade-in value is the motivator for noncaptive returns.

In order to understand the complex computations necessary for determining wholesale requirements, it is helpful to visualize the buildup of several levels of stocking requisites that add up to the total requirements. This was explained in chapter 13 on Level Setting. Review now will probably provide much better understanding than was possible at first contact with the concept.

22 *MULTIVENDOR OPPORTUNITIES*

Many products labeled and sold by companies like Genicom, Lanier, Lexmark, IBM, Kodak, and Xerox are manufactured by other companies to the distributor's specifications. Those companies likewise will make OEM (original equipment manufacturer) products available to others to sell. Inside those products are many standard components including central processing units, mother boards, disk drives, power supplies, and laser engines. In modern business the same company may be a customer, a competitor, and a collaborator on various projects. For example, Motorola may cooperate with IBM and Apple to produce Power PC integrated circuits. At the same time all three companies compete against each other to sell finished computers, and they use each other's products to fill voids in their own product lines.

Characteristics of multivendor parts

Multivendor parts for open systems have characteristics that make them very different to plan and manage from proprietary, legacy parts. The unique properties include:

1. Short design, production and life cycles
2. Little advance knowledge of field replaceable units
3. Rapid configuration changes
4. Multiple sources
5. Installed product units range from a few hundred to hundreds of thousands
6. Complex variations in product families
7. Same part often in many OEMs' products
8. Manufacturers provide overnight advance exchange and full support
9. Warranties to three years with liberal replacements
10. Functional substitutes frequently possible
11. Economies of scale reduce costs with high volumes
12. Low failure rates
13. Few facts until field experience
14. Contracted restore times vary from one hour to two days
15. Priority of need may vary depending on specific equipment use, not universal
16. Service contracts are assumed on short notice
17. Knowledge of installed base—*what is where*—is not adequate
18. Contract discipline lacking so a defective part from noncontract equipment may be claimed against a contract equipment
20. Many customers can replace their own parts
21. Replacement modes increased by users' omissions and commissions
22. Equipment subjected to high-failure environments and lack of care
23. Diagnostics lacking so many parts requested and replaced unnecessarily
24. Field technicians' skill, training, documentation, and discipline relatively low

25. No dominant 3rd or 4th party parts supplier today
26. No single supplier for all parts
27. Far more parts in service channels than are needed, due primarily to many competing organizations procuring parts rather than a few centralized supplies.
28. Many competitors have similar concerns
29. Considerable outsourcing
30. Costs and related book values decrease rapidly
31. Depreciation 18 to 84 months, or based on use, or as percent of revenue
32. Planning requires more hand adjustments where automated systems cannot work effectively
33. Variations contribute to lower sales discipline and more undercharging for service
34. Dynamic pricing for contracts not understood so contacts are often bid emotionally to beat competition, without much regard for profits
35. Complexities of MVS service and logistics business models are not well understood.

MVS growth and complexity

The ratio of proprietary to open systems depends entirely on the company. Until recently, the "WINTEL" (MicroSoft Windows[R] and Intel) alliances have been the leaders for open systems. Apple was at the opposite extreme until recently they realized the problems with closed operations and opened licensing of the Macintosh[R] operating system to anyone interested. Mainframe companies including Amdahl, Hitachi Data Systems, and IBM are also now opening doors to many opportunities. Present relative volumes for parts in those companies is about 90 percent proprietary and 10 percent open systems. That is double the MVS business of last year (1995), and is expected to double again in the current year. As that percentage doubles and the relative amount of manual effort is perhaps ten times more for MVS, the effect is greatly multiplied. Solutions must be quickly found for the MVS challenges before they overwhelm companies and cause severe customer trauma. It should be noted that many improvements generated for the

MVS business will also bring improvements to the proprietary business.

Sharing parts

There is major concern over the high investment required for open systems parts. Parts ownership is the most costly item for a computer service organization, other than labor. For one large company, proprietary parts consume 16 percent of the revenue, but parts for the desktop business exceed 50 percent and should be less than 30 percent. Service logistics operations often handle product as well as parts. There is an interlocking commitment. Several companies have established a partnership with fourth party parts suppliers so ownership of parts can be concentrated.   Their criteria for a parts partner include:

1. Independent
2. Two-way logistics and distribution expertise
3. Expertise in computer parts
4. Existing relationships with manufacturers
5. Capitalization and stability
6. Repair capability.

The concept for effective parts support categories is arguably evolving to:

1. Slow moving, necessary parts—carrying cost shared between servicer and parts providers
2. Medium activity parts—parts stocking broker carries for profitable resale
3. High activity or unique parts—service organization owns

Suppliers are in this business to profit, so the more volume they can get, the more willing they are to pass price reductions on to their customers. There is opportunity for manufacturers to share availability of parts by local OEM stocks that are available to authorized service vendors. Various pricing options include percent of revenue and percent of parts or product. There is interest in setting prices to share the potential profit or loss.

There is opportunity for a consortium of service vendors to share parts with prearranged pricing and access.

Economies of scale and high product density bring reduced unit costs and improved profits. Service organizations are beginning to realize that owning assets is not necessary when they can be rented, borrowed, consigned, leased, advance exchanged, and otherwise obtained without cash outlay. From the financial perspective, any parts that are purchased outright or obtained on capital lease must be shown on the balance sheet. This means that the measure Return on Assets (ROA) will be reduced by the dollars employed in parts assets. If the resources can be obtained without balance sheet investment then less initial cash or debt is required. There is an axiom in service parts that once you invest cash in parts you are rarely able to retrieve nearly as much value for those parts in the future. Obviously you want to invest as few dollars as possible for parts but still have a high support capability. Be careful that, in a rush to avoid balance sheet investment, you don't spend considerably more on the profit and loss statement for transportation, expediting, and higher acquisition costs. Like most things in service parts, this requires a balance. Today, and even more in the future, the opportunity to utilize third and fourth party suppliers for multivendor, open-system parts presents the chance for reduced cost while providing fast response and high level of support.

Independent parts suppliers

A major business has arisen called "Fourth party parts support." Initially these companies provided mostly repair for monitors, printers, CPUs, disks, tapes, and similar common components. They were able to effect repairs less expensively than individual companies can because their volume is much greater through combining the repairs for many companies. As microcomputers became popular and equipment proliferated, the opportunities expanded. Service organizations also began to realize that they should do internally the things they do best and that they should outsource the activities which are not in their core expertise. Thus, specialist organizations emerged in call management, help desk technical support, documentation and training, courier strategic stocks, "feet on the street" field operations, depot repairs, and parts support. Whereas a typical service company stocking their own parts may turn those assets two or three times a year, an independent part supplier (IPS) will average over twenty times a year. The IPS also has the ability to buy or barter excess parts, bring together companies interested in sharing inventories, and otherwise broker cooperative activities in the marketplace.

OEM opportunities

To the OEMs this shift means demand will be for far fewer parts than have been previously produced. In the past, parts were (are) owned by every service company and stocked in every location that might need them. Moreover, safety stocks were kept at most of those locations. By the *laws of large numbers*, consolidation of parts means that fewer parts can serve more need. Fast transport, rapid access, expedited pipelines, and consolidated parts management all combine to reduce the demand for quantities of SKUs.

OEMs have the opportunity to do many of these same functions with their assembled or proprietary parts. Industrial instrumentation, for example, may be very similar in many oil refineries. Rather than requiring each refinery to buy a complete set of "spares," the OEM could bring together four users and establish a centralized stock of common parts. Each user would lease that capability for, perhaps, one-third the cost of the parts. The first company needing the part would receive it quickly and the OEM would replenish the used part quickly so it would be available for any other partner needing one.

Parts to be obtained from an IPS should have that IPS listed on the master part record as the source. The concern is often expressed that, "Nobody outside of my company can do as good a job of parts support as I can do." That may be true. Evidence, however, shows that in most cases, an IPS with proper sharing of need information will do a better job than a service company was doing themselves. Several key elements exist. Note that there is nothing different about these key elements for an IPS versus any well-run logistics operation.

1. Direct electronic communications between order entry and the IPS supplier.
2. Sharing of information regarding forecasts, potential changes in design, marketing surges, new product uses, and other information that will allow the IPS to effectively plan.
3. Direct ship repairable carcass from the point of failure to the IPS
4. Use the IPS as the stocking facility and ship direct from them to the point of need.

Ready for issue

The IPS should have an ASL (authorized stock list) agreement with their clients that requires the IPS to always have at least one of every part they support on the shelf ready for instant shipment. Some innovators will say that they can plan to have essential subassemblies ready to modify and complete assembly to the desired configuration within the required time. This is fine for low need criticality parts, especially where different modifications of a base product exist. Waiting for final assembly until you know the exact configuration makes sense; if you have time. Experience indicates that theory often separates from practice. When time is of the essence it is often difficult to interrupt other projects for a new priority, to find the documentation, set up the testers, and do the other activities within a short period of time. If a commitment is missed, then confidence in the total parts support system is degraded. Thus, the rule is to always have a part on the shelf. This standard gains significantly in the level of confidence personal users have for our total support system. The few additional dollars invested to have parts on the shelf are more than offset by fewer parts being horded in the total system. It is much better to have one safety stock at a central location than for each field technician to have his own (frequently hidden) stock.

Courier stocks

An option for stocking echelon parts is to consolidate some parts at depots run by a courier service. Associated Distribution Logistics, Choice Logistics, FedEx Logistics, and UPS' SonicAir are examples of companies providing this service. Parts support is frequently provided by three echelons:

1. Frequently used, essential parts should be carried by field technicians.

2. Low and moderate use, critical parts with high cost that require rapid delivery response (within six hours) should be located at a courier stock.

3. All other parts should be in central stock, which may include independent parts suppliers as the direct source.

As a rough guideline, a part in courier stock should have a response requirement of six hours or less, and be used at least $1,000 worth a year. This means that a part costing $1,000 should be used at least once a year, a $2,000 part might be used every other year, and a $250 part should be used at least four times a year. Every company can calculate their own guideline based on the negotiated agreement with the courier for storage space, receiving, shipping, reports, and other necessary services as compared with the company's own internal capabilities. Remember that fast delivery situations are the courier's main business. Even though the costs of outsourcing to a courier appear higher, the courier can probably do the job better and your organization may suffer from hidden expediting costs, frustration, diverted efforts, and other costs than are not apparent on service call reports or financial records.

Courier companies will usually establish stock locations wherever customer business justifies. Standard locations typically range from 15 to 80 in North America, with additional overseas. If the courier's own drivers can not get the part on the ground in time, they may arrange next flight out (NFO) air transport or even charter aircraft if the requirement dictates and the customer approves.

A complete parts support option is for an external organization to take over the supply of all parts. This is generally being resisted by current mind-sets, but is seen as developing in the near future. Companies like Arrow Electronics, CompuCom, and Grainger can expand to stock and supply a company's parts to the company's own technicians as well as to outside customers.

Parts knowledgebase

The evolution of "open" systems requires more sophisticated tools for effective, profitable operations. As producers become assembly shops rather than complete manufacturers, a functional component like a disk or motherboard is probably manufactured by only a few facilities around the world, and may be assembled into hundreds of products and model variations. The assemblies are treated as commodities. The same, or similar components are used in most clone products. The current design cycle is under 9 months, and the useful life at customers is shortening. This presents new challenges and also opens new opportunities to find substitutable parts fast and at low cost.

The objective is to establish a base of knowledge about service parts that will enable a servicer to quickly identify and obtain needed parts. If I need a controller board for a Brand X Model Y PC, typical questions asked by service personnel will include:

What is the original part number?
Are there any substitutable boards?
What options or alternatives do we have in our own inventory?
Is there anything that makes one of the other options advantageous?
Which one can I get fastest?
Which one will cost less?
Can we get repair credit?
Will the supplier ship me a good part overnight if I return the bad one later?
I want to support a new product, what parts will I need?

The following words outline requirements for a parts knowledgebase. Rapid identification of the affected part will utilize computer-based query on the alphanumeric OEM part number, revision, description, cost, visual diagrams or photographs, and significant form/fit/function parameters to identify the field replaceable unit (FRU). Replacement parts can then be quickly identified for substitution based on standard units, interchangeable, superseded by, next higher assembly, and related criteria.

Direct replacement versus rules

Information is most easily gathered initially by direct relationships of one OEM part to others. Judgment is that, for future success, the system must become rule-based so the many variables which affect a specific part, such as clock speed, mouse yes or no, operating system, special applications, and accessories, can direct a wider variety of options than is possible with merely direct substitution. Hypertext, artificial intelligence, and fuzzy logic will be utilized in the rule-based version.

MEDIA
PC-based, with options for magnetic disks, CD ROM, and on-line searches of bulletin boards and Internet web pages
Screen-based
Auto-Fax, e-mail, voice response, and digital ASCII interfaces
Both single-user and network versions

CHALLENGES
Software for alphanumeric data with graphics interface
Knowledge acquisition and updating from representative, credible sources
Cooperation of OEMs, designers, and systems integrators, who create the devices that need service parts
Specifying initial format with growth steps
Sign up significant subscribers and sell subscriptions fast to build cash flow
FRU level parts for the field; and repair component level for repair centers
Prioritize initial product coverage

SOFTWARE FEATURES

Space for tech notes to be entered by users

When a part is selected on a diagram or photo, a mouse-click should display the alphanumeric information relating to that item; the reverse should also be possible

Relational database so modification can be easily invoked

Software will be self-contained and not require an added expensive database or language

Security will be implemented so the information can be only used by authorized persons

DATABASE ELEMENTS

Manufacturer

Product

Model number

Serial numbers range (flag option)

FRU list—field

Stock List—repair center

Original PN

Manufacturer PN

Noun description

Suppliers, supplier PN, unit $, flag preferred source

Supplier record: name, address, phone, contact, terms, transportation

Repairable flag, repair supplier(s), repair cost $, special arrangements

Significant parameters by function

Other products and models used on

Superseded by PN, revisions, and engineering change notice (ECN)

Interchangeable with PN and revision

Revision IDs and descriptions (by parameter)

Next higher PN

Drawing and grid coordinate location

Mean time between failures (MTBF)

MTBR (calculate replacement from product density/parts usage)

Mean time to repair (MTTR)

Recommended stock levels (rate/supported units)

List cost

Next cost
Special instructions and precautions freeform notes

MARKETS

Anyone supporting computer/electronic equipment made by someone else.
ISO/TPM
IPS/Fourth party repair center
Self-maintainer
VARs and systems integrator

LICENSES AND SUBSCRIPTIONS

Initial charge plus options ranging from annual/quarterly/ monthly updates on-line

Bulletin board and Internet searches charged by time or by search.

Participants who submit data to the knowledgebase manager in standard format can receive reduced rates.

Based on value gained, usage, etc.

High price for high value

Will-fit replacements

How about replacing a 100 MB disk with a 500 MB that is superior and costs less? Would you like a Pentium/133 Hz CPU board instead of the 486/33 Hz you now have, for the same repair charge? Since you obviously use Windows 95, would you like a new keyboard with the special Windows keys as direct exchange for your defective board? These are some of the opportunities that exist to replace defective items with superior capabilities that are truly faster, better, and cheaper. Unfortunately, designers and product managers short-circuit many approaches by use of unique connectors, mounting, or software. That, too, will change as people realize they can sell more and profit more by designing for the mass markets.

The opportunities in multivendor, open parts will expand as technology and human thought facilitate the evolution. The ripples caused by dropping the big MVS stone in the service logistics lagoon will amplify into waves of change. The concepts being developed for MVS parts will bring improvement also to management of all service parts.

23 ASSET RECOVERY

Control excess

At least ten times more service parts are produced and sold than are ever used. Most stock locations today have excess parts that can and should be eliminated. But, when we try to sell those parts to recover some of our investment, we typically find that they are obsolete, defective, and worth very little. Elimination of excess parts is one of the most difficult things that any part manager has to do. Getting barter or financial benefit in return for those excess parts is harder still. Elimination of excess infers the challenge to get maximum value out of those parts as quickly as possible. The important thing is, however, to get rid of excess parts so they no longer take up space, people's energy, data collection, taxes, cash, and other resources that are better focused on the parts we really need.

Value for excess

In the service parts business asset recovery might be viewed as a pretentious term for excess management. That may be correct, but it puts the emphasis in the right place. There is a tendency to regard excess parts as valueless just because they are not immediately useful. This is often not the case. Unlike our manufacturing counterparts who plan to have no excess, the service parts manager cannot avoid excess since the nature of random demand makes it necessary. (See chapter 13 on Level Setting for the rationale of this.) Managing excess should be as much a part of the daily routine as management of acquisitions. When it comes time to dispose of excess, however, we need to squeeze as much value out as possible. Here are some ideas about where to find opportunities for recovering value.

Sell at full price.

There is an old cliché about one person's refuse being another person's treasure. Often we don't consider that what we have in over abundance (in this case excess parts) can be of great value to others. Here are some places to look:

PRODUCTION—The production department is not likely to want to pay full price for parts that they manufactured, but what about the parts that they would have to buy from other suppliers? True it is just internal "funny money," but it is certainly fair to ask them to pay as much as they would pay an outside company.

THIRD PARTY COMPETITORS—It is often difficult to think about helping your competition with any thing, but let's think again. If they are willing to pay you full price (including your profit) for excess parts, who is helping whom? We suggest it is a win-win situation.

SUPPLIERS AND BROKERS—Suppliers and brokers are sometimes willing to pay above your cost for parts that are excess to you. They do this, of course, because they see the opportunity for a profit. You may be tempted to try to find out where they intend to sell the items so that you can make a larger profit. It usually isn't worth the effort. If you are selling excess for a profit already, don't get greedy.

Return to manufacturing or supplier at cost.

If the product is still in production, the manufacturing department may be willing to give return credit at cost for items that they made. Suppliers too will take returns at full credit under many conditions. Charging a restock fee is a customary practice for returning parts to external suppliers. Paying a restocking charge should be resisted between internal organizations.

Disassemble for components.

When disposing of excess parts it is important to think creatively. The parts may be excess, but what about the components? Always think of yourself first. Do you need them for your repair operations? Do your repair vendors need them? Does production need them? Can you sell them to anyone? Often you can recover more value by selling components than by selling the items at full price, but don't forget to consider the cost of disassembly.

Disassembly, of course, is the problem area with this approach. Are the facilities, personnel, skills, and tools available to do it? If not, can it be out-sourced? One of the biggest impediments to disassembly is the original assembly technique. The basic design of the part or product may preclude effective disassembly. This is good if you are trying to minimize production costs and protect your technology, but not so great if it keeps you from capitalizing on recovering usable components. (We also note that ease of disassembly helps the entire service process.)

Consign to a broker.

Sometimes parts brokers will take excess parts on consignment. This means they will sell it for you for a fee, but will not buy the parts directly. This is a reasonable approach for some items. Selling an item is invariably a better option than scrapping it, even if the value received is below cost. Don't forget depreciation. If the accounting organization has been depreciating items so that book value is lower than the original cost, then any amount higher than the book value of the asset will be profitable! .

To whom do you sell it? Just about anyone, assuming that there are no concerns about keeping the items out of the hands of the competitors. Basically you go back around the list of places where you tried to sell the items for a profit and ask them to bid on the items as outright purchase or as a share of revenue. The object is to gain as much benefit as possible from those assets. Negotiate the terms and conditions of a consignment carefully, remembering that, if you need a part while it is on consignment, you may wind up paying a brokers fee to use a part that you technically own. Most important, establish stop-loss lower selling price limits and an expiration date for the consignment.

Barter.

Often overlooked in the world of asset recovery is barter. We tend to think of recovering value in terms of money and not to consider that value takes other forms. The most familiar form of barter is trade credits. This is the situation where a supplier or other company accepts our excess parts but, instead of cash, gives us "credit" against the purchase of other parts and services. Barter is common in many cultures. If your company has off-shore contacts, it may be possible to obtain raw materials, finished goods, or assembly labor with credit from excess parts. This may require cutting through some red tape but it can be worth the effort.

Partner with an asset recovery dealer.

Dealers presently pay pennies per pound for typical circuit boards and electro-mechanical assemblies, but are often willing to share risks and revenues with the seller. A seller has the option of selecting items from the bulk containers that can be separately sold for relatively high prices versus selling the entire load at lower revenue. Even taking into account the profit they hope to make, recovery dealers will probably pay you more than you can make when all your time and costs are considered.

Parts reclaiming is a specialty business with only a few wheelers and dealers who know the market and where things can best be sold, handling all returned materials for customers and dealer reseller channels. Returned materials are received, processed, tested, refurbished, and either returned to the manufacturer or reissued as service parts.

Historically, separation of circuit boards into valuable components amounted to melting off gold fingers and small amounts of other precious metals. While rapidly changing product designs can make whole boards obsolescent, the component integrated circuits (ICs) still have long useful lives and can be recycled into different applications for a worldwide customer base. IC recycling services involve removal, reconditioning, testing, packaging, and marketing of memory devices and standard microprocessors. The process includes erasing software contained in programmable memories, removing labels with solvent baths, straightening leads, solder dipping, and packing for production. Material separation equipment has been developed which grinds the remaining components into small pieces and then uses centrifical force, filters, fluids, and other media to separate the remaining metals and plastics into material with recycling value.

Donate for tax write-off.

Hopefully your company is profitable. The down side of profitability is taxes. Donate excess parts to a not-for-profit organization and take full book value write-off. How much you will actually recover for the parts is a function of what your company's tax situation is, but it is usually better than scrap value. Finding a nonprofit organization that can use service parts is sometimes a problem. One of the best places is schools. Vocational training programs can often use parts to train students on assembly and disassembly techniques. Charitable organizations often rely on older equipment, so you may find customers that need older excess parts to keep their old equipment running. There is excellent public relations value in donating parts to charitable use, and you might even need to charge (or take an additional donation) for the skilled labor to install those donated parts. Remember, if you ship items somewhere for donation, the shipping costs are usually a write-off also.

Scrap.

One interesting thing about scraping items is how complicated it can be. To sell or even donate items requires minimal documentation. Be sure that the requirements of your accounting organization and corporate auditors are met. Scrap dealers must be authorized to provide the necessary accounting, OSHA, legal, and environmental documentation. Don't be surprised if it costs you as much in administrative costs as the value recovered from scraping.

Accounting and hazmat obligations

A corporation's auditors must certify that the assets claimed on the balance sheet are actually present and that the assets scrapped were actually disposed of. There have been situations in which parts were allegedly scrapped but showed up again in the illegal markets. IBM, Digital, and many other corporations have been victimized by these covert and overt actions. (Parts thrown into a dumpster have mysteriously reappeared for credit. Allegedly defective parts scrapped after several no trouble found tests can appear in customer's equipment for you to replace with a good part at no charge under a support agreement.) A responsible manager should visually assure that parts being scrapped are physically smashed beyond use before signing the property book that those parts are destroyed.

Then come environmental concerns. If batteries, oil, mercury, paint, rubber tires, selenium cylinders, solvent, or any allegedly hazardous materials (hazmat)should be found with any identification related to your business, you can be held liable for civil and criminal misdeeds. EPA charges can be very expensive to resolve. Failure to follow hazmat regulations carries enormous penalties. With environmental regulations the seller does not always transfer liability when it transfers ownership of goods. (If you think that we are trying to scare you into being very careful, you are right.) The best answer is to work only with licensed asset recovery companies.

Reverse logistics

Reverse logistics is the name given to recovering materials from customers and internal operations. There are six R's involved: recognize, recover, review, renew, remove, and reengineer. Some warehouses are specially setup for the purpose of receiving, sorting, and redistributing items to gain maximum value. A specialty operation not only saves money but can add value to products. Several companies, including Sears, have outsourced returns. Other companies have dedicated part of their warehouse for returns.

Interesting combinations of advantages have evolved. Hewlett Packard, for example, was being pestered by toner cartridge refurbishers who would refill the used cartridge from the HP LaserJet® printer for less cost than a new cartridge. Unfortunately, some of these small business people did not use the correct toner, reused the photoreceptor too many times, and caused problems that reflected poor quality on HP. There was nothing effective that could be done to prohibit this entrepreneurial business. HP took the approach that, as a good corporate citizen, it did not want cartridges cluttering up landfills, so they made it easy for the user to return empty cartridges directly to HP for reclamation. The new cartridge box is plainly marked as reusable. A preaddressed, no charge UPS label is enclosed. All the customer has to do is put the used cartridge in the box, stick on the UPS label and drop the box at a UPS pickup point. HP gets the bulky plastic components back at low cost to recycle, it gets good will from purchasers for the ease of recycling, and recovers cartridges that might otherwise be refurbished in less-than-high-quality condition.

As recycling increases and even becomes mandatory, many service companies will benefit by reclaiming, refurbishing, recycling, rejuvenating, and remanufacturing durable service assets.

24

COMPUTERIZATION

$\mathbb{A}$computer system is a tool that supports and disciplines Management's strategy and tactics. While preparing this chapter, the authors reviewed the material on computerization in the *Service Parts Management* book that Joe Patton wrote in 1983. It is amazing how much the world of computers and electronics has changed! Then the emphasis was first on hardware and second on process and capabilities. Technology has developed so much that with few exceptions, hardware has become a moot point. Let's start with the history.

Logistics systems history

Service parts management is the material support of the service function. It provides the same role as the material management organization in a manufacturing organization. But, for the reasons covered earlier in this book, the management processes must be significantly different. The history of the development of manufacturing management processes is well known and documented. Starting early in this century and perfected during World War II an "American Standard" approach to managing manufacturing was perfected. When in the 1960s, computerization of this production function started, the function itself (and most of the subfunctions) were well defined. To be sure there are differences such as continuous process manufacturing versus job shop manufacturing, but these can be viewed as variations to an underlying process that the vast majority of manufacturing companies practice. When the individual comprehensive manufacturing systems were put together in the 1970s and dubbed MRP (material requirements planning) there was little difference between them except the bells and whistles.

Service Organization

Service organizations are quite different. There are few "Standard" approaches to date. Every company practices service of durable products somewhat differently. For this reason service managers in search of packaged software to help manage their function rarely find better that a 70 to 80 percent match to their requirements. Interestingly, the systems themselves are standardizing the management practices in the industry. One role of a computerized management system (CMS) is to implement and discipline management's policies and procedures, but, to date, the most different area from company to company is still service parts management. Most of the CMS software vendors offer inventory control functions, and a few offer some stock management tools at a tactical level. None to date offer a fully integrated materials management system for both tactical and strategic implementation which requires some explanation about the varying levels of complexity and sophistication.

INVENTORY CONTROL The system knows precisely where all the parts are, all the time, on a real time basis.

TACTICAL PLANNING The system computes stocking requirements based on history, forecasts, and installed products for selected stocking locations. The CMS dynamically updates requirements in all stocking locations. Stock distributions and stock location performance reports are produced on request, and stock levels are automatically maintained at appropriate levels.

STRATEGIC PLANNING The system actively aligns logistics performance goals to support changing service and service support goals and conditions. On demand the CMS generates what-if? estimates of staffing and funding required for material management and service support based on input service performance scenarios. Selected logistics support strategies are converted to budgets and resource requirements in selectable formats.

Pie-in-the-Sky

For readers who are currently familiar with the state of service parts management systems, this may be viewed as pie-in-the-sky. The point is that manufacturing systems are reaching this level of refinement. The service systems and subsystems that support them should be improving as well. Unfortunately, a great deal of effort has gone into the development of GUI front ends and elegant charts and graphs instead of pushing the envelope from a management system point of view.

Service parts computerization issues

The challenge to achieve inventory control of material that is spread out all over the world and constantly moving is a major effort. It was initially trivialized because basic inventory control is a straightforward process. Service parts inventory control is, however, tremendously complex because of the number of stocking locations involved and the unpredictable movement of the stock. Systems are now available to perform this function in a "bullet proof" manner thanks to system developers who have now fully integrated logistics data collection with service management systems and other corporate functions. Improvements in remote data entry techniques have also contributed immeasurably. The remaining implementation challenge is the human one. Corporate culture changes slowly. Field operations that have traditionally been semiautonomous and used to "taking care of themselves" are not flocking to the band wagon of central inventory control. It will take at least the rest of the millennium to implement these systems.

Better planning can help ease the implementation planning by improving confidence in the system. It is interesting, however, that in the last 15 years of service parts systems evolution the development of sophisticated and adequate logistics planning subsystems has been sorely missing. Those that have been put forward are adaptations of manufacturing materials management and usually fall short of the state-of-the-art in service parts planning theory. To be sure this a complex area to address. Some people consider it the most mysterious of the "black arts" that logisticians practice, but still one would have expected at least a few fully developed integrated planning systems by now.

Fortunately, the need for an integrated planning system at this point has been overcome by events and by a technology that now allows users to develop the tools they need on an ad hoc basis without perturbation of Corporate MIS plans and functions. Unfortunately, systems developers who are now spending great sums to computerize the planning function for resale may be wasting their money since an increasing sophisticated used community is liable to eliminate the market before the product is ready. Let's discuss some of this technology.

Mainframe or not to mainframe

That is the question. *But what is a mainframe these days?* The hardware no longer distinguishes the difference. Physical size used to be all you needed to know! For the purpose of this book let's agree on a slightly unusual definition. The mainframe is a collection of hardware and software designed and implemented to collect detailed transactions over large geographical areas. Think of order entry or service call posting or billing information. One might say "Corporate Mainframe" because it is a central company repository of data. It is the back bone of the process of documenting what persons in the company do. It certainly is where the financial data is kept. It is very capable of collecting and storing large amounts of information. It is not particularly good at the "number crunching" necessary to analyze data. Even today, in an age of inexpensive processors and mass memory, companies limit the amount of analytical work on mainframes because it slows down transaction processing.

When you think about it, this feature of "Main Frame" computers was always there. What is different is that ten years ago we had to pick our hardware carefully to obtain a system that could do an adequate job of both collecting and analyzing the data. Today, it is a slam dunk. See Figure 24-1. The "Main Frame," whatever technology it is constructed of, is the transaction recorder. Parts management information and guidance is best derived from the central data by analysis done on microprocessor-based systems—that is, personal computers (PCs), local area networks(LANs), and wide area networks (WANs).

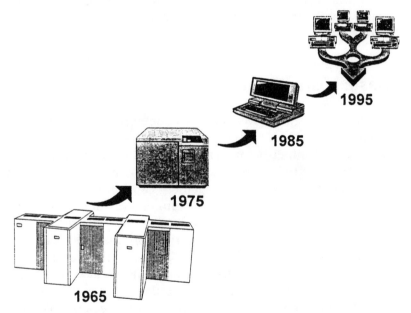

FIGURE 24-1 Your desk computer is more powerful that a room full 30 years ago.

The data transfer problem

Until recent years the biggest problem with integrating systems was the problem of transportability of data. That is, data just wasn't very transportable. Herb Feldmann still tells horror stories about what it took to get data from a Corporate IBM onto a Data General minicomputer for analysis in the early 1980s. The reason for this was obvious even though few people admitted it. If data were transportable then equipment should be interchangeable. Manufacturers did not want customers buying any other equipment except theirs. The solution turned out to be microprocessors. When PCs first arrived on the scene they were not a threat to the manufacturers. The irony is that the solution to the problem also wound up replacing minicomputers and many of the larger systems. These small, multivendor, micro-based systems took on a life of their own. The standard quickly became the IBM PC and to a lesser extent the Apple Macintosh. Now manufacturers were forced to establish rapid data transfer to the PC because their customers demanded it. The PC became the quickest way to transfer data from one computer to another. More importantly, customers now demand rapid transfer of data between different vendor's hardware.

Basic system requirements

How then should we view the issue of computerization for service logistics? How should we think about the system requirements for logistics management for the 21st century? The essential components of a service parts management system should be viewed as the management capabilities that the system provides to users. These requirements are operational tools, planning capabilities, wholesale (central) and retail (field) requirements determination, distribution management, and operational and financial performance planning and assessment. While these issues have always existed, at earlier times they were viewed separately or secondary from a systems perspective, while discussions focused on hardware or data comparability.

Operational tools

Operational logistics systems are essentially control processes. If "bullet proof" inventory control is the primary consideration for any operational tool being developed or evaluated, you can't be far from the mark. Let's talk about where these tools are and how they are applied.

CENTRAL WAREHOUSE The central warehouse is the stocking location through which most material flows. Typically, it is also a collection point for defective material and items to be scrapped. It provides parts to replenish retail level stocking locations and may operate a retail level sale function direct to customers. Inventory control is an imperative here. Please note that in future logistics the physical facilities may be in suppliers, repair depots, and other locations removed from, (and replacing) central warehouses. Information will also be located on many different databases, but should be instantly available to any authorized person anywhere in the world.

If inventory cannot be tracked in the warehouse—all is lost! The system imperative is that if you want to do anything with a part, you must have a transaction for that event in the system or you cannot act. Suppose, for an example, the Vice President for Marketing wants to schedule a demonstration for perspective customers of how the service process works. Suppose he wants to use some real parts from the warehouse for a "couple of hours" as props for the demonstration. There must be a transaction *in the system* to cover this eventuality and know where the parts are all the time.

REPAIR OPERATIONS This includes both in-house and vendor repair. It is composed of a planning function that decides what, how many, and at what repair center, specific parts are to be repaired. At a minimum the system should be able to track specific parts in and out of repair rigorously enough so as to be able to compute repair throughput time by part number. Of all the applications that involve serialized tracking of parts, using bar code or similar technology, repair processing is the application that most justifies the technology investment. The system should also assist shop managers to control the flowthrough of work through the shop. This can be done by expanding the transactions to track from station to station within the shop but care should be taken not to overcomputerize this. First, it is not realistic to do for off-site repair vendors even though it may now be technically feasible. Further, there is a tendency to overdefine stations. For example, do not track items through cleaning, initial inspection, component replacement, testing, final quality assurance, and packaging when the entire process takes less than an hour.

REPLENISHMENT This is the function that keeps the central logistics system "full." It is done in conjunction with repair planning and with ordering from manufacturing (or outside the company) those items that are needed but cannot be supplied from internal resources. The system must dynamically adjust central warehouse and logistics pipeline requirements based on continuous analysis of trended transaction data. Further, it should automatically initiate purchasing and repair transactions in time to keep stock on the shelf ready to meet demands.

USE REPORTING The parts management system should be integrated with service management, order entry functions, and other processes that reflect the consumption of parts at the end of the supply chain. This interface is once again transaction data of the usage as it occurs. The system evaluation/and design criteria are based on the question "Are all parts usage scenarios captured and do they flow smoothly to the service parts data base on a real time basis?"

INVENTORY CONTROL Those actions necessary to assure that all assets in the retail segment of the logistics system are properly accounted for at all times.

Role of bar code and remote data entry

The term *Bar Code* is used here to mean any technology employed to capture data without human key strokes. (for example, Bar Code, Optical Character Readers, and On-board Electronic Signature). Its primary function is to make entering transactions faster and more accurate. Unfortunately it does not correct flawed transaction programming or the lack of transaction discipline on the part of the people that work with the system.

Accuracy of the records and the maintenance of perpetual paper or computer information consistent with physical realities are vital. If the data-collection methods are awkward and time consuming, the data will not be collected. An uncontrolled stockroom, (meaning that anybody can take the parts) rarely will have accurate information on parts status. Someone must be in charge of assuring that the right parts are on hand, and a good record system provides the necessary tool. *Improved technology will not solve system or process problems!*

Planning capabilities

This aspect of planning is the capability to determine resource requirements beyond the parts themselves. It should probably be the last system capability to be mentioned since many of the other capabilities go before into making plans possible. It is listed first so that readers will understand the direction and level of detail required in the other capabilities. To a large extent the process of capabilities planning is an extension of wholesale level parts planning as it should be done by the wholesale level planners. To aid in understanding, we cite an example. Most of our clients are involved in planning the flow of parts through repair operations. More than one of these clients fell into the trap of scheduling to the shop capacity rather than the logistics needs. This obviously becomes a self-fullfilling prophecy and no one learns what the shop capability *should* be or where the bottlenecks are. This is the type of capability planning that must be enhanced by the system. Just as sophisticated manufacturing systems do this type of analysis for the users, so should service parts management systems determine the requirements for repair, purchasing, staffing, and other needs. Let's shift our thoughts back to the planning of the parts themselves.

It is trite to say that planning is important. Trite, but necessary! Glory and praise may go to the masters of the "diving catch" who get the parts there just in time—at the last possible minute, but higher honor should go to the unsung heros who sit in a corner and routinely order parts to arrive when they are needed. The reality is that the "diving catch" is often late, and invariably costs more to execute. The CMS should provide the tools and facilitate the routine planning processes as much, if not more, than the emergency processes. To accomplish this, the system should enhance macro and micro level planning at central and field levels; currently being referred to as Wholesale and Retail level planning.

Wholesale requirements determination

Wholesale parts planning processes are:

REQUIREMENTS FORECASTING The wholesale logistics system must serve as the primary logistics interface with other functional areas of the company. It must provide short and medium range forecasts in monetary terms to the financial organization and at the part number and quantity level to the manufacturing and/or procurement organizations. MRP/DRP type systems are adequate for this and should be an integral part of the system at this level.

PRODUCT SUPPORT PLANNING The wholesale logistics system contains the planning arm of logistics for products that have yet to be introduced. It should have direct access to engineering and marketing data for products being developed, with rapid communication of logistics requirements to these systems. The CMS should be designed to provide immediate feedback to these other functions (engineering and sales) on failure rates, service levels, logistics demands, and life cycle impact of changes that they make.

EXCESS MANAGEMENT The system should have the ability to instantaneously identify excess parts and materials (both local and global) by part number, location, investment, book value and cost-to-retain.

Retail distribution

This field support function determines what parts are to be stocked where and in what quantities. Selections are based on requirements to provide a specified service level. The primary feature of the distribution plan is that each stocking location has a list of parts that are authorized to be stocked there and at what levels of inventory to be maintained. These lists are called Authorized Stock Lists (ASLs). The system should provide an automated capability to establish these ASLs and then allow them to be overlaid and adjusted based on information that human judgments must add. Further, the CMS should have the capability to estimate the impact on changes in service plans (typically reorganizations, new product introductions or changes in major contracts) on field distribution requirements. This capability should be available on an ad hoc, what-if? basis. The system should also facilitate field upgrade planning and scheduling by identifying quantities, locations, workload, and resource requirements.

Operational and financial performance planning and assessment

The system should generate the key measurements to manage all aspects of logistics performance and planning effectiveness. These metrics include:

THE FIRST PASS FILL RATE (FPFR) FPFR is the primary measure of stocking location performance. At the central, wholesale level the stock list is the complete list of parts that may be replaced in the field; that is, Field Replaceable Units (FRUs.)

CYCLE TIMES DISTRIBUTIONS Process cycle times are imperative to logistics operations and the containment of unnecessary investment. A primary feature of the management systems are tools to measure these pipelines. The variation of cycle times in a demand-driven environment is what dictates safety level requirements. The critical metrics are the statistical *mean, median* and *standard deviation* of the following cycle time distributions:

Repair Time The time it takes to return an item to *ready for issue* (RFI) condition once the decision to repair it has been made. This is recorded for every part number and repair location.

Return Time   The time it takes to return an unserviceable part to the repair facility. This is a retail level management responsibility but the data is collected at the wholesale level. The system should provide summary and detailed data at the transaction level based on the activity or person responsible for returning the item.

Procurement Time   The lead time to acquire a new item. The CMS should provide summary and detailed data at the transaction level by part number and vendor. Note that Procurement Time is the total time from the initial request until the part is in hand. The lead time quoted by a supplier is only part of the sequence.

Demand Interval Time   The time between demands for a particular part at a particular stocking location. The system should provide summary and detailed data at the transaction level by part number and stocking location. Note that this calculation is a variation on *demands over time*. Demands of three parts per month translates to ten days between demands, but may have slightly different meaning if all three parts are needed at the same time.

Repair center productivity

Repair center productivity is measured in much the same way that manufacturing productivity is measured at a person-hour level. Labor standards must be developed for each unit repaired and productivity assessed against the standard. The noticeable exception to the manufacturing approach is that repair times are exponentially rather than normally distributed. This dictates that the system must be capable of performing different mathematic algorithms compared to manufacturing measurements. Further, the CMS should produce summary reports (perhaps weekly) on productivity effectiveness and utilization at the shop, part and technician levels. It should further provide automated analysis of "production" delays and, as noted earlier, capacity requirements.

Service level/response time/investment

The relationship between service level, response time, and inventory investment is driven by numerous factors. The system should assess these factors and predict the trade-off between performance and investment. Further, the CMS should also assess its own effectiveness by comparing predictions with actual data after the fact. The CMS should present actual and predicted data in terms of days of supply, number of parts, and level of financial investment for each segment of the logistics pipeline and every stock location.

TABLE 24-1
CMS Report Guidelines

KISS (Keep It Satisfyingly Simple.

Arrange information in human thought sequence.
Put the most commonly used information first.
Allow easy correction of user mistakes.
Plan for expansion.
Build in flexibility.
You set the rules, and let the computer do the work.
Edit all possible entries.
Establish logical hierarchies, e.g., part-equipment-product-system-site-customer-contract.
Display all selections on the screen at one time, rather than one-at-a-time.
Use consistent terms and mnemonics that a human can directly identify.
If you must print, do so on 8.5 × 11 inch plain paper.
Use graphics and illustrations that are easier to interpret than numbers.
Use Word messages as positive direction to the solution.
Strive for guidance, knowledge, and wisdom through comparison with goals, variance analysis, and identification of the critical few.
Let computer experts provide you the computer tools, so that you can concentrate on effectively managing the service business.

Table 24-1 lists major considerations for evaluating the human-friendliness and guidance abilities of logistics reports.

Database requirements

Database requirements for a service parts management system can be thought of as a collection of data tables. A discussion of database structures (hierarchal, indexed, sequential) is no longer germane. Regardless of what happens behind the screen, the database can be represented as a set of data tables related by key elements such as *Part Number* or *Stock Location ID*. This is called a "relational" database and is the modern standard database technology. Following is a list of data tables organized by table type. (Please note that field length and field character type are not identified because those should be whatever makes sense for a company. The only requirement is that fields be internally consistent and validated whenever possible.)

Table types

Following is a list of database table types with a discussion of the purpose, use, and listings, typical of that type.

KEY TABLES These tables are used to identify and validate key identifiers and codes within the system. For the most parts these "codes" are the keys that relate the data tables. They were formerly thought of as "master files," but relational databases do not contain the long records that were necessary in previous data structures. These tables include:

Part Number
Manufacturer
Supplier
Stocking Location
Customer ID

INFORMATION TABLES These tables contain information related to one key value in a key table. Examples:

Part Description
Product Used on
Supplier Terms
Part Number Cross-reference
Customer Address

CURRENT STATUS TABLES The current location and condition of all parts is established in Current Status tables. This data is the focal point of all inventory control actions.

TEMPORARY TABLES These tables are the results of partially manipulated data for use in management reporting or for interface with other systems. Data here is temporary in nature since the accuracy of the information degrades with time. Such tables might be forecasts, budgets, shop loading details, or Field ASL lists. These tables are retained only until the next one is generated. The data that generated the table is retained so that any table can be regenerated as required.

HISTORY TABLES These tables provide the history data necessary to analyze historical action and to trend and forecast future occurrences. These tables may include.

Orders History
Direct Sales
Purchase   History
Repair History
Defective Return Material Assets (RMA)

Please note that many of these history tables require two entries. For example, a Repair History Table implies two entries—one for when a part entered repair and one for when it was completed—necessitating two tables.

SUSPENSE TABLES These are also temporary in nature and, as the name implies, they are used for pending actions. For example, if stock is loaned to sales for a demo, a separate "Loan" table should exist. This enables building two transaction history tables and facilitates the tracking and return of the material. Other examples of suspense files are:

Stock on Order
Pick Pending
Stock Allocation
In Transit
Stock in Repair
Defective Due-In
Stock Reservation

AUDIT TABLE In an earlier technology this was the "Audit Tape." It is a permanent record of every transaction in the system. It should be complete enough to be used in a recovery process for the system. Recovery would involve starting with a historical database and "playing" the transactions from the audit table one at a time to bring history up-to-date. It is important that a complete audit trail be maintained on every important part, from the time someone needs it until that part is used. Checks and balances should be provided to assure that all ordered parts are, in fact, received; that they are paid for on time, and only once; and that they are effectively used for the purpose for which they were intended. A parts record system should include audit controls and safeguards that preclude mistakes or dishonest intentious. For example, one person should request and order parts, a separate person should confirm their receipt, and a third person should authorize the payment. Cycle counts of physical versus perpetual inventory should be conducted with emphasis on the essential high cost parts which have uses outside the business and therefore might be subject to disappearance.

Off-the-shelf system selection

With all the criteria that have been discussed in this chapter the reader will be tempted to think that a system with all the sophistication and functionality that has been discussed is not likely to exist for off-the-shelf purchase. You *are correct!* Manufacturing systems with all of the tools that they could possibly have still don't exist in an off-the-shelf mode either. So, what should users look for if they are shopping for the best possible fit?

In another scenario, service parts managers are left with a situation where Manufacturing and perhaps Finance and possibly Service Operations have selected software that is good for them and compatible with one another. The problem is that the selected system often lacks logistics planning tools that even come close to the ones described in this chapter. What should service parts managers do then?

The answer to both of these questions is the same: *Hang your hat on inventory control and transaction integrity!* Then hang as if your business life depended on 100 percent control accuracy, because it does.

As noted earlier in this chapter, corporate systems (once called mainframe systems) are excellent for collecting and storing data. If the system that you acquire off-the-shelf (or the one that is pushed on you without much choice) does your transactions accurately and on a real time basis—all else can be overcome. If you have to put your job on the line by insisting on accurate, easy, timely capture of the transactions necessary to manage parts—you should. After all, accurate, complete data it is little enough to ask for. Moreover, if the system is so bad that it does not adequately capture transactions, your job is in trouble anyway.

In an environment where adequate and timely transactions are available, all of the other capabilities discussed in this chapter can be efficiently developed and implemented, if necessary, using available personal computer (PC) techniques. The logistics organization in this case will have to employ at least one "power user"—someone who is a "Whiz" with PCs. (To help them survive now, there are usually several PC-skilled planners in logistics organizations. The management challenge of this approach is that the processes to manage parts that are developed around PC technology must be institutionalized. This means that the principles and practices have to be recognized by a company as the formal way to do business and this standard operating procedure (SOP) has to be prepared and followed to insure continuing benefits from the process. The old adage, "It is easier to obtain forgiveness than to ask for permission" might apply, but, in this case, what is to be obtained is praise, not forgiveness, because of the cost savings and service parts performance improvement which will result.

System implementation

Considering the discussion thus far, it is not hard to imagine that when it comes time to implement a service parts management system (or to implement enhancements to an existing one), there are a menage of systems to be tied together. Let's assume the worse. Suppose that the various necessary corporate level systems are not integrated. As long as the data transactions exist somehow somewhere in the company, we can proceed. Let's look at the implementation process one step at a time. *Document as you go!*

SPECIFICATIONS The focus of specifications is on the management capability desired by management. Separating management's desires into what will be derived from corporate systems and what will have to be added locally is a systems integration challenge. The output goals and objectives must be established before the inputs and data manipulation can be determined. This leads to an investigation of where the data will come from and what computations will be made. (Recommended computation metrology is discussed else where in this book and is not addressed here.) The data sources will trigger interactive, ongoing discussions that take place in parallel with the design of the management capability. Stay focused on:

1. Plan and Measure. The finished system will be part of a process wherein action is planned to produce performance results and the performance is measured against what was planned. We must therefore document what we will measure, how we will measure it, and what tools will be needed to help move measurements in the desirable direction.

2. The "Routine" System. Emergencies can be handled manually and documented after the fact. The purpose of the CMS is to improve control over the environment in order to eliminate, or at least reduce, emergencies. Don't be distracted by outlandish *what- ifs?* that happen once a year.

3. Inventory in Motion. The largest shortcoming of most material management systems is managing only the static inventory on the shelf. The dynamic pipeline inventory is just as important, and often more so. Remember that we want to avoid owning assets that sit idle. The best possible situation is to gain the use of a part precisely when we need it. Don't forget to include pipeline management in your processes and as a major tactical advantage of your system.

REVERSE PLAN Start with the desired results. Then step to the controls necessary for the result, the reports necessary for the control, the transactions necessary for the reports, and the procedures necessary to capture the transactions. Document as you go. Appoint a patient person as a scribe to record all decisions and document the processes as they are developed.

"FREEZE THE DESIGN" There is a cliché that says, "If system development is allowed to change without constraint; then the rate of change will exceed the rate of progress." At some point the design must be frozen for implementation. At this point no further modifications are allowed. Suggestions go in a folder for the next revision of the process. "Make it work" changes to "fixing bugs is permitted," but these are limited to system crashes or incorrect calculations.

KISS "KEEP IT SATISFYINGLY SIMPLE" Please note that we are not developing a system or even writing system specifications. We are designing *and documenting* management processes. Pretend that activities must be done manually. Go to the point of manual, hands-on "dry runs" and pilot tests. Who knows, you might have to stop there. You might want to stop there because simple, variable situations are often handled better by a quick human judgment than by computer. You rarely overcomplicate a process if you will have to do it manually—even for a short period of time as a test.

Simple physical methods are sometimes better than computer processes. Instead of counting from the bin every resistor used in repairs, locate a box containing the safety stock in back of a parts bin with a reorder card attached. When the main supply of resistors is all used, the safety stock box can be opened and the reorder card simply dropped into the purchasing agent's basket. Parts that are hung on a pegboard hook can utilize the same principle, with a reorder tag suspended on the rod at the point where the reorder quantity of items will remain after the reorder card is moved.

HARDWARE The hardware required to perform logistics transactions is usually fixed by the corporate systems in which data resides. The planning hardware depends on how much of the planning capability is resident in the corporate system. Beyond that is the PC-based technology primarily intended for "number crunching" of down-loaded system transactions. Herb Feldmann has computed a complete logistics distribution plan for central logistics and 120 field locations on a single 286, 20 MHz PC. It did take 4 hours to generate, but was achievable. A small LAN system is recommended with as many work stations as necessary. These need to be state-of-the-art but not necessarily the "hottest" or "coolest" (meaning the fastest CPU with the most RAM and disk memory) computers available. The same distribution plan that took 4 hours to calculate on the 286, took 20 minutes on a 486 66 MHz machine, and takes only a few minutes on a P5/120 processor. In addition to the work stations, laser quality printers for most reports and a color printer for presentation work are advisable.

SOFTWARE As with hardware, whatever software is needed to operate the corporate system must be provided. Beyond that script, programs to extract transaction data from corporate systems will have to be developed. Ad hoc query language should also be provided. These tools and training on their use should be provided by the Corporate Information Systems (IS) function. Additionally, PC-based productivity tools should be provided to work station users. The most common of these are spreadsheet, word processing and presentation applications software. These are best provided as a suite of integrated programs that work well on the work station hardware. Training is usually provided for these products by Corporate IS. The authors have found that formal training is usually not necessary if individuals are afforded the time to work through the tutorial programs that come with the packages. Proficiency comes with experience. For the development of the "number crunching" programs, a database system is recommended. There are many available in the market place and most office suite packages have one. The authors use a compilable version of FoxPro® since there are versions available for DOS, Windows and Apple Computers and all work is therefore transportable.

TRAINING By the time we get to training of users, much of the training has already been done by active participation. This assumes that Planners, Stock keepers, and other Logistics personnel helped develop the process, wrote the procedures for their processes, and participated in the trials. The challenge is keeping the staff current as the system evolves and the staff turns over. Training should be ongoing in the operational system functions that collect the data in places like the Warehouse, Repair Centers, Shipping and Receiving, Help Desk, and for Field Technicians. Assistance will be available from the IS organization for initial implementations, but post-implementation refresher training and training new personnel must be done in conjunction with the training department or internal to the logistics organization itself.

Start with an overview and then teach people only what they need to know to do their job. Then go back in a week or two with refresher training to assure they can use all available capabilities. In a month, begin to expand their horizons with cross-training and expansion into related functions, as well as assuring details on their own applications.

SYSTEM IMPLEMENTATION IS NEVER FINISHED The process is never finished. There is always more polishing that can be done. There are always new issues in the environment to be confronted. The process and its procedures and computer systems are in continuous evolution. This is true for manufacturing systems. Change is ever greater in the chaotic and evolving world of Customer Service.

What to do when the computer fails

Everything made by humans will fail sometime—lightning storms, squirrels chewing wires, coffee spilled into electronics, disk crashes. If you have experienced a computer failure then you know there should be frequent data backups kept off site and procedures ready to use if the computer quits. Have written procedures and practice them in slack periods. Murphy's Laws usually strike at busy times. "The computer is down" should never stop you from supporting your customers. Inventory records have been kept for centuries without computers. Electronic tools provide magnificent aides to logistics, but artificial intelligence is no substitute for the real thing.

Section III

PULLING IT ALL TOGETHER

25 PERSONNEL AND ORGANIZA- TIONS

People are the most important asset

People are the major expense to most organizations. The major profit generators in most organizations are also people. Every business organization relies on people to provide the ideas, plans, and leadership. As Bill Davidow says, "In the old economy, 80 percent of most companies' assets were tangible. Nowadays, 80 percent of a company's assets are likely to be intangible—people, knowledge, customers. The challenge is to capture the value of those intangible assets and turn them into profits."

We emphasize again that service parts management is a people business, in case the point is not already clear. All the technology of computers, sophisticated equipment, and models cannot accomplish much if good people are not involved. The abilities and motivation of logistics personnel is of vital importance. Good people can overcome any problem. Successful organizations realize the synergistic influence of proper parts management multiplying the effectiveness of other service personnel. Since people and parts are the producers of effective service, tradeoffs can be made to pay a little more for rapid delivery of the right part to save valuable technician time. For example, a modern tactic is for the logistics experts to supply parts to the point of need so the technician can stay on site and concentrate on fixing the equipment and satisfying the customer.

This approach accentuates the positive. There are magnificent opportunities available to the service manager who looks for ways to increase revenues, build the business, implement new technologies, and provide career opportunities for a few more good people.

A parts manager should have hands-on experience with parts—understand statistics and risk taking, be highly motivated, know where different kinds of parts are used and what the necessary storage conditions for them are, and be able to manage any subsidiary personnel. It has been suggested that automated warehouses can replace humans, which may be true in manufacturing where large quantities of materials are moved at a time, but in service where an order averages 1.2 parts, humans can beat automation several times over.

Change, the constant in service

As this oxymoronic subtitle suggests, change is a continual part of the service environment. Unfortunately, people resist change. Executives have difficulty dealing with change but, rather than always reacting, let's take Vince Lombardi's approach that the best defense is a strong offense. Remember that suggestion because many business organizations have recently been on the defensive—cutting costs, terminating people, eliminating investments, and generally acting like turtles pulling head and feet into a closed shell. A major change has occurred in the field technician force. As Figure 25-1 dramatizes, technicians of years ago were thoroughly trained and equipped with oscilloscopes, soldering irons, and component parts so they could fix anything in the field. The skill sets now are shifting to apply the most skills at front end serviceability and at the back end help desk/technical assistance center. This trend is expected to evolve even further so that more field technicians will become parts changers who follow the guidance of diagnostic devices and product experts.

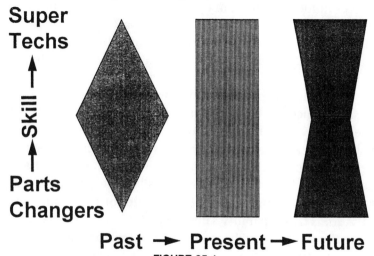

Super Techs

↑

Skill

↑

Parts Changers

Past ➤ Present ➤ Future

FIGURE 25-1
Technician skills are no longer emphasized in the field

One business principle shattered in recent years is the expectation of lifetime employment with a company. It used to be that if a person joined a company after school, he expected to remain there until he got his gold watch on retirement about forty years later. Now, how many of you expect to be with the same company all your working days? Even if we were to be with the same organization for an extended time, its name would have changed several times through mergers, acquisitions, spinoffs, and similar organizational gyrations. We would see other changes in management philosophy including teams, partnerships, outsourcing, flat-broad organizations, greater span of control for managers, subcontracting instead of full employment, restricted medical and other benefits—all of which create the need to look out for yourself. Most employer organizations are no longer paternalistic. Have you noticed that when you ask a person what he or she does for a living, the answer is no longer, "I work for GE, or Kodak, or IBM"? Instead, the career response is, "I am a service manager, a medical equipment technician, or a help desk supervisor."

Technology or people?

Technology in the form of computers, telecommunication, and transportation enables us to do more with fewer people. *Better, Cheaper, Faster* are banner words used by many organizations. Most successful service organizations have invested major funds in their computerized service management systems and in wireless communications with their field representatives. One medical OEM is giving its sales people laptop computers with multimedia, virtual reality capabilities. These enable the "sales person" to go to a medical facility, rearrange the equipment in the most effective manner, and then allow the doctor to walk through and literally "use" the equipment in virtual reality. Impressive? High value for the money? You bet! And, is this capability sales or service? Who really cares? It thrills the customer, who commits to more products and services with this progressive company. It is win-win! The best "sales people" most of our companies have now are called *Service Representatives*.

It is an interesting dichotomy that this same company is having major problems implementing its new computerized service management system to eliminate paper forms and to close calls by remote control. Some people suggest that management's priorities are on the frills rather than the foundation, that management is putting its money on potential revenue increases rather than on what the executives consider expense reduction. Management needs only to be persuaded that service data can be a gold mine with nuggets of wisdom to be intelligently mined.

Examples abound of the service transition from pure hardware installation and repairs to software, professional services, and comprehensive support. Chain saws, lawn mowers, ovens, and safes can all be better sold and supported using technology and management concepts which are changing rapidly. People at all levels recognize the transforming, complex world in which they operate and appreciate insights on how to provide positive direction for improved success.

New appraisal systems

Old rules often counter productive change. Let us consider two Service Parts operations. One has twenty people on a mainframe, plus five supervisors and a manager who constantly complains about the excessive workload. A comparable organization in another company achieves consistently good results with seven total people on a local area network with direct electronic links both to suppliers and the field. Should the manager with more people and the larger budget get the higher salary, or should the more effective manager be paid more? How should their performance be measured? Those challenges of change are similar across most service functions.

When cutting takes place, people are usually the first targets. Many of us have been involved with the activity termed *down sizing, right sizing, reduction in force, termination,* or *firing.* With the benefit of 20/20 hindsight, the authors judge that cutbacks have proven, on the whole, to be detrimental to affected individuals and to the organization. There is also strong evidence that corporations run by financial-based executives concentrate too much on cost reduction, when they should be pushing the generation of new revenues.

It takes a leap of faith to understand how replacing an experienced, (but expensive) manager or teacher or service technician with a fresh-out-of-college youngster who is willing to work for lower wages, gains in any way other than the short term payroll expenses. If you look at value over time, most experienced people can accomplish more in a given time. Their productivity per dollar is higher than the new person who must be trained and then fumbles through a service call taking more time, wasting parts, and aggravating customers. Consider that we should strive to increase revenues and profits rather than concentrating on reducing short term expenses.

Personnel need to know when they are doing well or badly. Publicly praising people when appropriate and providing private constructive criticism is necessary. One of the best techniques for motivating stockroom personnel is providing a large wall chart that tracks number of orders picked, packed, and shipped, percentage on time, percentage error-free, and so forth. A typical chart in reduced form is shown in Table 25-1.

TABLE 25-1
Motivation by posting performance

Orders requested	530
Orders shipped	525
Number of line items	1575
Percent on time	99
Percent error-free	99.8
Percent demands filled	97
Number of complaints	0

Current data can be entered on the chart at the midday break and again at the end of shift. The previous day's data is left until noon of the next day. (Some things are beyond the control of stock personnel, such as the number of requests.) You do not pack orders that have not been requested, but on high order days the orders shipped becomes a goal to strive for and helps motivate personnel to work faster to get the new record on the board. An example of the need for improved goals and motivation is the United States Postal Service (USPS) where people are over 80 percent of its costs. The USPS may be the best in the world, but when bragging that on time delivery performance has risen to 90 percent, it shows they do not understand the value of the missing 10 percent. It is small wonder that people are willing to spend more money to ship via FedEx, UPS, or another courier who assure on-time delivery. (Do note that if you need weekend delivery the USPS now delivers Express Mail Next Day Service on Saturday and Sunday for the standard charge.)

Logistics functional organizations

The major functions of most service parts organizations include the following which are often names of organizations as well as the functions:

Part Master
Planning and forecasting
Procurement
Inventory control
Warehouse
Repair
Finance
Administration

The activities and results of these functions interface with each other and with external functions including engineering, production, marketing, sales, and other partners. These are the top level functions, under which come many subfunctions. For example, the "Part Master" should be a proud title for the person or organization in charge of establishing and enforcing procedures for cataloging new or revised parts, standardizing FRUs, identifying parts for field technicians, and assuring that the computer database of parts is always current.

Where these functions are physically located depends on the objectives of the service organization but prime consideration goes to the warehouse. Since its function is to supply parts quickly to field persons, the warehouse should be located near a major airport, and preferably at an overnight shipper hub. If many products are proprietary, then another consideration is to locate near the production facility. It is desirable to have all parts functions near each other to facilitate the informal exchange of information that inevitably covers more than formal communications. Put all logistics functions in the warehouse facility if you can to help the Part Master, planners, and forecasters to easily lay hands on a part under discussion. Word descriptions are a start, pictures are better, but best is holding the part in your hand to understand its size, weight, fragility, complexity, connections, switches settings, and other consider- ations. Close proximity improves responsibility and account- ability because a Part Master can easily assure if the promised last-minute order can be processed and shipped that night.

Parts representatives should be located with new product developers, marketeers, project managers, and in the Technical Assistance Center. Logistics must influence the early stages of product development and acquisition to assure that part sup- port can be effectively provided. Marketing, left to its own de- vices, might go off and sell products with same-day restore times in Resume Speed, Iowa, without realizing that support will cost far more than the product revenue. Program managers have been known to cut parts plans drastically to lower the quote price, and then expect the original high level of support without the funding. These are negative examples with a defen- sive air. In fact, if logisticians take a proactive stance and are available to provide analysis and advice, their rationale is usu- ally welcomed. Plans done right in the beginning are much better than changed after the course is set.

Parts expertise is vital to facilitating technician results. There can be advantages to locating a representative in the Technical Assistance Center (TAC) to help with parts concerns. Again, the advantage of face-to-face contact improves perfor- mance. With e-mail, fax, phone, and electronic data inter- change (EDI) individuals can be located almost anywhere. Experience shows that, with proper goals in place, the nonware- house members of a service parts team can function in various locations with other members.

Part Master qualifications

The Part Master function should be located at the point where new parts enter the organization. In a company servicing products that they design, the Part Master function may be in Design Engineering with strong oversight from Logistics. In an independent service organization (ISO), also termed third-party maintainer (TPM), parts enter from the new product planners and from technicians who encounter new parts for the first time. Personnel qualifications include:

1. Education—College BA or BS with emphasis on numbers and technology.

2. Experience—Hands-on work as a stockkeeper or technician working on similar equipment.

3. Special qualifications:

□ Computer literate in database, spread sheet, and word processing applications.

□ Touch type at least 50 characters per minute on computer keyboard.

□ Stickler for details to discipline data entry and validation of Part Master database.

4. Responsibilities:

□ Establish standard process and procedures for cataloging parts with noun nomenclature and necessary data details.

□ Assure computer software enables the above process and procedures so many people can simultaneously search to find a needed part, or add required details if the part is not already entered and create a new part identifier.

□ Work with product planners and TAC to assure that a part is not duplicated under multiple identifiers.

□ Analyze parts to establish the proper ABC classification for each based on demand, cost, essentiality, shelf life, control, and use patterns.

□ Establish links to interchangeable, substitutable parts with the same form, fit, and function.

□ Classify parts for engineering evaluation that are candidates for substitutes if they had slight modifications such as connectors, firm ware, or mounting modifications.

□ Identify logical configuration changes to maintain accurate records. For example, a technician may install part 456 and return defective 345, which will be repaired to a 567. The part record needs to convert identifiers to assure accurate transfer accounting and control.

□ Standardize field replaceable units (FRUs) to meet the criteria outlined in chapter 10.

◻ Aid TAC analysts, technicians, and customers to correctly identify parts.

◻ Work with product design and production to stimulate use of existing standard parts.

◻ Purge unneeded obsolete and superceeded parts from the active database.

Planning and forecasting analyst qualifications

Planners and forecasters identify which parts should be stocked where. They provide the directions for the operations people to implement. A typical job description for an Inventory Analyst is as follows:

1. Education—a Bachelor degree or the equivalent in business, engineering, mathematics, or a scientific field with emphasis on numerical analysis.

2. Experience—at least two years' related experience such as production inventory control, field service management, or with a parts distributor or retailer.

3. Special qualifications:

◻ Hands-on experience, which should provide knowledge of what kinds of parts are potential problems.

◻ Ability to relate part names to the physical objects and the conditions under which they are used.

◻ Able to sit at computer monitor for long periods of time and concentrate on complex tasks.

4. Responsibilities:

◻ In cooperation with technical personnel, analyze new products to determine which parts will need to be replaced and at what rate.

◻ Based on response and restore requirements, desired support level, and finances, develop provisioning strategy including where stocks should be located.

◻ Generate authorized stock lists (ASLs) for every inventory location.

◻ Establish initial economic order quantity.

◻ Request parts through purchasing channels.

◻ Determine initial reorder point.

◻ Work with the computerized parts management system to assure that data entered is complete, timely, and valid. Use that data to provide guidance for improved parts support.

◻ Establish automated procedures to place normal resupply orders without human intervention.

◻ Coordinate with engineering and marketing to assure that inventories are adjusted for revisions to parts, special projects, end-of-life buys, and other changes.

◻ Provide input to life-cycle costing and trade-off analyses that involve parts.

◻ Produce ongoing measurements to determine when parts are above or below control limits.

◻ Calculate, dynamically analyze, and revise safety stock levels for critical parts.

◻ Document logic, reasons for change, and audit trails so that other people can understand the rationale and could rapidly assume the responsibilities.

◻ Prepare budgets and operate within approved limits.

Procurement qualifications

Parts procurement in a small organization may be embodied in the same person who does the inventory analysis, and probably brews the coffee too. In larger organizations purchasing may be a completely separate function to which the inventory management simply forwards purchase requests. There should be checks and balances by the Finance function, but the action people should be organized under Service Parts for motivation and technical control. The term procurement is preferred over the term *purchasing* because modern parts managers should arrange advance exchange, consigned parts, supplier direct shipment, and other tactics that will avoid the need to purchase parts with balance sheet money. Procurement in a multivendor organization must be more flexible, responsive, and results controlled (rather than process detail controlled) than is purchasing for proprietary products. Note that Procurement is charged with getting parts from outside the company, including from repair vendors. Operations people are responsible for gaining the best use of assets already owned, and then handing the baton to Procurement if additional parts are needed from external sources. Responsibilities of the part Procurement function, regardless of where it is located, include:

1. Education—College Associate or Bachelor degree with emphasis on human relations.
2. Experience — Retail buying and selling or technician work with similar industries is helpful.
3. Special qualifications:

☐ Ability to juggle several tasks at once, under time pressure.
☐ Able to weigh considerations of price, delivery, quality, and other factors for on-the-spot decisions.
☐ Enjoy communicating with people, be pleasant to deal with, and an effective negotiator.

4. Responsibilities:

☐ Contact and qualify a small group of vendor-partners who can together fill all parts needs.
☐ Track vendors' performance to determine the recommended vendor for each part.
☐ Provide reports to suppliers and internal customers of performance and areas for improvement.
☐ Arrange for technical and other assistance as necessary to help vendors perform at desired levels.
☐ Process purchase requests for necessary approvals.
☐ Create purchase orders from the approved requests.
☐ Consolidate purchase orders to get the best possible combination of vendor performance and benefit/cost.
☐ Evaluate benefits and costs of blanket purchase orders, bulk buys, and outsourcing alternatives.

□ Contact prospective vendors to determine whether parts are available and get quotes.

□ Prepare formal requests for proposals or quotes, where required.

□ Negotiate any discrepancies, such as shortages or quality rejects.

□ Assure tracking of receipts to accounts payable and authorization of payment.

□ Acquire communications and computer systems that enable instantaneous, paperless transactions.

Inventory control personnel qualifications

Inventory control is responsible to assure that every part is where it should be. They assure accountability.

1. Education—Associate, technical school, or college degree
2. Experience—Production material control, stockkeeper, and/or warehouse work in a related environment.
3. Special qualifications:

□ Type at least 80 characters per minute on computer keyboard.

□ Able to work under pressure in a high volume, time-sensitive facility

4. Responsibilities:

□ Assure that the authorized stock list (ASL) parts are always good and ready for issue.

□ Monitor parts at outside vendors for repair to assure timely availability for use.

□ Assure that parts used by field technicians are promptly shipped to repair.

□ Stimulate the return of excess parts.

□ Calculate the dollar-time value of parts in pipelines and publicize opportunities for improvement.

□ Develop and gain auditor's approval for cycle count process to avoid shut-down physical counts.

☐ Track down count discrepancies and resolve them through management approval.

☐ Maintain close relationship with Procurement to assure supplier quality of new and repair parts.

☐ Expedite special part and equipment needs.

☐ Identify unmarked parts and equipment and assure accurate accounting transactions.

☐ Spot check pick, pack, and ship to assure accuracy of order fulfillment

☐ Issue, record, and followup on return material authorizations (RMAs).

Warehouse personnel qualifications

Warehouse operations are often referred to as the muscle of the parts organization. Pickers and packers need good minds too. This can be an entry-level position for people who can read and write and pay attention to detail. One of the most important characteristics of a parts person is attention to quality that will assure picking the proper part and handling it safely so that the correct item arrives at the user's location in good condition. The qualifications listed can serve as a check list for the various jobs:

1. Education—high school or equivalent.
2. Experience—helpful, but not mandatory, to have worked with equipment using parts similar to those supported.
3. Special qualifications:

☐ Physically able to lift and move heavy objects.

☐ Qualified to operate fork truck, material handling equipment, and packaging machines.

☐ Read accurately and write legibly.

☐ Can accurately enter data on keyboard terminal with at least two fingers at a time.

☐ Ability with numbers generally equivalent to balancing a checkbook.

4. Responsibilities:

□ Establish and care for parts-keeping facilities.

□ Receive parts from shippers or plant receiving, assure that proper items and quantities are received, and report the transaction.

□ Determine correct location for incoming parts and stock them to the proper bins.

□ Maintain accurate parts records.
Note when high moving parts in a bin drop below the reorder point and assure that an order has been placed.

□ Obtain parts to meet special needs.
Expedite parts for emergency repairs.

□ Obtain and support consumables and supplies purchased in bulk but issued in smaller quantities.

□ Issue parts to authorized requesters.

□ Receive unused parts back into stock.

□ Arrange transportation for parts as required.

□ Return repairable parts to center; assure requested data are provided and that credits are accounted for.

Training

Formal training with on-the-job follow-up is vital for qualified parts personnel. As many procedures as possible should be developed to show the "one best way." The descriptions should be written and used as a core for the training program. It is easy for someone long experienced in the parts business to say that things are "intuitively obvious and anybody can do that," but quite often that is not true. As Figure 25-2 illustrates, there can be a major knowledge and motivation gap to be filled by training.

When a person is assigned to a service parts function, an initial orientation walk through the warehouse, call management center, technical assistance center, and parts planning should be provided by the supervisor. Then a classroom session should be conducted to outline all the activities that go on and how the procedures meet those demands. Forms should be completed during training to assure that all entries are complete and legible. If a computer terminal is used, the available programs should be exercised with training that will point out

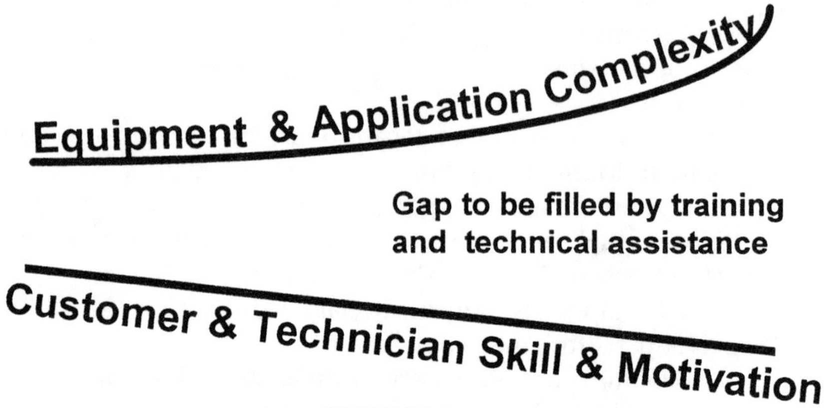

Equipment & Application Complexity

Gap to be filled by training and technical assistance

Customer & Technician Skill & Motivation

FIGURE 25-2
Effective use of modern technology requires extensive training

any errors. Self-paced instruction is possible for much of this training. If the turnover in personnel requires frequent training, then an investment in programmed instruction, either written or on a computer, will be helpful.

Parts management pointers

Since training is only a means to the end result of better performance, improvements in work processes can come from informal encounters. Solicit ideas from the people who are doing the job. Many managers are surprised at how much employees really have to offer when the manager requests their help. Suggestion boxes are useful in a large organization, but the most effective approach is from the supervisor who says, "We ought to be able to do this better. Do you have any ideas?" Good follow-up is necessary, of course, and the good ideas should be put to use whenever possible. Soliciting ideas and then not doing anything will put an end to the ideas. Publicly acclaiming such ideas usually brings out more. Participation groups such as a quality circle are also effective. Employee groups can address specific problems or may address broad issues that can then be narrowed down into specific challenges. Participative approaches by a facilitating leader can further more good parts management than any amount of dictatorial demanding.

The management techniques of providing authority commensurate with responsibility and delegation are also effective. A human tendency is to do something yourself because it is quicker and more accurate than taking the time to explain it to someone else. The result for employees can be a very dull work situation. People usually work harder if their jobs are enriched by opportunities to do special projects and stretch their talents. As many tasks as possible should be delegated to the lowest level person who has the ability and knowledge to accomplish them.

Authority, responsibility, and accountability should go hand in hand. A manager can delegate authority but will not be relieved of the ultimate responsibility to assure that the job is accomplished. The person who is given and accepts the task is made responsible and accountable for accomplishing what he/she has agreed to do. There are many difficult situations in managing parts where someone is responsible for something without having the necessary authority. For example, a supervisor is told to do everything necessary to get a job done, but then is restricted as to the personnel and resources available. Or the parts manager is held responsible for a 98 percent stock level but is not given authority to determine which parts are to be ordered and how many dollars can be spent. If a job is to be accomplished, then authority must be given that is commensurate with responsibility. The complete combination of authority, responsibility, and accountability will help provide strong motivation for parts personnel. Be sure that the person assigned the task has access to the necessary authority, personnel, and resources in order to perform successfully.

26 LOGISTICS PERFORMANCE ENVELOPE

The Logistics Performance Envelope (LPE) is a term that expresses the concept that a successful balance for every service parts situation can be found between the major logistics performance metrics. The value of the metrics at this "balance" point can then be used to express a logistics support policy in quantitative terms. As a quick reminder, the following metrics will be used in this chapter to explain the Logistics Performance Envelope concept.

First Pass Fill Rate (FPFR) is the percentage of time that the part needed is available for issue in the stocking location that is planned to provide first level support for that part. For the purpose of discussing the LPE at a corporate policy level, the first pass fill rate is the aggregate first pass fill rate at the end of the supply chain. (This means at stocking locations that directly serve the ultimate customers.)

Logistics Service Level   is the percentage of time that a needed part is delivered to a customer site within the prescribed time period, regardless of the number of passes it takes at the logistics system.

Response Time   is the amount of time that it takes logistics to provide the part once the need is identified. For Logistics Performance Envelope purposes this is the aggregate average response time to customers. (Note that contracts rarely specify the part response time alone, but rather include it as part of Restore Time.)

Required Investment   is the financial investment level for assets required to provide the desired performance levels of the these three metrics.

Bounding the envelope

The Logistics service level as defined above can not be planned for directly. Ultimately it is the result of human effort on a case-by-case basis and for this reason the logistics service level is inconsistent and difficult to plan. Fortunately, it can be planned for indirectly. The FPFR can be planned and measured at both an individual stocking location and at aggregate levels. The FPFR defines the part availability without additional human efforts. Simply, it is the percentage of the time the part is where it should be when the need for it arises there. Obviously FPFR supports and is the basis for overall logistics service level. It is also one of the three curves of the logistics performance envelope. The other two are the Response Time and the Financial Investment. Figure 26-1 is a representation of the LPE.

Notice that there is an area bounded by the curves for FPFR, Response Time and Investment. This is the area where the goals for all three of these metrics are met (ergo the term *performance envelope*). A couple of things should be understood:

• The envelope portrayed is a single implementable combination of the three main metrics. There are other influencing factors. In fact, the solution is three-dimensional and each of

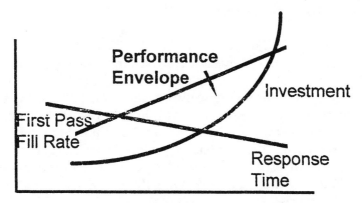

FIGURE 26-1
The logistics performance envelope is bounded by the range of acceptable metrics

these three parameters is really a plane that is affected by additional variables. (We feel very progressive to be able to model the situation in two dimensions and gain major improvements at that.) Additionally, there are combinations of the three metrics which are beyond the envelope of reasonable performance. The most often quoted is "Stock everything everywhere with no investment."

• There are no scales shown in the diagram because the relationship between the metrics is not absolute or constant. The actual numbers are unique to each enterprise and are driven by complex factors including product mix, financial condition of the company, customer expectations, competition, past performance, and contractual obligations. Performance envelopes are therefore different from company to company, and often even product to product within a company. Moreover, they change over time as business conditions change.

These factors reveal that the development of a Logistics Performance Envelope is not a one time occurrence. It is the macro level of a logistics business model and a management tool that should be used on an ongoing basis. If properly developed and implemented, the Logistics Performance Envelope will assure optimal levels of investment for any logistics performance level selected by company management.

Planning fill rate

Many procedures have been devised over the years to contain service parts inventory growth. Since the "growth" that concerns most people is inventory financial investment, most of these procedures are fiscally oriented controls. An example is to assign an investment dollar limit to each field manager and then track the actual investment to assure that the limit is not exceeded. This approach has the benefit of assuring that corporate investment is controlled while permitting stocking flexibility in the field. Unfortunately, it also has some major disadvantages.

Fiscal controls do not tie the stock performance to the dollar limits. Deciding what to stock is a separate process from deciding what the total value of the stock should be. While the concept of "maximum flexibility" sounds good from a human resource perspective, field personnel can only see part of the big picture and their stocking decisions are often suboptimal from a corporate logistics point of view. When carried to an extreme, fiscal control (which might include a bonus structure for field managers who stay under their planned dollar limit) can result in degradation of field logistics support at the expense of the customer, and an increase in labor costs. Overall, the concept of direct financial control of service parts investment is putting the cart before the horse. It is much better to decide what logistic service level is desired, come up with a list of parts to do that, and then look at the investment. If it isn't what it has to be, then restructure the list or adjust the service goal. Once a balance has been reached, the parts can be managed and controlled directly and the investment will follow.

The process is usually managed with an Authorized Stock List (ASL), which is a list of parts that are authorized to be retained in a particular stocking location. The ASL contains the reorder point and order quantity for each part number. The list is needed to plan and manage stock. Without ASLs, we can't tell specifically what we need to have in place and where; neither can we determine the required investment or potential excess. To plan an authorized stock list for any inventory location there are two questions that must be addressed—What parts to stock? How many of each part to stock?

What to stock?

We discussed in chapters 5 and 8 the use of Pareto analysis for the purpose of identifying the critical few parts. This prioritization minimizes management problems as we stock the fewest parts that create the greatest benefit. This is a relatively straightforward process, but first we must select the data that is used in the analysis. Here are the trade-offs:

USE VERSUS DEMAND Should consumption at the end of the supply chain be used as a basis for stocking or should we use the demand data or even the issues data? To quickly understand the difference, consider that technicians typically order more parts than they ultimately use. Not all parts demanded (ordered) are available to issue. Not all issued parts are consumed (used). Since the function of logistics is to support the field technicians, who in turn support the ultimate customer, it is recommended that logistics stock be based on *demand*.

REQUESTS VERSUS QUANTITY A request is an order, which may contain many part numbers and multiple quantities of each. The initial inclination of most people is to use demand quantity, but consider the "Principle of Dissatisfaction" which states that if someone asks once for ten of a nonstocked item they leave disappointed once. If a technician asks ten times for one of a nonstocked item, then he leaves disappointed ten times. For this reason it is recommended that the demand pattern be analyzed. If the average quantity demanded per request is greater than 1.5, then use the request rate as a basis to decide what parts to stock.

FORECAST VERSUS HISTORICAL Historical data is much easier to use in an "untreated" form and can be used as a forecast for low demand items because of the problems of forecasting for small numbers . For other items we should go to the trouble of formal statistical forecasting. This will assure that stocking decisions are forward looking rather than backward looking. New product plans should be folded in, as well as factors that planners know are not reflected in the historical data. Once the data has been manipulated we can apply Pareto analysis, Figure 26-2.

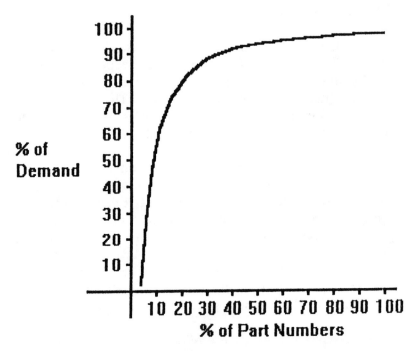

FIGURE 26-2
Pareto diagram shows cumulative percents of parts and filled demands

The Pareto curve illustrates the same relationship we have seen before. A very high percentage of the demand is generated for a very small percentage of the parts. Therefore the most straightforward approach to planning field stocking is to stock the high demand items in the field and retain the low demand items centrally. The spreadsheet format of Table 26-1 shows information for 12,900 demands on 2,900 part numbers.

In this example if you wanted to fill 86 percent of the demands you would only have to stock 700 of the 2,900 parts in the field. This is the beginning of the stock list. It will need a lot of work and coordination before it is done (see the process discussed in chapter 27), but it is a good start. (You may also want to review information on level setting from chapter 13.)

Controlling fill rate

The key to controlling fill rate in any stocking location is to control it the way you plan it. The critical metrics are Demand

TABLE 26-1
Pareto calculations show the most important items first

Incremental No. of Part Numbers Demanded	Incremental Number of Demands	% of Demand	% of Part Numbers	Cumulative % of Demands	Cumulative % of Part Numbers Demanded
100	4,350	33.72	3.45	33.72	3.45
200	3,375	26.16	6.90	59.88	10.35
200	2,025	15.70	6.90	75.58	17.25
200	1,350	10.47	6.90	86.05	24.15
200	900	6.98	6.90	93.03	31.05
200	375	2.91	6.90	95.94	37.95
200	225	1.74	6.90	97.68	44.85
200	150	1.16	6.90	98.84	51.74
400	75	0.58	13.78	99.42	65.53
1000	75	0.58	34.47	100.00	100.00
2,900	12,900	100.00	100.00		

Accommodation and Demand Satisfaction. When the Pareto analysis was done to determine what parts were to be on the authorized stock list (ASL), Demand Accommodation for that stock location was being planned. When the stock levels were assigned (Order Point and Order Quantity), Demand Satisfaction was being planned. Since first pass fill rate (FPFR) is the product of Demand Accommodation and Demand Satisfaction, control of fill rate is directly related to planning. Here are the rules:

• If Demand Accommodation is low, you have the wrong list of part numbers. Do the Pareto analysis again and increase the planned accommodation level

• If Demand Satisfaction is low and Demand Accommodation is adequate, you are stocking the right items but not enough of them. Review the safety stock calculations and increase the probability of success.

• Never stock items (in any stocking location) which are not on the ASL or in greater quantities than are permitted by the ordering policy. The exception is at central logistics where low use, high value, insurance and excess parts should be consolidated.

Planning investment

Required investment is a function of field level First Pass Fill Rate (FPFR), Logistics response time, and "pipeline" requirements. Calculations start with the usage profile for *one* item on the stock list of *one* inventory location. If we multiply this by the average cost of the item, we have the planned investment for that one item. If we add the planned investment for all the items on the stock list, we have the planned investment for the stocking location. If we add the planned investment for all the stocking locations then we have the planned investment for all on-hand stocks.

Remember that the pipeline quantity for the item is the reorder point less the safety level, plus one-half of the order quantity. This is the quantity of the item that is needed for the replenishment pipeline to assure that levels are maintained in the stocking location. If we multiply this quantity by the average cost of the item we have the planned pipeline investment for *one* item. Again, by adding the planned pipeline investment for all parts at all stocking locations we obtain the planned pipeline investment for the replenishment pipeline.

There are other pipelines to consider, most notably the return and repair pipelines for repairable items. The point is that investment is directly related to the FPFR and computable from the same data. If we can plan and control our field fill rate, then we can plan and control our investment.

Investment reduction

Many ways have been tried to reduce parts inventory costs. Suffice it to say that for any FPFR and response time combination there is *one and only one* optimal investment level. Within the context of the logistics structure presented, here are principles that work:

SHORTEN (SPEED) PIPELINES This reduces the pipeline investment requirements. It is most effective when applied to the repair and defective return pipelines. It may require some organizational restructuring and process changes. This is *the major improvement opportunity* for most organizations.

EXCHANGE HIGH COST ITEMS that are demand supported for lower cost items with equivalent demand to reduce the required on-hand and pipeline investment. The higher cost item was on the list to begin with because it was justified by the demand rate. Watch out, it may take several low cost items to reach an equivalent level of demand accommodation, so the investment savings may be eaten up with administrative costs for the additional SKUs and the emergency transportation costs for those removed from the list. Push for the lowest possible number of SKUs, and allow greater quantities of the fewer items.

REDUCE THE SAFETY LEVEL This reduces the on-hand investment requirement but also reduces Demand Satisfaction since there will be a higher out-of-stock rate. This in turn will reduce FPFR unless more items are added to the stocking list—another Catch-22.

REDUCE ORDER QUANTITIES This reduces the on-hand and the replenishment pipeline investment requirements but increases the number of replenishment orders. This is effective if the desire is to trade off investment costs for expense costs or if the logistics administration and warehouse personnel are underutilized.

Planning response time

Logistics response time is the last of the performance envelope parameters and it is the most difficult to change. It is a direct function of how near the parts are to the customers. Since response is a matter of time and distance, it dictates how many field stocking locations are needed and thereby drives on-hand and pipeline investment requirements. Obviously, if we wish a two hour response to our customers, we need more stocking locations (and a higher investment) than if we were happy with a four hour response. As a matter of fact, if we can operate our business with a three-day routine response time and overnight for emergencies, we need only one stocking location. Response time has a predictable relationship with required investment.

The stock distribution that is currently most cost effective in high-tech service organizations on North America is called strategic stocking. Under this plan local stocking is reduced to a lower level (perhaps 60 to 85 percent of the demand) and then augmented with centrally controlled, strategically placed stocking locations. These strategic locations are usually operated by a third party and located near airports. They do not replenish the local stocking locations but rather provide for the next increment of demand. Typically the planning is for 97 percent of the demand to be satisfied from the local or strategic levels. An example of strategic locations is shown in Figure 26-3.

These locations are within two hours commercial flying time and/or four hours ground drive time from most US locations. Additionally, all but two major metropolitan areas (Minneapolis and Miami) are covered by more than one strategic location. Many areas are covered by three or four of these locations. Of course the placement of these locations, like the local ones, is driven by where the customers and their equipment are located.

Response from multiple stocking locations

Planning the over all logistics response time is a matter of computing a weighted average from the various levels from which parts are supplied. This easily fits in a spreadsheet format. For example, a response time estimate for a logistics strategy that provided 85 percent FPFR from the local level and 10 percent from the strategic level might look like Table 26-2.

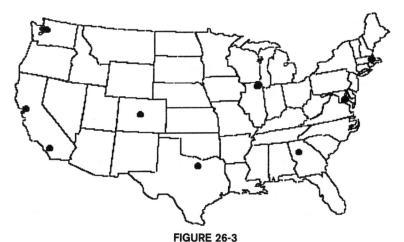

FIGURE 26-3
Typical strategic locations to provide same day delivery

Atlanta, GA	Dallas, TX	San Francisco, CA
Boston, MA	Denver, CO	Seattle, WA
Chicago, IL	Los Angeles, CA	Washington, DC

This produces a 2.7 hour mean logistics response time, with 85 percent occurring within 15 minutes. In order to reduce the response time, the stock is moved closer to the customers. In the following example in Table 26-3 the local FPFR has been increased to 95 percent and the strategic level has been reduced to 3 percent.

This dramatically reduces the mean response time to 1.2 hours, with 95 percent within 15 minutes. With the response time improvement of course comes additional investment.

TABLE 26-2
Part response times can build from multiple stock locations

Level	% of Fill	Response Time (hrs)	Aggregate (hrs)
Local	85	.25	0.21
Strategic	10	8.00	0.80
Central	3	24.00	0.72
Other	2	48.00	0.96
Total	100		2.69

TABLE 26-3
Parts response is speeded by placing more parts closer to the customers

Level	% of Fill	Response Time (hrs)	Aggregate (hrs)
Local	95	.25	0.24
Strategic	3	8.00	0.24
Central	1	24.00	0.24
Other	1	48.00	0.48
Total	100		1.20

How much logistics is enough?

We have presented the computations for the three parameters that drive logistics performance and interrelate to one another mathematically—First Pass Fix Rate (FPFR), Required Investment, and Logistics Response Time. In narrative the relationships are as follows, assuming that you want fast response time, a high level of support, and low costs:

• Raise FPFR: Investment goes up (bad), Response Time goes down (good)
• Lower FPFR: Response Time increases (bad), Investment decreases (good)

• Lower Investment: Response Time lengthens (bad) and FPFR go down (bad)
• Raise Investment: Response Time speeds (good) and FPFR increases (good)

• Reduce Response Time: FPFR declines and Investment goes up (bad, bad)
• Lengthen Response Time: FPFR improves (good) and Investment decreases (good).

Ideally, the optimal balance is a point where three lines intersect. Alas, there is friction in the real world, planning is not perfect, and execution is not perfect. But suppose that we build a business model of what were trying to achieve with our logistics strategy and leave room for the real world friction and for management flexibility. Then we create on the chart an area to operate within the Logistics Performance Envelope. Stated as a policy direction it might sound like this, "Keep the investment under X, keep the field FPFR up to Y, and don't let the response time exceed Z." *(We have defined quantitatively without bias how much logistics is enough!)*

Calculate logistics requirements to drive financial needs

Many service organizations respond to requests for proposal, (RFPs) without knowing how much the required parts will cost, what of those costs are incremental or what parts may already be available. The process should be in the following steps.

1. Establish Response Time based on the RFP contractual terms. Any products on same-day response should be specifically identified. Determine if response desired is mean (average) or maximum. Many customers expect all calls to have action in progress by the expected response time. Also determine how much restore time will be used before parts are requested.

2. Establish several related levels of support. Typically 85, 90, 95, and 98 percent are good draft levels.

3. Calculate the financial costs of each support level, and for any variations in response or restore time.

4. Gain management decision for the one best level (or variations) to be offered.

5. Price the proposed contract accordingly.

6. When selected, generate the authorized stock list (ASL) of parts for the selected level.

Planning a logistics strategy

Many companies have a logistics strategy, but few have proactively built them. It usually evolves over time and is the result of a tenuous equilibrium of external and internal pressures. The steps that are necessary to build a logistics strategy, or to examine the one you have, are outlined below. It is not a quick or easy process.

- Build a business model. Since every business is unique, the model has to be unique. The foundation programs exist but tuning is required for most situations. No canned software exists that will do the job at the level of detail required to achieve accurate results. It will require a great deal of data and some programming. From personal experience, a typical business model requires about 25 megabytes of data and 4,000 lines of code. The mathematics involved has been explained in chapters 8, 9, 12, and 13. The really good news is that with the appropriate download of data, the model can be built on a PC.

- Use the model to develop alternative logistics strategies. Each strategy should reflect a feasible combination of FPFR, Response Time and Financial Investment. Other outputs of the model will depend on the needs of the business and the management that will ultimately approve the strategy.

- Decide on a strategy. It is probably not surprising that this is the most time consuming and painful step. The decision will affect the Service and Finance organizations directly. It is likely to have an indirect affect on Sales, Manufacturing and Engineering as well. Getting the right people together to understand the issues and agree on the solution will be problematical. Once they have agreed, it is imperative that the strategy be communicated throughout the company so that there is no confusion about the logistics charter and expectations. Especially train and discipline salespeople that same-day response and restoration is much more expensive for both parts and labor than is next-day response.

- Put together a detailed implementation plan to fulfill the selected strategy. Since things typically have to change, project management techniques and software are usually necessary for planning and management of the changes.

- Retain top management involvement throughout the process. The visible interest and participation of corporate executives is essential because of the cross-functional impact of the strategy. Keep them stage center. Permission is not enough. Proactive support is vital!

• This is not a case where half a loaf is better than none. Remember, if tempted to settle for less than a complete implementation, you just wind up with spoiled dough.

27 *PERFORMANCE ASSESSMENT*

$\mathbb{P}$erformance assessment in the service parts business can be a tricky business. Sometimes parts operations that look busy, thrive on accomplishing the impossible in the face of chaos, and are the heros of the hour, are in fact in very bad shape. This type of organization gets caught up in the "diving catch" syndrome and is usually driven by the personality of one individual. It cannot last forever. A crash is inevitable. The damage can be severe and will be at your customer's expense. For this reason it is important that management assess the quality and potential of a service parts operation beyond the reputation of the organization. Figure 27-1 outlines the process for performance improvement.

Assessment process

BASIC FAMILIARIZATION The first step is to become thoroughly familiar with the physical facilities. Tour the central logistics

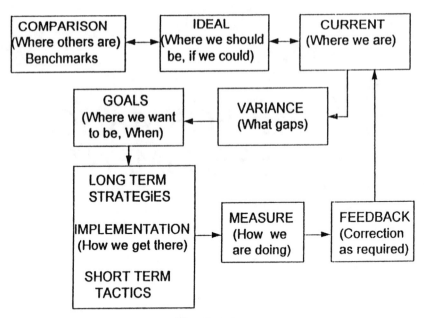

FIGURE 27-1
A defined process aids performance improvement

facilities in detail. Spot check field and subcontract facilities. Look at the areas that the staff wants to show, but also randomly look at areas that are not suggested. Second, have the staff present a briefing on strategies, plans, goals, measurements and all pertinent situations concerning logistics support services. What they say (and don't say) speaks volumes. Interview senior management of related functions including headquarters service managers and senior people of engineering, manufacturing, quality, finance, marketing, sales, purchasing, and anyone else who has ideas and challenges to share. Third, determine the industry benchmarks for comparable service parts logistics functions. Don't concentrate solely in your own industry. Comparison with mediocrity is of little value. Look to the "best of breed" performers in each segment of the business and reason how L. L. Bean's pick techniques or Land's End's packaging might improve your parts operation.

PLANNING Make a formal project of the assessment. Prepare a plan and timetable. Schedule an appointment with management at a specific time in the future to present your findings and recommendations. If this seems like a trick to force completion of the assessment; it is!

SELECTING SAMPLES Most emergency processes work well. It is more important to discern if the routine processes are working well. Historical data is needed for accurate evaluation. Quantify as much as possible and get as much data as possible. When complete data sets are not available, randomly select sample data. A statistical analyst can help to set up the data analysis. Main considerations for selecting sample locations and functions include:

1. Representative
2. Influence
3. Inclusion of extremes in geography, customers, products, environment, and perceived performance
4. Image
5. Cooperation expected
6. Size
7. Convenience of access
8. Cost in money and time

If an organization is geographically dispersed, then assure that a suborganization is evaluated in every area. This helps to cover the objection, "It might be that way in their area, but it is different in mine." (Note that regional differences have been found to be very small, generally within 1.5 percent of each other.) Individual managers and their people are the biggest effect. It also helps to visit and interview influential personalities. The informal communications network will quickly spread the word that this guy is really trying to help us.

Thorough preparation is obviously required so that you walk into that first location ready to ask the right questions and then quietly listen. When conducting an assessment, keep your senses alert. There is nothing as useless as solving the wrong problem, so make sure that the facts are accurate. It is easy to make premature judgments based on initial impressions.Most good managers will welcome the evaluation with open arms, recognizing that they need all the help they can get. A few people, however, will be defensive, usually because of their fear of being criticized. It can be very helpful to sit down with the affected managers and let them know in businesslike fashion why you are conducting the investigation, and that the objective is to improve service performance for everyone's benefit. The improvement team leader must be a good salesperson with public relations abilities in order to sell the activities in a positive fashion, yet be backed by top management who will dictate compliance if necessary.

FACE-TO-FACE, ON-SITE EVALUATION Talk with the people that do the work at all levels. Listen to their frustrations. (Most of the time these are just the result of human nature.) Sometimes, however, there are windows on problems and keys to solutions in what they say. Be patient. Listen to understand before you even consider suggesting a solution.

PRESENTATIONS AND BUY-IN Service parts logistics permeates a company, but at a very low level. The key to improvement may lie outside of logistics' responsibilities or even beyond service's functional areas. For this reason it is important to obtain top management understanding of problems and *buy-in* to solution. *Permission is usually not enough.* Getting management's attention is usually difficult, but it is mandatory for success. (See chapter 5 for techniques to use.)

Indicators

The following are things to look for during the actual assessment. Please note that what you don't see can be just as important as what you do see.

INVENTORY CONTROL Inventory control is the basic imperative. It is the foundation on which everything else is built. If there are problems here, efforts to improve the process elsewhere will be marginal at best. On the surface, inventory control means that you don't loose things. You are able to track your inventory at all times and know exactly where it is on a real time basis. But inventory control is an indicator of something much more than that; it means *DISCIPLINE*. Are the processes and people disciplined enough to assure sound operations? What does it look like? At inventory time, it means less than 1 percent variance at the piece count level. It means continuous cycle counting, inventory accuracy greater than 99 percent and location accuracy at least that good. What you should not see is surprises and people panicking to find parts that are needed to fill orders!

LACK OF CHAOS   Chaos is disruptive and counterproductive. The problem is that untrained people find it difficult to discern a chaotic environment from a merely busy one. We see the activity and motion, but need to go beyond the hustle and bustle to assure effective results. Even "productive" activity may not be the best utilization of that effort. Possibly the activity is not needed at all. For example, the people putting parts on the shelf may be very efficient, but perhaps those parts should be directly moved from Receiving to Shipping because they are backordered for rush projects. Question if steps such as put-away can be eliminated. Is most effort directed at routine/nonemergency work? Is routine work delayed or put off by the emergencies? The indicators are emergency order rates and overtime costs. The best visual measure is a level of activity that is consistent throughout the day and not concentrated at the end of the day trying to get things ready for overnight priority shippers. Do remember that the same number of parts are going to be shipped whether we have the three day backlog or process them all to ship the same day. Customers are far happier if we ship everything today.

SUFFICIENT INVESTMENT   Are orders delayed pending receipt of in-bound stock? Are there enough parts in the right places to provide the desired fill rates? Do we know what the right fill rates are to fulfill the logistics objective? We can't even begin to answer these questions unless there is a way to quantify desired performance and further to translate the desired performance into required investment. Do these tools exist? Are they used to define *How much Logistics is enough?* Another indicator is the interaction between the logistics organization and other elements of the organization. Is the logistics organization part of business planning? Can they readily assess the logistics impact of business decisions and vise versa? Can alternative logistics strategies at either the product level or business level be objectively assessed as part of a "best balanced" business decision? Conversely, are there conflicting opinions about the appropriate level of investment, but no numbers are truly defensible? If the tools do not exist within logistics to facilitate quantitative participation in business decisions, what you hear is "Trust me, that's what it will take" and what you get are decisions that don't accurately consider logistics costs on either the high or low side.

SHORT AND CONSISTENT PIPELINES The biggest generators of excess inventory are the pipelines that the parts flow through. If they require days or weeks, then additional financial investment has to be made to fill them up. If time can be reduced, then the money saved goes mostly to profit. These pipelines are:

Procurement
Repair
Defective Return
Field Replenishment

Managing pipelines requires a double focus. The first is length—creating the need to buy stock to fill up the pipeline. The second is variance—creating the need to buy stock as safety level to cover the variability in the flow. While the importance of the pipeline length is generally understood, managing the average cycle time is not enough. Both the average and the variance of each pipeline must be managed and controlled. (Pipeline levels is covered in chapter 13.) Do logistics planners know the average time for each of these pipelines? Do they know the variance in them (or at least the maximum time)? Can they support their numbers with data? Does the Field Organization take responsibility for these two parameters of the defective return pipeline? The answers to these questions will paint the picture.

DEPENDABLE PROCESS This is the combination of people, training, policies, procedures, software, management and information that exists to plan and control logistics operations. They exist to assure that today's operations happen properly and that tomorrow's go equally well. In other words, their job is to make sure that the smooth running operations can be sustained indefinitely. The indicators here are indirect. Are the logistics planners confident or do they hedge their measurements and predictions with too many caveats? Is there a forecasting process that functions in an acceptable manner? What is the trend in the emergency order rate? Is Logistics proactively participating in product support planning?

POSITIVE CONTROL This means that Logistics can control and predict with confidence what will happen to all logistics performance parameters when one of them is deliberately changed. Expected results should happen as planned. This indicates whether we are in control of the logistics environment or are being driven by it. If the process contains a hierarchy of performance metrics that are interdependent on one another, this can be done. To test this, ask, "What would happen if we reduced the investment in parts by X dollars?" A confident and defensible answer with supporting data should be available within 24 hours.

CONTINUOUS IMPROVEMENT As in most endeavors, that which does not move forward, falls behind. Improvements in logistics process should be continuous. What you see is constant effort to improve performance, reduce costs, enhance information flow and training, *frequent training*. You also see trend charts on the wall that are up to date and being used. What you should hear are requests for resources to improve systems and to attend seminars and conferences on state-of-the-art logistics issues. What you won't hear is "That's the way we've always done it."

Checklist for assessment

There are other indicators that can be used to assess the condition of a parts operation. Some of these are general in nature and can be applied to most organizations. Those which we have discussed, are targeted at the technical aspects of work that is being performed. Table 27-1 is a checklist that summarizes the above discussion.

TABLE 27-1

A process check list helps quantify metrics

Logistics Process Checklist		
CONDITION	INDICATOR	COUNTER INDICATOR
INVENTORY CONTROL	• 99% Inventory Accuracy. • Small variances in fiscal inventories.	• Frequent efforts to locate stock to fill orders at the last minute.
LACK OF CHAOS	• Consistent level of effort all day. • Appropriate Emergency Order Rates.	• Intermittent "panic" activity.
SUFFICIENT INVESTMENT	• Service levels met. • Order filling not delayed for stock in pipelines. • Accurate predictions. • Logistics included in product planning.	• Excess stock for current product. • "Trust Me" estimates.
SHORT & CONSISTENT PIPELINES	• Internal pipelines not longer than 2 weeks. • Procurement pipeline not longer than a month. • Pipeline variances being aggressively managed. • Field Organization accountable for defective return pipeline.	• Excessive activity and cost to expedite parts movements. • Excessive investment
DEPENDABLE PROCESSES	• Good forecasting accuracy. • Shifts in business and products supported do not create chaos.	. Personal lack confidence. • Estimates are provided with excessive caveats.
POSITIVE CONTROL	• The results of stocking policy decisions can be predicted with accuracy and are supported with quantitative data.	• Surprises. • Stocking plans that do not produce desired result. • Minimal "what-if" capability.
CONTINUOUS IMPROVEMENT	• Process continuously being "worked on." • Priority given to personnel training.	• "That's the way we have always done it."

Moving from assessment to improvement

Once the assessment is done, the conclusions drawn, the recommendations made and the go-ahead received; the really hard part begins. *Making the changes.* Service parts logistics is fraught with panics. The old adage about it being difficult to remember that the object is to drain the swamp when you are up to your buttocks in alligators applies quite well. Several techniques apply here.

First, don't be over aggressive. It is human nature to underestimate how long things take to accomplish. Remember that normal operations must continue in the mean time. Allow much more time and person hours to make the changes than you initially think it will take.

Second, keep top management involved. Schedule periodic updates to management on plan progress. This may be a forcing function to keep people focused on progress, but it works. At times it is essential.

Finally, seek an outside consultant expert to guide and stimulate changes. Your people probably do know what to do. But, if they are capable, why haven't they made the improvements already? (The answer is probably a combination of having too many other priority activities, career bias toward maintaining the status quo, human ego that resents inference that their way was not good enough, and feeling overworked from the other "right-sizing" activities going on around them.) Experience shows that change comes hard to service organizations. But, time is money. The authors can show that one organization left over $2 million on the table because of trying to do activities themselves over many months which could have been done in about two months with some outside assistance. After twenty years in the consulting business the authors understand a desire to do-it-yourself, but observe that a professional consultant can push change rapidly so that the results pay for the investment many times over.

28 MATHEMATICAL BUSINESS MODELING

Logistics is both an art and a science. As one might suppose from the title of this chapter, business modeling is the science. This is quite correct, but even in the structured world of mathematics there is room for art. No model can expect to take in all the likely occurrences of the real world; particularly a complex world like service. Therefore a business model that quantitatively delineates this world is an art form in its own right. *Business modeling is the artful combination of scientific tools so that they collectively predict the real world.*

Art or science

Some mathematical models are quite simple. For example "Where will we be at 4:00 p.m. if we are traveling east at 55

425

miles per hour?" We use a simple mathematical model to figure this out:

$$\text{Distance} = \text{Speed} \times \text{Time}$$

Based on our model we determine that we will be 110 miles east of our current location in two hours. Or so our model tells us! What if we get lost or have a flat tire? Those factors are not in our model. More sophisticated models would allow for these contingencies. Adjustments and flexibility are frequently needed in modeling service logistics.

An example of a service parts logistics model is the calculation of spare parts required for the initial provisioning of a product See Figure 28-1

```
==================================================================
         Enter Number of Parts:    50 (0 to exit)
         Enter Days of Service:    90
    Enter # of Expected Failures:  25 per Million Hours of Service
 Enter Level of Support Desired:   98%

         Spare Parts Required =    7
==================================================================
```

Figure 28-1
Initial provisioning demonstration

This is obviously a computerized model. Complex models require the processing power of computers to make them useful in the real world. This is particularly true of "what-if?" models that use multiple input configurations to generate predictive output. The processing power afforded on PC based systems makes this kind of modeling available at all levels of modern organizations.

As the complexity of a model increases, it becomes harder to understand all of the relationships that are interplaying within the model. Figure 28-2 is a medium complexity model that addresses the transportation costs associated with service parts logistics.

In this example, the data is between the upper lines in the "what-if" configuration and the predicted output is below the second line.

Another example of this type model, somewhat more complex, is demonstrated in Figure 28-3.

```
=========================================================================
Part Volume/Year:   50000 items   Internal Carrying Cost:   30 %
Average Unit Cost:  200.00 $      Strategic Carrying Cost:  40 %
                                  Repairable Returns:       20 %
Fill Rate Plan
   Local Level      :  85 %       Shipping Costs/Line
   Strategic Level  :  10 %          Routine:    10.00 $
   Central Level    :   5 %          Emergency:  75.00 $

Response Time                     Order Costs/Line
   Local Level:   0.25 hrs        Internal Routine   : 10.00 $
   Strategic:     4.00 hrs        Internal Emergency: 50.00 $
   Central:      24.00 hrs        Procurement        : 30.00 $
=========================================================================
```

FIGURE 28-2
Transportation tradeoffs

```
=========================================================================
Annual Contract Fee $   4500.00   Phone clear time:      0.50
Phone clear percent %     10.00   Dispatch time    :     0.25
Mean hrs between srvc:   2880.00   Travel time      :    15.00
                                   Diagnostic time  :     1.50
Equipment down percent%   90.00   Fix time         :     0.50

Logistics percentage %    80.00   Loaded Labor Cost$ 145.00
Log Cost per Event    $  500.00
Logistics levels/ fill rate / time(hrs)       Call back percentages
                       ======      =======
         Level 1   %    85.00  :    0.25   First call clears %   85.00
         Level 2   %    10.00  :   24.00   Second call clears%   10.00
         Level 3   %     5.00  :   48.00   Third call clears %    5.00
=========================================================================
RESPONSE TIME    :   13.73        UPTIME %   99.15
REPAIR TIME      :    1.80
LOGISTICS TIME   :    4.01        CONTRACT PROFIT $  1350.85
CALL BACK TIME   :    7.73        PROFITABILITY   %    30.02
AVERAGE DOWN TIME :  27.32
         Copyright by Patton Consultants, Inc.   214/539-0598
=========================================================================
```

FIGURE 28-3
Uptime analysis model integrates parts with labor

This is the same type of "what-if?" model but is used to predict the impact of logistics performance on higher level service performance goals. Complete business models are more complex still. They require extensive input data and months to build.

Logistics business models

A mathematical model that accurately portrays the logistics business environment of a particular company is a valuable resource and guide to management. Most complex enterprises do some modeling and the manufacturing function has a business model built into the Materials Requirements Planning (MRP) systems. MRP is such an ingrained part of the process in manufacturing that we tend to forget that models are involved at all. Philosophically, manufacturing acquires materials to meet preplanned requirements. Service logistics acquires materials to ensure that parts are available if and when the need occurs.

There is a standard approach to manage manufacturing that, with the exception of variations for different types of manufacturing processes, is common through out the western world. There is no such "common approach" to managing a service organization and the logistics function is especially different from company to company. For proof, try buying "off the shelf" software. An MRP system is easy to buy. MRP systems all have essentially the same in underlaying structure. Shopping for MRP software is a matter of finding one with the interfaces and "bells and whistles" that most closely meet your needs. If the package requires more than 5 or 10 percent modification, then you haven't shopped enough. Shopping for a Service system, however, is a much different matter. Here you will be lucky to find 80 percent commonality and the area that requires the most modification is logistics. As a matter of fact, most systems available today only provide inventory control as the standard offering; logistics planning is assumed to be part of the modifications.

Logistics planning and operations are further complicated by the fact that they touch so many other functional areas of the company, but at lower levels in the organizations. This usually means that the complexity and extent of the service parts impact is not understood at the senior management level. Worse perhaps, is the tug of war that takes place over logistics between Service and Marketing/Sales, both close to the customer, and Finance. A typical argument might concern not enough parts versus too much investment with both Sales and

Finance believing that their issue is with the Service Logistics organization. The real problem is management's need to set goals which balance support level and response time against financial investment. The logistics organization, in reality, is the one party involved that is unbiased with respect to this issue. Of course, this conflict should be resolved by management in the form of clear cut, quantitative logistics support policies but, Lacking unemotional alternatives, management is ill prepared to make such decisions. The logistics Organization, although positioned to develop the alternatives, frequently does not have the tools to do so. Herein lies the need for a Logistics Business Model.

Model components

The parts of a logistics model change from company to company. They have to because every company, their products and their customers are unique. To conceptually explain logistics does not require a unique structure, but to accurately portray the logistics environment of a company in mathematical terms requires something very original. Nonetheless there are certain components that must be included in any model to assure completeness. These components are:

Response time

Response time is a function of how many field stocking locations there are, how close these are to the customers, and the stock list of each of the locations. Obviously, this directly impacts on the investment and operating costs of logistics support. The business model should be able to alter the field stocking location configuration to assess the impact that a varied structure would have on response time, investment, and operating costs.

Stocking locations

There are several kinds of stocking locations. Some support the customers. Some (central logistics) replenish those retail locations, and some support the logistics process. (Examples of the latter are defective storage and receiving.) All stocking locations need to be included in a business model. Each stocking site needs to be modeled separately in terms of what part numbers and quantities are (should be) there to achieve the desired First Pass Fill Rate (FPFR). Again, these stock lists should be changeable so that the impact of alternate stock lists on the business parameters such as response time or investment may be quickly assessed.

Pipelines

Managing the inventory on the shelf is not enough! The model must also include the inventory in motion. If investment is to be predicted (and controlled) then the conduits that the parts flow through must be part of the measurements. These pipelines are procurement, defective return, repair, and field replenishment. The appropriate measurements for each pipelines are the cycle time and the variance in that cycle for each part number at the aggregate level. Once more, these parameters should be changeable so that the impact of variations in pipeline performance on other model parameters can be determined.

Investment

Of course no business model would be complete without a financial investment forecast. While it is easy to understand that there is a relationship between the parts you buy and investment, computing what those parts are and where they should be for a desired logistics service level is the real work of the model. This is unique to a company and the environment in which it operates. The model must be capable of running "backwards" to answer questions like "What would the impact be on our service level if we reduced investment by ten percent?"

Operating costs

Perhaps more important than the investment from a cash flow point of view are operating costs. These costs, generically, are holding costs, ordering costs and transportation cost. Below this level are a myriad of lower level details. From warehouse expenses to postage, everything needs to be integrated into the model and related to the other metrics. The most difficult thing to model is opportunity costs. The cost of being out-of-stock can be the subject of considerable disagreement having more to do with customer satisfaction in a service contract scenario than it does with lost revenue, and it is usually left out of the modeling effort. If opportunity costs are to be approached, then they should be categorized as part of operating costs.

Model capabilities

In order to be truly effective, the logistics business model must function simultaneously on two levels—the macro level and the micro level. There relationship between the two levels must be seamless. If the macro level does not translate directly to the micro level and vice verse then the model ceases to be a true business tool.

Macro level

This is the level of policy determination and "What-if?" analysis. At this high level, the model assists in business strategic planning. The model outputs summary level data on alternate stocking strategies, investment requirements, procurement and operating budgets, repair shop plans, and loadings. It presents options for logistics strategies so that management can better select the logistics support policy that, on balance, is the best for the business. Since the parameters of overall logistics performance are established in quantitative terms they can now be tracked and a complete picture is generated for each segment of the logistics milieu. Annotated with the dollars and part piece count for each segment,it might look something like Figure 30-4. Please not the distinction between the wholesale and retail levels. This is a useful concept when structuring planning effort.

Micro level

At this level the model drives detailed logistics planning. The model generates recommended stock lists for all inventory locations at the part number level. This is also the level at which actual performance data is brought in and analyzed against the outputs of the model.

Data file requirements (Sample Formats)

Business models require vast amounts of data. In the "What-if?" type model discussed above, the input data was keyed to the screen and was a matter of conjecture. In a fully developed business model, reams of data are utilized to develop these same input factors. The following are representative logistics business model input file structures. The letters after the file name indicate the type of digit: C = character field, D = date, L = logical, and N = numeric. A "Father" file is the currently preferred part identifier, which may be any or several of the next higher assembly, supercession, or chained part. The numbers are typical file size, which will vary by company. For example, we recommend part numbers of only five or six numeric digits, but many companies still have 12 digit part identifiers with alphanumeric characters. Not all of these files will be required all of the time. As a matter of fact, there is considerable variance in data requirements between models developed for different companies.

MASTER FILES

FILE NAME - PMAST		
PN	C	12,0
DESC	C	20,0
PROD	C	4,0
UNIT	N	6,2
FRU	L	1,0
REPAIRABLE	L	1,0
WASHOUT	N	3,0
PARTTYPE	C	1,0
CRIT	L	1,0
FATHER	C	12,0

FILE NAME - ORGN		
ORGN	C	4,0
NAME	C	20,0
CITY	C	15,0
STATE	C	2,0
ZIP	C	5,0

FILE NAME - FE		
FE	C	6,0
ORGN	C	4,0
NAME	C	20,0

PROD	C	4,0
QTY	N	6,0
LOCA	C	4,0
CONTTYPE	C	2,0
CITY	C	15,0
STATE	C	2,0
ZIP	C	5,0
ORGN	C	4,0
FE	C	6,0

FILE NAME - CUSTOMER		
ORGN	C	4,0
NAME	C	20,0

```
FILE NAME - LOCA
LOCA          C          4,0
DESC          C         20,0
ORGN          C          4,0
FE            C          6,0

FILE NAME - PROD
PROD          C          4,0
DESC          C         20,0

FILE NAME - INSTALLD
CUSTOMER      C         10,0
SITE          C          4,0

FILE NAME - SITE
CUSTOMER      C         10,0
SITE          C          4,0
LOCA          C          4,0
CONTTYPE      C          2,0
CITY          C         15,0
STATE         C          2,0
ZIP           C          5,0
ORGN          C          4,0
FE            C          6,0
```

CROSS REFERENCE FILES

```
FILE NAME - FATHERS
PN            C         12,0
FATHER        C         12,0

FILE NAME - LOCADELTA
LOCA          C          4,0
NEWLOCA       C          4,0
ASOFDATE      D          8
```

TRANSACTION HISTORY FILES

```
FILE NAME - ORDERS (FIELD)        FILE NAME - DIRECT
PN            C         12,0       CUSTOMER      C         10,0
LOCA          C          4,0       SITE          C          4,0
QTY           N          6,0       PN            C         12,0
ODATE         D          8,0       QTY           N          6,0
RDATE         D          8,0       SDATE         D          8,0
ORGN          C          4,0
FE            C          6,0       FILE NAME - USAGE
                                   PN            C         12,0
FILE NAME - ORDERS (PROCUREMENT)   CUSTOMER      C         10,0
PN            C         12,0       SITE          C          4,0
LOCA          C          4,0       PROD          C          4,0
QTY           N          6,0       LOCA          C          4,0
ODATE         D          8,0       UDATE         D          8,0
RDATE         D          8,0       QTY           N          6,0
                                   ORGN          C          4,0
                                   FE            C          6,0
FILE NAME - RETURNS
PN            C         12,0       FILE NAME - REPAIR
LOCA          C          4,0       PN            C         12,0
QTY           N          6,0       QTY           N          6,0
UDATE         D          8,0       INDATE        D          8,0
RDATE         D          8,0       OUTDATE       D          8,0
ORGN          C          4,0
FE            C          6,0
```

CURRENT STATUS FILES

```
FILE NAME - STATUS
PN            C         12,0
LOCA          C          4,0
CONDITION     C          1,0
QTY           N          6,0
```

Not all of these files will be required all of the time. As a matter of fact, there is considerable variance in data requirements between models developed for different companies.

Data integrity adjustments

Arguably, the most demanding aspect of a business model is that it requires an absolutely "tight" database. No holes—No dead ends—No nonexistent relationships. This is much more stringent than is required for operational systems. For example, you don't need a standard cost to transact a part, but to model investment requirements against part volumes you do. Even when such fields are "required" in an operating system, an acceptable "work around" is usually possible to register a transaction. In the case of analytical models, which must have accurate inputs, this flexibility is not so. This presents two opportunities when building business models. The first is the chance to clean up your database. The second, is the chance to find out where the real holes are and where the transaction system needs to be "tightened" or more discipline needs to be added.

Another opportunity for data quality improvements that usually presents itself while building business models, is assuring the accuracy of part cross-reference data. No one intends to stock the same part under two different numbers, or to plan future requirements for obsolete parts. Here is the opportunity to make sure that old part numbers and revision numbers roll together to the currently preferred number for planning purposes,

Model configuration

The first major modeling decision, for which there are several options is: "What is the purpose of this model?"

One-time analysis

A singular analysis may be done for many reasons: for stock distribution planning, for investment planning, or perhaps for both. The single advantage to a one time analysis is that is does not have to be repeated. For this reason the data preparation does not have to be "institutionalized." Holes and data inconsistencies in the input data can be fixed or patched quickly in the analytical database without disturbing corporate data. The disadvantage is that to repeat the process, you must go though the complete sequence again from the beginning with new data.

"What if?" modeling

This type of modeling is usual approached as a middle ground so far as data preparation is concerned. In this approach, as problems are identified with the data, the problems are "fixed" in the corporate data structure and transferred again to the analytical database. This assures that at least the base data is not corrupted for analytical purposes. These corrections mean that the model can be repeated using new data for several months before the corporate data becomes corrupted again.

Integrated model

In this approach, the model is used not only for "What-if?" analysis but also becomes an integrated part of the logistics management process. In this scenario, field service levels are stipulated to the model, the model generates stock distributions to the part number and quantity level, and the operating system produces reports of actual performance. The data integrity required by the model presents major difficulties. Not only does the historical database have to be corrected, but the transactions must be "tightened" so that the data does not become corrupt as a result of transactions.

Options for generating forecast demand

Planning always requires some method to generate a forecast of the demand for parts that will be experienced in the future. Several situations and options and presented.

Preplanned requirement

There is no better forecast than a preplanned requirement. It is this type of requirement that makes Just-in-Time manufacturing feasible. In spite of the fact that the most common kind of part demand in the service world is demand that results from the random (and therefore not preplanned) failure of a piece of equipment, still, there are those demands that can and should be preplanned. Most typically these are parts that are used for equipment installations and for engineering change orders. From a planning perspective, these parts should be provisioned over and above those needed *Just-in-Case* to support random demand. From a modeling point of view, the use (demand) for those parts should be considered nonrecurring and categorized separately in the forecasting database.

Modeling factors

Every model contains modeling factors that are not dynamically derived from the input data on an ongoing basis. These factors are the result of separate studies or may be convenient estimates that everyone agrees to. Such factors include holding costs, ordering costs, default values for unit costs, repair yield and unit shipping cost.

What to use

With all the data available the question might well be asked "What do we use for the model?" The answer is, "The best available data that at any given time is appropriate." We don't mean to evade the answer, but this is where the "artful" application enters the equation. Modeling is a dynamic process. It is never really finished. Data must be continually purged, modified, reconfigured, and updated.

Selecting balanced strategy

The most important objective of modeling is that it adequately portrays the real world at both a macro and micro levels. Models should be used by management to establish the tradeoffs between logistics support strategies and also to assure that whatever strategy is selected flows seamlessly to the required stocking levels of all parts at all locations.

Revolution, not evolution

It takes a lot of effort to put a logistics model together. Moreover, it takes a lot of effort to maintain one. As the conditions of the business change over time, the validity of the model is degraded unless it is continually updated. This is the last criteria for the model. It must be dynamic. It must update and reconfigure itself automatically.

Service parts logistics operations is both an art and a science. The business model is the science. But even as complex as these models can be, they cannot foresee all the variables that may occur in an environment in which demand is generated by random equipment failure. Beyond the science is the art applied by logistics planners and business models give them a qualitatively better starting point. Just the fact that a model defines "How much logistics is enough?" is a quantum leap in many companies. Our experience has been that a well tailored business model invariably reduces investment by at least 20 percent over the historical investment. Most often this reduction is accompanied by a reduction in operating expense and a significant improvement in logistics performance. Typically, a 20 percent to 30 percent improvement is gained in both! **It's worth it!**

29 *LOOSE LINKS AND LOGISTICS LIMITS*

T he saying, "A chain is only as strong as its weakest link," is especially applicable to service logistics. Integration of many functions is necessary for success of the whole. Service Parts performance assessments consistently reveal problems and neglected opportunities. This chapter presents ten loose links and suggests improvements that can increase revenues, reduce costs, and gain profits. It also suggests that logistics is limited by the burdens that other organizations inflict by incomplete lists of products to be supported, unreasonable customer expectations, and financial constraints that hinder the logistics mission. The ten "loosest" links are:

1. Management support
2. Installed base
3. Field replaceable units (FRU) standards
4. Authorized stock lists (ASLs)
5. Diagnostics
6. Asset valuation
7. Pipeline speed
8. Business models
9. Integrated electronic guidance
10. Metrics and goals

Management support

This is the same item that appears as Number One on my list of "Top Ten Techniques for Managing Service" and several other advisories. Service logistics has particular challenges because there are at least fifteen major differences from the production parts with which many people are familiar. The three main supports for the business of service are people, parts, and information; as illustrated in Figure 29-1.

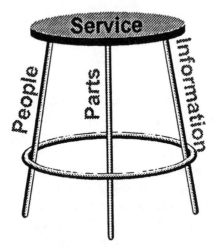

FIGURE 29-1
Service requires a balance of people, parts, and information

Parts are becoming increasingly critical and a higher percentage of the total costs of service as multivendor products predominate over proprietary equipment. Chief Executives and Chief Financial Officers, especially, should be educated in the linkages of logistics so they can direct the proper balance of the related functions. Hold a monthly briefing breakfast for executives across service plus finance, marketing, sales, production, quality, and engineering to help them understand the underlying principles and practices that interface with their functional responsibilities.

Installed base

In order to proactively plan the right part at the right place at the right time, logistics must know what product models are installed where, and what response and restore time requirements are contracted for each piece of equipment. Without that knowledge, logistics will always be reactive, late, and expensive. Accurate knowledge of the installed base is important for billing accuracy. When I tell people about finding large organizations underbilling by 23 and 28 percent, the typical comment is, "I'm surprised it's that low." That stimulates the equation shown in Figure 29-2.

**Ignorance
X
Complacency
=
Decline**

FIGURE 29-2
An equation for failure

Recommendation is to make accurate knowledge of the installed base a company priority, hopefully driven by the CFO. Go ahead and agree to service contract rates for product families, with the insistence that accurate product inventory by location and response time will be committed within thirty days.

Knowledge of the hardware and software assets has values beyond service logistics. Effective management of technology requires that assets be utilized where they are most needed. For example, if a researcher takes hours to process data on her 386 while a secretary in another group has a Pentium with a 2 Gb hard drive and a 17 inch monitor used only for word processing, the equipment should probably be switched between users. Assurance that all software is properly licensed will also avoid future legal problems. Technology asset audits and continuing database maintenance can be a profitable product to offer customers, and is a value-add that can be most effectively provided by the organization who does installation, moves, systems integration, repairs, and user training

FRU standards

A set list of field replaceable units (FRUs) forms the foundation for stock lists, technician requirements, documentation, diagnostics, training, technical assistance, and parts forecasting. The FRUs in turn are dependent on the support strategy, i.e., should every fuse, nut, and integrated circuit be replaced in the field, or should FRUs be major components or even whole units? Yes, there is one best way to do most service tasks. Standardized FRUs will stock one part, and only one part, to accomplish each job. The actual selections of which parts should be FRUs are somewhat subjective, and should be made by experienced field technicians based on failure modes, size of the units, speed of repair required, etc. Using well-known technicians helps gain buy-in of their compatriots.

A good FRU list will reduce the number of parts stocked at least 25 percent. When you consider that every stock keeping unit listed costs several thousands of dollars just to determine and enter the data, reducing the number of listings saves considerable effort and money.

Start your process by establishing the FRUs for every new product so that the parts are available before the first customer installation. Minimize the number of FRUs so that you can achieve close to 100 percent availability of those parts. In other words, *concentrate on the critical few*. Then go back and designate

FRUs for existing high volume products. Make sure that your Master Part Record has a field that can be flagged as "Repair Center Part Only" since the Repair Depot will need a lower level of parts than will be permitted in the field.

ASLs

Authorized Stock Lists (ASLs) are a means of specifying which parts and quantities should be carried by every field engineer, strategic parts bank, and the central warehouse. The target is to identify at least 95 percent of all parts that will be needed and have them on the ASL and on hand. The ASL for each location can be computer-generated using logistics business modeling. Those results should be presented to each field engineer and manager for their adjustments and approval. A scientifically determined ASL will usually remove significant dollars and units of parts from the field for consolidation at the central warehouse. The reaction of most technicians is, "It's about time!" One organization pulled 85 percent of their parts units and dollars from the field. They added about 20 percent new parts. The First Pass Fill Rate that was about 70 percent will, with tuning, exceed 90 percent. Both logistics' customers - the field engineers - and their customers - the end users - notice significant improvement.

Diagnostics

One client of Patton Consultants found that 50 to 90 percent of all parts ordered "Priority 1 - Emergency" are not used within the next two weeks. There are some reporting deficiencies, but one interpretation is that up to nine out of every ten parts that were expensively expedited to the field, were not really needed. Some field engineers probably ordered parts *Emergency* when what they really needed was routine replenishment; but they lacked confidence in the normal system. In most cases it is felt that the extra parts were ordered because poor diagnostics failed to proactively determine the one or few parts that were probably needed to fix the failure. We can blame inadequate documentation, faulty technical assistance, lacking remote diagnostics, inability of the field engineer to properly talk with the user and determine the real problem and possible solutions in advance, and a multitude of smaller reasons. The opportunity here is for improved support engineering and field operations, both normally not under direct control of logistics, to greatly reduce the number of parts required and related expenses, and also to improve speed of repair, reduce broken calls, and improve customer satisfaction. while improving profits.

Asset valuation

The challenge is to accurately value the parts and units used for service so that financial books are accurate, taxes are minimized, and correct values are used in trade-off analysis. The need is to maintain part operating values at the *lower of cost or market*. For example, when a new network server is introduced, you must buy a mother board to support fast repairs even though the warranty will replace a defective part overnight. That critical part may never fail, but if it does you must have a replacement ready for fast restoration.

How fast should that part value be financially depreciated? Many companies have reduced the period to 18 months straight-line. Others have tied the term to actual need for, and value of, those parts. Consider basing the part value on a percentage such as 25 percent of revenue forecast from maintaining products on which those parts are used. Or, if a SKU has not been used in the last year and is not expected to be needed in the future, write it off 100 percent. If use is less than on hand, write off 50 percent. Keep the rest at current market value. We realize that many business people want their parts valued as high as possible. Bank loans to small service companies often depend on the balance sheet value placed on those parts. However, if *repair or buy* and similar decisions are based on artificially high values, then poor decision will be made. Add a field to your part record for *Next Cost* to accurately value parts for management decisions. Keep your values of at least class "A" (high cost, high quantity) parts in line with what those parts could be sold for in the marketplace.

Pipeline speed

The four pipelines of concern are:

—Procurement of new parts
—Order, pick, pack, and transport
—Return of defective and excess parts from the field
—Repair of defective parts

The first improvement recommended is to go beyond measuring average performance and also compute the range and standard deviations of individual vendors and field technicians. Reduce the variance before trying to reduce the mean. This will identify problems in process and will detect quantification of changes.

Return of defective parts from the field is almost certain to be a problem. "It's not under my control," claim the logisticians. Maybe not completely, but operations management will usually help if we give them tools to work with. You already own these valuable assets and can have them rejuvenated for 20 to 30 percent of the cost for a new part. Assure that *Return parts promptly* is a formal item on every technician's job description, with individual quantification on *promptly*.

Direct ship failed parts from the point of failure to the repair facility. When a repairable part is reported on-line as used, message the technician where the part is to be shipped. Make the tech's job easy by providing repacking tape, shipping labels, and pre-paid shipping in the reusable package of the good part. Create an electronic *Due-In* list. The timing from use until the part should be received at Repair can be based on the individual technician's geography and also the need for that particular part. "Round-trip" pickup of defectives may be arranged with the courier service, or drop off at a convenient Mail Boxes, Etc., or at least once a week pickup by your contract delivery service can be arranged direct from the tech's van or garage. If the Due-In is not automatically cleared by the part arriving at Repair, a message or phone call from the manager provides stimulation. At performance appraisal time, evaluate the technician on the time-value of the dollars in parts returned. You will be impressed how the pipeline that used to be months can be reduced to a few days. The other pipelines should be addressed in similar aggressive fashion. Fast turnaround can greatly reduce the need for safety stocks and additional part purchases since a few expensive parts can be kept in useful service.

Business models

Service logistics is a very complex combination of art and science. "Seat-of-the-pants" management will result in inefficient failure. Pure science is not the whole answer either since mathematics and technology must be smoothed with people skills. Logistics business models can be major aids. It many cases, modeling has provided the directions to reduce inventory 10 to 40 percent, reduce pipelines from months to days, increase support levels from 70 percent to above 95 percent, and improve both customer satisfaction and profits. The Logistics Performance Envelope statistically ties Response Time to First Pass Fill Rate to Financial Investment so that management can play "What if?" and make rational decisions about goals.

Integrated electronic guidance

Handwriting, phone calls, and manual faxes have their place, but not in logistics operations. Computer and telecommunications technology applied to service logistics pays for itself many times over. For example, when a technician needs a part, that data should be keyed or scanned into his wireless portable teletransaction computer (PTC) and instantly transmitted. Within seconds the response should show that the part is available and expected time of arrival. Any purchase or repair orders or courier delivery directions should be electronically transmitted directly to the supplier's computer.

Computerized Management Systems (CMS) have come a long way in recent years from merely processing transactions to providing wisdom and guidance. Unfortunately, no CMS yet provides adequate logistics management, forecasting, planning, and improvement analysis. Those capabilities are coming. Control is a start, but most of the Loose Links already discussed are facilitated by effective systems.

Metrics and goals

Where is your line in the sand? The big three goals for parts supporting overall service are:

☞ Operational availability >=98%

☞ First Call Fix Rate >=90%

☞Restore Time >=98% per contract.

A package of about ten parts-specific goals will support these. Many organizations have conflicting goals. The executive gives the service organization a goal to increase MVS (multivendor service) $100 million and gives the logistics organization a goal to cut investment $25 million. Does anyone realize the inconsistency? Does anyone stand up and show that those goals can only be achieved by blowing acquisition, expediting and transportation expenses sky high? Goals should be written, measurable, understandable, challenging, and achievable. Only with goals can the desired result be clear. Logistics is not Wonderland. Logistics can be logical, rational, and stimulated by leadership that strengthens these loose links and recognizes the limits.

30 PULLING IT ALL TOGETHER

The intent of this chapter is to gather all the ideas discussed elsewhere in the book into a comprehensive explanation of how the entire logistics function should be managed. The reader can visualize the entire service parts logistics environment, see how the pieces fit together, and how to manage all the factors simultaneously. This chapter is divided into two parts. The first is a discussion of the logistics environment stated in terms of whether the parts are moving or not moving between and within wholesale and retail functions. (Figure 30-1 illustrates this movement.) These parts are the same SKUs in either state. Sometimes they are dynamic in a logistics pipeline and sometimes they are static sitting in a stocking location. This distinction provides two different focuses and mind sets, both of which are needed to understand why all the functions discussed in this book are necessary. The second part of the chapter deals with the functions of a comprehensive logistics management organization, designed to address both moving

449

and static inventory and how to use the tools presented in this book.

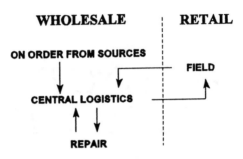

FIGURE 30-1 Wholesale is central logistics and Retail is the field

Static inventory (fixed asset control)

This is the stock that is (at least for the moment) in a stocking location rather than being in transit. This stock can be central (main, wholesale) or field retail stock. There are some further distinctions and subtleties.

Central stocking locations

This is the stock that is under the direct control of the corporate level logistics organization. The function of this stock is to replenish field stocks and to satisfy customer demands directly for low volume or critically short parts. It is typically segmented by the following locations.

WAREHOUSE—This is the central stock of parts for the corporation. Although there can be multiple locations for large organizations, there is usually only one. It is historically the funnel that new parts flow through. Often it is the collection point for defective and excess parts before they are repaired or scrapped. The funnel collection concept is being diminished by direct ship to and from suppliers, but it will probably not completely disappear.

STRATEGIC REMOTE STORAGE—These locations usually contain medium volume, critical items. There are typically several of these and may be operated by a fourth party storage, courier, or freight forwarder company. These locations exist to reduce the response time to customers for items that should not be stocked in field stocking locations because of cost or low demand. Central control is retained over this stock to allow rapid shipment from any location to any customer site.

"ON CALL" SUPPLIERS—This is the use of vendors' parts to directly fill current demand. This has the obvious advantage of not having to invest in the stock until it is needed. The major disadvantage is that it requires long term relationships with single vendors, thereby reducing flexibility. This approach is often best for volume parts since most vendors are reluctant to undertake the risk of stocking low usage parts without contractual assurances of profitability. As the market for independent parts suppliers develops, they will handle a broader line of parts and provide more effective use (turns) of parts by sharing the parts among many potential users.

Field stocking locations

These locations function under the control of the field service organizations to meet immediate customer demand for parts. Typically the person (there should be a single person responsible even though other persons may help) in charge of this stock is not a full time logistics expert. Typical field stocking configurations include:

VEHICLE STOCKS—These parts are in the hands of Customer Service Engineers for use on service calls. The CSE is responsible for physical safekeeping, inventory control, usage reporting, periodic inventory taking and the return of defective inventory. Vehicle stocks are often referred to as car, trunk or van stocks depending on the type of conveyance. It is not uncommon for some of these parts to be in the technician's garage or a rented self-storage area. The intent is to enable the technician to have with him the parts he most frequently needs to fix customers' equipment.

OFFICE STOCKS—This is an area in the service office that is used for storage of service parts. It may be a cage, closest or a desk drawer. These can exist with or without the use of vehicle stocks. They can be open to all or, preferably, controlled by an administrative person as an additional duty.

FORMAL FIELD STOCKING LOCATIONS—These are controlled stock rooms manned by full time logistics personnel. The important distinction is that the personnel staffing these locations report to the field organization. (If the staff reports to the logistics organization at corporate headquarters, these locations would be considered part of central logistics.)

FOURTH PARTY STORAGE—These are formal controlled stocking locations staffed and operated by an external vender. These are considered field stocking locations if field personnel have access to the stock without requiring prior approval of central logistics. The contract to pay for these services may, however, be centrally administered.

Whatever the level and function of a stocking location, they all share one thing: parts must be managed. This means that there must be a formal Authorized Stock List (ASL) designed to provide a specified level of logistics support from that location. Finally, the actual performance of the stocking location is monitored periodically and the SKUs with levels adjusted to assure that achieved performance comes up to what is planned. As part of a complete logistics support policy, the performance metrics of all stocking locations are integrated to form a "multi-echelon" fill plan. This plan is devised to achieve the best business balance between Response Time, Fill Rate and Required Investment. (See chapter 26 on The Logistics Performance Envelope.)

Inventory in motion (pipeline control)

Inventory in motion is the parts in transit between stocking locations and repair facilities. Surprisingly, adequate management of pipelines is often overlooked. These pipelines are all time-based process cycles. The variation of cycle times in a demand-driven environment dictates safety level and investment requirements. The critical metrics are the statistical mean, median, and standard deviation of the following cycle time distributions:

RETURN TIME—The time it takes to return an unserviceable part to the repair center. This is a retail field level management responsibility, although the performance data is collected at the wholesale level.

REPAIR TIME—The time it takes to restore an item to ready for issue (RFI) condition once the decision to repair it has been made.

FIELD REPLENISHMENT TIME—The time it takes on a routine basis to replenish retail field stocks from central logistics.

PROCUREMENT TIME—The lead time required to acquire a new item, measured from the time the need is identified until the part is in the hands of the person who needs it.

Consistent management of logistics pipelines is the real secret to providing a desired level of logistics service at optimal cost. Pipelines must not be permitted to function by default. They need to be managed, with the goals, measurement and discipline that infers. Managing a pipeline means to monitor the statistics of that pipeline and take actions to assure that parameters stay within limits. Most of the time we are dealing with cycle times where shorter is better. What we must do is manage the situations in the environment and drive the average to the goal that we want to achieve. The standard deviation of the pipeline distribution can be more important than the average. Here are the process steps:

1. Compute the average and median of the pipeline times. If they are more or less equal go to step 3.
2. Attack the tail and eliminate the conditions that cause "outriders" to skew the distribution. Drive the distribution to normality. As you do this the standard deviation of the pipeline distribution will be reduced. So will the average. Also, the median and average will move closer together. You will often find

that a few technicians or parts are causing most of the late results.

3. Compute the standard deviation. Note that the plus (slower) side from the mean is probably more of a problem than the minus (faster) side. If the deviation is not excessive go to step 5.

4. Work for consistency. Eliminate the things that cause variance. This is usually done with policy changes to assure consistency of effort.

5. Go after the average and drive it toward your goal.

When faced with a choice between the average you want and consistency (small standard deviation), often the best choice is consistency—at least consistent events and times can be planned for. Most importantly, realize that managing averages alone is not enough to plan and control logistics pipelines. If you want confidence and predictability, then you must also manage the variances.

Logistics organizations and processes

The mechanism by which quality is introduced into our efforts has been described as *Plan what you do—then do what you plan.* This should be no less true for service parts management. The tradition in the service industry has been to respond to emergencies rapidly, and although necessary, it has induced a culture where planning is an additional duty for material expediters. In fact, if planning is done well, then much less expediting is required. By contrast, persons with a manufacturing background quickly grasp the need for a material management function as a result of their experience. Cost effective service management requires an organization dedicated to proactive service parts management.

Active management of logistics function requires two focuses (mind sets). One is directed at field level operations and what has to happen at the end of the supply chain to satisfy the ultimate customer. The other is directed at central logistics and what has to happen to keep the flow of parts moving and the field replenished. We refer to the former as retail level management and the latter as wholesale level management. Both are necessary to assure proper supply and both are beyond the expedited responses to emergency situations.

A third skill set is required to perform administrative and business functions. Before we discuss the management functions, we need to address the skill sets required for the staff.

ANALYTICAL THOUGHT—Persons who plan and manage proactive parts operations proactively must be problem solvers. They must be capable of analyzing complex situations for root cause and devising solutions that will work and are pragmatically implementable. This requires people who are both math smart and people smart.

KNOWLEDGE OF STATISTICS—Since the majority of part requirements are driven by random equipment failure, the planning process is quite different than planning to a required date. Service parts requires the ability to model both just-in-time and just-in-case. A basic understanding of statistical processes and measurements is essential.

COMPUTER LITERACY—Much of the analytical work must be done on an ad hoc basis. It is best performed on a PC or work station equipment using data downloaded from corporate systems. The ability to query large databases and download data into local files provides the foundation. The capability to manipulate this data using database tools builds the new structure. While many analytical tasks can be done in spreadsheet programs, the ability to use PC database application programs is the critical framework.

These skills do not require a college degree although some academic preparation, such as an Associates in Science degree, is desirable. They do require knowledge, attitude and an approach that is unique.

There are two common hiring errors. The first is to hire personnel from service operations (typically the warehouse or a technical area) based on the assumption that, because they have handled the parts and products, that they know how to plan for them. The second is to hire personnel from manufacturing material planning based on the assumption that the planning skills are the same. Both of these assumptions are incorrect. Without assessing the individuals for the specialized service parts skill sets described above, their transition to service parts planning will be painful for them and probably costly to the company.

Wholesale logistics management

Wholesale logistics management is the engine that drives and supports all subsequent logistics operations. It is the sustaining function of central logistics management and includes the following responsibilities:

Requirements forecasting

Wholesale logistics serves as the primary logistics interface with other functional areas of the company. It must provide short-range and long-range forecasts in financial terms to the financial organization and at the part number and quantity level to the repair, manufacturing and/or procurement organizations.

Central fill rate management

This function decides what items should be stocked within the central system, where (if there is more than one location in central logistics), and how many of each SKU. This provides the *should-be-on-the-shelf* information necessary to make repair and procurement decisions on a week-to-week basis. The primary goal is to achieve a predetermined First Pass Fill Rate in central logistics for routine orders. Finally, the effectiveness of the process must be assessed against actual fill rates and appropriate adjustments must be made based on the feedback.

Pipeline management

Wholesale logistics performs pipeline management as described previously for the procurement, repair and field replenishment pipelines.

Parts sourcing

Determining the source for new parts entering the logistics system is the responsibility of wholesale logistics. Parts sourcing and acquisition should be done only at this level in order to assure economies of scale and optimal distribution of assets. Local buys can be an effective process for multivendor parts that are rapidly available at a local computer store, but the procedure and authorization must be centrally controlled. The sources for parts include manufacturing, procurement, repair, de-manufacture, and return from the field.

Procurement

The acquisition of new, direct exchange, borrowed and other parts from external sources and the contract administration of external repair vendors.

Repair management and direction

Wholesale logistics functions as a "production control" for internal and external repair operations. Wholesale logistics decides what should be repaired, when and in what quantity. It issues the appropriate work direction to implement these decisions.

A common error is to try to run repair operations with economies of scale and process as if in high-volume manufacturing. This looses sight of the fact that the sole reason for repair operations is to keep stock on the shelf in central logistics. Repair operations are fully cost justified by procurement avoidance and therefore shop efficiencies are not the primary concern as they are in manufacturing. Another common error is to plan repair work based on the capacities of the repair operations. We frequently find situations where repair managers and planners have to be reminded that they must plan based on demand, rather than on capacity to supply. In this case wholesale logistics and shop management loose the ability to identify process bottlenecks in repair which then precludes proper repair capacity planning.

Product support planning

Wholesale logistics, working in coordination with engineering and field personnel, determines what items are FRUs in accordance with the product support plan. It also develops the logistics support plan for the initial fielding of new products. In the absence of a product support plan, wholesale logistics management should define structured product FRU lists in coordination with field management.

Central inventory control

Wholesale logistics is responsible for assuring that all assets in the wholesale segment of the logistics system are properly accounted for at all times.

Excess management

Because of the random nature of most service parts demands, some excess and obsolete parts are inevitable. Wholesale logistics should deal with excess disposal and value recovery on an ongoing basis.

Order Entry

This is the function in central logistics that receives and validates orders. These orders may be from internal personnel or directly from customers. The orders can be taken manually, automatically generated, or passed from the call management system. Field orders should be validated against the ASL for the ordering stocking location and against the appropriate product FRU list.

Retail logistics management

Retail logistics is the part of central logistics management that is dedicated to managing what happens at the end of the logistics supply chain. It includes the following responsibilities:

Distribution planning

This is the determination of which parts are to be stocked where and in what quantities. The selections are based on the requirements to provide a specified service level. The primary feature of the distribution plan is that each stocking location has a list of the parts that are authorized to be stocked there and at what levels of inventory they are to be maintained. These lists are the field Authorized Stock Lists (ASLs). The field organization has input to the number and location of field stocking locations, but the overriding consideration is the tradeoff between logistics fill rate, response time, and required financial investment. If the field distribution is at or near optimal level, it directly drives required investment. At that point, inventory investment reduction cannot be effected without impacting adversely on logistics service levels.

Field stock list development

It is tempting to believe that the best people to determine what parts should be stocked at the end of the supply chain are the people who work there. The reality is that decisions at that level tend to result in over stocking. Moreover, even when the location is removed, the people in the field do not process the global view of demand patterns that greatly impact stocking decisions for low and medium demand parts. The best approach for developing a field stock list is first to generate a part number list in central logistics using statistical analysis tools, and then to coordinate the list with field personnel. Part numbers can be added when sufficient rational justification exists. Computer programs are very good at analyzing history, but need humans to add information about coming changes. For example, if a technician often covers for another technician with unique equipment, then critical parts should be positioned where they are available to both technicians, or if the parts' cost is low, then both technicians could carry the parts. Finally, however, the quantities to be stocked are determined by central logistics using statistical methods.

Field stocking location performance evaluation and adjustments

Planning the stock list is only half of retail logistics' job. The stock list performance must be monitored and the list adjusted on an ongoing basis to assure that the desired performance metrics are achieved and sustained. The tools to do this are Demand Accommodation and Demand Satisfaction that were discussed earlier in chapter 4. Do note that planners should not be asked to do operations' tasks of identifying parts and expediting shipments.

Field redistribution management

The retail logistics management function of the central logistics organization is constantly working with individual field stocking locations. They are ideally positioned to see where local shortages can be filled by the redistribution of local excess in another field stocking location. Whether these parts are sent directly from field site to field site is a matter of company policy. What usually works best is for nonrepairable parts to be shipped site to site in the field and for repairable parts be returned to central facilities for testing and repackaging.

Defective return pipeline monitoring

Given the focus of retail logistics management, it is also well suited to monitor the defective return pipelines. Due-in reports should be automated directly from the call management system. Responsibility for the control of the return pipeline belongs to field management. The retail logistics function should gather the data, compute the appropriate pipeline parameter, distribute performance reports and make necessary recommendations to management.

Administration and operations functions

The following responsibilities do not fit well with the operational focus of either the wholesale or retail functions. They are therefore grouped into a third function called administration and operations.

Strategic logistic policy development

Discussed at length in several places throughout this book has been the concept that there should be a Logistics Support Policy stated in quantitative terms. Described as the Logistics

Performance Envelope, this approach is to provide, on a sustained basis, the best balance between First Pass Fill Rate, Response Time and Financial Investment. This balance is dynamic since the product configuration and customer environment is always changing. In other words, *the envelope must be revised periodically*. The central logistics organization should have a tool (computer model) capable of *what-if? macro level analysis* of the envelope parameters.

Investment management

Investment is driven by the distribution plan and logistics pipeline requirements. The investment levels must be monitored closely to assure that the investment limits are not exceeded. Often the first indication that there is a physical distribution or policy problem is that the investment levels start to shift unpredictably or inappropriately.

Performance metrics coordination and reporting

The collection and dissemination of logistics performance metrics is a function of logistics administration. The following metrics outline a minimum set to measure the results of proactive planning.

    Static Sites
        Central Locations
            Overall Service Level
            First Pass Fill Rate
            Throughput Time (average and 98th percentile)
        Field Locations (individually and by organization rollup)
            Overall Service Level
            First Pass Fill Rate
            Response Time (average and 98 percentile)
    Pipelines
            Procurement (by part number, vendor and rollup)
                Mean, medium, mode, and standard deviation
            Repair (by part number, repair location and rollup)
                Mean, medium, mode, and standard deviation
            Routine replenishment (by part number, field stocking
                location and rollup)

Mean, medium, mode, and standard deviation
Defective return (by part number, field stocking location
   and rollup)
Mean, medium, mode, and standard deviation

Database responsibility

Logistics data is often difficult to maintain since the logistics organization must rely on other organizations to input the data. Nonetheless logistics administration has both the global view and the vested interest. It must take responsibility for monitoring the collection of this data and its retention.

TRANSACTION HISTORIES Part usage, ordering, return and repair transactions are the primary drivers of forecasting and planning and are therefore essential.

MASTER FILES These are the tables that define the logistics world. They include information about the parts, installed products, customers' field sites, etc. This information changes slowly, but a constant effort must be applied to assure that it remains current.

FRU LIST MAINTENANCE Logistics is responsible for the maintenance of the comprehensive product FRU Lists.

AUTHORIZED STOCK LISTS Logistics is responsible for the maintenance of the ASLs for all stocking locations in the company. Typically, replenishment of field ASL items is based on usage reporting and is "pushed" without an order.

INVESTMENT BY LOGISTICS SEGMENT Wholesale logistics should gather and publish planned and actual investment data by logistics segment both static and moving. (See Figure 30-1.) When used in conjunction with the business model described above it is useful to compare actual data in terms of days of supply, number of parts and level of investment for each segment of the logistics pipeline.

System support

Logistics administration is responsible for computer support interface within the central logistics function and between Logistics and the Management Information Systems Functions. This support has a broad range of tasks from the development of specifications for main frame transaction processing to developing a spreadsheet template.

Contract quote support and ad hoc queries

From time to time Logistics must respond to the informational needs of other internal organizations. Most frequently these are either impact assessments required to quote service contracts to perspective customers or an unanticipated question from management. Logistics administration should have the tools to generate the information directly from logistics data without interrupting wholesale or retail management functions.

Part identification and expediting

This function draws much attention since it is usually done under a time constraint and with a great deal of management interest. It is part of logistics administration rather than wholesale or retail planning management because it requires different skill sets and we want to preclude expediting from disrupting proactive efforts.

Field organization's logistics responsibilities

It must be remembered that all persons in the company who come into contact with service parts are responsible for them. Specifically, just because there is an organization called "Logistics," does not mean that other organizations do not have logistics management responsibilities. This is particularly true for the field organization. The obligations of the field are few but very important. Here are the most critical:

Inventory control

The location of all service parts in the hands of field personnel should be known and visible to all levels on a real time basis. Items should never be lost!

Transaction reporting

Hand-in-hand with inventory control is transaction discipline. Indeed it is the vehicle by which inventory control is effected. Transactions need to be complete, accurate, and timely.

Defective part return

This pipeline is the effort most often overlooked, perhaps because the items in this pipeline are not immediately usable. The longer term impact is, however, that excessive length or variability in this pipeline has a severe adverse impact on investment and fill rate. Investment grows because parts must be bought to fill up this pipeline and the fill rate drops because the parts have not been processed through repair and returned to the shelf before the next requirement is received.

Total logistics management (TLM)

We conclude this book with the outline for a Total Logistics Management Process approach to service parts management. All elements of this process have been covered in this book. You will want to choose and tune the pieces of this complex puzzle to fit your unique needs. Do remember, however, that there is one best way to do most service tasks.

- Systems and procedures are not enough for real change in logistics support. A corporate level process perspective is required.
- Multi dimensional process views are needed:

Macro versus Micro	Wholesale versus Retail
Routine versus Emergency	Planned versus Random
Static versus Dynamic	Pipeline versus Shelf

Myopic and single-focus thinking is what causes most organizations to fail to develop processes for Total Logistics Management.

- Total Logistics Management includes:

Authorized stock lists	Inventory control
Balanced business perfor-	Investment quantified
mance	Logistics policy determination
Business models	Operations tools
Continuous training	Performance goals and mea-
Dynamic knowledgebase	sures
Formal processes	Pipeline management
FRU standards	Planning engine
	Responsibility and account-
	ability
	Standard operating procedures
	Strategic uses of logistics
	Structured support planning
	Transaction discipline
	Wholesale and retail perspec-
	tives

Interfaces include:
  Manufacturing
    Manufactured parts
    MRP interface
    Procurement
    Repair-sometimes
    Warehousing-sometimes

  Finance
    Funding of part buys
    Investment planning
    Depreciation

  Marketing and Sales
    Supported equipment
    Sales persons' understanding of tradeoffs
    Customer entitlement and expectations
    Field parts distributions

Engineering
　Product support planning
　Reliability information
　FRU definition and standardization.

Top management support is critical because logistics cross-functional interfaces are extensive and complex. The pervasive nature of service parts logistics requires the highest level of participation to make substantive changes. Permission is not enough - management must lead!

Appendix A

RELATED PROFESSIONAL SOCIETIES AND PUBLICATIONS

American Institute of Plant Engineers (AIPE)
   3975 Erie Avenue
   Cincinnati, OH 45208-9971
   (513) 561-6000
   Publication: *AIPE Facilities*

American Production and Inventory Control Society (APICS)
   400 West Annondale Road
   Falls Church, VA 22046-4274
   (800) 444-2742
   Publications: *APICS - The Performance Advantage* and others

American Productivity and Quality Center (APQC)
    123 North Post Oak Lane
    Houston, TX 77024-7797
    (713) 685-4666
    International Benchmarking Clearinghouse and other offerings

American Society for Quality Control (ASQC)
    611 East Wisconsin Avenue
    P O Box 3005
    Milwaukee, WI 53201-3005
    (414) 272-8575
    Publications: *Quality Progress* and others

American Society of Transportation and Logistics
    216 East Church Street
    Lock Haven, PA 17745-2010
    (717) 748-8515

Annual Reliability and Maintainability Symposium (ARMS)
    Proceedings available from IEEE

Association for the Advancement of Medical Instrumentation (AAMI)
    3330 Washington Boulevard, Suite 400
    Arlington, VA 22201-4598
    (703) 525-4890
    Publications: *Biomedical Instrumentation & Technology*

Association for Services Management International (AFSMI)
    1342 Colonial Boulevard, Suite 25
    Fort Myers, FL 33907
    (800) 333-9786
    Publications: *The Professional Journal* and others

Automatic ID News
    7500 Old Oak Boulevard
    Cleveland, OH 44130
    (216) 826-2559

Canadian Association of Logistics Management
    610 Alden Road #201
    Markham, ON L3R 9Z1 Canada
    (416) 513-7300

Computer Industry Technology Association
    450 East 22nd Street, Suite 230
    Lombard, IL 60148-6158
    (708) 268-1818 ext 321 or (800) 77MICRO
    A+ Certification testing program

Council of Logistics Management (CLM)
   2803 Butterfield Road #380
   Oak Brook, IL 60521-1156
   (708) 574-0985
   Publications: *Bibliography on Logistics Management* and others

Independent Service Network International (ISNI)
   494 Ansley Walk Terrace
   Atlanta, GA 30309
   (404) 885-9908, Fax -9909

Institute of Industrial Engineers (IIE)
   25 Technology Park/Atlanta
   Norcross, GA 30092
   (404) 449-7900
   Publications: *IIE Solutions* and others

Institute of Electrical and Electronic Engineers (IEEE)
   345 East 47th Street
   New York, NY 10017
   (212) 644-7900
   Publications: *IEEE Spectrum* and others

Instrument Society of America (ISA)
   POB 12277
   67 Alexander Drive
   Raleigh, NC 27709
   (800) 334-6391
   Publications: *InTech* and others

International Customer Service Association
   401 North Michigan Avenue
   Chicago, IL 60611-4267
   (312) 321-6800

Maintenance Technology
   An Applied Technology Publication
   1300 South Grove Avenue, Suite 205
   Barrington, IL 60010
   (708) 382-8100

Modern Materials Handling
   275 Washington Street
   Newton, MA 02158
   (617) 558-4548

National Association of Service Managers (NASM)
   1030 West Higgins Road, Suite 109
   Hoffman Estates, IL 60195
   (708) 310-9930
   Publications: *Service Management* and others

Second Source Publications
   10 Risho Avenue
   East Providence, RI 02914-1215
   (401) 434-1050, Fax -1090
   Publications: *Medical Equipment Services Directory* and others

Service Management Europe
   Service Management Publications Ltd.
   Weybourne House
   2 London Street, Chertsey
   Surrey KT16 8AA, United Kingdom

Service and Support World
   Publications and Communications, Inc.
   12416 Haymeadow Drive
   Austin, TX 78750-1896
   (512) 250-9023, Fax (512) 331-3900

Service News
   United Publications
   P O Box 995
   38 Lafayette Street
   Yarmouth, ME 04096
   (207) 846-0600

Software Support Professionals Association (SSPA)
   11828 Rancho Bernardo, Building 123-161
   San Diego, CA 92128
   (619) 745-2271

Society for Maintenance and Reliability Professionals
   500 N. Michigan Avenue, Suite 1920
   Chicago, IL 60611
   (800) 950-7354

Society of Logistics Engineers (SOLE)
   8100 Professional Place, Suite 211
   New Carrollton, MD 20785
   (301) 459-8446
   Publications: *Logistics Spectrum* and others

Society of Reliability Engineers (SRE)
    P O Box 392
    Wilsonville, OR 97070

Systems Dealers Association (SDA)
    1601 N. Bond Street, Suite 302
    Naperville, IL 60540
    (312) 983-8444

Warehousing Education and Research Council
    1100 Jorie Boulevard, Ste 170
    Oak Brook, IL 60521
    (708) 990-0256

Appendix

LOGISTICS BESTMARKS™ QUESTIONNAIRE L6

PATTON CONSULTANTS INC.

If you have any questions about this survey please call Joe Patton at 803-686-6650

1. What are your annual service parts shipping volumes from the central warehouse?

Number of items (pieces) _____

SKU lines (different part numbers) _____

Number of shipments? _____

Dollars? $ Cost in million _____

2. Parts Usage - Value of parts reported as used in the last 12 months, at cost:

$ _____

3. Net Parts Cost - The last 12 months total P&L costs for parts used plus direct and indirect planning and logistics expenses necessary to support the parts system:

$ _____

4. Logistics operating items included in Net Parts Costs (enter % or 0 where appropriate):

Warehousing, Pick and Pack	$ ____	% ____
Obsolescence Central Spare	____	____
Obsolescence Field Spares	____	____
Freight - routine	____	____
Freight - expedited	____	____
Cost of material planning	____	____
MIS Support	____	____
Purchasing	____	____
Order entry	____	____
Repairs	____	____
Other (detail)	____	____
Total $ ____		100%

5. The above Logistics operating costs total $_____M, which is ____% of the net parts costs.

6. Parts total inventory value at cost - The pure materials cost from the Balance Sheet (based on original parts cost):

$ _____

7. Parts total value at book - The cost less depreciation and reserves per the Balance Sheet:

$ _____

8. Are defective parts awaiting repair valued on your balance sheet?

Yes / No

9. Hardware maintenance revenue - The money received for all equipment maintenance supported by the parts, including service contracts, time & materials business, and direct parts sales:

$ _____

10. Does the ratio of service parts investment to service revenue vary by product or product life cycle?

Not managed that way: _____

Varied by product based on: _____

Varied by product life cycle based on: _____

11. Approximately how many dollars of product (at cost) does the parts inventory support?

$_____Million

12. Basis for inventory valuation (x where appropriate):

a. Expendable or consumable parts

Actual Cost _____

Average Cost _____

Standard Cost _____

Other _____
If "other," please detail :

aa. What is the average cost of a non-repairable item? $ _____

b. Good repairable parts

Actual Cost _____

Average Cost _____

Standard Cost _____

Other (detail) _____

473

bb. What is the average cost of a good
repairable part? $ _____

c. Defective repairable parts

    Actual Cost   _____

    Average Cost   _____

    Standard Cost   _____

    Other (detail)   _____

13. Do you use financial reserves for obsolescence?

                                     Yes / No

14. Do you formally depreciate parts?   Yes / No

15. How many months are typically used to fully reserve/depreciate parts?

                                     _____

16. Are reserves varied by product life cycle?

                                     Yes / No

If Yes, detail:

17. What % of parts were scrapped last year?

    From repair: _____ %

    others   _____ %

    Total Scrap   _____ %

18. Is scrap a planned process?   Yes / No

19. What are your annual turn rates for all parts per year?

                 Dollars: _____   Units: _____

20. Is "turns" a significant measure to management?

                                     Yes / No

21. How many parts stock locations do you have?

    Customer Sites   _____

    Single FE Stocks   _____

    Multiple-FE / Office Stocks   _____

    Major Warehouses   _____

    Other (detail)   _____

22. How many SKU lines (different part numbers) do you maintain in your service parts master file?

                                       _____

23. How may SKU lines have been active in the last year?

                                       _____

24. What is your parts investment percentage by logistics pipeline segment?

    Central Warehouse (Serviceable)   _____ %

    Central Warehouse (Unserviceable) _____ %

    In Repair   _____ %

    In Field Stocking Locations   _____ %

    In Transit   _____ %

25. What percent of customer trouble calls are cleared remotely, without having to dispatch a technician?

    Hardware Calls   _____%

    Software Calls   _____%

26. When a technician is dispatched, what percent of the time is the problem resolved without a "call back" (i.e., First Call Fix Rate)?

                                     _____%

27. What is the first pass fill rate from your lowest level logistics operation to the customers (% of parts instantly available to the technician)?

                                     _____ %

28. What is the First Pass Fill Rate from the central (wholesale) facility (% of all parts ordered that are good, on hand)?

                                     _____ %

29. What is the average part response time from order to delivery if a part is not available in the field but is ready for issue at the central stock?

                                     _____ Hours

30. What is the average part response time if a part is *not* available in the field and *not* good, on hand at the central stock?

                                     _____ Hours

31. What is your Service Staffing?

    No. of Field Technicians   _____
    No. of Repair Technicians   _____
    No. in Tech Assistance
    No. of Administrative Personnel   _____
    No. of Logistics Planners   _____
    No. in Logistics Operations   _____

32. Do you conduct customer service satisfaction surveys?

                            Yes / No

33. What was your last overall satisfaction rating on a scale of 1= poor to 10= perfect?   _____

34. How did your customers rate your logistics process on a scale of 1(poor) to 10(perfect)?   _____

35. What is your Dead on Arrival (DOA; defined as a part unusable for any reason) rate for parts received in the field?   _____%

36. What is your No Trouble Found (NTF) rate for parts received in repair?

                            _____%

37. Do the Help Desk and Technical Assistance Center perform effectively to guide technicians in ordering the correct parts? (Rate on scale from 0= no help at all to 10 = perfect guidance):   _____

38. What percent of shipments to the field are "expedited"?

                            _____%

39. What percent of field service calls are claimed to be late response due to a lack of needed parts?

                            _____ %

40. Do you use third/forth party storage or "parts bank" facilities?

                            Yes / No

41. What is your central warehouse throughput time from the time the order is received until it is shipped?

    Routine shipments.   _____ days

    Expedited Shipments.   _____ hours

42. What methods do you use for expedited shipments?

    Next flight out (NFO)   _____%

    Carrier next morning   _____%

    Carrier next day   _____%

    Carrier second day   _____%

    Other   _____%

43. What carrier do you primarily use?

    Expedited: _____

    Routine: _____

44. What is the cost of a two pound next morning shipment?

                        $ _____

45. What is the average cost for a routine shipment, and how many pieces are in an average routine shipment?

            $ _____ for ____ pieces

46. What is the average cost for an expedited shipment, and how many pieces are in an average expedited shipment?

            $_____ for ____ pieces

47. What percent of field return parts are picked up at a customer site by courier for return to repair or good stocks?   ____ %

48. Prioritize the information (data) you use to plan parts provisioning for new products.
(0 - not used, 1 - considered, 2 - primary data).

    Sales forecasts   ____

    Manufacturing forecasts   ____

    Engineering MTBF data   ____

    Other: ____

49. What standard period of time do you provision for?   _____

50. Rate your accuracy at generating initial provisioning forecasts on a scale of 1 = poor to 10 = perfect. _____

51. Do you use mathematical modeling for initial provisioning?

Yes / No

If yes, what model? _____

52. Do you provide parts warranties ?   Yes / No

If yes, for what period of time?   ____ days

53. What are your parts warranty costs as a percentage of your parts investment?

_____ %

54. How do you support self-maintaining customers? ("X" as applicable)

No support   _____

Time and Materials   _____

Tech Assist. & Parts Contract   _____

Parts only Contract   _____

Parts as Required   _____

Other   _____

55. Where were repairs done, last 12 months?

	Units	$ 000
Company repair center	____	____
Original manufacturer	____	____
Fourth party repairer	____	____
Other (describe):	____	____
Total	____	____

56. What is average return days of a repairable part from the place of failure to the repair facility?

_____days, with variance of_____ days.

57. How many days of backlog parts with repair orders waiting to be repaired do you have now?

____ days

58. Organizationally, where does the repair center report?

Logistics   ____

Service   ____

Manufacturing   ____

Other: _____

59. Do field organizations perform any screening tests on removed parts prior to sending them to repair?

Yes / No

60. The pipeline route for return parts is:

a. Parts are shipped directly from the field technician to the facility that will do the repairs

Yes / No

b. Parts are collected at field offices and then forwarded to a central facility that then sends parts to the facility that will do the repairs

Yes / No

c. Other (describe):

61. What is the average repair cost as a percentage of new part cost?

____%

62. Parts usage for repairable parts is valued at (choose one):

New build part cost   ____

Repaired part cost   ____

Other (detail):   _____

63. Given the FPFR in question 28, what is the Demand Accommodation at the central stock (% of parts on the Authorized Stock List)?

____ %

64. What is the related Demand Satisfaction (% of parts on ASL and on hand) ?

_____ %

65. Ratios

a. Inventory Cost / Revenue (Calculated % of [Q6 / Q9) * 100] _____%

b. Inventory Book / Revenue (Calculated % of [Q7 / Q9) * 100: _____%

c. Months of inventory at cost (Calculated [Q6 / Q2) / 12]) _____ months

d. Parts Usage / Hardware Maintenance Revenue; (Calculated % of [Q2 / Q9) * 100]) _____ %

e. Net Parts Cost / Hardware Maintenance Revenue (Calculated % of [(Q3 / Q9) * 100]) _____ %

66. Service Level - Response time for delivery of parts to the end user site. Note that this should be the time required from when the need for parts is identified until they arrive. (This may be different from contracted response time.)

Customer/Part Availability	% of Service Calls		
	A. Proprietary Products (high cost / low volume)	B. Open, Commodity (low cost / high volume)	C. Total (all calls)
0-1 hour	% _____	% _____	% _____
1-2 hours	_____	_____	_____
2-4 hours	_____	_____	_____
4-24 hours	_____	_____	_____
> 24 hours	_____	_____	_____
	100%	100%	100%

67. What are the major issues you see in Logistics Management in the next five years?

68. What is the most pressing logistics issue you face near term?

###

Please return the completed questionnaire by Fax to 803-686-6651, by e-mail to jdpatton@aol.com, or by mail to:
Patton Consultants, Inc.
4 Covington Place
Hilton Head, SC 29928-7665
Phone 803-686-6650

Appendix C

BIBLIOGRAPHY

Unfortunately, there are relatively few books or magazine articles written in the 1990s on the subject of service parts logistics. Topical searches of computerized databases do not list many articles published in professional journals, so recent articles are added by manual search. Many published articles are by Herb Feldmann and/or Joe Patton, and have been incorporated in this material, so those articles are not referenced. *Books in Print* does not list several of the texts known to the authors, so those are also manually added. There is major need for good articles and books about your experiences with service parts. The authors are available to give advice to anyone who would like to write articles or a book that will help build a body of knowledge for our profession.

Books

Anderson, R. T. *Reliability-Centered Maintenance,* ISBN 1–85166–470–X, Elsevier, 1991.

Balm, G. J. *Benchmarking: A Practitioner's Guide for Becoming and Staying Best of the Test,* QPMA Press, Schaumberg, IL, 1993.

Bell, Chip R. and Ron, Zemke. *Managing 'Knock Your Socks Off' Service.* AMACON, New York, 1992.

Bleuel, William H. and Joseph D. Patton, Jr. *Service Management: Principles and Practices* (Third Edition). Instrument Society of America, Research Triangle Park, NC, 1994

Blumberg, Donald F. *Managing Service as a Strategic Profit Center,* ISBN 0–07–006189–0, McGraw-Hill, Inc., USA, 1991.

Collier, David A. *The Service/Quality Solution: Using Service Management to Gain Competitive Advantage,* ISBN 1–55623–753–7, 1994.

Davidow, William H. *The Virtual Corporation: Customization and Instantaneous Response in Manufacturing and Service: Lessons from the World's Most Advanced Companies,* ISBN 0–88730– 593–8 Harper-Business, 1992

Defense Logistics: *Requirements Determinations for Aviation Spare Parts,* ISBN 0–7881–2865–5, Diane Pub, 1996.

Dovich, Robert A. *Quality Engineering Statistics,* ISBN 0–930206–05–3, 1992.

Hallows, Richard. *Service Management in Computing and Telecommunications,* ISBN 0–89006–676– 0, Artech Hse, 1994.

Hanan, Mark. *Profits Without Products: How to Transform Your Product Business into a Service,* ISBN 0–8144–5132–2, AMACON, 1992.

Heskett, James L., W. Earl Sasser, and Christopher W. L. Hart, *Service Breakthroughs, Changing the Rules of the Game.* The Free Press, a Division of Macmillan, Inc., New York, NY 1990.

Holmberg. *Operational Reliability and Systematic Maintenance,* ISBN 1–85166–612–5, Elsevier, 1991.

Kaynak, O. (Editor) *Intelligent Systems: Safety, Reliability and Maintainability Issues,* ISBN 3–540– 56993–6, Spr. Verlag, 1993.

Kececioglu, Dimitri. *Reliability Engineering Handbook, Volumes 1 and 2,* ISBN 0–13–772302–4, 1991.

Krezevic, J. *Reliability, Maintainability and Supportability: a Probabilistic Approach,* ISBN 0–07– 707423–8, McGraw, 1992.

LaBounty, Char. *How to Establish and Maintain Service Level Agreements,* ISBN 1–57125–009–3, Help Desk Institute, 1995.

Lochner, Robert A. and Joseph. E. Matar, *Designing for Quality,* ISBN 0–527–91633–1, 1990.

Military Handbooks are available from: Defense Documentation Center, DSA, Cameron Station, Arlington, VA 22314, or the Naval Publications and Forms Center, 5801 Tabor Avenue, Philadelphia, PA 19120.

Mobray, John. *Reliability Central Maintenance,* ISBN 0–8311–3044–x, Industry Publications, 1992.

Murdick, Robert G., Barry, Render, and Roberta S. Russell, *Service Operations Management.* Allyn and Bacon, London, Sydney, Toronto, 1990.

Orsburn, Douglas, K. *Spares Management Handbook,* ISBN 0–8306–7626–0, McGraw-Hill, 1991.

Pasco, Ivan. *A Practical Guide to Service Management,* The Graphic Print Centre Pty. Ltd., Victoria, Australia, 1994.

Patton, Joseph D. Jr. *Maintainability and Maintenance Management* (Third Edition). Instrument Society of America, Research Triangle Park, NC, 1994

Patton, Joseph D. Jr. *Preventive Maintenance* (Second Edition), Instrument Society of America, Research Triangle Park, NC, 1995.

Rautmann, Harley. *Full Spectrum Service Marketing.* Strategic Services, Beaverton, OR, 1990.

Smeitink, E. *Stochastic Models for Repairable Systems,* ISBN 90–5170–135–7, IBD Ltd/Thesis Publications, 1993.

Smith David J. *Reliability, Maintainability and Risk,* 4th Edition, ISBN 0–7506–0854–4, Butterworth-Heinemann, 1993.

Society of Automotive Engineers *Reliability, Maintainability and Supportability Handbook,* ISBN 1–56091–244–8 SAE, 1992.

Thomopoulos, Nick T. *Strategic Inventory Management and Planning With Tables* ISBN 0–933931– 11–5, Hitchcock Publishing Co., Carol Stream, IL , 1990.

Villemeur, A. *Reliability, Availability, Maintainability and Safety Assessment (2 volumes)* ISBN 0- 471-93054-4, Wiley, 1992.

Whiteley, Richard C. *Customer Driven Company, Moving from Talk to Action.* Addison-Wesley Publishing Company, Inc. Reading, MA, 1991.

Zeithaml, Valerie A., A. Parasuraman, and Leonard L. Berry, *Delivering Quality Service, Balancing Customer Perceptions and Expectations.* The Free Press, A Division of Macmillan, Inc., New York, NY 1990

Articles

Aftermarket Business. "Retailers Looking for More Hard Parts Growth - and Getting It," February 1, 1992, p 22.

American Metal Market. "Recycle Technology Center Planned by US Automakers," September 1, 1993, p 1 (2).

Aaron, Lauric Joan. "Deflating the Cost of Expedited Service," *Inbound Logistics,* October, 1995, p 34.

Automotive Industries. "The Recycling Gap," February 1994, p 97 (3).

Beddingfield, Thomas W. "Reducing Inventory enhances Competitiveness," *APICS - The Performance Advantage,* September 1992, p 28.

Bell, Chip and Ron. Zemke, "The Performing Art of Service Management," *Management Review,* July 1990, pp 42-45.

Bindra, Ramnik, Richard, Garver, and Mike McElhone, "Achieving ISO 9000: From Minefield to Meadow," *Council of Logistics Management Annual Conference Proceedings,* October 1995, pp 251-264.

Brown, Luther M. "The Art of Avoiding Damaged Freight," *Distribution,* March 1995, pp 60-62.

Bulmann, R. Allan. "Quality in Transportation and Distribution," *Logistics Spectrum,* Fall 1995, pp 30 - 36.

Buxbaum, Peter A. "When Your Shipment Doesn't Arrive Intact," *Transportation & Distribution,* August 1995, pp 43-46.

Caplice, Chris and Sheffi, Yossi. "A Review and Evaluation of Logistics Performance Measurement Systems," *International Journal of Logistics Management*, Volume 6, Number 1, 1995, pp 61–74.

Carlsson, Tommy and Anders Ljundberg. "Measuring Service and Quality in the Order Process," *Council of Logistics Management Annual Conference Proceedings*, October 1995, pp 313–332.

Childs, Joel. "Transportation and Logistics: Your Competitive Advantage or Your Downfall?," *APICS - The Performance Advantage*, April 1996.

Cina, Craig. "Five Steps to Service Excellence," *The Journal of Services Marketing*. Vol 4, No. 2, Spring 1990, pp 39–47.

Clausen, Larry. "Electronic Commerce Through Electronic Catalogs," *EDI World*, September 1995, pp 46–48.

Cogger, William A. "Managing and Maximizing Part Value," *Service & Support Management*, July 1994. p 22 (4).

Construction Equipment. "Remanufacturing Restores Reliability," January 15, 1992, p 9.

Cooke, James Aaron. "How Moore Keeps Its Operations in Top Form," *Traffic Management*, September 1995, pp 23–27.

Customer Service Newsletter. "Does a Remote Work Program Suit Your Company?" January 1996.

Customer Service Newsletter. "Empowerment: Get Your Reps Thinking Like Managers," February 1996.

Defense Daily. "Army Uses Unreliable Data Bases to Track Spare Part Inventories," February 12, 1996, p 213.

Defense Daily. "Millions Wasted Due to Poor Maintenance Data - GAO," April 15, 1996, p 88.

Distribution. "A Breakthrough in Reverse Logistics," November 1994, p 14.

Distribution. "A World Without Wires," September 1995, pp 58–62.

Evers, Philip T. "Expanding the Square Root Law: An Analysis of Both Safety and Cycle Stocks," *The Logistics and Transportation Review*, Vol 31, Number 6, pp 1–20.

Flight International. "Dodgy Dealings (Unauthorized Spare Parts for Aircraft Maintenance Becoming Increasingly Available Worldwide with Governments Seeking to Stem Trade)" March 17, 1993, p 26.

Forger, Gary. "UPS Starts World's Premier Cross-Docking Operation," *Modern Materials Handling,* November 1995, pp 36–38.

Frieswich, Kria. "10 Ways to Improve Your Warehouse . . . Now," *Industrial Distribution,* December 1995, pp 39–40.

Gibson, Brian J. and Ray A. Mundy, "Developing an Effective Logistics Benchmarking Program," *Council of Logistics Management Annual Conference Proceedings,* October 1995, pp 43–60.

Gillis, Chris and Robert Mottley. "Rebooting the Supply Chain," *American Shipper,* December 1995, pp 57–59.

Giuntini, Ron. "Managing an OEM Parts Business to Support and Out-of-Production Product Line," *AFSMI The Professional Journal,* January 1996, pp 13–17.

Gooley, Toby B. "Finding the Hidden Cost of Logistics," *Traffic Management,* March 1995, pp 47– 53.

Government Computer News. "AF Automates Parts Requisition Process," September 16, 1991, p 6.

Government Computer News. "DoD Technicians Bartering for Z-248 Parts," September 30, 1991 pp 3 (2).

Government Computer News. "DoD Spare Parts System to Undergo Its Final Test Runs," June 8, 1992, p 64.

Gustin, Craig M, Patricia J. Daugherty, and Theodore P. Stank, "The Effects of Information Availability on Logistics Integration," *Journal of Business Logistics,* Volume 16, Number 1, 1995, pp 23–40.

Hamilton, Karen. "Asset Tracking Tools: The First Step to Overall Asset Management," *Service News,* October 1995. p 2 (2).

Harler, Curt. "Logistics on the Cutting Edge of Wireless," *Transportation & Distribution,* March 1995, pp 30–40.

Harrington, Lisa. "The Outsourcing Decision," *Inbound Logistics,* June 1995, p 18.

Harrington, Lisa. "It's Time to Rethink Your Logistics Costing," *Transportation & Distribution,* July 1995, pp 27–30.

Harris, Terry. "You Make the Choice: Optimizing Inventory for Customer Service or for Investment Amount," *APICS - The Performance Advantage,* June 1996, p 54.

Harvey, Sid. "Wholesaler Streamlines Parts Inventory for Customers Trucks," *Air Conditioning, Heating, & Refrigeration News,* December 4, 1995, p 25.

Hotchkiss, D'Anne. "Industrial Age Evolves to Computer Age," *Warehousing Management,* November/December 1995, pp 21–22.

Hovencamp, David P. "Where is it? The Cost Accountant Deals with Inventory Shrink," *APICS - The Performance Advantage,* July 1995, p 50.

IIE Transactions "Multiple Failures in a Multi-Item Spares Inventory Model," April 1995, p 171 (10).

IIE Transactions "On the Implementation of a Control-Based Forecasting System for Aircraft Spare Parts Procurement," April 1995, p 210 (7).

Industrial Engineering. "Smooth Landing at Air Canada for 140,000 Aircraft Parts," June 1994, p 28 (2).

Industry Week. "Electronic Catalogs: Parts Online," June 3, 1996, p 39.

Landeros, Robert, Robert Reck, and Richard E. Plank, "Maintaining Buyer-Supplier Partnerships," *International Journal of Purchasing and Materials Management,* Summer 1995, pp 2–11.

Langen, Robert. " Xerox Automates Parts Warehouse," *ID Systems,* December 1995, pp 15–17, 41– 42.

Lincoln, Sarah and Art Price. "What Benchmarking Books Don't Tell You," *ASQC Quality Progress,* March 1996, pp 33–36.

Maintenance Management. "World-Class Maintenance: Values and Beliefs" (Last of a ten-part series), May 1996, p 47.

Modern Materials Handling. "A Guide to Powered Small Parts Storage," November 1991, p 52 (7).

Modern Materials Handling. "Small Parts Storage: The Basic Options," October 1993, p 50 (2).

Ness, Joseph A. and Thomas G. Cucuzza, "Tapping the Full Potential of ABC," *Harvard Business Review,* July-August 1995, pp 130–139.

Noa, Jack. "Making Warranty Work More Profitable," *Computer Service & Repair,* March/April 1996, pp 12–13.

Nonnemacher, Michael. "Set Up a Locator System That's Simple and Easy To Use," *APICS - The Performance Advantage,* December 1991, p 32.

Peck, William F. "Motivating Technical Employees," *Civil Engineering*, April 1993, pp 68–69.

Pine, Joseph B. II, Don, Peppers, and Martha Rogers. "Do You Want to Keep Your Customers Forever?" *Harvard Business Review*, March-April 1995, pp 103–114.

Pohlen, Terrance L. and Bernard J. La Londe, "Implementing Activity-Based Costing (ABC) in Logistics," *Journal of Business Logistics*, Volume 15, Number 2, 1994, pp 1–22.

Pollock, William K. "Necessities for Authorized Service Providers," *Service & Support Management*, December 1995, pp 13–14.

Purchasing. "MRO Buyers Take Few Bows for Their Accomplishments," September 8, 1994, p 34 (2).

Rautmann, Harley. "Parts Marketing Programs," *AFSMI The Professional Journal*, November 1995, pp 25–27.

Rayport, Jeffrey F. and John J. Sviokla, "Exploiting the Virtual Supply Chain," *Harvard Business Review*, November-December 1995, p 75.

Reynolds, Michael P. "Spare Parts Inventory Management," *APICS - The Performance Advantage*, April 1994, p 42.

Rothmeier, Craig. "Meeting Business Objectives Through Logistics," *Service & Support Management*, July 1944, p 12 (4).

Saba, David. "Taking Necessary Steps to Motivate Quality Programs," *Industrial Engineering*, January 1993, pp 43–44.

Semejin, Janaap and David B. Vellenga, "International Logistics and One-Stop Shopping," *International Journal of Physical Distribution and Logistics Management*," Volume 25, Number 10, 1995, pp 24–26.

Smith, Richard. "Motivation is the Key to Effective Performance," *Management Accounting*, March 1993, p 50.

Stern, Willy. "Warning! (Bogus parts have turned up in commercial jets. Where's the FAA?)," *Business Week*, June 10, 1996, p 84 (7).

The Tax Advisor. "Eighth Circuit Affirms Honeywell Decision - Rotable Spare Parts are Depreciable," January 1995, p 29 (2).

The Tax Advisor. "Rotable Spare Parts," March 1996, p 137 (2).

Traffic Management. "American Public Warehouse Register," 14th Edition, 1995.

Tyndal, Gener R. "Logistics Costs and Service Levels," in *Emerging Practices in Cost Management*, Brinker, Barry J. editor, Waren, Gorham, & Lamont, Boston, MA, 1990, p 215.

Verespej, Michael A. "The Psychology of Entitlement: It Must be Broken," *Industry Week*, April 5, 1993, pp 35–36.

Ward's Auto World. "Recycling or Reuse: The Long and Short of It," April 1994, p 16.

World Wastes. "Spec'ing Replacement Parts: The Buyers Beware," August 1992, p 50 (3).

Young, Donald. "Considerations in the Design of Electronic Commerce Solutions," *EDI World*, *Part I* in August, 1995, pp 46–48; Part II September 1995, pp 43–45.

Zemke, Ron. "The Emerging Art of Service Management," *Training*, January 1992, pp 36–42.

Zuckerman, Amy. "Logistics Lights Up Philips," *Inbound Logistics*, September 1995, pp 24–28.

INDEX

ABOUT THE AUTHORS

Joseph D. Patton. Jr. is President of Patton Consultants. Inc., the leading advisors to management on equipment service, logistics, and support systems. Before founding Patton Consultants. Mr. Patton was a Regular Army Officer and spent eleven years with Xerox Corporation. He is author of over a hundred published articles and five other books including *Service Management (now in 3rd edition), Maintainability and Maintenance Management (also 3rd edition), Preventive Maintenance (2nd edition), Service Parts Management,* and *Logistics Technology and Management.* Joe Patton earned a BS from Penn State and a MBA in marketing from the University of Rochester. Joe is a Registered Professional Engineer (PE) in Quality Engineering, a Fellow of both the American Society for Quality Control and the Society of Logistics Engineers, a Certified Professional Logistician (CPL), National Association of Service Managers Life-Certified Service Executive, and a twenty-year member of the Association for Services Management International.

Herbert C. Feldmann has been associated with field service, maintenance management, and logistics for over thirty years. He started his career as a military logistics officer and has worked for General Electric Company and Patton Consultants, Inc. He is President of Management Metrics Services, Inc., a firm providing out-sourced service parts planning. Based in Dallas, Herb travels the world assisting clients with service logistics and support system improvements. Herb earned a BS in mathematics from the University of Buffalo and a Masters Degree in operations research from the University of Alabama. He is a Certified Professional Logistician (CPL), and author of over 25 published articles.